# THE MARRANOS OF SPAIN

# THE MARRANOS OF SPAIN

From the Late 14th to the Early 16th Century

*According to Contemporary Hebrew Sources*

*by*

## B. NETANYAHU

*Third Edition, Updated and Expanded*

Cornell University Press

*Ithaca and London*

LIBRARY OF CONGRESS CATALOGING-IN-PUBLICATION DATA

Netanyahu, B. (Benzion), b. 1910
    The Marranos of Spain, from the late 14th to the early 16th
century, according to contemporary Hebrew sources / by B. Netanyahu.
—3rd ed.
        p.   cm.
    Includes bibliographical references and index.
    ISBN 0-8014-3586-2 (cloth : alk. paper). — ISBN 0-8014-8568-1
(pbk. : alk. paper)
    1. Marranos—Spain—Historiography.   2. Rabbinic and polemical
literature—History and criticism.   I. Title.
DS135.S7N39   1999
946'.004924—dc21                                                98-55165

PRINTED IN THE UNITED STATES OF AMERICA

Cloth printing 10   9   8   7   6   5   4   3   2   1

Paperback   10   9   8   7   6   5   4   3   2   1

To

CELA

*for toil, and faith, and dedication*

# FOREWORD

This study is part of an inquiry designed to establish what we can learn about the Marranos, as well as about the genesis of the Spanish Inquisition, from non-Inquisitional sources. In pursuit of this aim, I have undertaken a dual approach — an analysis of all the evidence on the Marranos contained in the Hebrew sources, and a scrutiny of all related testimony contained in the non-Hebrew documents. As I had expected, these investigations, though schematically disparate, proved to be interrelated — and, in fact, to an extent larger than I had thought. This made it all the more apparent that the full objective of my inquiry will have been attained only when the parallel study, now in an advanced stage of preparation, is completed and made public.

The conclusions I have arrived at in these researches differ so widely with commonly held views, that I do not delude myself with the hope that they will be easily accepted. No doubt they will encounter, apart from fair criticism, that opposition which seems to be the fate of every new idea. I dare to believe, however, that they will withstand these objections and, in the course of time, will serve to develop a better grasp of a subject whose importance is admittedly great. For, indeed, owing to its bearing upon the Inquisition and the latter's international repercussions, the Marrano problem is of paramount significance not only to the histories of the Jewish and Spanish peoples, but also to the history of the world.

At this point I would like to express my gratitude to the American Academy for Jewish Research for undertaking the publication of this work after having published the first two chapters in its *Proceedings* of 1963. I am also grateful to the Lucius N. Littauer Foundation, so noted for its meritorious aid to scholarship, for having shared with the Academy the financial burden involved.

B. N.

*September 30, 1965*

# PREFACE TO THE SECOND EDITION

This edition is only slightly revised, but considerably enlarged—that is, by twenty-five pages. It includes a new chapter on the number of the Marranos in Seville in the 1480s, and another on the Marranos' countries of refuge in the decade preceding the establishment of the Inquisition. Both relate to topics discussed elsewhere in this study, and both offer, as I see it, considerable support for the conclusions reached in those discussions. Similarly, the section dealing with the dates of composition of Profeit Duran's polemical works was amplified and expanded to include new evidence. In this instance, however, the broadened inquiry led to a somewhat revised conclusion.

Apart from this revision, and some minor corrections, the text as a whole has remained intact. Several notes, however, were modified or restructured to permit the inclusion of new material. Such, for instance, is the note on page 59 dealing with the origin of the term *Marrano*.

While all these additions may be considered marginal to the *main* theme of inquiry pursued in this book, they bear directly upon some major questions related to the history of the Marranos generally. It is my hope, indeed, that the added discussions will help throw some light on these questions, and also elucidate other developments which are outside the strictly Marrano sphere. Perhaps, in justification of this hope, I may mention my identification of a leading church figure who aided the Jewish people in times of trouble and is referred to anonymously in Duran's *Epistle*. His identity has hitherto eluded the scholars who dealt with that particular document, and his name has to this day not been mentioned in Jewish historical literature.

The reaction to the book thus far has been such as to offer me no little encouragement. When its opening chapters appeared for the first time (December, 1963), the thesis propounded in its pages was little known, and even to a lesser extent, accepted.

Since then matters have considerably changed. The author's views on the subject, at least in broad outline, are now common knowledge to students in the field, and the current of scholarly opinion has been shifting—gradually, to be sure, but not imperceptibly—from the old, conventional view of the Marranos toward a new understanding of the Marrano sources and a new grasp of the Marrano problem. Independent research has led other authors, too, to reach conclusions similar to my own, and the views they expressed in recent years have no doubt contributed to the same trend. Nevertheless, I believe that the present book has played an appreciable role in this development. It dispelled, in part, the mist of myth and legend that had shrouded the historical evolution of Marranism, and allowed for a more realistic view of the whole succession of related events. Other vantage-points for such observation will doubtlessly be offered in the course of time; and the process of re-evaluation, once started, is not likely to cease.

I had hoped that my parallel study of the Marranos according to the *non*-Hebrew sources would have been published by this time. But the vicissitudes of life and the needs of research, which turned out to be more intricate than I had expected, have set much of the pace for my progress in the work. I mentioned that study in the Foreword to this book, and now I feel I owe the reader the information that its completion is already in sight.

*B. N.*

*October 20, 1971*

# PREFACE TO THE THIRD EDITION

When I prepared this book for the present edition, I carefully reread all of its parts and the comments made on it by various scholars. My survey confirmed the impression I had gained from some of the relevant researches I pursued in the period following the book's publication. Only isolated statements touching marginal points appeared to be in need of correction, while several new works on Castile's urban population led me to reexamine solutions I offered to unsettled problems concerning the number of the Marranos, which I discussed in the appendices. I found, however, nothing that called for any change either in my view concerning the Marranos' number or in the content of the main body of the book, which unfolds the religious history of the Spanish Marranos across the entire fifteenth century and a short time thereafter. Not a single testimony I included in this account has ever been proven to be misinterpreted; none of the arguments I advanced has been overthrown; and none of the conclusions I reached has been refuted.

I have, of course, corrected the few errors I referred to, included some new data in the notes, and added some remarks that fortify, in my judgment, my view concerning the size of the Marrano population. I have also added an Afterword in which I reviewed some of the scholarly reactions to this book since its first appearance in 1966. This review enabled me to take into consideration the new opinions expressed about the thesis of this work in the light of my studies about the Marranos according to the *non*-Hebrew sources. Consisting of detailed and large-scale inquiries, these studies are included in my *Origins of the Inquisition in Fifteenth Century Spain* (1995).

As I said in the Foreword, the inquiries referred to form an integral part of my overall investigation into the Marrano problem. For what we gather about the Marranos from the Hebrew sources can be checked and examined in the light of the lessons derivable from the *non*-Hebrew documents. Convinced as I am that these lessons agree with the conclusions arrived at in this book, I feel I can now state without hesitation that the Hebrew sources dealing with the Marrano question reveal the transformation of the Marranos' religious attitudes as they evolved in the ninety years preceding the Inquisition, as well as in the first decades of its operation. Thus they throw much needed light on one of the great chapters of Hispano-Jewish history, which had hitherto been half-befogged and misconceived.

B. N.

*July 12, 1998*

# CONTENTS

PAGE

Foreword ............................................. vii

Preface to the Second Edition .......................... viii

Preface to the Third Edition .......................... x

I. The Problem ..................................... 1

II. The Responsa .................................... 5

III. The Philosophic and Polemic Literature............... 77

IV. The Homiletic and Exegetic Literature ............... 135

V. Conclusions ..................................... 204

Appendices:

1. The Saloniki Rabbinical Decisions on the Marranos ..... 211

2. The Destinations of the Fugitives from the Inquisition ... 216

3. The Dates of Composition of Efodi's Polemical Works.... 221

4. The Book of Complaints........................... 224

5. The Number of the Marranos in Spain ................ 235

Post Scriptum to Second Edition:

1. The Marranos' Countries of Refuge .................. 251

2. The Number of Marranos in Seville in the 1480s ........ 255

Addendum ............................................ 271

Afterword ............................................ 275

Index................................................ 295

# THE MARRANOS OF SPAIN

# I. The Problem

One of the still unsettled questions related to Spanish-Jewish history is the measure of Jewishness to be attributed to the Marranos at various periods of the 15th century. Since both Spanish and Hispano-Jewish history are closely bound with the history of the Marranos, any answer given to this question necessarily bears upon our interpretation of much of what transpired in Christian Spain in that era. It is especially so when we consider the developments in the century's last three decades, for then we are confronted with two momentous events that were intimately connected with the Marrano problem. The first was the establishment of the Inquisition, whose avowed and, originally, sole purpose was to solve that problem in its own prescribed manner; the second was the expulsion of the Jews from Spain and the territories then controlled by it — a measure officially defended on the ground that the presence of the Jews in those countries was a factor militating against that solution. What is more, as the Edict of Expulsion indicates, the Inquisition was instrumental in procuring that measure, and thus the major events referred to were linked with each other in more ways than one; both stemmed from the same source: the forces that occasioned the establishment of the Inquisition and steered its course of action.

Now, it is on the assumed Jewishness of the Marranos that the whole case of the Inquisition rests. Therefore, the results of our inquiry must touch, among other things, upon both the moral and practical impulsions of the entire inquisitorial drive. To realize how far-reaching are the implications of some of the possible conclusions, it is sufficient to reflect, even in a cursory manner, upon the following two alternatives. If the Marranos, or most of them, were Jews, as the advocates of the Inquisition have repeatedly claimed,[1] one may censure the practices of the

[1] Among the most recent and most determined of these advocates, I shall mention here only Bernardino Llorca, *La Inquisición Española*, Comillas

1

Inquisition, but one cannot negate a moral basis for its activities — at least, from a medieval point of view; more clearly, one may rightly maintain that in its struggle with the Jewish "heresy" the Inquisition showed excessive zeal, perhaps even undue virulence and rancor, but one cannot deny all justice to those who, being aware of that "heresy," saw the need for *some* form of struggle, and thus one can hardly question the basic honesty of the Inquisition's declared aims. If, however, the assumption made regarding the Jewishness of the Marranos is wrong, it can hardly be claimed that the Inquisition was, or could for long remain, unaware of this fact. Consequently, we must seek other reasons — apart from those officially announced — both for the establishment of the Inquisition and the particular policies it pursued. How Jewish were the Marranos? Indeed, upon the answer to this question depends not only our correct understanding of the motives, goals and procedures of the Holy Office, but also the proper reconstruction of what truly happened in Spain at that crucial period of Spanish and Jewish history.

Jewish historians have, on the whole, accepted the first proposition, namely, that the Marranos, or most of them, were Jews. On the general reasons for this stand, as well as on its relationship to Spanish and other historical writings on the Inquisition, we have dwelt in some detail in the following.[2] Here we shall limit ourselves to presenting the most extreme view as expressed on the question, i. e., that of Professor Baer. As Baer sees it, "the majority of the conversos were real Jews" (יהודים ממש);[3] and although this is a clear-cut statement, it may be further elucidated by Baer's additional and even more sweeping assertion: "Conversos and Jews were *one people*, bound together by

(Santander), 1953, p. 18; id., "La Inquisición Española y los conversos judíos o 'Marranos,'" in *Sefarad*, II, p. 116; id., "Los conversos judíos y la Inquisición Española," *ibid.*, VIII, and other works; N. López Martínez, "El peligro de los Conversos," in *Hispania Sacra*, III (1950), pp. 3–63; id., *Los Judaizantes Castellanos*, Burgos, 1954, pp. 52–56; and M. de la Pinta Llolernte, *La Inquisición Española*, 1948; id., *Las Cárceles inquisitoriales Españolas*, 1949.

2 See below, pp. 276–287.

3 I. F. Baer, *Toledot ha-Yehudim bi-Sefarad ha-Noẓrit*, Tel-Aviv, 1959², p. 365.

ties of religion, and fate, and messianic hope."[4] Accordingly, Baer does not hesitate to say that "essentially the Inquisition was right in evaluating the character of the conversos."[5]

From this view I differ radically. I adhere to the hypothesis I have advanced elsewhere that (1) "the overwhelming majority of the Marranos" at the time of the establishment of the Inquisition were not Jews, but "detached from Judaism," or rather, to put it more clearly, Christians; (2) that "in seeking to identify the whole Marrano group with a secret Jewish heresy, the Spanish Inquisition was operating with a fiction," and (3) that "it was driven to this operation by racial hatred and political considerations rather than by religious zeal."[6]

On all these statements I still stand — in fact, I am now convinced of their veracity more than ever. What I can now add by way of clarification, and am better able to substantiate, is that the minority that still adhered to Judaism in the three decades preceding the establishment of the Inquisition was, save for temporary and inconsequential reactions, constantly diminishing in size and influence; that it would have, in all likelihood, soon faded into nothingness, had not the process of assimilation been violently interfered with by the repellent and bewildering actions of the Inquisition; and that thus it was due to the Inquisition itself that the dying Marranism in Spain was given a new lease on life. As I see it, therefore, what actually happened was the reverse of what is generally assumed: *it was not a powerful Marrano movement that provoked the establishment of the Inquisition, but it was the establishment of the Inquisition that caused the temporary resurgence of the Spanish Marrano movement.*

If this hypothesis is correct, my contention that the Inquisition was based upon, and operated with, a fictitious charge must emerge as a necessary conclusion. And, what must be equally obvious in this event is that this fiction was in no way a product of misinformation or self-delusion, but of deliberate and careful calculation. If the case as presented by the Holy Office grossly exaggerated a situation which was in itself quite insignificant, those who used these tactics knew precisely what

---

[4] *Ibid.*, p. 464.     [5] *Ibid.*, p. 463.
[6] *Don Isaac Abravanel*, Philadelphia, 1953, p. 275.

4 THE MARRANOS OF SPAIN

they were doing. The fact that there was a striking difference between the official campaign slogans of the Inquisition and the real, unpublished aims of its advocates should surprise no one at all familiar with the history of persecution. Campaign slogans of mass persecution movements rarely agree with their actual aims since persecution habitually claims, in self-justification, motives more noble than those that prompted it. Now, religious motivation, however distorted, has always some nobility to it, and in the Middle Ages in particular it had, besides an appeal, also an explosive force. That it was brought to the fore in the campaign against the Marranos was, therefore, merely part of a *modus operandi*, a means for attaining a certain end; but it was not really the religion of the Marranos with which the Inquisition was concerned. Its concern were the *bearers* of that religion. Its purpose was to degrade, impoverish and ruin the influence of the Marranos in all spheres of life, to terrorize and demoralize them individually and collectively — in brief, to destroy them psychologically and physically so as to make it impossible for them to rise again as a factor of any consequence in Spain. The aim of the Inquisition, therefore, as I see it, was *not to eradicate a Jewish heresy from the midst of the Marrano group, but to eradicate the Marrano group from the midst of the Spanish people.*

All these contentions represent so radical a departure from the theories hitherto accepted as valid, that their foundation — namely, the non-Jewishness of the Marranos, or at least of their overwhelming majority — must be conclusively proven before they can claim to be something more than a mere hypothesis, however plausible. When I first advanced this hypothesis, I supported it by a number of proofs and arguments that appeared to me cogent and decisive.[7] Yet, an all-inclusive examination and analysis of the sources related to this question — both Jewish and non-Jewish — was obviously called for. What I could not do in the framework of a biography, I propose to do here. The present study represents the first portion of the task at hand.

[7] *Ibid.*, pp. 41–45, 275.

## II. THE RESPONSA

### 1

Our interest in the Hebrew sources relating to the Marranos centers, first of all, in the responsa of the 15th and early 16th centuries. This is so not merely because of the general character of these documents, containing as they do decisions of legal authorities based on Jewish law and precedent, as well as on a careful examination of the facts; it is so also for another reason. What we seek to establish here is the *religious* position of the Marranos, and first of all their attitude toward Judaism, and this is precisely where the responsa, judging by the general field of their concern, should be expected to provide an answer. In fact, all the cases related to the Marranos which we find in the responsa of the period deal with religious questions touching upon the border line between Jew and gentile, Jew and convert, and, above all, between a *real* convert and an unwilling and fictitious one.[8]

Several matters, however, must be borne in mind when we deal with the responsa concerning the Spanish Marranos. First, we must consider the position, both theoretical and practical, taken by the Rabbis of the period toward *forced* conversion as such. Since by this we mean, particularly, what they thought of the phenomenon from a religious standpoint, awareness of their views in this regard may help us better to evaluate their statements on the Jewishness or non-Jewishness of the Marranos. Second, we must consider their attitude, again the theoretical

[8] The available studies on the Marranos in the literature of the responsa (S. Asaf, "Anusei Sefarad u-Portugal be-Sifrut ha-Teshuvot," in *Zion*, Jerusalem, V, 1932/33, pp. 19–60; H. J. Zimmels, *Die Marranen in der rabbinischen Literatur*, Berlin, 1932) offer important contributions to the subject, but consider the position of the responsa on the Marranos from a halakhic rather than an historical point of view.

and practical, towards conversion in the real and full sense. The fact is that Marranism was rarely dealt with by them independently of conversion, and their views on the latter issue necessarily affected their stand on the Marrano question.

When the catastrophe of 1391 suddenly presented Spanish Jewry with the problem of crypto-Judaism — a problem which had not been known in Christian Spain for almost eight hundred years — the rabbis nevertheless could fall back on legal precedent, formed in other countries to meet similar situations. These precedents, however, were not all of the same order; their underlying concepts often differed; in fact, they bore the earmarks of two traditions, which were fundamentally antagonistic. One of these was the product of Franco-German Jewry, the other had its inception in Spain's Moslem dominions. Both, then, originated outside Christian Spain, and in different social and religious climates. Whether either of them was substantially fit to meet the problem of forced conversion under the particular Spanish conditions of the time, and if so — to what extent, are questions not hitherto discussed. The Spanish rabbis, in any case, saw no other alternative, it appears, but to follow these traditions in some fashion. The influence of the latter upon the rabbinical authorities alternately wavered in opposite directions; yet, it was primarily these traditions, and no newly developed attitudes, that shaped the Jewish policies toward the Marranos.

The basic elements of the attitudes toward the question owe their origin to ancient Jewish law. A tannaitic dictum of the second century states clearly and without ambiguity that the sacrifice of one's offspring to idolatry — a most hideous crime on all counts — does not entail the prescribed punishment when the act was committed under duress, in error, or through deliberate misguidance.[9] At the root of this opinion no doubt lay the conception that a man can be held responsible for his actions only when done of his own free will.[10] The question of compul-

---

[9] Sifra, *Qedoshim*, X, 5, 3, 13. Cf. Nahmanides on Lev. 18.21, 20.5. The position remains fundamentally unchanged also if Maimonides' view is preferred, namely, that the reference is not to "sacrifice," but to another heathen cult (*Hilkhot 'Akum*, VI, 3; Comm. on San. VII, 7; in accordance with Rashi, Comm. on Lev. 18.21 and on San. 64b).

[10] The broad interpretation of the limitations which negate free operation

sion, however, was singled out for special scrutiny and consideration, since certain circumstances, which were regarded as compelling, e. g., the threat of death, were not held sufficient to paralyze free will, and one seemed capable of *choosing* death instead of performing a blasphemous act. According to Rabbi Ishmael, therefore, when one faces the alternative of death or the performance of idolatrous worship, one should choose the latter course, since the Law was given "to live by it and not to die by it;"[11] but this procedure was limited by him strictly to cases in which the forbidden act was meant to be performed *privately*; when it was to be performed *publicly*, i. e., in the presence of at least ten Israelites, he considered it one's duty to choose death.[12] To make the gravity of this instruction appear in its full, awesome light, two commandments were invoked: one — to sanctify the name of God, the other — not to profane it.[13] Both commandments were considered violated when the ruling under consideration was transgressed; the threat of death was not to be considered, in this case, either an excuse for the crime committed or a mitigation of the punishment due.[14] Although apparently radical on the twofold crime issue, this notion represented, in reality, a compromise, an intermediate position between two extremes. One was the view exposed above, disclaiming *any* responsibility for *all* acts committed under *any* form of duress. The other extremity in this controversy was embodied in the opinion, originating, in all likelihood, in the school of Rabbi Akiba, according to which death should be preferred to idolatry under *all* circumstances, whether private

---

of the will, as indicated in the above quoted dictum, was not limited to Jewish law. Cf., for instance, Aristotle, *Nicomachean Ethics*, III, 2, where acts done out of ignorance are regarded as non-voluntary, just like acts done under compulsion, and consequently do not involve any punishment for their author.

[11] Sanhedrin 74a.

[12] *Ibid.*, and 74b; cf. 'Avodah Zarah 27b.     [13] Sanhedrin 74a.

[14] The extent to which actions held as profaning the Name were considered criminal by this school of thought is evident from its view of *repentance* which, in the cases of such offenses, cannot earn the sinner divine pardon. Repentance is merely the first step for cleansing the soul of its sin, whereas the end result can be attained only by death itself. See Tosefta (ed. Lieberman, New York, 1962), Kippurim, IV (v), 8; Yoma 86a.

or public. In conformity with this opinion, a tannaitic decision, probably adopted during the Hadrianic persecutions, states definitely and without reservations: where the transgression of the Law implies death, one should violate the Law and stay alive, except in instances where the violation implies idolatry, incest, or murder; in such cases one should prefer death to the violation of the Law.[15] Nevertheless, the controversy was not abated and continued even in amoraic times. Rav Ze'ira, the Amora of the fourth century, objecting to the extreme view that idolatrous worship is criminal under *all* circumstances, evidently maintained that *any* violation of the Law committed under compulsion is not liable to punishment,[16] while Rava, his contemporary, took the intermediate position of Rabbi Ishmael and declared idolatrous worship under the threat of death to be a crime only when performed in public.[17] Now these opinions as well as their motivation, with their apparently contradictory approaches and principles, formed the core of the dualistic attitude toward forced conversion manifested by the Jewish authorities in the Middle Ages.

Let us now consider the essentials of the first tradition whose origin must be associated with two of the first and foremost rabbinical authorities in Germany and France, i. e., Rabbenu Gershom, the Light of the Exile, and Rabbi Solomon ben Yiẓḥak (Rashi). It is quite clear that the major aim of their policy was to facilitate, as far as possible, the return of the forced convert to the Jewish fold. Thus, according to Rashi, not only should the forced convert, so long as he is secretly devoted to Judaism, be regarded and treated as a full-fledged Jew,[18] but special concern should also be shown for the state of mind in which he

---

[15] Sanhedrin 74a.

[16] 'Avodah Zarah 54a; the principle enunciated in this instance is אונס רחמנא פטריה; cf. Nedarim 27a (where instead of אונס the reading is אנוס); cf. also Yoma 85a and Bava Qamma 28b.

[17] 'Avodah Zarah 54a.

[18] This is implied in his position on *anusim*, as expressed in his responsum, quoted in Judah ben Asher's *Zikhron Yehudah*, Berlin, 1846, 50a; similarly, *anusim* who had illicit relations with Christian women are treated by him on a par with Israelites. See Rashi's *Responsa* (ed. I. Elfenbein, New York, 1943), No. 171 (p. 192).

necessarily finds himself. Every caution should be exercised in avoiding offense to the forced convert, both before and after his return, a hostile attitude, according to these authorities, being likely to alienate him from the community and weaken his desire to return to the fold.[19] The matter was considered of such importance that Rabbenu Gershom would excommunicate any one who would remind a returning convert of his conversion,[20] while the responsa of Rashi generally refrain from using the offensive title *convert* when referring to forced converts, and employ instead the term *anus* (the forced one), which highlights merely the element of compulsion.[21]

This attitude of special consideration for the forced convert's feelings and difficulties, however, was expected to be reciprocated on his part by a demonstration of proper behavior. To begin with, he was expected to realize that his forced conversion did not absolve him from punishment for any misdemeanor he might have performed while ostensibly a convert. As with the initial act of conversion, so each action or inaction violating the Law for which he might be held responsible thereafter, must, in order to be exempt from punishment, be a result of the same kind of compulsion; more specifically, whenever not evidently threatened

[19] See *Teshuvot Rabbenu Gershom Meor ha-Golah* (ed. S. Eidelberg, New York, 1955), 4; Rashi, *Responsa*, No. 170. Both responsa insist on the restoration of the full rights to a converted priest who returned to the fold; cf. the opposite stand taken in the Geonic period (see L. Ginzberg, *Genizah Studies*, II, New York, 1929, p. 107). See also Rashi, *Responsa*, No. 168 (חלילה לפרוש מן יינן של אנוסים ולביישן); the same attitude is expressed also in the ordinances of Rabbenu Tam; see L. Finkelstein, *Jewish Self-Government in the Middle Ages*, New York, 1924, pp. 126 (שלא להזכיר), 175, 179 (שלא לבייש אדם אנוס ובעל תשובה) (פשעו לבעל תשובה; שלא לבייש בעל תשובה מעוונו).

[20] See Rashi's responsum in J. Müller, *Teshuvot Ḥakhmei Ẓarefat ve-Loter*, Vienna, 1881, No. 21 (p. 11b).

[21] It appears that it was through the responsa of Rashi that the title *anus* was first introduced into the responsa literature as a technical term for forced convert. Not before decades passed, however, was this use generally accepted. In the chronicles of Solomon ben Simon about the first crusade (written in 1140) the term *anusim* still alternates with *ne'enasim* (see A. Neubauer and M. Stern, *Hebraeische Berichte ueber die Judenverfolgungen waehrend der Kreuzzuege*, Berlin, 1892, pp. 13, 21, 29; the same is true of the chronicles of Ephraim ben Jacob of Bonn about the second crusade (see *ibid.*, pp. 64, 73).

with loss of life, he must perform the commandments, both the positive and negative, as all faithful Jews do;[22] second, he must seek all avenues of escape from a situation which recurringly subjects him to the violation of the Law and return to the fold as soon as possible.[23] Then, upon his return, he should repent "with all his heart" and behave as all penitents of this category should.[24]

This, then, was the second half of the Franco-German policy toward the forced convert, and what it aimed at and what it implied from the standpoint of the relationship between the latter and the community can be easily seen. The idea that each of the convert's transgressions must be judged independently, and not automatically as a direct result of his status, inevitably led the convert to realize that his undergoing forced conversion did not end with the initial, formal act, but was actually being renewed again and again with every performance of the prohibited religious worship. While this was bound to deepen his consciousness of sin, the insistence upon his obedience to Jewish law whenever not clearly threatened with death was aimed, among other things, at defeating the tendency toward detachment from Judaism which was bound to develop out of the habitual departure from Jewish law and custom.[25] As far as the forced convert was concerned, however, this dualism of life and performance placed him in a situation which was as agonizing

[22] See Rashi's responsum in *Zikhron Yehudah*, p. 50a. Proper *anusim*, who can be considered qualified witnesses, i. e., who are in good standing as Jews before a Jewish court, are, according to him, those who "secretely practiced the Law of Moses and were not suspect of transgressing any of the commandments which they violated under compulsion."

[23] This is clearly implied in Rashi's description of *anusim* who behaved properly. See his *Responsa*, No. 168 (p. 189).

[24] *Anusim* must perform, according to Rashi, "proper repentance" (תשובה הוגנת), that is, one which must be effected "with all their heart and all their soul and all their might" (בכל לבבם ובכל נפשם ובכל מאודם).

[25] That deviations from Jewish law became customary among *anusim* in the Franco-German countries, too, although undoubtedly in smaller measure than it later appeared in Spain and Portugal, is evident from various responsa. See, for instance, Rashi, in *Zikhron Yehudah*, 50a (ואם הוחזקו האנוסים מופקרים); id., *Responsa*, No. 169, p. 190 (ואנוסים שחללו שבת בפרהסיא); (בעבירות שלא אנסום); R. Ḥayyim ben Isaac of Vienna, *Responsa*, No. 91 (ed. Leipzig, 1860, p. 28b).

as it was dangerous. He had to weigh his every action and decide whether it involved danger to him or not, and he had to guard himself not only from the opinion of his Christian neighbors, but also from the judgment of his fellow Jews. That he was often misjudged by them can be taken for granted, since the borderline between the violation of Jewish law through fear and its violation for other reasons could not always be clearly discerned. Then, his motives, even if justifiable, could not always be explained to, or understood by those who had not experienced his predicament. The inevitable result was that the attitude toward the forced convert was mingled with a growing distrust, and this distrust, plus the tension it generated in his relationship with the Jewish community, was bound to diminish the standing of the forced convert in the eyes of the faithful.

In fact, distrust of him was so great that his behavior was carefully watched by the community for a long time even after his return.[26] What is more, his behavior was a yardstick of his repentance which, in his case, could be considered accomplished only after a long period of penance and self-denial. The importance attached, in this tradition, to this form of repentance cannot be over-stated, for forced conversion was viewed by it not as a transgression to be treated lightly, or even as a serious misdemeanor, but as a degrading and grievous sin.[27] While

---

[26] Rashi, *Responsa*, No. 168 (שאלו לפני ר' על האנוסים אם יש לפרוש מן יינן עד) שיעמדו בתשובתם ימים רבים ותהיה התשובה שלהם מפורסמת; *ibid.*, No. 169 (ונ ל ו י ה. ואילו האנוסים שבאו מחדש אין אנו בקיאין בהם ותשובתן לא ראינו (אנוסים שחיללו שבת בפרהסיא ותשובתם לא נתפרסמה — עד מתי מותרים לשתות יין עם אחיהם?).

[27] Even Jews converted not under threat of death, but by sheer physical force, as was the case of the Jews of Regensburg during the first Crusade, were held guilty and consequently in need of repentance (see Neubauer and Stern, *op. cit.*, p. 28). The extent to which the sin involved in a conversion effected not by violence, but in *mortal fear* was considered deplorable by this school of thought, is indicated in the demand of Asher ben Yeḥiel for the sinner not only to repent, but also to subject himself to "suffering." See his *Responsa*, xxxii, 8 (p. 32c). On the gravity of the sins that require, to be cleansed, "suffering" in addition to repentance, see Maimonides, *Sefer ha-Mada'*, *Hilkhot Teshuvah*, I,4; and cf. above, note 14. The difficult, almost crushing, purgatorial procedure, recommended for a returning convert in the *Darkhei Teshuvah* (see Meir of Rothenburg, *Responsa*, Budapest, 1895, p. 161c) —

stipulating that this sin should never be used to taunt the returning convert, it insisted that he should always and at all times be conscious of his guilt.[28] He should deeply regret his action both before and after his "return," and repeatedly give vent to his regret in expressions of anguish and prayers for forgiveness.[29] None of the romantic heroism which in later times and other countries was associated with the life of the forced convert is evident in this tradition. On the contrary, there was nothing, according to it, for the forced convert to be proud of — certainly not his deed in saving his skin — and a great deal to be humble about. Perhaps the best expression of this attitude is to be found in the responsa of Rabbi Asher ben Yeḥiel. Comparing the believers in Judaism to the soldiers of a king, he avers, in all seriousness, that it is on those prepared to fight to the end that the God of Israel can rely for the maintenance of His kingdom; therefore, he who fled in fear before a life and death

a compendium of Franco-German origin — alludes to no distinction between the two kinds of converts, and most likely was meant for both. The compendium, which is based on Eleazar ben Judah's *Sefer ha-Roqeaḥ*, significantly changes the title כופר בעיקר, the subject of the corresponding passage in the latter work (see *ibid.*, Hilkhot Teshuvah, xxiv, Jerusalem, 1960, p. 31, and *Yoreh Ḥaṭa'im*, Lemberg, 1837, xix), to the mere external description: נשתמד ועובד ע"ז, which puts the stress not on beliefs, but on the bare facts of conversion and worship. Perhaps also indicative in the same direction is the omission of Eleazar ben Yehudah's directive: ואם יאמר לו מומר רשע ישתוק.

[28] In conformity with this doctrine was the emphasis placed upon Sanctification of the Name as a duty incumbent upon every Jew under practically all conceivable circumstances (see R. Eliezer of Metz, *Sefer Yere'im ha-Shalem*, Vilna, 1901, cclxx [128b]). Although thus presented as an "every-day" precept *from which no deviation was permissible*, the difficulty in fulfilling this precept could, of course, not be ignored. R. Meir of Rothenburg was clearly trying, in his campaign for Sanctification, to make that difficulty appear less frightful (see his *Responsa*, ed. Sudylkow, 1835, No. 517; and cf. *Kol Bo*, Fürth, 1782, 56d). On the other hand, to increase the attraction of Sanctification, stress was placed upon the great honor which the name of the Sanctifier was to earn: he was to be mourned by the entire people and, out of respect for his memory and for Heaven, his widow was never to remarry. See R. Ḥayyim ben Isaac of Vienna, *Responsa*, No. 14 (p. 7b).

[29] See Rashi's responsum in *Zikhron Yehudah*, 50a: while in a state of conversion, the *anusim*, in order to qualify as Jewish witnesses, should be not only "God fearing" (יראי השם), but also בוכים ומצטערים על אונסם ומבקשים מחילה.

struggle could not expect, upon returning after the storm, to be treated as if nothing had happened.[30] The conclusion: the forced convert is not an outright traitor, as the real convert was considered to be, but he is nevertheless a cowardly deserter; he should realize that he has committed a disgraceful act and his bearing should be one of shame and humiliation; only a long process of repentance through sufferance could obliterate his shame and sin.[31]

These then were the essentials of the Franco-German tradition with respect to the attitude towards the forced convert. Opposed to it in spirit, as well as in content, was the tradition originated in Moslem Spain, as reflected in the various expositions of Maimonides. As far as theory is concerned, Maimonides too regards Sanctification of the Name, i. e., the preference of death to conversion, as the highest form of religious devotion and as a directive which the believer is duty-bound to obey.[32] From a practical point of view, however, when he comes down to the concrete case before him — that is, of the Almohadan persecution, he strongly advocates forced conversion on the ground that the Law was made "to live by it and not to die by it."[33] As for the status of the forced convert, not only does he consider him a full-fledged Jew — as the Franco-German rabbis did — but also one in good standing as far as the requirements

[30] Asher b. Yeḥiel, *Responsa*, xxxii, 8 (p. 32c).

[31] Thus, according to Asher ben Yeḥiel (*ibid.*), those converted out of fear of death require, in order to be forgiven, to go through three stages of purification: self-reproach (חרטה), repentance (תשובה) and suffering (יסורים). Cf. above, notes 14 and 26.

[32] *Iggeret ha-Shemad*, in *Ḥemdah Genuzah* (ed. Z. H. Edelmann), Koenigsberg, 1856, 9b, 10b, 11a; *Hilkhot Yesodei ha-Torah*, V, 1, 4.

[33] See *Iggeret ha-Shemad, ibid.*, 11b: לפיכך כל מי שנהרג כדי שיודה בשליחות אותו האיש לא יאמר עליו [אלא] שהוא עושה הטוב והישר ויש לו שכר לפני השי"ב . . . אבל מי שבא לשאול אותנו או יהרג או יודה אומרים לו שיודה ואל יהרג. The extent to which Maimonides was definite in this matter can be seen from his criticism of his opponent who advocated Sanctification of the Name under the Almohadan persecution. He regards him as "a sinner and rebel who deserves the death punishment," for he ignores the admonition of the Sages: "Let him transgress and not be killed" and the divine injunction of "to live by them, and not to die by them" (*ibid.*).

of the Law are concerned.[34] Considering the formal act of forced conversion valueless from a legal point of view, he brings to the forefront the old dictum that absolves misdeeds committed under compulsion from any penalty whatsoever.[35] As Maimonides apparently understood this dictum, the wrongdoer is free from any penalty because he is free from any guilt; and, indeed, nowhere in the tannaitic or amoraic literature, he says, is the forced convert called "sinner, or wicked, or unqualified to serve as witness."[36] On the contrary, what the tradition of the Sages indicates is that people of this category were regarded as "most righteous" (צדיקים גמורים).[37] In any case, what counted heavily with Maimonides was not so much the act of conversion itself, as the clandestine devotion of the convert to Judaism in the face of mortal danger. No one, he emphasizes, can claim greater

[34] *Ibid.*, 11a. Maimonides defines here the forced convert as an "involuntary profaner of the Name" (מחלל שם שמים באונס) who, as he puts it, "bears no similarity whatsoever to the voluntary profaner" (ואינו כמו מחלל שם שמים ברצון בשום פנים). The forced convert, he agrees, failed to perform an explicit commandment: to sanctify the divine Name; it seems, however, that despite his recognition of Sanctification as a commandment directed to the whole people (see above, note 32), he did not see in it a generally performable precept, but rather an opportunity to *excel* in doing good, which only the extra-pious are capable of grasping. This is, possibly, indicated by his use (*ibid.*, 10b) of Ps. 50.5 to describe the Sanctifiers (אספו לי חסידי כורתי בריתי עלי זבח), although he follows here Sanhedrin 110b, and by his carefully phrased appraisal of the forced convert as merely one who "failed to do good": לא היטיב לעשות (*ibid.*, 11a); in contrast, see the evaluation of Asher ben Yeḥiel: מאד הרעו לעשות (*Responsa*, xxxii, 8, 32c). In *Hilkhot Yesodei ha-Torah*, V, 4, Maimonides' formal position on forced conversion appears to be stricter: here he defines the forced convert (under certain circumstances) plainly a "profaner of the Name;" his fundamental attitude, nevertheless, appears to have remained unchanged.

[35] *Iggeret ha-Shemad, ibid.*, 11a.

[36] *Ibid.*: ולא נקרא לא פושע ולא רשע ולא פסול לעדות אלא אם כן עשה עבירות יפסל בם לעדות.

[37] *Ibid.*; Maimonides classifies here the faithful Jews during the Hellenistic persecution in the category of forced converts, using as a basis for this classification a statement from *Midrash Ma'aseh Ḥanukkah* (עמדו וגזרו: כל בן ישראל שעושה לו בריח או מסגר לפתחו ידקר בחרב; see the various versions of this midrash in J. D. Eisenstein, *Oẓar Midrashim*, I, New York, 1915, especially pp. 189, 192), but attributing to it quite a different meaning from the one implied in the midrash itself.

idealism and purity of purpose in performing the commandments than the *forced* convert, for assuredly he was impelled to this performance by religious motives only, and not by lesser considerations such as the desire for public acclaim and the benefits following therefrom.[38] Consequently, "he who performs the commandments secretly may well expect a much greater reward than he who performs them openly."[39] Yet the forced convert deserves a "higher premium" for still another reason, which is truly preponderant: in Maimonides' opinion, "there is no comparison between the reward awaiting one for performing a commandment *without fear*, and that which is assured to him who does it *knowing* that discovery would bring forfeiture of life and property."[40] According to this conception, then, not only is the forced convert free from sin and guilt, but he also deserves high praise and admiration, second only to that befitting the one who sanctifies God's name. No wonder, therefore, that nowhere does Maimonides indicate the need for the forced convert to do penance. Only in one instance does he consider the convert who is secretly practicing the Jewish religion justifiably subject to heavy censure — that is, when he refuses to leave the land of persecution and settle in a country where he can worship in freedom. He considers such transfer so important for the believer that in his opinion nothing should stand in its way, not even love for wife and children — let alone considerations of a pecuniary nature.[41] Indeed, he says, he who is prevented from taking this step by such considerations and desires (משאלות לבו) "should see himself as a profaner of the Name" of a category "akin to one who does it willfully," or more clearly, he should regard himself as a transgressor "incurring divine dissatisfaction, who must expect punishment for his evil deed."[42]

---

[38] *Iggeret ha-Shemad, ibid.,* 12b.

[39] *Ibid.*

[40] *Ibid.*

[41] *Ibid.,* 12a.

[42] *Ibid.*: וכל העומד שם הרי הוא עובר ומחלל שם שמים והוא קרוב למזיד; see also *ibid.,* 12b: חייב הוא כל מי שאינו יכול לצאת מפני משאלות לבו וכו' שיראה נפשו מחלל שם שמים לא ברצון ממש, אבל קרוב הוא להיות ברצון ושהוא נזוף מלפני המקום ברוך הוא ונענש על רוע מעשיו. In *Hilkhot Yesodei ha-Torah,* V, 4, Maimonides takes a more severe attitude toward those who can escape and refuse. Here they are

It was this heritage, then, of the two schools of thought, with their conflicting attitudes toward the forced convert, that the Spanish rabbis were confronted with when they had to deal with the problem in Spain. The difficulty in choosing one of these approaches, or in modifying it for their particular purposes, was enhanced by the fact that in Spain the borderline between convert and forced convert was much less firm and less clearly noticeable than it was in Germany or France or the Almohadan domains. Spanish Jewry had been hit by a wave of conversion already before 1391,[43] and when the catastrophe of that year occurred, the *real* converts, substantial in number, were not slow to mingle with the newly converted so as to form one social entity. Such mingling was no doubt facilitated by the fact that already during the riots, and especially shortly thereafter, although fear was clearly still in the air, many were converted more out of despair than out of direct threat of death, and, within the first few decades after the catastrophe, the number of such "voluntary" converts increased by leaps and bounds.[44] The growing merger between real and fictitious converts made it increasingly difficult for the rabbis to deal with the one without touching upon the other, and in dealing with the *real* convert, as with the *anus*, the rabbis had to resort to the legal position taken by the earlier authorities on the question. An examination of this position shows us, first of all, that it,

---

defined not merely as being *close* to the category of deliberate profaners, as they are regarded in *Iggeret ha-Shemad*, but as deliberate idolaters, pure and simple. The more radical position Maimonides took here on this question may have been — at least partly — the result of an intent to weaken the rather negative impression which his defense and, indeed, solicitation of forced conversion must have made on many. And see below, note 92.

[43] See introduction to *Even Bohan* of Shem Tov ben Yiẓḥaq ben Shaprut of Tudela, written in 1386 (Breslau Manuscript at the Hebrew University Library, No. 753, p. 2).

[44] On the conversion movement as it developed after the riots (1391–1415) under the impact of terror, pressure and persuasion, see Amador de los Ríos, *Historia de los Judíos de España y Portugal*, II, Madrid, 1876, pp. 400–407, 424–431, 443–445, and I. F. Baer, *Toledot ha-Yehudim bi-Sefarad ha-Noẓrit*, Tel-Aviv, 1959², pp. 323–324, 347, 357–358, and the sources cited in both these works.

too, was far from uniform and that, just as in the case of the forced convert, it embodied two conflicting traditions, one aiming at the attraction of the convert, the other at his rejection. Dating back to the Geonic period,[45] and possibly to earlier times, these two attitudes manifested themselves in the Middle Ages not so much in crystalized policies as in two distinct approaches, one upheld by Rashi, the other by Maimonides. Rashi, who based himself on the maxim that "an Israelite, although he sinned, is still an Israelite,"[46] strove to emphasize the convert's identity with the Jewish people, while Maimonides, for whom an Israelite turned "idolater" was a gentile in every respect, declared the convert to be "excluded from the community of Israel."[47] The practical difference implied in these theories

[45] The dualism of attitude toward the convert in the Geonic period is especially expressed in the struggle over the question of levirate marriage (see below, notes 102/4). On the question of money lending on interest to a convert we have the opinion of Shalom Gaon, prohibiting such a transaction as well as the borrowing of money on interest from a convert by a Jew (R. Meir of Rothenburg, *Responsa*, ed. Budapest, 25a). Contrariwise, a tradition transmitted by Alfasi, which was no doubt rooted in a Geonic view, *permitted* money-lending on interest to a convert, although only to a defiant one (see *Teshuvot ha-Geonim*, Jerusalem, 1960, No. 284, p. 80). Regarding inheritance, the prevailing opinion in the Geonic period was that a convert does not *inherit* from his father, although he can bequeath his property to his descendants; see *Otzar ha-Geonim* (ed. B. M. Lewin), IX (Qiddushin), pp. 30–34, 200; ibid., part IV, pp. 61–62; see also L. Ginzberg, *Genizah Studies*, II, New York, 1929, p. 122. Although the position may have been inspired by Moslem law, as L. Ginzberg has pointed out (*ibid.*, pp. 168, 636; and see also Lewin, *Otzar ha-Geonim*, IX, pp. 7–8, 200, and *ibid.*, part IV, pp. 61–62), the acceptance of this position and the reasons offered in its defense (in a responsum of Rav Natronai Gaon, *ibid.*, p. 31: משומד ע"י מתעברת נחלה מאומה לאומה), and especially in the formulation in which it is found in Rashba, *Responsa*, VII, No. 292, where it is attributed to Rav Hai Gaon (משומד יצא מאומה לאומה), indicate the dominant Geonic view that conversion does not change only one's religion, but also one's peoplehood, and therefore all ties with the convert must be cut, or loosened as much as possible.

[46] Sanhedrin, 44a; see Rashi's *Responsa*, Nos. 171, 173, 175; on Rashi's novel application of this dictum as an halakhic rule see A. Berliner, "Zur Charakteristik Raschi's," in *Gedenkbuch zur Erinnerung an David Kaufmann*, Breslau, 1900, pp. 271–273, and recently: Jacob Katz, "Israel af-'al-pi she-ḥata," in *Tarbiz*, xxvii (1958), pp. 203–217.

[47] *Hilkhot 'Avodat Kokhavim*, II, 5; see also *Hilkhot Mamrim*, III, 2: והמוסרין והמומרין . . . שכל אלו אינם בכלל ישראל. In keeping with this position is Maimon-

involved both family and economic relations. According to the first school of thought, judged by its extreme position, the convert is on a par with a Jew in all marital and extra-marital relations, while, economically, he is equally so as to the vital matters of inheritance and money lending.[48] According to the second tendency, however, the convert is treated on a Jewish level only with respect to his marrying a Jewish woman under Jewish law; otherwise, he is considered a non-Jew for all intents and purposes.[49] Between these two extremes there were a variety of intermediary positions, and opinion wavered between the two, at times leaning toward the Maimonidean approach and, more

ides' view that a convert, unlike the rest of Israel, has no share in the world to come. In this category, moreover, he places not only a convert to the entire Law, but also a defiant convert to *one* of the commandments (*Hilkhot Teshuvah*, III, 6, 9).

[48] Rashi's position on these questions is stated in the following sources: on marriage — in his *Responsa*, No. 171; on Levirate marriage — *ibid.*, No. 173; on money-lending on interest — *ibid.*, No. 175; on inheritance — *ibid.*, No. 174; the latter responsum, however, deals only with the convert's right to bequeath property; as for his rights to inherit property, Rashi's opinion may be gathered from his general statement on the issue of inheritance and his reference to Qiddushin 18a, where it is clearly implied that a convert does inherit his Jewish father. Had Rashi thought differently and taken the position of Rav Ẓadoq Gaon, namely, that the passage referred to in Qiddushin 18a postulates the convert's right to bequeath, not to inherit (see *Otzar ha-Geonim*, IX, pp. 31–33, 34), he would have undoubtedly found it necessary to comment on this, as did Rabbenu Gershom Meor ha-Golah when he adopted the Gaon's view (see R. Meir of Rothenburg, *Responsa*, Budapest, 1896, No. 928, pp. 129bc).

[49] Although I have associated the second tendency with Maimonides, because of his clear cut stand on the convert's exclusion from the community of Israel, Maimonides was not the most typical representative of the principle he enunciated. When it came to the practical issues involved, Maimonides saw himself often forced to yield his principle to the Talmudic ruling, both the explicit and implied. Thus he felt compelled to agree that a convert does fall under the law of levirate marriage (*Hilkhot Yibbum va-Ḥalizah*, I, 6), although according to one opinion, Maimonides may *not* have referred here to a full-fledged convert, i. e., to one who habitually violates the *entire* Law (see R. David ha-Kohen, *Responsa*, IX, 6, Ostrog, 1834, p. 28b). On the question of inheritance, again, he had to admit that a convert does inherit his Jewish father, but minimized the practical meaning of this privilege by emphasizing the right of the Jewish court to confiscate the inheritance (see *Hilkhot*

often, toward that of Rashi.[50] Yet nothing was really considered final in this matter, except one point on which all agreed, namely, that a marriage between a convert and a Jewess was valid when contracted under Jewish law. Hence, it was the task of the Spanish rabbis, while taking a stand on this issue, to decide upon a choice between the tendencies, or otherwise upon their adaptation in some fashion to the problem they now had to cope with.

To understand more fully what was involved in the adoption of either policy both toward the forced and real convert, a few more remarks are called for. In France and Germany when Jews underwent, during riots and under direct threat of death, a formal conversion to Christianity, they knew that they committed a dishonorable act which was *not* in conformity with the community's principles and traditions. That the community would then disparage their behavior, that they might be judged as failures and weaklings, must have honestly been regarded by

*Neḥalot*, VI, 12, and especially his *Responsa*, ed. Freimann, Jerusalem, 1934, No. 202, p. 198).

[50] On the question of money lending on interest to a convert, the preponderance of opinion appears to have been against Rashi's position. Rabbenu Tam, who took the lead in this direction, on the ground that a convert cannot be considered "thy brother" (*Sefer ha-Yashar*, No. 536 [ed. Vienna, p. 59c]), was followed in this regard by R. Eliezer ben Samuel of Metz, who, nevertheless, permitted the lending of money on interest only to a defiant, not a lascivious convert (*Sefer Yerē'im ha-Shalem*, No. 156, pp. 73b-74a). The same position was taken by Eliezer ben Yoel ha-Levi of Bonn (*Sefer Rabiah*, ed. Aptowitzer, I, Berlin, 1918, pp. 158–159). R. Isaac ben Samuel of Dampierre permitted money lending on interest to a convert, claiming that the injunction to assist one's brother in his livelihood (Lev. 25.36) cannot apply to one whose downfall should be sought; at the same time he prohibited to borrow money from a convert on interest, since the convert is not free from the obligation to assist *his* Israelite brother in his livelihood, and thus he should not be misled into violating a commandment (*Mordekhai*, on Bava Meẓi'a, No. 335; and see E. E. Urbach, *Ba'alei ha-Tosafot*, Jerusalem, 1955, pp. 204–205). Along the lines of these arguments many other authoritative opinions were formed in defense of taking interest from a convert, including those of Naḥmanides (*Ḥiddushei ha-Ramban*, II, 1959, p. 66ab), R. Meir of Rothenburg (*Responsa*, ed. Budapest, Nos. 164, 799), and Solomon ben Adret (*Responsa attributed to Nahmanides*, Warsaw, 1883, No. 224). Among those who upheld Rashi's view on this question was R. Eliezer ben Nathan of Mayence (*Even ha-'Ezer*,

such backsliders, by virtue of their upbringing and religious outlook, as not only understandable, but also justifiable. In addition, since they were relatively few in number, these forced
converts were naturally inclined to gravitate toward the majority,
i. e., the faithful, and, consequently, were prepared to bow to
the majority's criticisms and instructions. Thus there was no
basic split between the forced convert and the community, and
the aforementioned position of the French and German rabbis
was, on the whole, both acceptable and effective.[51] In the case
of the Almohadan persecution, on the other hand, the *entire*
community underwent forced conversion, and the individual
forced convert saw himself acting in full conformity with the
community's decision. Thus here, too, there was no cleavage
between the forced convert and the community, and the positive
view taken of him by Maimonides was in complete harmony
with the convert's self-evaluation and calculated to increase his
steadfastness in the faith. What transpired in Christian Spain,

Prague, 1610, 97a). —On the question of inheritance options were more inclined
toward favoring the convert with this right. Such was the attitude not only of
Isaac ben Asher ha-Levi (*Or Zaru'a*, III, Jerusalem, 1887, No. 103, p. 32b)
and Eliezer ben Yoel of Bonn (*Mordekhai*, on Qiddushin, 492), but also of
Naḥmanides (see Asaf, *Mi-Sifran shel Rishonim*, Jerusalem, 1935, 56–57),
Asher ben Yeḥiel (*Asheri*, on Qiddushin 18a [chap. I, No. 23]) and Jacob ben
Asher (*Tur, Ḥoshen Mishpat*, 283). Rashba, who subscribed to Rav Hai's
responsum on this question (Adret, *Responsa*, VII, 292), and R. Meir of
Rothenburg (*Responsa*, ed. Cremona, No. 82) were among the few rabbinical
authorities in the Middle Ages who denied the convert the inheritance of his
Jewish father. The gap between the opposing views, however, was considerably narrowed by the fact that most of the pro-convert advocates in this matter
favored the confiscation of his inheritance by a Jewish court (see Joseph Caro,
Responsa, *Avqat Rokhel*, ed. Saloniki, 1891, No. 90, p. 61c). — On the question
of levirate marriage, see below, pp. 39–40.

[51] It is significant that practically all the responsa dealing with forced conversion in France and Germany refer to cases of forced converts who *returned* to
the fold. See Rashi, *Responsa*, Nos. 168, 169, 171; *Zikhron Yehudah*, p. 50a;
R. Ḥayyim b. Isaac of Vienna, *Responsa* (Leipzig, 1860, 91, p. 27d); Asher
ben Yeḥiel, *Responsa*, xxxii, 8, p. 32c); Isserlein, *Terumat ha-Deshen*, I, No.
241 (Fürth, 1778, p. 7a). And comp. A. Neubauer and M. Stern, *op. cit.*,
p. 28.

however, was a case apart both in scope and character. Here neither the *minority* nor the *whole* community was converted, but the *majority*, and possibly the overwhelming one.[52] Backed by the performance of the majority body which included many, or most, of the community's leaders,[53] the ordinary forced convert in Spain could hardly develop feelings of shame or regret, the action of the majority tending to bolster his natural tendency to self-justification. Here, therefore, if the minority looked down upon him, or regarded him with disdain or reproach, it would become automatically subject to *his* censure, if not to his reciprocal scorn and aversion.[54]

In these circumstances it is indeed quite dubious whether any of the policies described above could very well fit into the Spanish scene. In fact, both the social and religious conditions in Christian Spain of the 14th and 15th centuries were so different from those prevailing centuries earlier in the countries to its north and south, that the problem of forced conversion in Spain clearly called for a policy of its own. The rabbis unquestionably sensed this need, and the responsa testify to their repeated — though hardly successful — attempts to fashion a new policy congruent with the times. Whether any such policy could in any degree have changed the course of Jewish history in Spain is, of course, extremely doubtful. The policy of the Spanish rabbis, however, to the extent it is reflected in the responsa of the period, was based on a *combination* of the above

[52] The reference here is to the number of the Marranos after 1415. After 1391, however, while possibly counting a quarter of a million, the converts were not the majority of Spain's Jewry. Nevertheless, even then, since they were a *large minority* and constituted a powerful group, their condition differed in this respect from that of the forced converts in Germany, for instance. Furthermore, also after 1391, the forced converts in Spain formed the *majority in a number of important urban or regional communities* as, for instance, in Seville and Valencia. On the number of the Spanish Marranos, see below, appendix E.

[53] See Baer, *op. cit.*, p. 285, 347, 526 (note 4), 527 (note 7).

[54] An indication of the secure psychological position in which the Marranos felt themselves vis-à-vis the Jews, can be found in the following words of Rashbaẓ (*Tashbeẓ*, III, No. 47 [15c]): ומה שלא קידשה בפני עדים כשרים הוא לפי שהוא האנוס אומר שהאנוסים הם יותר כשרים בעיניו מישראלים.

outlined traditions,[55] its various elements changing, as we shall
see, under the impact of the shifting conditions of the age. Uni-
formity or full consistency could hardly be expected in such a
complex and difficult problem, and practical attitudes, as manifested in real life, had their share of influence, too. There is a
great deal more that could be said in this connection. For our
present purpose, however, it will suffice to indicate that awareness of the policies on forced conversion, pursued by the authors
of the responsa under consideration, is necessary to judge correctly their views of the Jewishness or non-Jewishness of the
Marranos.

2

The great rabbinical authority, Isaac bar Sheshet Perfet
(Ribash), escaped from Valencia, where he had served as Chief
Rabbi, during the riots of 1391 and, shortly after having settled
in North Africa, became Chief Rabbi of the city of Algiers.[56]
Between the Jews of North Africa and those of Spain, especially
those of Valencia and the Balearic Islands, there existed a

[55] The basis of this combination was already laid by Rashba who, in his
treatment of forced conversion, applied the principles employed for this case
both by the Franco-German and the Maimonidean schools of thought. In
applying the maxim of "an Israelite, although he sinned, is still an Israelite"
to the case of the *forced* convert (prior to that, to my knowledge, it was applied
only to cases of *real* conversion), Rashba ascribed greater weight to the *sin* of
the forced convert, and, in fact, classified forced conversion as a species of
conversion. On the other hand, by bringing to the fore, as he does, the principle that the "Law was given to live by it, and not to die by it," in explanation
of relieving the forced convert from punishment and of considering him a full-
fledged Jew, Rashba was clearly trying to reconcile two contradictory approaches. See his *Responsa*, VII, 41.

[56] And not of all the communities of the Tlemcen Sultanate, as Graetz
thinks (*Geschichte der Juden*, 4th ed., VIII, p. 99), or of the Hispano-
Jewish community in that sultanate, as suggested by Epstein (*The Responsa
of R. Simon b. Ẓemaḥ Duran*, London, 1930, pp. 19, 35); see A. Hershman,
*R. Yiẓḥaq bar Sheshet*, Jerusalem, 1955/6, p. 168. On Ribash see also H.
Jaulus, "R. Simeon ben Zemach Duran," in *MGWJ*, xxiii, pp. 255–259,
308–314, and E. Atlas, "Ribash u-Benei Doro," in *Hakerem*, Warsaw, 1887,
1–26.

regular, lively traffic, prompted primarily by commercial interests, and when the bloody outbursts occurred in Spain, North Africa was the main sanctuary for those who managed to escape the holocaust. Also, for years after the riots, and probably throughout the first decade, groups of forced converts fled to North Africa, where they could return to their ancestral faith and enjoy the freedom of religious worship. These circumstances, and the authority of Ribash, as well as of his successors of the Duran family, made Algiers an important clearing house for all questions arising from the Marrano situation that had to be decided by a Jewish religious court. It is owing to this fact that we are now in a position to take a closer look at the Marranos' religious life — at least from a Jewish point of view.

The North African responsa, with few exceptions, carry no dates. But the approximate time of their composition can be established, in most cases, by internal evidence. As for Ribash, it seems very likely that those of his responsa which concern the Marranos appear in their present published collection more or less in the order they were issued.[57] Thus it appears that responsum #4 is one of the first documents in which Ribash expressed his opinions on the issue. In fact, it contains his basic concept of forced conversion and the policy he proposed to meet this problem. We shall therefore consider this responsum first.

According to Ribash, the forced convert, in yielding to the act of formal conversion, violates three fundamental commandments: (1) to love God more than life, (2) to sanctify His name, and (3) not to profane it. He is thus guilty of three heavy offenses; yet he must be considered a full-fledged Jew, first, because, "an Israelite, although he sinned, is still an Israelite" and, second, because he committed these transgressions under the impact of the fear of death. In addition, since the Law excludes from punishment any transgression committed under duress, he is also absolved from any penalty, whether

[57] On the problem of the historical order of Ribash' responsa, see Jaulus, "Die Responsen des R. Isaak ben Scheschet chronologisch geordnet," in *MGWJ*, xxiv, pp. 320–325; Atlas, *loc. cit.*, pp. 6–9; Hershman, *op. cit.*, pp. 10, 137–151, 153–154, 165.

human or divine, and in support of this position Ribash employs both the maxims of אונס רחמנא פטריה and "to live by it, and not to die by it."[58]

We see, then, that his policy toward the Marranos is based upon a set of principles borrowed from the Franco-German school as well as from Maimonides. The emphasis of the *transgression* committed by the forced convert in submitting to the formal act of conversion, and the application to his case of the principle "although he sinned," is clearly in accordance with the Franco-German attitude, while the argument for absolving the sinner from punishment is presented along the lines followed by Maimonides. In proposing this eclectic policy, Ribash trod the path beaten out by Rashba;[59] but this did not comprise *all* the fundamentals of Ribash's position on the question. For beyond the initial act of conversion, there was the concrete behavior of the forced convert, and this behavior constituted to Ribash a major factor in determining the convert's status. To make his position, therefore, clear beyond doubt, Ribash adds the following significant passage:

"Nevertheless, it should be understood that this [namely, the consideration of the forced convert as a full-fledged Jew and his being freed from any penalty] refers to one who, when left to himself, does his utmost to avoid any of the sins enumerated in the Law. However, if, even when left to himself [i. e., where gentiles cannot see him], he commits a transgression which entails the penalty of lashes, as when he eats defiled food, whether to satisfy his appetite or out of defiance, he is unfit to offer testimony and is suspect of violating that commandment habitually. Indeed, he is considered a convert with regard to that commandment, which, however, does not make him a convert with respect to the entire Law. Needless to say, if [when left to himself] he worships a foreign deity, or violates the Sabbath

---

[58] Perfet, *Responsa*, No. 4 (ed. New York, 1954, 1c). Some of these ideas of Ribash are expressed through quotations from Maimonides and Rashba. His own presentation of his basic position is summarized by him as follows: דע שכל מי שעבר על כל מצוות התורה באונס ואפילו עבד עבודה זרה שהדין שיהרג ואל יעבור — אם עבר ולא נהרג לא נפסל לעדות וכישראל הוא לכל דבריו.

[59] See above, note 55.

publicly, he is a renegade from the entire Law and should be considered an idolater in every respect."[60]

This insistence upon the need of the forced convert, in order to be considered a Jew, to perform the commandments fully and meticulously is, of course, in line with all earlier traditions, but there is a new strictness here which should not be overlooked. The application of the term מומר לאותו דבר to a forced convert who habitually violates a commandment is not found in the earlier responsa on *anusim*, and it evidently came to remind the forced convert that by habitually violating one commandment after another he was well on the road toward full conversion. By declaring that the habitual violator of the Sabbath must be considered a full-fledged convert, Ribash was certainly voicing a strong tradition,[61] but also here he goes beyond Maimonides' position toward the *anus*,[62] if not beyond that of the Franco-German school.[63] Yet the reason for this attitude can be readily understood. What Ribash was trying to accomplish here was *to draw a clear line of demarcation between the real and the forced convert*, and public violation of the Sabbath by the convert when no apparent danger was involved could well serve, to his thinking, as such a line — a distinct mark of alienation from Judaism and concurrence in the principles of the foreign faith.[64] For what was now uppermost in his mind

---

[60] Perfet, *Responsa*, No. 4 (1c).

[61] See Maimonides, *Hilkhot Shabbat*, xxx, 15: המחלל שבת בפרהסיא הרי הוא; *Hilkhot Gerushin*, III, 15: ישראל שנשתמד כעובד עבודה זרה ושניהם כגוים לכל דבריהם. לעבודה זרה או שהוא מחלל שבתות בפרהסיא הרי הוא כעכו"ם לכל דבריו. According to the 'Iṭṭur, I (Lemberg, 1860, 63b), the early Geonim maintained that one who habitually violates the Sabbath publicly is unlike an Israelite (משומר לחלל שבתות בפרהסיא אינו כישראל). And see Ḥullin 5a, 'Eruvin 69ab.

[62] See *Iggeret ha-Shemad*, in *loc. cit.*, 12b: וגם כן אינו ראוי להרחיק מחללי שבתות [בין האנוסים] ולמאוס אותם אלא מקרבם ומזרזם לעשות המצוות.

[63] Rashi, however, repudiated the ruling that a public violator of the Sabbath is equal to an idolater and saw in the opinion expressed in this regard in the Talmud ('Eruvin 69ab; Ḥullin 5a) an isolated view which does not determine the Halakha (see *Responsa*, No. 169; see also Rashi's commentary on Ḥullin 5a (on the phrase אלא לאו הכי קאמר) and 'Eruvin 69b (on רב אשי אמר).

[64] That public observance or violation of the Sabbath by a *forced convert* in circumstances involving no danger could serve as a line of demarcation between Jew and "idolater" was also the view of Rashi (*Responsa, ibid.*, p. 190), despite

was not the problem of *false conversion*, but rather the problem
of *false anusiut*.

The latter problem presented itself to Ribash not as a theoretical possibility, but as a concrete reality — the product of
the growing religious confusion in the conversos' camp. Ribash
did not doubt that the conversion of 1391 was effected under
compulsion, but he could not help noticing among the forced
converts a change of heart on the entire question. The paramount fact, as he saw it, was that *the convert violates the law
also when left to himself*, namely, "where no [hostile] eye sees
him to inform upon him and deliver him to the authorities,"[65]
and, for Ribash, this was sufficient proof that "the conversion,
which at the beginning was compulsory, turned into a willful
one."[66] What is more, the cases of such *voluntary* converts
became among the conversos so common as to cast a serious
suspicion upon the attitude toward Judaism of the entire Marrano group. In fact, as Ribash sees it, there is no more an *anus*
who can automatically be considered faithful to the religion of
Israel either in theory or in practice; and the practical conclusions he derives from these observations are therefore as
follows:

"Those *anusim* who have remained *all this time* (כל זה הזמן)
in the lands of persecution (בארצות השמד) and did not leave
[those countries] to save their souls, as many, rich and destitute,
did, have already forfeited the *ḥazakah* of being proper Jews
[or, for that matter, real *anusim*], and an investigation of an
expert is required to determine (1) whether they behave as real
Jews when among themselves, and (2) whether they are unable
to escape from the country [of persecution] to a place where
they could practice their religion without fear. Now, if they
fall under this category, they are like full-fledged Israelites;
[consequently,] their slaughtering can be relied upon and wine
touched by them should not be prohibited [for Jews]. If, [on

---

his general objection to having a Jew who violated the Sabbath regarded as an
idolater (see above, note 63).

[65] Perfet, *Responsa*, No. 4 (p. 1c).

[66] *Ibid.*: ואע״פ שתחילת ההמרה היתה באונס, הרי הוא עתה עובר ברצון.

the other hand,] even when left to themselves, they willingly commit the sin of worshipping a foreign deity or of publicly violating the Sabbath laws, they must be considered complete idolaters, and [consequently] their slaughter should be regarded like that of a gentile and their touch prohibits the wine.[67] However, if the sin committed [habitually] belongs to other categories, [the transgressor] should be considered a convert with regard to that particular law, but not in other respects as well. He does not defile wine by his touch, for [in that case] he is not to be regarded as a complete gentile."[68]

The important element in the convert's problem, presented in the passage just quoted, is, of course, his required departure from the Spanish domains to other countries. The remedy advocated by Maimonides — flight at all cost — is evidently adopted by Ribash, too, but the obstacles that stood in the way of this plan were much greater in Christian Spain than in Germany or in the Moslem Spanish principalities which were

[67] From Ribash' responsa on the issue of *yein nesekh* it is clear that he took the Maimonidean position (*Hilkhot Ma'akhalot Asurot*, xi, 4–5) that the deliberate touch of wine by a Christian forbids the wine for a Jew to drink, or otherwise benefit from it (*Responsa*, No. 12, 6a), while if it was so touched by a Moslem it was forbidden for drinking only (*ibid.*, No. 424, 268a). The position of Rashi who tried to mitigate the severity of the ancient ruling on *yein nesekh* insofar as the touch of Christians was concerned (see Tosafot on 'Avodah Zarah 57b; Tur, *Yoreh De'ah, Hilkhot Yein Nesekh*, 123; Rashi, *Responsa*, Nos. 58 [p. 56], 155 [p. 177]; Berliner, *loc. cit.*, pp. 273–275) — a position supported among others by Asher ben Yeḥiel (*Asheri*, on 'Avodah Zarah 57b [chap. IV, 7]; Tur, *Yoreh De'ah, ibid.*) — was obviously rejected by him. In this connection it should be added that his religious-legal evaluation of Christianity in this and other instances was not only in conformity with the opinion of most earlier Jewish authorities, including Maimonides (*Hilkhot 'Akum*, ix, 4), but also in accord with the mutual religious attitudes prevailing in the Middle Ages. Thus Christians considered Moslems as heathen (see, for instance, the Latin epitaph on the sepulcre of Fernando III in Seville [cf. Américo Castro's "Las Castas y lo Castizo," in *La Torre*, Puerto Rico, July-December, 1961, pp. 72–73], which includes the statement: "et metropolis tocius Hispanie de manibus eripuit paganorum"), while Moslems regarded Christians as polytheists and idol worshippers (see, for instance, A. Huici Miranda, *Las Grandes Batallas de la Reconquista durante las invasiones Africanas*, Madrid, 1956, pp. 120, 129).

[68] Perfet, *Responsa*, No. 4 (1c).

overrun by the Almohades. The main difficulty lay, it appears, not so much in the prohibitive orders issued against such emigration,[69] as in the expense of transportation across the sea and in the economic prospects offered the immigrants by their prospective countries of destination. That Ribash had these impediments in mind, we know from at least two indications,[70] although it is not clear that he assessed them in the light of a large scale solution. In any case, when writing the above-mentioned responsum, he believed that the opportunities for flight were still far from exhausted, and that failure to use these opportunities was caused not by the objective conditions, but by the subjective attitudes of the converts themselves. The majority of those who *wanted* to leave Spain, he was sure, could have done so and settled elsewhere, and thus those who remained there *all this time* (which means, it seems, at least several years) were, in most cases, not really concerned, or rather determined to stay where they were. Now, since these people did have the possibility of departing from the land of persecution, they can no longer invoke the pretext of coercion as excuse for practicing the foreign religion. This fact, plus the slighting of the commandments, noticeable among many of the Marranos, places the Jewishness of *each* of them in grave doubt, according to Ribash. Therefore, whenever a case of an *anus* is brought before a rabbinical court, that *anus* should be subjected to an investigation to determine what kind of *anus* he is, i. e., whether he is (a) one who acts secretly as a real Jew, but has no possibility of leaving for another country, or (b) one who violates such precepts of the law whose violation does not place him in the category of a gentile, or (c) one who freely worships a foreign God or publicly violates the Sabbath, who is a non-Jew to all intents and purposes.

What can be deduced from all this regarding the shifting attitudes among the conversos toward both Christianity and

[69] Baer, *op. cit.*, p. 300; id., *Die Juden im christlichen Spanien*, I, Berlin, 1929, No. 451.

[70] See Perfet, *Responsa*, Nos. 11, 61. On the economic difficulties that developed in North Africa as a result of the influx of the refugees from Spain, see also *Tashbeẓ*, III, Amsterdam, 1738, No. 45 (14c); 46 (14d).

Judaism can be safely summarized as follows. The attachment to Judaism was weakening; the trend toward Christianity was intensified. The migration of the forced converts from Spain, which at first was not inconsiderable, was, after a few years, reduced to insignificant proportions. The conversion of many, which was at first forced, ended as a voluntary one. The number of those who had undergone a change of heart could not yet be determined; there were still many devoted Jews among the Marranos, but the number of real renegades was alarmingly increasing. No longer were the latter an insignificant minority; had they been so, they would not have subjected the entire group to such a grave suspicion.

This position of Ribash is further clarified in a responsum which was apparently written some time later. He now describes the stay in Spain of those who failed to leave the country not in the vague phrase of "all this time" (כל זה הזמן), but in the more definite term of "a long period" (ימים רבים),[71] and he not only insists that they be subject to an inquiry, but that their cases call for a *thorough* investigation (וראוי לחקור הרבה בענינם)[72] which is clear evidence that, in his opinion, there was now room for greater suspicion. Indeed, suspicion for Ribash is already partly replaced by certainty when he now says quite definitely that some of them "had the possibility of escaping," but refused,[73] and he explicitly attributes that refusal to no other motive than their changed attitude toward Judaism. "For, after having been converted at the beginning under compulsion, they later threw off willingly the yoke of Heaven, broke the bonds of the Law (ניתקו מוסרות התורה מעליהם), and of their own free will they follow the laws of the gentiles and violate all precepts of the Torah.[74] Furthermore, they persecute the unfortunate Jews who live in their midst and [repeatedly] cast aspersions upon them in order to eliminate Israel from among the nations and bring a total end to its existence. In addition, these wicked elements deliver to the authorities those *anusim* whose heart is devoted to Heaven,

---

[71] Perfet, *Responsa*, No. 11 (3b).
[72] *Ibid.*      [73] *Ibid.*
[74] *Ibid.*: ומרצונם הולכים בחוקות הנויים ועוברים על כל מצוות התורה.

[i. e., who are faithful to the Jewish religion] and who endeavor to leave the land of persecution, as we heard about some in Valencia and Barcelona. Now these and all those who resemble them have no share in the God of Israel, and not only are they disqualified as witnesses, but they must be classed as inferior to gentiles, [i. e., as heretics and real converts whose downfall should be sought,] *albeit their conversion was originally a forced one.*"[75]

With all this it is still clear to·Ribash that the converts who have undergone a change of heart do not comprise the *entire* Marrano group. "There are others," he says, "who would have left the land of persecution wholeheartedly, but could not afford the large expense involved in removing themselves and their families to another land."[76] They do not escape *without* their families, as Maimonides advised for such cases, "since they fear that if they left their family members behind, the latter would assimilate among the gentiles, follow their behavior and will never leave those lands." Therefore, "they prefer to delay their departure in order to hold the members of their family in the bonds of the Law and its commandments, until they are pitied by Heaven and the gates of salvation are opened to them. In the meantime, they take care not to defile themselves in transgressions except at *times* of peril and in *places* of danger."[77]

These statements implicitly offer us a new view of a social panorama which was rapidly undergoing a fundamental change. The camp of the conversos was now split wide open into two conflicting factions. One faction comprised those who earnestly desired to retain their Jewishness, or who still had Jewish interests at heart; the other consisted of renegades from Judaism who not only practiced Christianity willingly, but also worked relentlessly to bring the rest of Jewry into the Christian fold. Until then the Jewish people knew the zealot convert who changed his religion of his own volition and then became a persecutor of his

[75] *Ibid.*: אע"פ שהיתה תחילתן באונס. The repeated emphasis of this point clearly indicates that the element of these zealot converts emanated from the *forced* converts, and not — or at least not only — from those who converted at will.

[76] *Ibid.*

[77] *Ibid.*, 3b–3c.

former brethren. Now the same type appears not individually, but in the form of a group — and among those who had changed their religion under *duress*. In consequence, many of those who were originally *anusim* (forced ones) were now to be regarded as ordinary *meshumadim* (apostates) — non-Jews in every sense of the word. As for the other segment of the Marranos, it still contained, to be sure, many crypto-Jews, but the Jewish position towards these could be determined only after establishing the reason for their continued stay in Spain. Many Marranos undoubtedly clung to the country for purely economic reasons; they either refused to exchange security and stability for the unknown possibilities of a foreign environment, or they realized that departure from their native land would mean loss of fortunes and possessions. Ribash did not take such considerations into account. As far as he was concerned, there was only one valid excuse for a Marrano not to leave the country of persecution — lack of means to uproot himself with his family and refusal to leave his family behind out of fear that it would be lost to Judaism. This is the only excuse which, in his eyes, still justifies the treatment of such a convert as a Jew. Lacking such justification, the converso who keeps on staying in Spain and violates the commandments out of *compulsion* must be considered, in his opinion, as one who violates them with *deliberation*.

These and other responsa of Ribash[78] concerning the situation in the Marrano camp leave us with the definite impression that Ribash had no faith in the future of Judaism in the mass of Spain's new converts. He was led to this conclusion by the increasing laxity in fulfilling the commandments even on the part of those who could still be identified as Jews, by the spread of intimate relations between conversos and Christian women[79] and, above all, by the growing tendency toward Christianization among the Marranos, and the rise of an aggressive element among them who conducted a determined anti-Jewish campaign. The only solution he saw for the problem was total and undelayed emigration despite all the difficulties involved. Later developments certainly demonstrated the far-sightedness of this advice.

[78] See, for instance, *ibid.*, No. 6.           [79] *Ibid.*, 2b.

All this, it should be pointed out, is related to what happened between 1391 and 1408, the probable year of Ribash's death.[80] The theory that the Marrano camp as a whole is to be regarded as a Jewish camp appears fictitious even when applied to that early period. Already then it was drifting away from the Jewish fold. What transpired *after* 1408 only intensified that drift.

3

Rabbi Simon b. Ẓemaḥ Duran (Rashbaẓ), who inherited Ribash's position in Algiers, was, like his predecessor, a refugee from Spain who managed to escape to North Africa during the persecution of 1391.[81] Because of his resolute leadership and scholarly pre-eminence, and the fame which he was not long in acquiring, as well as because of his important connections, both personal and communal, with Spain's Jews, and especially with those of Majorca, his former dwelling place, Rashbaẓ was no doubt kept well informed of the internal developments in Spain; and, indeed, his responsa on the Marrano problem at times offer us important information that we can find nowhere else.

The development of Duran's view of the Marranos was, in a way, similar to that of Ribash. He, too, began his summary of the theory he initially formed about their religious stand by emphasizing the full-fledged Jewishness of the forced converts, and, in fact, when he first tackled this problem — while still a member of Ribash's court — we see him take on an even more lenient attitude toward the *anusim* as a group. While by that time Ribash had already abandoned his unreserved faith in the

[80] On the date of Ribash' death see the detailed discussion by Graetz, VIII 4th ed., note 2 (II), pp. 404–406; D. Kaufmann, *MGWJ*, xxxi (1882), 86–91; xxxii (1883), 190–192; *REJ*, iv (1882), 319–320; id., *Ha-Kerem*, Warsaw, 1887, p. 25; Atlas, *loc. cit.*, pp. 4–5. I believe, however, that Hershman clinched the argument in favor of the assumption that Ribash died in 1408 (see *op. cit.*, pp. 155–157).

[81] On Duran see H. Jaulus, "R. Simeon ben Zemach Duran," in *MGWJ*, xxiii (1874), 241–259, 308–317, 355–366, 398–412, 447–463, 499–514; xxiv (1875), 160–178; I. Epstein, *The Responsa of R. Simon ben Ẓemaḥ Duran*, London, 1930; Hershman, *op. cit.*, index.

Jewishness of the Marranos and began to limit their validity as witnesses before a Jewish court, Rashbaẓ still insisted on treating them as Jews without any reservation whatsoever, and considered them trustworthy to testify on all the prohibitions of the Law, let alone of those prescribed by the Sages.[82] In addition, he parts company with Ribash on the evaluation of the *conversos'* failure to emigrate en masse from Spain, and, to justify his position, he takes great pains to explain away Maimonides' admonition against *anusim* who failed to escape the land of religious coercion and are defined by Maimonides as "deliberate worshippers of a foreign deity" and thus as non-Jews in every respect.[83] "It appears," agrees Duran, "that the *anusim* [who stay in Spain] could have escaped from the country, as many of them did. Nevertheless, it is difficult to state this [with certainty] for many reasons." As a matter of principle, we should refrain from attributing their stay to their own will, but rather should we relate it to "one of the compelling circumstances, [namely,] either to their inability to procure the high cost of travel by sea, or to their fear that their intent would be discovered, and [in consequence] they would be classified as criminals and subjected to physical punishment. We may also assume that they did make strenuous efforts to flee [the country of persecution], but failed to achieve this aim because of unpropitious circumstances" (נטרפה השעה).[84] Maimonides' designation of the lingerers, he maintains, should be understood as referring only to situations where no such obstacles exist, i. e., to cases where it is clearly known that one *could* have escaped, but *refused*.[85] Hence it cannot serve as a guide for the action to be taken by the *anusim* of Spain, nor as a yardstick for their evaluation. In thus disposing of Maimonides' opinion, however, Duran does not consider the question settled, and in his effort to disqualify the Marranos' stay in Spain as proof of their religious insincerity,

[82] *Tashbeẓ*, I, lxiii (31d): נאמנין הם להעיד בכל איסורין שבתורה וכ״ש באיסורין דרבנן כסתם יינם והרי הם כישראלים גמורים.

[83] *Hilkhot Yesodei ha-Torah*, V, 4; and see above, note 42.

[84] *Tashbeẓ*, I, lxiii (31a).

[85] *Ibid.* (31d); that is, could have escaped without any danger to himself (שאם הדבר ברור אצלנו שאין לו שום אונס וכו').

he employs a number of further arguments. Evidently impressed by the atmosphere of persecution that engulfed Jews and Marranos alike in Castile and Aragon in the last decade of Ribash's life, Duran does not hesitate to state that even if the king issued a decree allowing all the Marranos to leave the country, he would not regard as sinner any Marrano who might fail to make use of this offer, for it can be argued that he was still afraid that the permit was a trap, a test of the Marranos' faithfulness to Christianity, so that if they followed the proposal they might be put to death.[86] In brief, says Duran, the mere fact of the Marranos' staying in the countries of persecution cannot serve as sufficient proof that they practice the new religion willingly. Since originally the conversion was a forced one, they should be further regarded as being under duress until actually seen transgressing the law when threatened with no danger.[87] Indeed, Duran believes that such matters should be classified among the things known only to one's self,[88] and since only God, and no outsider, can read the innermost secrets of one's soul, the continued stay of the Marranos in Spain should be interpreted positively rather than negatively. What is more, even if the anusim themselves admit that the main motive for their continued stay is financial (מחמת אונס ממון שלא יגזלוהו מהם), namely, their refusal to lose their possessions, they still cannot be regarded as deliberate worshippers of a foreign deity;[89] and he goes into a lengthy argument to prove his point. Thus he takes quite an opposite stand not only to Maimonides, but also to Ribash who, as we have seen, completely disregarded economic considerations (save for travel expenses) as justification for a continued stay. The basic difference between Duran and Ribash at that early stage of Duran's career can thus be summarized as follows: while Ribash considered the anusim suspect in non-Jewishness unless they were proven faithful Jews, Duran considered them

---

[86] Ibid. (31a).

[87] Ibid. (31d): והילכך העולה לנו מזה הוא שאלו האנוסים בחזקת כשרות הם מסתמא אא״כ נתברר לנו שהורעה חזקתן והיותם בלתי נזהרים בדברים אסורים, אבל מן הסתם אין לנו להוציאם מחזקתן.

[88] Ibid. (31a); see also 31d (toward the end of the responsum).

[89] Ibid. (31d).

full-fledged Israelites until proven justified to be considered suspect.[90]

This position toward the *anusim*, however, changed in the course of time. In a subsequent responsum, written years later, we find a stiffening of the attitude toward the Marranos and a clear intention to consider them suspect rather than trustworthy in matters of religious law. Like the earlier responsum, the one now under discussion deals with the validity to be attached to the Marranos' testimony regarding wine they offer to Jews. While in the earlier responsum we saw him take a clearly positive stand on this issue,[91] in the later responsum he writes as follows:

"And with regard to the reliability of the *anusim*, as well as with regard to their touch [in matters concerning the purity or impurity of wine], a great difficulty is involved. I shall not indulge in conjecture in this matter, but shall present to you the words of Maimonides on the *anusim*, as they are written in the fifth chapter of his *Foundations of the Law*, namely, that if he, the *anus*, can escape from the rule of the wicked king and does not do so, he is like a dog that returns to its vomit and should be defined as a deliberate worshipper of a foreign deity, who is denied a share of the world to come and goes down to the lowest part of Gehinom."[92]

What we see here is nothing less than the complete reversal of the stand described above. We find here none of his former liberal interpretations of Maimonides' statement on the need for every *anus* to leave the country of persecution; none of his justification of, or attempts to justify, the continued stay of the

[90] See above, note 87.
[91] See *Tashbeẓ*, I, lxiii (31bc), and above, note 82.
[92] *Tashbeẓ*, I, lxvi (33d). ‏לא אסבור. מ א ד. ק ש ה ד ב ר ומגען נאמנותן בענין ויש‎. Duran's ‏וכו' התורה יסורי מהל' [ד'] בפ"ה ז"ל הרמב"ם לשון לך אכתוב אבל בזה, סברות‎ citing of this passage, not found in some ancient manuscripts of the Code, may be added to other proofs attesting to its Maimonidean authorship. The use Miamonides makes here of the simile in Prov. 26.11 ("like a dog that returns to its vomit") to describe a convert who tarries in the land of persecution was made, curiously enough, centuries before by the Council of Agde (506) in its denunciation of converts from Judaism to Christianity who relapsed into the practice of Jewish religion (see Jost, *Geschichte der Israeliten*, V, Berlin, 1825, p. 64, and cf. J. Starr, *The Jews in the Byzantine Empire*, pp. 6, 140, n. 77).

Marranos in Spain; none of the argument that God alone can decide whether an *anus* is staying out of will or out of compulsion. Duran simply takes here the stand that an *anus* who stayed in the country of persecution beyond a reasonable span of time must be defined as עובד עבודה זרה במזיד, a deliberate worshipper of a foreign deity — the worst definition that can be applied by a Jew to a fellow-Jew who failed in his religious duties.

The reason for this blunt reversal is clearly indicated in the same responsum: it was the increasing volume of evidence on the change of attitudes among the *anusim* themselves. To begin with, he points out, "we see among those *who come over here* full-fledged idolaters (עכו״ם גמורים), and since this is the case, who can say who among the *anusim* is in reality a Jew (כשר) and who is not (פסול)."[93] Furthermore, "according to what we hear about the *anusim, most of them or almost all of them* violate the Sabbath publicly, and even those who used to be careful about this became heterodox (החמיצו) and do not care about this at all."[94] What is more, "it appears," he writes to the inquirer in Majorca, "that you are not troubled at all by their continued stay in Spain *after the permission for departure has been granted*[95] and you do not take exception also to those who do not even think of leaving the country (אפילו לאותן שאין[96] מהרהרין בלבם יציאה כלל), [which thing is evident by the fact] that they built for themselves new houses and married off their sons and daughters [obviously to *anusim* of their own kind who do not plan to depart]. Then, there are those who came here [to North Africa] and of their own will returned [to Spain] — how should *they* be regarded? Should they be considered as those who failed to leave, or not? *All this requires a revision.* It appears that

---

[93] *Tashbeẓ*, I, lxvi (34c).

[94] *Ibid.*: לפי הנשמע ר ו ב ן ו ק ר ו ב ל כ ו ל ן ואפילו אותן שהיו נזהרים מזה [מחלול שבת בפרהסיה] ה ח מ י צ ו ו א י נ ן נ ז ה ר י ם כ ל ל. Rashbaẓ, of course, refers to those who violate the Sabbath out of disregard for the Law, and not out of desire to appear as good Christians in the eyes of the gentiles. That Rashbaẓ saw in *such* violators of the Sabbath real converts, as Ribash did, is indicated in his statement on the subject: וענין החילול [של שבת] בפרהסיא הוא משומד לכל התורה כולה וכו' (*ibid.*, 34d).

[95] *Ibid.* (34c).

[96] This is of course the correct reading instead of שהן.

you believe that their lingering there does not exclude them from the status of a forced convert and does not place them in the category of deliberate worshippers of a foreign deity, *contrary to what Maimonides said and to what appears to me.*"[97]

It is quite clear that the cardinal fact which influenced his view of the Marranos was their reaction to the new policy enabling them free departure from Spain. No strings, it seems, were attached to the permit and no measures were taken against those who left Spain and returned to Judaism; but those who made use of the opportunity were, it is obvious, extremely few, while the rest of the Marranos continued to stay in the "land of persecution," as if nothing had happened. There were some, we gather from Duran's responsum, who interpreted the new policy toward the *anusim* — i.e., the freedom of movement granted them by the authorities and the relaxation in the surveillance of their behavior—as an indication that the Marranos could retain their Judaism in Spain while merely behaving superficially as Christians. *Duran rejects this opinion.*[98] Evidently he saw in the whole conduct of those Marranos a cynical and disrespectful attitude toward Judaism, and he may have also assessed the government's policy as an indication of its belief that the assimilation of the Marranos was well under way and that the freedom of movement was granted them on the assumption that only few of them would abuse the permit for departure for the purpose of returning to their ancestral faith. This assumption was justified by the facts. What Duran now saw was the twofold phenomenon—no emigration movement to speak of and an increased trend toward total assimilation. All this finally convinced him that the *anusim could* leave Spain, but refused to, and all the excuses that he himself advanced to justify their continued stay in Spain against the opinions of Maimonides and Ribash were now completely discarded by him. Not only does he now fail to mention them, but he clearly identifies himself with Maimonides' position, and although he still shows some

---

[97] *Ibid.*

[98] *Ibid.* (34cd): ונראה לי שאתם סבורים שאין עיכובן מוציאן מחזקתן ולעשותם עובדי עבודה זרה במזיד וכו׳ . . . לא שיהא כן דעתי (It seems you assume that their prolonged stay in Spain does not annul their status as forced converts and does not make them deliberate worshippers of a foreign deity. . . . Yet this is not my opinion.)

hesitance regarding the policy to be pursued toward the *group*, one thing is quite obvious: he does not regard the attitude of trust and tolerance hitherto shown most of its members as justifiable any longer. On the contrary, he advocates a *revision* of this attitude. It is clear to him that almost all of the Marranos are violators of the Law, of the kind akin to "deliberate renegades," and all of them, because of their refusal to leave Spain, are regarded by him as perverse sinners. In any case, he emphasizes that the *anusim* can no longer be automatically considered faithful Jews merely on the ground of their forced conversion. Life has shown that they are no longer what they were. Duran is now coming closer to the position taken by Ribash.

In another responsum, the disqualification of the *anusim* as witnesses is extended also to cases of marriage. His opinion is that if a marriage between *anusim* was performed according to Jewish law, in the presence of Jewish witnesses, the marriage is valid. But if it was performed in the presence of *anusim*, it must be regarded, from the standpoint of Jewish law, as if no marriage had been contracted at all. Hence, an *anusa* who married in such a manner and wants to marry a Jew, needs no divorce, "for the *anusim* are certainly no more trustworthy than an Israelite sinner who is not fit to serve as witness."[99] In fact, their status is incomparably worse. "Since they have stayed there [in the country of *shemad*] of their own free will and act licentiously to violate the rules of the Law even when among themselves, in such things as the eating of defiled food and the violation of the Sabbath, apart from serving a foreign deity (מלבד השתחוויתן לעבודה זרה), there is no question about their being disqualified as witnesses in all matters that concern the Law."[100]

By taking this unqualified position on the crucial question of Marrano testimony in matters of Jewish law, Rashbaẓ really classified the Marranos as converts. If a Jewess married to a

[99] *Tashbeẓ*, III, 47.
[100] *Tashbeẓ*, III, 47 (15c): וא"כ זה האנוס שקידש אנוסה זו אם קידשה בפני עדי ישראל צריכה גט ואם קידשה בפני עדים אנוסים דכוותיהו אין קידושיו קידושין דודאי פסולים לעדות הם, שכיון שעמדו שם ברצונם ומתפקרים לעבור על דברי תורה בכמה דברים א פ י ל ו כ ש ה ן ל ב י ן ע צ מ ן כגון אכילת נבילות וחילול שבת מלבד השתחוויתן לעבודה זרה אין ספק שפסולים הם לעדות דבר תורה והמקדש אשה בפניהם אינה מקודשת כלל. Cf. the precisely opposite view cited above, notes 82, 97.

Marrano not before Jewish witnesses was free, according to Rashbaẓ, to remarry a Jew without first obtaining a divorce[101] — and, what is most important of all, without having the need first to establish whether these Marranos were behaving secretly as Jews or not, — it was because Rashbaẓ was convinced that the Marrano camp as a whole was Christianized and that the time had come to draw conclusions from this decisive fact. If most of the Marranos were already converts, or very close to the state of full conversion, they should, he thought, be treated as such, and not as unfortunate crypto-Jews, "whose heart is devoted to Heaven" and who seek every way and avenue both to practice Judaism secretly and return to it openly. To judge by both his diagnosis of the case and his proposals for treating the malady, such treatment should consist first of all in establishing an unequivocal and efficacious partition between Jews and Marranos. This conclusion is especially apparent in his discussions of cases of levirate marriage in which Jews and Marranos were involved.

The applicability of the law of levirate marriage to a convert — or more precisely, the measure of that applicability — was a question on which opinion had differed since the Geonic period. In the solutions proposed to this question, the changing policies toward conversion often played no less a part than purely legalistic meditations or interpretations of the ancient laws.[102] Levirate marriage was a strong bond that held the convert attached to the community, and those who favored the convert's ouster from the fold, looked for arguments to curtail that law's applicability to the convert. In the Geonic period there were several Geonim — notably Rav Yehudai and Rav Naḥshon —

---

[101] It must be pointed out, however, that Duran found it necessary to mitigate his position with regard to the validity of marriages performed by Marranos. Although the need for having Jewish witnesses at the ceremony remains for him a *conditio sine qua non* for the validity of the marriage, he is satisfied to recognize the marriage as binding if cohabitation of the married couple took place in a locality where Jews qualified to testify were available at the time and where it was brought to their knowledge (*ibid.*, 15). This regulation, it seems, was honored in Spain until the Expulsion. The disqualification of Marrano marriages which we find later in the decision of Saloniki's rabbis (see below, appendix A) was in line with this policy.

[102] See above, pp. 16–19; and see on this: L. Ginzberg, *Genizah Studies*, II, 166–169; B. M. Lewin, *Otzar ha-Geonim*, IX, 7–8.

who proposed to limit such application only to cases where the deceased, or his brother, was converted *after* the marriage.[103] But Rav Sherira Gaon objected to this limitation,[104] and so did Rashi,[105] on good halakhic grounds, no doubt, but also because they looked with disfavor upon the severance of all ties between the convert and the community. Maimonides, who declared the convert to be automatically excluded from the Jewish community by his very act of conversion,[106] could not help, nevertheless, recognizing the validity of the convert's rights as a *levir*.[107] This was also the position of Rashba, and of other rabbinic authorities in the Middle Ages.[108] Yet the voice of the opposition was hardly silenced,[109] and R. Meir of Rothenburg did not hesitate to declare that, were it not for the prohibitive authority of Rashi, he would have sided with the Gaon Rav Yehudai on this question.[110] The applicability of levirate marriage to the convert thus remained in full force.

[103] On the opinions of Rav Yehudai and Rav Naḥshon see *Otzar ha-Geonim*, VII, Jerusalem, 1936, 36–37.

[104] See B. M. Lewin, *Otzar ha-Geonim*, VII, 77 (p. 34); cf. *Sefer ha-'Iṭṭur*, Lemberg, 1860, I, 32d; it is not excluded, however, that Rav Sherira shared the opinion of Rav Yehudai and Rav Naḥshon, namely, that if the brother of the deceased converted *before* the marriage, no *ḥaliẓah* was required. Cf. *Bet Josef*, on *Even ha-'Ezer*, 157, and see L. Ginzberg, *Genizah Studies*, II, 168, and B. M. Lewin, *Otzar ha-Geonim*, VII, 36 (note 11). In any case, it is clear from Rav Sherira's own formulation of his position that he limited the application of this law to a convert *born as a Jew*. Cf. *Sefer ha-'Iṭṭur*, *ibid.* This seems to have been also the opinion of the author of *Halakhot Gedolot* (see *ibid.*, *Hilkhot Yevamot*, end, ed. Tel-Aviv, 1962, p. 102a).

[105] See his *Responsa*, No. 173.

[106] See above, p. 17. [107] *Hilkhot Yibbum va-Ḥaliẓah*, I, 6.

[108] Solomon ben Adret, *Novellae on Yevamot*, 22a (ed. Josefouv, 1874, p. 7c); Jacob ben Asher, *Even ha-'Ezer*, *Hilkhot Yibbum*, 157; Isserlein, *Terumat ha-Deshen*, No. 223 [61a]).

[109] Isaac ben Moses of Vienna, for instance, sided, as it appears, with Rav Naḥshon Gaon, according to whom levirate marriage does not apply in cases where the brother-in-law was a convert before the marriage (*Or Zaru'a*, I, Zhitomir, 1862, 605, 163a). His son, R. Ḥayyim ben Isaac, adopted the same position (*Responsa*, Leipzig, 1960, No. 116, pp. 36d–37a), while R. Abraham of Regensburg maintained that a childless widow is free from any tie to her brother-in-law if the latter converted either before or after the marriage (see R. Meir of Rothenburg, *Responsa*, Budapest, 1895, No. 1022, p. 158a; cf. Isserlein, *op. cit.*, p. 60a).

[110] *Mordekhai*, on *Yevamot*, No. 30.

That Rashbaẓ found it necessary to reopen the discussion of this seemingly settled question is in itself a clear indication of his dissatisfaction with the accepted procedure, and the strong support he offered the view favoring the limitation of the levirate law in conversion cases leaves no room for doubt as to where he stood on this question. According to him, a childless widow should be bound to her brother-in-law, under the provision of levirate marriage, only when either her husband or his brother was converted *after* the marriage. However, if either the husband or the brother-in-law had been converted *before* the marriage, the levirate law should not be invoked. This law applies, insists Rashbaẓ, only to cases where real "brotherhood" — not merely in origin, but also in attitudes — could be claimed to have existed during the marriage between the bridegroom and his brother, "but one who assimilates among the idolaters (הנטמע בעכו"ם) comes into the category of a heretic," and since we are obliged to seek the latter's downfall, it is obvious that "if one of the parties had converted, he could no longer be considered a brother."[111] In support of this position, he cites Naḥmanides, who permitted money to be loaned on interest to a convert's son since the Biblical law prohibiting usury applies to a "brother," which means, according to Naḥmanides, not merely an Israelite, but also a brother in feelings and attitudes.[112] It is obvious, then, that Duran completely rejected the idea of "brotherhood" between Jews and Marranos, except in a purely ethnic sense, and that he favored separation between the groups as the only way out of a harmful entanglement. As he saw it, the Marranos ought to be treated realistically according to what they actually

---

111 *Tashbeẓ*, III, 15b.

112 *Ibid*. It goes without saying, argues Rashbaẓ, that if the brother-in-law was a convert when the marriage took place, the woman married her husband on the understanding that she would *not* have to have recourse to her brother-in-law in case of her husband's demise. The reverse halakhic decision in case of the brother-in-law being a leper already at the time of the marriage is not comparable in this instance, for a Jewish woman may agree to live with a leper (who is affected physically) but not with a convert (who is affected morally and whose downfall should be sought); *ibid*., 15bc. The argument Rashbaẓ employs here is similar to that of R. Meir of Rothenburg; see his *Responsa*, Budapest, 564 [76c], 1022 [157d–158a]; also *Responsa*, Berlin, 1891, ms. Prague, No. 130, p. 280).

were — not *unwilling*, but *willing* converts, and consequently, traitors to the Jewish religion and enemies of the Jewish people.[113]

The following responsum (III, 312) throws light on another phase in the *conversos'* situation and their relationships with the Jewish camp. It deals with the "latest converts" (אנוסים אחרונים) "who do not yet (עדיין לא) have the notoriety of violating the Sabbath publicly" and who testify to the ritual purity of wine which was prepared in their homes.[114] Duran, in his reply to the query, takes a severer view of the situation than he had on earlier occasions. Years before, he would permit not only the touching of wine by *anusim*, but also the use of wine sent by them to Jews.[115] Later on, he forbade the touching of wine only by those among the *anusim* who were known to be real apostates (משומדים גמורים).[116] Now, however, he maintains that even if the new *anusim* are not known to have violated the Sabbath publicly, they must be considered suspect of having violated it, and as such they may not even be permitted to touch wine intended for Jews.[117] Furthermore, "even if you forego this general suspicion, it will mean only that their touch does not contaminate the wine, yet their testimony regarding its purity cannot be trusted."[118] In justification of his opinion, he mentions the early

[113] Since the phenomenon of Marranism touched practically every Jewish family in Spain and went deep into family relationships, Rashbaz' position on the attitude to be assumed by the Jewish relatives of a convert in the case of the latter's death, is also indicative of the stand he took on the issues of Marranism and the rift within the Jewish camp. Thus, according to him, the death of a convert should nɔt be mourned by his Jewish brother or other close relations, but should rather be regarded as a joyful event and celebrated in accordance with the prescribed custom (*Tashbez*, II, 139, p. 31d; cf. Maimonides, *Hilkhot Evel*, I, 10 on the basis of *Evel Rabbati*, II, 10; cf. R. Meir of Rothenburg, *Responsa*, No. 544; and see also Asher ben Yeḥiel, *Responsa*, xvii, 9, who seems to have taken a milder attitude since his reply is limited merely to stating that the death of a convert should not be mourned). The same behavior is also recommended in the case of the death of a convert's son, provided he passed the age of minority and had a chance to learn of his real origin. Rashbaz thus rejects *de facto* the notion that converts' sons should be regarded as *anusim* since they were not to blame for their upbringing (a notion derived from Maimonides' attitude toward the Karaites, *Hilkhot Mamrim*, III, 3), although *de jure* he considers it debatable.

[114] *Tashbez*, III, 312 (63b).
[115] *Ibid.*, I, 63 (31bc).
[116] *Ibid.*, I, 66 (34d).    [117] *Ibid.*, III, 312 (63bc).    [118] *Ibid.*, 63c.

converts (אנוסים ראשונים), who certainly were converted under direct threat of death, and yet were not careful to avoid drinking wine with gentiles, and therefore could not be trusted regarding wine; all the more so those who were not converted under total compulsion (שלא נאנסו אונס גמור), there is no doubt that they are not careful in avoiding the drinking of wine of gentiles (אין ספק שאינם משמרים מלשתות סתם יינם). "Therefore I forbade the use of wine coming from them [i. e., from *anusim*] even when it was prepared before the persecution (הגזרה); all the more should we now forbid such wine after the persecution has taken place." And he concludes with the following note: "*And what we saw of them and heard from their own mouths, and what was written to us about them from over there, makes them absolute suspects*; and since they are suspected, they cannot be trusted."[119]

Duran then places the new *anusim*, too, in the category of the distrusted. By these "new anusim" the reference is, it seems, to the Jews in Majorca who went over to Christianity during the persecution of 1435.[120] Now, these converts are placed by him on a level lower than that of the *anusim* of 1391. If the latter, whose religious sincerity could not be questioned at the time of their conversion, became in the course of time violators of the law, i. e., renegades from Judaism and "worse than gentiles," how much more so were the former converts, whose faithfulness to Judaism must be questioned by the very act of their conversion which, although a result of pressure, was not made under the direct threat of death. The experiences of the past led him to assume a severe attitude toward the new converts, an attitude based on a pessimistic outlook which was evidently shared by the Jews of Spain. The phrase "who do *not yet* have the notoriety of violating the Sabbath publicly,"[121] found in the question addressed to him, speaks volumes in this respect. "*Not yet*"

---

[119] *Ibid.*; cf. the more lenient attitude he maintained on the same question, *ibid.*, II, 60 (14ab).

[120] See M. Kayserling, *Die Juden in Navarra, den Baskenlaendern und an den Balearen*, Berlin, 1861, pp. 173–177; Amador de los Rios, *Historia de los Judíos de España y Portugal*, III, pp. 85–87; Graetz, *Geschichte der Juden* (4th ed.), VIII, pp. 184–186; *Tashbeẓ*, II, No. 225 (45b); III, 227 (on the internal relationships in the community of Palma and the relations between the community and the Marranos), pp. 48c–49a.

[121] See above, p. 42.

indicates clearly the general expectation that these converts *will* in the course of time turn renegades as their forerunners did.

Indeed, Simon ben Ẓemaḥ Duran's responsa are replete with testimonies to this effect, i. e., that Marranism was turning relentlessly into apostasy and that the circle was soon to be closed. We shall quote only one more passage. In summarizing the contents of a question addressed to him from Majorca, Duran speaks about "one of those who are called *anusim* and who doubtlessly kneel to a foreign deity and violate the Sabbath publicly."[122] The name *"anusim"* is thus for him clearly a misnomer for the members of this group who, in all propriety, should be called apostates (משומדים). And, indeed, in discussing the *converso* who is the subject of the inquiry, Duran says that "witnesses testified that he was not like the *rest of the converts* (המשומדים) who take off the yoke of the Law, and his heart was directed to Heaven."[123] So the "rest of the converts," namely, the overwhelming majority, were considered Christianized and their hearts were *not* directed toward the God of Israel.

## 4

Simon ben Ẓemaḥ Duran died in 1444. By that time more than half a century had passed since the great conversion. Already two generations of crypto-Jews had lived within the Christian society, at least formally and ostensibly as full-fledged Christians, and practically as a camp whose Jewish underground was gradually weakening and disintegrating under the pressures of environment and education. We have already noticed this trend in the responsa of Ribash and Simon Duran. In the days of Solomon Duran (better known as Rashbash), Simon Duran's son and successor to the rabbinate, this trend was further intensified. We shall later present the reasons for this continual intensification, abetted not merely by the increasing lapse of time since the original conversion (of 1391), but by other important factors as well. At the moment, we are trying to draw whatever testimony

---

[122] *Ibid.*, III, 43 (14a): אחד מהנקראים אנוסים ובלי ספק משתחווים לע״ז ומחללים שבת בפרהסיא.

[123] *Ibid.*, 14b: שאין זה כשאר המשומדים פורקים עול ולבו היה לשמים.

we can from the responsa literature on the Marrano situation, and especially on the attitude of the Marranos toward Judaism and that of the Jews toward the Marranos. The responsa of Solomon ben Simon Duran offer us additional clues in this regard.

Rashbash already had to deal with the third generation of converts. This generation whom he generally describes as "sons of apostates known as uncircumcised *anusim*"[124] — a description which in itself indicates the state of Marranism in his time — presented, he felt, a new problem and called for a new approach. Brought up by parents who were themselves converts or, in many cases, converts' sons, and educated to believe in Christianity and practice it, this generation, taken as a whole, was so thoroughly steeped in the Christian way of life and so completely detached from Judaism that the Jews came to consider them as gentiles. Therefore, when any of this group wished to return to Judaism, the tendency was to judge such a person not as a repentant convert, but as a gentile proselyte. Rashbash was strongly opposed to this position. As he sees it, the gentilehood of the Marranos — even of the third generation of converts — cannot be determined by their religious status, but by their ancestral source and by that alone. As long as they are of Jewish stock, that is, as long as their origin can be traced to a Jewish mother, albeit a converted one, they must be considered members of the Jewish people and, as such, regarded as "our brethren."[125] In support of this position he presents Rashi's view prohibiting the lending of money on interest to a convert, indicating that the pentateuchal concept of "thy brother," from whom alone the taking of usury was forbidden, includes, according to Rashi, the convert as well. Then he takes pains to prove that even in the opinion of Rabbenu Tam and Naḥmanides, who permitted money-lending on interest to a convert, the latter was in no way disqualified as a member of the Jewish people; their ruling, too, was based on the conception of the convert as a "brother," except that they considered him a brother who sinned heavily, "whose downfall should be sought," and therefore must be denied the general privilege of obtaining

---

[124] Rashbash, *Responsa*, Livorno, 1742, No. 89 (17a): בני אלו המשומדים הנקראים אנוסים הערלים.

[125] *Ibid.*, 17a.

help toward his livelihood.[126] Rashbash does agree with the view that any one who has deserted the faith of Israel must be classified, so long as he persists in his deflection, among those "whose downfall should be sought," but such treatment deserve, in his opinion, only those who were fully aware of the truth and willfully rebelled against it. These, and these alone, are the real apostates. Those, however, "who were *born* in heresy, misled by their parents to believe in it and educated on it from their childhood" must be considered, in all justice, "forced ones" (*anusim*). These could not help accepting the new concepts, since "every man, convinced that his father would like him to believe in truth, not in falsehood, believes in the teachings of his father more than in those of a hundred other people."[127]

In thus attempting to divide the *conversos* into these two groups, Rashbash was evidently probing his way toward the formation of a new policy which, in his opinion, the times called for. By broadening the *anusiut* concept of those "born in heresy" — originally proposed by Maimonides for the Karaites[128] — so as to include sons of converts as well, Rashbash was clearly trying to exonerate the overwhelming majority of the Marranos of his time from the crime of outright apostasy. Since they could be taken as having been misled by their parents to believe in the foreign religion, they could be considered as "babes in captivity" who must be treated with patience and understanding. What is more, by applying even to the "rebellious" type of convert the epithet of "our brother," Rashbash was trying to foster more leniency toward the group as a whole — a leniency, which, we may assume, he hoped, might ultimately attract the Marranos to Judaism and facilitate their return to it. In any case, the strictness with which they were regarded by his predecessors (Rashbaz and Ribash), and undoubtedly by many of his contemporaries, must be abandoned, he felt, as unworkable

---

[126] *Ibid.*, 17ab; Rashbash' interpretation of Naḥmanides' position, as well as that of Rabbenu Tam, may be open to question since both these authorities rather insist that a convert cannot be defined as a "brother" (see *Sefer ha-Yashar*, No. 536; *Ḥidushei ha-Ramban*, II, 1959, p. 66a); he similarly appears to be in the wrong when he thus interprets the position of Rashbaz. See above, p. 121.

[127] *Ibid.* (17b).

[128] Sefer Shofetim. *Hilkhot Mamrim*, III, 3.

in the new circumstances, if not as having been ill-advised for the earlier times as well. As he put it, the Marranos "should not be frightened away, but rather be drawn back by an attitude of gentleness" (ואין ליראו ולבהלו אבל למשכו חסד).[129] Every indication should be given them that they are considered by the Jews not as gentiles, but as Israelites, and, as far as their majority is concerned, not even as ordinary converts, but as a group apart, to whom special consideration and extra facilities are extended for their return.

Yet, what is even more typical of his attitude toward Marranism, and what is highly symptomatic of the general situation, is his complete silence on the issue of emigration. That it was useless and ludicrous to advocate flight to die-hard converts, by choice or by education, was of course one reason for this silence, and since by then most of the Marranos were known for what they were, there was no point in mentioning their "stay" as proof of their apostasy either. But what about those "devotees of Heaven" that Rashbash still found among the Marranos, those who "grieved and groaned" under the yoke?[130] Ribash and Rashbaẓ would have undoubtedly fulminated against these delinquents from the obvious duty of "leaving the country of the vicious king" for having remained so long in this sinful state and in that religiously untenable position. Rashbash, however, does not utter even a single word of criticism to this effect against these Marranos either; nor does he offer them any *friendly* advice aimed at the same objective. The demand for emigration is clearly abandoned by him as something unacceptable by the group as a whole and, in all likelihood, as an irritating factor that could bring no good results. Instead, he tries to cooperate with these "devotees" and alleviate their feeling of guilt.[131]

---

[129] Rashbash, *Responsa, ibid.,* 17b.

[130] *Ibid.,* No. 90 (17c).

[131] *Ibid.* On its face value, the responsum appears to testify to the existence of a large Jewish underground among the Marranos. Nevertheless, his statement: אלו האנוסים אשר לבם לשמים . . . אפילו אם לא יאכלו בפסח אלא אורז ודומה לו, יעלילום הנוצרים לאמר: עדיין אתם מתנהגים בחוקת אבותיכם לאכול אורז בפסח כי בכל הבתים מבשלים אורז (*ibid.*) no doubt repeats the argument presented to him by the questioners, who represented, in all likelihood, their local group only, and therefore should not be taken as clue for evaluating the Marrano attitude generally. Accordingly, the responsum was directed to a locality, where

All this clearly indicates a reversal of attitudes in dealing with the Marranos. But it indicates also something else, which, from the standpoint of our inquiry, is of paramount importance. It shows that the policies proposed and practiced earlier to meet the problem raised by Marranism met with no apparent success, if not with total disaster; and this defeat, whatever its measure, *spelled the victory of the assimilationist faction.* Nevertheless, the new attitude, conceived in a spirit of compromise and conciliation, meant retreat, but not total despair. In proposing it, Duran, as we have indicated, must have assumed that ways could still be found in winning back at least a fraction of the Marranos.

But this hope could not be maintained. The lenient policy referred to above was formulated, it appears, at the beginning of Rashbash's career, and from that time there seems to emanate also the report on the remaining "devotees of Heaven" who still sought ways of practicing Judaism, even though in a defective and dubious manner. Yet, in the course of time it became clear to him that even this element had greatly diminished and that the trend toward total Christianization among the Marranos had become more dominant than ever before. In the face of this development, apparently, Rashbash abandoned his policy of leniency either as ineffectual, or perhaps as historically outdated. In any case, in his last responsum on the subject (probably written toward the end of his life, perhaps at the beginning of the sixties), there is no hint of any special consideration for the Marranos as a group, or for any particular part of them. In contrast, there is every indication that he reverted to the position taken by Ribash, and especially by his father in the later stage of his life.

Because of the importance of this responsum to our argument, we shall touch briefly upon the circumstances that evoked it. The question again concerns the ritual purity of wine coming from Marrano sources. The Marrano who, in the case under consideration, sent the wine from Majorca to North Africa, had

such Marranos may have constituted a distinct group, possibly forming even a majority among the local conversos, or its author may have had in mind a few localities where the same condition prevailed. As for the time of composition of this document, the order of Rashbash's responsa collection, if it can be taken as a clue, suggests an early period in his career.

presumably received it from a Jew in Tortosa. Another Marrano, who came from Majorca to North Africa in the same ship that brought the wine, testified to the effect (a) that, while in Majorca, he saw the wine taken off a ship coming from Tortosa and then held to be ritually fit for Jews; (b) that the Marrano who received the wine read a letter sent to him from Tortosa. Besides the testimony of this Marrano, there was evidence that, when the wine was examined in the African port of Bougie, its vessels were found to have been doubly sealed, the external seal carrying the inscription: "Ritually fit wine from Tortosa." Despite this latter evidence, and the fact that a note, confirming the contents of the inscription, was found in a cane attached to the seal, the recipients were doubtful about the purity of the wine, since they received it from an *anus* in Majorca, although they were inclined to dismiss this suspicion owing to the fact that another *anus* corroborated the statement about the arrival of the wine from Tortosa. In this they relied on the old maxim that one who may be suspected of giving false testimony when his own interests are involved, is not suspected of such testimony when it affects the interests of others.[132]

We have presented here the entire case in order to understand more fully the position taken by Solomon Duran. He completely rejects the reliance on the testimony of the Marrano who came from Majorca, since all the Marranos of his time are considered by him untrustworthy as witnesses in any matter that concerns Jewish law. It is true, he says, that Ribash and Simon Duran, his father, once took a different stand; they decided that Marranos could be trusted in testimonies that concern the interest of others, although not in those involving their own interest.[133] But this, he says, referred to the "early *anusim*" (i. e., to Marranos shortly after the conversion of 1391), who did not violate the Sabbath publicly when among themselves; but "today when *all of them violate the Sabbath publicly* [even when left to themselves], *they should not be trusted at all.*"[134]

[132] Rashbash, *Responsa*, No. 553 (109a).
[133] See Perfet, *Responsa*, No. 4 (2a), No. 12 (6a); *Tashbez*, III, No. 312 (63ab).
[134] Rashbash, Responsa, No. 553 (109c): ואע"פ שנמצא בתשובת הרב ר' יצחק בר ששת ז"ל גם בתשובת אדוני אבי מורי הרב ז"ל שיש להאמינם על של אחרים, זהו בראשונים שלא היו מחללי שבתות בפרהסיא, אבל היום ש כ ו ל ם מחללי שבת בפרהסיא אין להאמינם כלל.

Habitual public violation of the Sabbath when conditions spelled no danger was for Solomon Duran, no less than for his predecessors, clear proof that the Marranos involved were real, and not ostensible converts. To assume that such Marranos were crypto-Jews would indeed stand no test of logic. Those who would violate the Sabbath *publicly* when such violation *was not called for* would not, by any reasoning, avoid doing so *privately*, which was the lesser offense of the two. In fact, as if to clarify his view of the Marranos beyond doubt, Duran found it necessary to voice his conviction that, besides being unfit to testify in cases involving Jewish jurisdiction, the Marranos are also capable of forging documents in such cases *as all apostates are*. As Duran saw it, the *anus* referred to in the question may have well falsified both the writing on the seal and the note within the cane.[135] Thus, in this regard, too, he believed the Marranos to be "worse than gentiles."

According to Duran, then, *all* the Marranos were public violators of the Sabbath, which meant, violators of the entire Law, or apostates and non-Jews in every respect, save for matters of marital relations (if we assume that in this respect he adhered to his father's opinion). In the course of his dealings with the Marrano question, Simon Duran, as we have noticed, came to consider the Marranos devoted to Judaism a small minority in that camp. It seems that in the days of his son, Rashbash, such devotees became so rare that they were regarded as virtually non-existent.

Nevertheless, this *total* exclusion of the Marranos from the camp of the "faithful" was, to some extent, exaggerated. The flame of Judaism among the Marranos was not yet completely extinguished, and here and there it still appeared to flicker, sufficiently to kindle new hope in the heart of an optimistic Jewish observer. Such an observer was Ẓemaḥ Duran, Rashbash's son,

---

[135] *Ibid.*, 109d: ומה שיש לחוש בזה שמא האנוס יכתוב כתיבה אשורית על פי ההבית ובקנה יכתוב גם כן פתק, ובאמת שזו חששה גדולה היא, ויותר יש לחוש בזה מן האנוסים ולא מן הגויים, שהגויים אין אנו חוששים להם שמא נמירי כמו שכתבו בשם ר"י ז"ל ו ב מ ש ו מ ד י ם אנו חוששים להם בזה, אלא שלא כל הדברים שווים; שאם אנוס שלחו או הביא יין עמו בספינה א נ ו ח ו ש ש י ם ש מ א ה ו א ז י י פ ו... Note the alternate use of *anusim* and *meshumadim* as synonymous terms. And see Tosafot on 'Avodah Zarah 69b and 31a.

who assumed the rabbinate of Algiers upon his father's death in 1467. For some time prior to that — from 1465 on, it appears — he stayed in Majorca to rid himself of an illness;[136] and it seems that what he saw or heard there led him to express an opinion considerably at variance with the above quoted from Rashbash.

In Majorca, we must remember, a group of Jews had been compulsively converted not only in 1391, but also in 1435, and it is possible that among the latter and their descendants, devotion to Judaism was still manifest. Apart from these there must have been other unmistakable cases of crypto-Jewishness both in and outside Majorca, so that Ẓemaḥ Duran gained the impression that there were still "many among the Marranos who preserve the laws of Sabbath."[137] By "many," however, we should not be misled to think of a majority or even of a large minority. This would too flagrantly contradict Rashbash, as well as what we have learned from all previous responsa regarding the course of Marrano Christianization. To Ẓemaḥ Duran, who was undoubtedly aware of his father's negative statement on the Marranos, it was exciting and indeed even reassuring to find, upon visiting Spanish territory, Marranos still practicing Judaism.[137a] Even if he found that several thousands of Marranos in Majorca, Valencia and Catalonia were still faithful to the old religion, it might have been for him sufficient justification to designate the number as "many." Yet, even several thousands of such Marranos would be but a small fraction of the hundreds of thousands of Marranos who then lived in Aragon and Castile.[138]

---

[136] *Yakhin va-Boaz*, I, Livorno, 1782, 34c (headline to question and responsum); see also *ibid.*, headlines to responsa 125 and 126 (35d, 36a).

[137] *Ibid.*, I, 125 (35d).

[137a] Significantly, the long overdue stay of these Marranos in Spain is completely ignored by him. Cf. above, p. 47.

[138] It must be pointed out that the responsum in which the above statement is found was addressed to a rabbi in Játiva where, it appears, a pocket of *real anusim* persisted up to R. Ẓemaḥ's time (on Játiva, see Baer, *Die Juden im christlichen Spanien*, I, Berlin, 1929, index, p. 1157, and *Sefarad*, VIII, 84; XV, 93–94). It is not unlikely that the favorable report he received about the conditions in Játiva, and about the *anus* who was the subject of the inquiry (אינו אוכל נבלות ולא חמץ בפסח ונמנע מכל האיסורין כפי יכולתו ואינו מחלל שבת לעולם), moved him to consider the Marranos *generally* in a more favorable light. His

The impression thus gained by Ẓemaḥ Duran in Majorca led him to take a more positive view of the Marrano camp as a whole. Some affection for Judaism, he believed, was hidden in the recesses of every Marrano soul, even in the apparently most assimilated one; but he could not of course ignore the fact that most of the Marranos behaved as Christians, "worshipped a foreign deity and desecrated the Sabbath publicly," and gave no sign of that presumably concealed feeling. In trying therefore to sustain the rights of the group in all matters relating to marital law, he could not do so on the basis of the assumption that the Marranos, or most of them, were *religiously* Jewish, that is, in spirit, if not in practice, but rather on the basis of the controversial claim that converts from Judaism should not be classed as gentiles. At variance with Maimonides on this issue, Ẓemaḥ Duran, like his father before him, insists that the Marranos belong to the Jewish fold, "even if we consider them not forced converts, but apostates."[139] The principle that "an Israelite, although he sinned, is still an Israelite," is advanced by him to prove this point; and to fortify his position against ancient opinion, excluding the convert from the Jewish people,[139a] Duran takes a further step which, under the circumstances, was daring indeed. Since that opinion was aimed, as he maintained, at converts to paganism only, it does not hold good for the Marranos, who are converts to Christianity; and he brings to the fore the opinion of Abba Mari, according to whom "gentiles living abroad" [i. e., outside of Palestine] could no longer be classed as idol worshippers.[140] In keeping with this, he

claim, however, that "these marranos are certainly not apostates to idolatry and never believed in it" may well reflect traditional opinion rather than objective observation. It was the prevailing view among Jews for generations that no convert from Judaism to Christianity (or for that matter to any other faith) actually believed in the new religion, and that conversion was, therefore, always a product of ulterior motives (see, for instance, R. Meir of Rothenburg, *Responsa*, Budapest, No. 1020, p. 155c, 155d).

[139] *Yakhin va-Boaz*, I, 107 (26c).   [139a] *Ibid.*; Ḥullin 5a, 13b; 'Eruvin 69b.

[140] *'Iṭṭur*, I, 63b; cf. Ḥullin 13b. Other Jewish authorities in the Middle Ages, who denied — to different extents and in varying degrees of clarity — the identification of Christians with pagans, did so, however, generally with the view of lessening the rigor of the ancient strictures applying to *yein nesekh*, or to business relations and social intercourse with gentiles, but not to conversion

upholds the position, already advocated by his father, that in no way should a "returning" Marrano be considered a proselyte, nor should his offspring be so considered so long as their mother is of Jewish stock.[141] Nevertheless, with all his insistence upon treating the Marranos as members of the Jewish people, Ẓemaḥ Duran, too, like his father before him, eventually reached the conclusion that, as far as Jewish religion was concerned, the Marranos as a group must be counted out. His original view about the considerable Jewishness still to be found among the Marranos was not, it seems, sustained by later evidence. In any case, it is nowhere reasserted, and, moreover, his later statements on the subject are obvious retreats from the original position. One such retreat is already implied in the words, "these Marranos, even if we assume that they are not forced converts, but apostates"[142] — an assumption which he does not reject, although at that time he was evidently still reluctant to concede the apostasy of the camp as a whole. The reluctance, however, was bound to fade away. Additional reports about the Marranos, that he must have received during the years of rabbinical service, compelled him further to revise his opinion, so that he finally reached the same conclusion arrived at by his father in his last years. In brief, Ẓemaḥ Duran, too, came to define the Marranos in their totality as "apostates," without any reservation whatsoever. "These apostates who are called *anusim*" is now a description repeatedly applied by him to the Marranos as a group.[143] And on this last

---

from Judaism. See, for instance, Rashi, *Responsa*, No. 327; and cf. above, note 67. This was also the position of Menaḥem b. Solomon of Perpignan who, despite his staunch advocacy against that identification (*Beth ha-Beḥirah*, on 'Avodah Zarah 6b [p. 9], 11b [p. 21], 21a [p. 53], 57a [p. 214]), accepted the old rulings on converts, including those proclaiming their gentilehood (see *ibid.*, 'Avodah Zarah 26b [p. 61]).

[141] *Yakhin va-Boaz*, I, 107 (26c); also *ibid.*, I, 75 (22d).

[142] *Ibid.*, I, 107 (26c).

[143] *Ibid.*, I; 75 (22c): אלו המשומדים הנקראים אנוסים; לאלו המשומדים או האנוסים and *ibid.*, 22d: אבל המשומדים הנקראים אנוסים אינם צריכים טבילה. The difference between Rashbaẓ and Ẓemaḥ Duran in the group's designation is significant. That of Rashbaẓ reads: "those who are called *anusim* and who doubtlessly kneel to a foreign deity and violate the Sabbath publicly" (see above,

convictive note, confirming what no longer could be denied, ends the discussion of the Marrano problem in the responsa literature prior to the establishment of the Inquisition.

## 5

The Inquisition effected a revolutionary change in the situation of the Marranos and, in consequence, served to heighten the interest in the relationship between them and the Jews. The events that led to this development can be summarized here briefly. The entire camp of the Marranos was violently shaken by the unprecedented terror to which they were subjected. While many of them fled to Christian countries, others escaped to the neighboring Moslem lands of Granada and North Africa.[144] Whether it was for opportunistic reasons, or because the Inquisition made them ponder their fate, their origin and the Christianity that treated them so harshly, some of these escapees from terror were led back to the camp from which their forefathers had come. What was the attitude of the Jews — or more exactly, of the Jewish authorities — toward these "returners"?

Two responsa dating from the years that immediately followed the establishment of the Inquisition can help us reconstruct some of the attitudes prevailing in that period. The first of these was addressed by the leaders of the Jewish community of Malaga, then still under Moslem control, to Rabbi Saadia ben Maimon ibn Danan, Chief Rabbi of Granada.[145] The other, from the Rabbinate of Mostaganem (in Algeria), was addressed to Simon Duran (Solomon Duran's second son), who succeeded his brother Ẓemaḥ to the Chief Rabbinate of Algiers.[146] Both questions revolve on the same theme — namely, the validity of the levirate marriage law in cases involving Christian Marranos — and both have such striking additional similarities, in style as well as in contents, that one is readily led to the conjecture that what we

note 122). In Ẓemaḥ Duran's description the apostasy is emphasized *first* as a fact known to all.

[144] See on this below, appendix B.
[145] See *Ḥemdah Genuzah*, ed. Edelmann, Koenigsberg, 1856, 13a–16b.
[146] See *Yakhin va-Boaz*, II, 31 (78–79).

have before us are two versions — one original and one modified
— of an identical presentation.[147] Since a comparison between
these versions will help us draw several conclusions, we shall here
present the question in both. They read as follows:

The version of the question
*in Simon Duran's Responsa*

מעשה שהיה כך היה שיש תשעים
שנה ויותר שבארץ הנוצרים מרוב
הגזרות והשמדות נשתמדו הרבה אנשים
ונשים וטף וזה הדור שנשתמד עם
היות שהיה להם מקום לברוח לא"י
[ = לארץ ישמעאל] הקרובה להם
לחזור לדתם הראשונה לא ברחו
אלא עמדו בגיותם והולידו בנים
ובנות בגיותם, וכן בניהם אשר קמו
אחריהם עמדו בגיותם כל ימי חייהם.
אח"כ קמו בניהם, מהם לדור שלישי
ומהם לדור רביעי, ונתעוררו לשוב
אל ה' אלהי ישראל וברחו מארץ
אדום לארץ ישמעאל וחזרו לדתם
הראשונה. ואלו האנשים בעודם
בגיותם רובם נשאו נשים כיוצא
בהם משומדות מזרע ישראל, והמיעוט
מהם נשאו גויות מזרע אדום, ועכשיו
בא לכאן מדור שלישי אחד או
מדור רביעי ונתגייר, ואחר שנתגייר
נשא אשה ומת בלא בנים. ועתה שואל
אני אם האשה הזאת זקוקה ליבם,
שנשאר אח מומר בארץ הנוצרים
לאותו הבעל ונולד בגיות הוא
ואביו, או נאמר שאינה זקוקה.[149]

The version of the question
*in Ibn Danan's responsum*

שלח שלחו אלי נכבדי הקהל
הקדוש מאלקה לשאול את פי במעשה
שקרה, והוא שאחד מאלו האנוסי'
הבאים מארץ קאשטיליא לחזור
בתשובה, והם שהוכרחו אבותם
ונ(כ) [א]נסו להמיר את כבודם ולצאת
מן הכלל, היום כמו תשעים שנה,
והנה אלה דור שני שלישי ורביעי,
כי זה האיש נשא אשה במאלקה
בכתובה וקדושין ומת בלא בנים,
וחיי לרבנן ולכל ישראל שבק,
ויש לו אחים מאותם המומרים שלא
שבו בתשובה, אם אשתו של זה השב
בתשובה זקוקה ליבום לאחיו המומר
הרשע ואם לאו, ואם אלה המומרים
יחשבו רשעים או גוים גמורים, ואם
קדושיהן תופשין בבת ישראל בעודם
בקלקולם ואם לאו; ואם הם נחשבים
כרשעי ישראל ולא כנויים, האנוסין
הם או משומדים.[148]

[147] Asaf's conjecture (*Zion*, V [1932–33], p. 56, note 1) that both questions
referred to the same case appears to me less likely, the questions having
originated in different countries, although, of course, not impossible.
[148] *Ḥemdah Genuzah*, 13a.
[149] *Yakhin va-Boaz*, II, 31 (78c).

*Translation*

| The version of the question<br>*in Simon Duran's Responsa* | The version of the question<br>*in Ibn Danan's responsum* |
|---|---|
| [The question refers to] a matter that happened as follows: it is more than ninety years that many men, women and children, apostatized in the land of the Christians as a result of the many [anti-Jewish] decrees and persecutions. Now, the generation which apostatized, although they could have escaped to the nearby land of the Moslems in order to return to their original faith, did not do so, but stayed on in their gentilehood and gave birth to sons and daughters while in that condition. Also their offspring who came after them persisted in that state of gentilehood all their lives. Then came the sons of these, some of them belonging to the third generation [of apostates] and some to the fourth and woke up to return to the God of Israel. They fled from the land of Edom [i. e., of the Christians] to the land of Ishmael [i. e., of the Moslems], and returned to their original faith. These men, while in the state of gentilehood, married, in most cases, | The notables of the holy community of Malaga addressed to me a question regarding a matter that happened. It concerned one of those *anusim* who are coming from Castile to repent. These are those whose forefathers were compelled and coerced to convert [to Christianity] and left the fold some ninety years ago. Now, those [who come to repent] belong to the second, third and fourth generation [of Marranos]. The person in question married a woman in Malaga according to Jewish law and died without issue. He has brothers who belong to those converts who did not repent. [The question is] whether the widow of the repentant is subjected to levirate marriage to the brother of the deceased, the wicked convert, or not. Also, whether these converts are to be considered wicked Israelites or complete gentiles, and whether their marriage rites affect a daughter of Israel while they are in their state of conversion; then, if they are to be re- |

## *Translation* (*continued*)

| The version of the question *in Simon Duran's Responsa* | The version of the question *in Ibn Danan's responsum* |
|---|---|
| their own kind, apostate women from the seed of Israel, while the minority married gentile women of Edomite [ = Christian ] stock. | garded as wicked Israelites, and not as gentiles, should they be considered as forced converts or as apostates? |

Presently came one of these here, a person from the third or fourth generation [of apostates], proselytized, and after having become a proselyte married a [Jewish] woman and died without issue. Now I ask whether this woman can remarry without being released, as the law of levirate marriage prescribes, by the brother of the deceased, who lives as a convert in the land of the Christians and whose father, let alone he himself, was born in gentilehood.

From both versions we learn, first of all, that the cases with which the question was concerned developed *after* the establishment of the Inquisition. This is clearly indicated by the references they contain to the general conversion as having occurred "some ninety years ago," or "more than ninety years ago." Since the Inquisition was established in 1481, exactly ninety years after the great conversion, it is clear that these statements date from the very first years of the Inquisition's activities. Second, both versions imply quite clearly that the cases under consideration were not isolated ones. Ibn Danan speaks about "*one of those conversos* who are coming from Castile to repent." Duran's version speaks even more impressively about those who return to the fold as substantially representing the latest generation.[150] It is obvious, then, from both versions that the tendency to "return" assumed shortly after the establishment of the Inquisition the character of a *movement*. Thirdly, both ver-

[150] Note the expression: אח״כ קמו בניהם של [המשומדים] מהם לדור שלישי ומהם לדור רביעי ונתעוררו לשוב אל ה' אלהי ישראל. This is also confirmed by another responsum of Duran, discussing "all those of the *anusim* who are coming to repent," etc., and describing their cases as "every day occurrences that take place everywhere" (מעשים בכל יום ובכל מקום; *ibid.*, II, 3 [68]).

sions indicate that this movement appeared as quite a new phenomenon to the Jews in the Moslem countries. Indeed, it was so novel and astonishing a phenomenon that the questioners felt it necessary to tell the rabbis, to whom they addressed their questions, the essentials of the Marranos' story which, they thought, might well be unknown to them. This means that "returning" Marranos were, at least for decades, a *rare* phenomenon, so that the Jews in the Moslem countries generally knew little or nothing about their past and present alike.[151]

Let us now take a look at the differences between the versions. The question as presented in Duran's responsum obviously maintains its original form, while the one we find in that of Saadia ibn Danan constitutes his own formulation of the case. We can see how Saadia ibn Danan, for reasons to be pointed out later, edited the question, abbreviated it, and even changed some of its terminology. In the first place, he does not, in discussing the Marranos, employ the term משומדים, but uses instead the term אנוסים which is not found in the version of Duran. It is true that we find in Ibn Danan's responsum the term מומרים, too, but he employs it here in an indefinite sense since, as he himself states, it is his task to find out whether these מומרים were unwilling converts (אנוסים) or apostates (משומדים). Secondly, instead of speaking of the return of the *conversos* to their original faith (לחזור לדתם הראשונה), as Duran's version does, he speaks of their *repentance* (לחזור בתשובה). In agreement with this, the term "proselyte" is not used by him at all, and instead he uses the term "penitent" (שב בתשובה).[152] Further, he eliminates com-

---

[151] This confirms what we said about the silence of Rashbash and his son Zemaḥ Duran on the migration issue (see above, pp. 127–128, 131). The few references to "returners" in the responsa of Rashbash and Zemaḥ Duran had obviously to do with isolated cases, and not with regular phenomena. — On the actual strength of the "return" movement *after* the establishment of the Inquisition, see below, appendix B.

[152] In his responsum, however, Ibn Danan mentions the fact that the returning Marranos are defined as "proselytes." The definition is attributed here to his anonymous opponent (see *Ḥemdah Genuzah*, 13b and 15b), but in view of the fact that the version addressed to Simon Duran II also includes that definition, the opponent may have merely supported the position expressed in the question.

pletely the all-too-significant charge about the Marranos' failure
to leave the country where they could not practice Judaism
openly (which charge implied an accusation of their willingness
to practice Christianity or, at least, their compliance with such
practice.) Instead, he emphasizes the element of *compulsion* in
the conversion of the original Marranos (<sup>153</sup>והם שהוכרחו אבותם ונאנסו
להמיר את כבודם). The claim found in Duran's version about their
own and their descendants' persistence in gentilehood is completely eliminated, and so is the reference to the "awakening"
that had occurred a short time before the responsum was written.
Instead, he merely mentions that the "repentants" belong to
the *second, third* and *fourth* generations. Significantly, Duran's
version mentions in this connection only "the *third* or *fourth*
generation" (and not the second), which is, of course, more
in accordance with the truth when the converts of 1391 are
considered.

Saadia ibn Danan presented in his responsum a passionate
defense of the Marranos, and his summary of the question addressed to him was obviously calculated to suit his views. Con-

<hr>

<sup>153</sup> Notice the repetition of the synonymous terms הוכרחו and נאנסו. — The
term להמיר which he employs here serves as an introduction to the term
מומרים which he uses later to describe the conversos (see above, p. 135),
the word *mumar*, then indicating all grades and forms of conversion, having
been somewhat less derogatory than *meshumad*, which generally meant a
*willful and complete* convert (for a view of the antithetical original meanings
of these terms, see S. Zeitlin, in *JQR*, LIV [1963], 84–86; on the absence of
*mumar* in ancient Hebrew literature, however, see S. Lieberman, in *H. A.
Wolfson Jubilee Volume*, II, 531–532). In line with this it may be assumed that
the appellation *mumar*, rather than *meshumad*, was often attached to the
forced convert, and this, in my opinion, may well have been the source of the
term *marrano:* a haplologic contraction of the Hebrew *mumar-anus* (which caused
the omission of the first syllable), effecting the transformation: *mumaranus,
maranus, marano, marrano*. Supporting this supposition is the form *murranus*,
found in a Latin document from 1291 (A. Farinelli, *Marrano*, Geneva, 1925,
29), and the forms *Marani* (Latin, pl., 1304; *ibid.*) and *marano* (Latin, dat.
sing., from 1220!—see Joaquim da Silveira, in *Revista Lusitana*, XXXV,
p. 138), all possible variants of that contraction. The derogatory meaning of
marrano-swine, stemming from accidental word similarity, if it did not serve
as catalyst in the transformation, may have been attached to the term soon
thereafter, or even much later, since *marrano* as vituperation cannot be
definitively shown before 1380 (*Cortes de Leon y de Castilla*, II, Madrid, 1863,
309). For other views on the origin of the term and the related literature,
see J. Corominas, *Diccionario Crítico Etimológico de la Lengua Castellana*, III,
Berne, 1954, 272–275.

trarywise, the version in Duran's responsum was not affected by
the opinion of the recipient, but presented the case as known to
the questioners who sought guidance and decision in an important religious matter. The facts enumerated, and the way
they are related, can hardly indicate a *personal* position; they
should rather be considered as what was *common* knowledge or
what was substantiated by reliable information. Such information was unquestionably based on authoritative Spanish sources,
and thus the Duran version no doubt represents what may be
defined as the *vox populi*, i. e:, the prevailing opinion about the
Marranos among the Jews of Spain.

Now, what are the particular things we can learn from this
"unedited" version? First, it emphasizes that the Marranos,
after having *apostatized* under duress, failed to leave Spain
although they *could* migrate to the neighboring Moslem countries, and that they and the generations after them stayed in a
state of *gentilehood*. The terms underlined are of the utmost
importance as they indicate that, at the beginning of the 80's,
the Jews generally regarded the Marranos not only as apostates,
but also as gentiles, and that they saw in their continued stay
in Spain definite *proof* of their willingness to practice Christianity, or at least that they did not mind such practice. Then
it tells us about an "awakening" that took place among the
Marranos at the time preceding the writing of the question,
i. e., shortly after the establishment of the Inquisition. The
description of the "awakening" is couched in terms indicating
a situation relevant to our inquiry. When the questioner tells
us that "they (i. e., the Marranos) *woke up* to *return* to the *God
of Israel*," his statement, of course, implies that prior to that
they were *estranged* from the *God of Israel* or, more clearly, had
no faith in Him. Had they belonged to those "whose heart was
devoted to Heaven," namely, who loved Judaism in their hearts
and recognized its truths even if they could not practice it
openly, such expressions ("woke up") would not have been used
to describe the "return." Similarly, the phrase "to return to
their *former faith*" indicates very clearly that the former faith,
i. e., Judaism, was not their faith prior to the "awakening," but
was rather replaced by another faith. The definition of the re-

turn as an act of proselytizing (נתגייר) is in full accord with this view of the Marranos as apostates turned gentiles who had nothing to do, prior to their return, with the Jewish religion and the Jewish people. The additional statement about the *majority* of the *conversos* having married apostate women of Jewish stock, comes to show that the assimilation of the Marranos was not only religious, but partly also ethnic, and was obviously given as further justification of the general view taken of them. All this offers us indisputable proof that at the time of the establishment of the Inquisition, the Marranos were regarded by Spain's Jews as Christians, as a camp that included no Crypto-Jewish movement to speak of (otherwise this fact would have been pointed out), and that the movement of "awakening" which suddenly resulted in an influx of Marrano refugees from Spain, took place *after* the establishment of the Inquisition, and no doubt under its impact.

Both Duran and Ibn Danan, however, disqualify this position and take an open stand in favor of the Marranos. Ibn Danan brushes aside the complaint of their continued stay under a government of coercion and their refusal to repent for such a long time as immaterial to the question. As far as the first generation was concerned, they should be classified, in his opinion, as "perfect *anusim*" (אנוסים גמורים) since they were obviously converted under duress, and as far as their offspring is concerned, "there is an element of duress in *their* existence" as well, and, therefore, "so long as they are separated from the gentiles and are recognized as the seed of Israel, they should be regarded as *wicked Israelites*, and not as *complete apostates.*[154] In any event, they should not be treated as gentiles, for even ordinary apostates cannot be so treated, since, in his opinion, they are equal to Jews in all matters that relate to lineage and usury.[155] The words of Maimonides and other great authorities who defined an Israelite who apostatized as a complete gentile

---

[154] *Ḥemdah Genuzah*, 13a.

[155] *Ibid.*, 14a; significantly, Saadia ibn Danan, in his attempt to defend the Marranos, takes an extreme position in favor of converts generally: אכן בענין היחס והריבית הם אחינו בלי ספק ר"ל לקידושי בת ישראל ולזקוק לייבום ולהתחתן בם לקחת את בנותיהם ושלא להלוותם ולא ללוות מהם בריבית.

(כגוי גמור), he interprets to mean *similar* to a complete gentile (כגוי גמור) but not actually a complete gentile (גוי גמור).[156] Furthermore, he takes the position that the offspring of an apostate should be classed as a "forced convert"[157] — a position which, as we have noticed, was already considered by Rashbaẓ[158] and initially accepted by Rashbash.[159] In that case, of course, the restrictions imposed on apostates could not be applied to them.

This entire line of defense confirms rather than denies the indictment of the Marranos as non-Jews in every respect, save for the ethnic one. But the argument, it must be pointed out, branches out also in other directions. As Ibn Danan sees it, the Marranos, taken collectively, cannot be classified as apostates or gentiles for additional reasons as well. In the first place, some of them do perform some of the commandments secretly, "while the wicked among them who are inclined to heresy and Epicurean thought cannot believe that the foreign religion has anything of value in it."[160] Proof of this he sees in the fact that they are "rejected by the gentiles who constantly abuse and denounce them as 'Jews' and hate them because of their inclination to Judaism."[161] Ibn Danan knows, however, that heretics and Epicureans are equally disliked by Jews and that the "many who do perform commandments" — like those who died in sanctifying the Name — constituted only a small minority of the Marranos.[162] Therefore, to offset their quantitative insignificance, he tries to bolster their value qualitatively. Surely, he says, *"that fraction of the Marranos* who endanger themselves to perform *some* commandments will enjoy greater reward than those Jews who live under no fear or danger, and do not perform the commandments properly."[163] At the same time, he

---

[156] *Ibid.*

[157] *Ibid.*: ולפי דעתי . . . זרע המשומד אנוס הוא, ויש לי ראיות על זה, וזרע האנוס גם כן אנוס הוא.

[158] *Tashbeẓ*, II, 139 (end); see above, note 113.

[159] See above, p. 126.

[160] *Ḥemdah Genuzah*, 14b–15a.          [161] *Ibid.*, 15a.

[162] See below, note 163; and see A. Marx, "The Expulsion of the Jews from Spain," *JQR* (O. S.), XX (1908), p. 252.

[163] *Ḥemdah Genuzah*, 15a; חי ה' כי יש שכר לק צ ת מהם, ר"ל לאותם המסכנים עצמם לשמור ק צ ת מצוות, יותר משכר היהודים האלה אשר אין להם פחד ולא סכנה, אבל

tries to prove that, even from a quantitative point of view, the adherence to a foreign religion by its majority does not divorce a group from the Jewish people. Ibn Danan reviews the history of Israel and shows that idolatry was practiced by the majority of the people, first, in the days of the Judges, then in the days of the prophet Elijah when, according to I Kings (19.18), there remained in the whole of Israel only 7,000 faithful who "have not bowed to Baal," and yet "we did not see that it occurred to any of our Sages that our forefathers who betrayed God, rebelled against Him and denied Him should be called 'complete gentiles' or 'worse than gentiles,' and that their sons who repented and worshipped God should be considered proselytes."[164]

What was the reason for this rather outstretched and obviously aggressive position of Ibn Danan? It is clear that from an halakhic point of view he had good precedents to sustain his judgment that the laws of levirate marriage should apply to the Marranos, even if all of them were considered apostates.[165] But the issues at stake were much bigger. What Ibn Danan was fighting for was the *recognition of the Marranos as members of the Jewish people.* In this he resembled Zemaḥ Duran and his father, at least in the earlier stages of their careers; but he differed from them in intensity and persuasiveness, theirs being a campaign based on dwindling hopes, his on rising optimistic expectations. The historic drama that unfolded before his eyes, and whose scenes followed each other in such rapid succession —

---

ישבחום הגויים אם ישמרו תורת ה' והוקיו והם אינם עושים המצוות כתיקונן. The point made here reflects the similar view expressed by Maimonides in *Iggeret ha-Shemad* (see above, pp. 13–14, and notes 38, 39). The phrase כי יש שכר לקצת מהם shows clearly that Ibn Danan realized that the "many" who adhered to Judaism in some fashion were a small minority among the Marranos (קצת מהם) and that even these would perform only *some* commandments (קצת מצוות).

[164] *Ibid.*, 15b. Also in this Ibn Danan follows in the footsteps of Maimonides in *Iggeret ha-Shemad* (*ibid.*, p. 12, end), except that he gives the argument a sharper edge. Similarly, his description of the Jews under the hellenistic persecution as *anusim* (*ibid.*, 16a) is borrowed from Maimonides (see *ibid.*, 8b, and above, note 37). To complete the comparison, one may add that even the way Ibn Danan treats his opponent is reminiscent of Maimonides' attitude toward *his* antagonist.

[165] See above, notes 48, 49, 107, 108.

the Inquisition, the awakening, and the mass flight of Marranos
from Castile — gave him every reason to believe that the great
event which was awaited so long and, indeed, so despondently —
the return of the majority of Spain's Jewry to the fold — was at
last at hand. The stand to be taken towards the Marranos
now, he thought, was one that would hasten and facilitate this
process, and not obstruct or retard it in any way. This consideration was the dominant motive in his argument, as is clearly
indicated by Ibn Danan himself. "If the Marranos are to be
considered as gentiles and those who return to Judaism as proselytes, their desire to return to the fold will weaken, so that
finally they will assimilate among the gentiles, add crime to
their sin, and even their name will be forgotten from Israel."[166]
To avoid this, the Marranos must be received not as strangers,
but as brethren. They should have a feeling that they are returning home, and what should be emphasized upon their return
is not their long detachment from the people because of their
religious miscarriage, but rather their steadfast attachment to it
because of their lineal relationship. This ethnic affinity must be
played up to encourage rapprochement between Marranos and
Jews. "Indeed, when it comes to lineage," he says, "all the
people of Israel are brethren. We are all the sons of one father,
the rebels and the criminals, the apostates and the forced converts, and the proselytes who are attached to the house of Jacob.
All of these are Israelites. Even if they left God or denied Him,
or violated His Law, the yoke of that Law is still upon their
shoulders and will never be removed from them."[167]

Ibn Danan's responsum is perhaps the most eloquent plea in
all Hebrew literature on behalf of the Marranos. Duran's reply
contains no such moving arguments, but is perhaps more thorough in its attempt to prove his point from a halakhic point of
view. He takes the same position as Ibn Danan, but goes out
of his way to defeat the claim that the *conversos* cannot be regarded as unquestionable Jews according to their lineage since a
minority of them married gentile women. According to him,
that minority is insignificant, and so long as we have no special

---

[166] *Ḥemdah Genuzah*, 16b.
[167] *Ibid.*, 15b.

testimony to the effect that the mother of a Marrano was a gentile, we should consider all those who come to repent as of Jewish origin.[168]

In a second responsum, written sometime later, after the establishment of the Inquisition in Aragon,[169] — that is, after 1484 — he again tries hard to disqualify the opinion that the Marranos are of impure Jewish stock. As he sees it, the Marranos were meticulous in keeping family purity by shunning mixed marriages. "The insignificant minority that intermarried with the gentiles is considered by them as an abomination."[170]

---

[168] *Yakhin va-Boaz*, II, 31 (79b). In his attempt to prove the Jewishness of the Marranos, Duran, as his brother before him (see above, p. 52), is also trying to find support in Abba Mari, according to whom "Gentiles living abroad [i. e., outside of Palestine] are not idolaters" (*'Iṭṭur*, I, 63b); consequently, even if conversion to paganism may turn a Jew into a gentile (as Maimonides believed), conversion to Christianity does not.

[169] See *Yakhin va-Boaz*, II, 3 (67d–69b). That this responsum was written after the establishment of the Inquisition in Aragon is evident from a statement included in the question (*ibid.*, 68d) wherein Catalonia is mentioned in the first place among the refugees' countries of origin (שבאין ממלכות קאטאלאן וקאסטיליייא ופורטוגל להתייר ולהכנס תחת כנפי השכינה). The question discussed earlier (*ibid.*, II, 31) mentions only the refugees from Castile (see above, p. 135). The reference to Portugal is, of course, no indication that the question was written after the forced conversion in that country (1497). Spanish exiles who had been compelled to embrace Christianity and *returned to Judaism shortly thereafter* would not have been called *gerim*. The question, therefore, was written between 1484 and 1492 (the expulsion not being mentioned in it!), when Portugal served as a haven not only for the truly Christianized Marranos (see below, appendix B), but also as a temporary station for *conversos* who decided to return to Judaism.

[170] *Ibid.*, 68cd. The discrepancy between the statement in the question addressed to him and his own assertions on the measure of intermarriage between Marranos and gentiles may be partly ascribed to the fact that Duran's main information regarding the Marranos was derived from Majorca and Aragon where intermarriage between New and Old Christians was much more limited, although the cause may not have been the "abomination" showed by many Marranos toward intermarriage with Christians, but the contempt with which marriage with Marranos was regarded by the Catalans (see Amador de los Ríos, *Historia de los Judíos de España y Portugal*, III, p. 88, note 1, and the sources quoted there). Despite claims to the contrary, intermarriage was practiced on a considerable scale. This is attested by every page of the *Libro Verde de Aragon*, written in 1507 (first published by Rios in

Similarly, he categorically objects to the definition of the returning Marranos as proselytes, a definition found also in the second question, which, incidentally, is another proof to the effect that the notion of the Marranos as proselyting gentiles was the commonly accepted view. According to Duran, the Marranos are not gentiles, but members of the people of Israel, and those among them who return to the fold are not proselytes, but penitents. That is why the latter can serve as priests which no gentile proselyte can do, and their being priests should be accepted on the strength of their own testimony, namely, the testimony of "returners."[171] But Simon Duran does not deny the charge that the Marranos of his generation were apostates, nor does he anywhere indicate in his responsa that a section of them was devoted to Judaism, even "in their hearts" only.[171a]

Revista de España, CV–CVI, and later by Isidro de las Cagigas, Madrid, 1929). What is more, already in 1449, as Lea has pointed out (on the basis of Caballero, Noticias de Doctor Alonso Díaz de Montalvo, p. 251), a petition addressed by the conversos of Toledo to Lope de Barrientos, bishop of Cuenca, enumerated "all the noblest families of Spain as being of Jewish blood" (A History of the Inquisition in Spain, I, New York, 1906, p. 120). The statements on intermarriage between Marranos and old Christians which we find in the questions addressed to Duran, as well as in the Responsa of Jacob Berav (see below, p. 70), must therefore have been founded on more authoritative information than that which served as basis for Duran's opinion.

[171] Yakhin va-Boaz, II, 3 (68c).

[171a] The one sign of Marrano Jewishness to be found in his responsa is the reference to the custom of marrying before Jewish witnesses, prior to going through the Christian marriage ceremony, which was prevalent in a Marrano group in Valencia (ibid., II, 19, [73c]). From the responsum dealing with this matter, as well as from the question that evoked it, however, we gain the impression that what was involved was an isolated Jewish rite that survived in a particular group whose members lived otherwise as non-Jews, so much so that they could well be regarded by Jews as apostates or even gentiles (ibid.). By signifying them as anusim, the questioner may have referred to those among the Marranos in the city of Valencia who still had some pro-Jewish leanings, manifested in the preservation of one or more Jewish rites, or to such a group in the neighborhood of the city, or somewhere else in the province. That the custom, in any case, was not practiced by all the Marranos in Valencia, can be gathered, among other things, by the fact that, in an inquisitorial trial of Valencian Marranos in 1464, some of the latter were charged by the Inquisition with entertaining hopes to remarry according to

Nor does he claim that the parents of these Marranos were Jews in practice or in spirit, or even partly so; and when the authors of the question which evoked his later responsum stated that "*the fathers of these Marranos who 'returned' were uncircumcised and worshipped idols willingly,* while the mothers were not married according to Jewish law", etc.,[172] he accepts this statement without protest — which is not at all his habit when he disagrees with the questioner — and presents his argument entirely on *this* foundation. In fact, his entire defense of the Marranos is based on the assumption that they are both converts and sons of converts, and it is only through protecting the rights of the convert that he sees it possible to safeguard the rights of the Marrano. Indeed, the position taken here, as in Ibn Danan, in favor of the convert,[173] and the emphasis upon the basic "brotherhood" between the convert and the full-fledged Jews,[174] are in themselves clear indications that Marranism could no longer be separated, even by its staunchest advocates, from apostasy.

Yet, something else should be said in this connection. Simon Duran and Ibn Danan, as we have seen, followed Rashbash and his son, Zemaḥ, with respect to one important issue, namely, the belonging of the Marranos to the Jewish people. But they

---

Jewish law, but not with having been so married (see Baer, *Die Juden im christlichen Spanien*, II, Berlin, 1936, p. 443).

[172] *Yakhin va-Boaz*, II, 3 (68d–69a).

[173] This position is summarized by Simon Duran as follows: העולה מזה שהמשומד והמשומדת נחשבים ישראל ובנים אשר יולדו להם בשמדוחם גם כן נחשבים מישראל, ואפילו עד כמה דורות (*Ibid.*, II, 3 [68c]); see also *ibid.*, II, 19 (73cd); the law of levirate marriage is also applicable to the convert regardless of whether the conversion took place before or after the marriage (*ibid.*, 31, 79a, 79c). He is obviously in error, however, when he claims that Rashbaẓ took in this instance a position against Rav Yehudai Gaon, whereas Rashbaẓ was trying to offer the Gaon support on this issue (see above, p. 121); on the question of interest, however, he is rather indefinite, although he seems inclined to accept Naḥmanides' position in the way it was interpreted by his father (*ibid.*, 78d, 79c; and see above, note 126).

[174] *Ibid.*, 79a: ומאחר שהמומרים יש להם אחוה זקוקה היא [אשת אחי המומר לחליצה; ואין לטעות ולומר מאחר שנולדו בניותן לא בקדושה היא לידתן...דישראל מומר דיניה כישראל אפילו לכמה דרי בקדושתיהו קיימי...דאחינו הוא מכל מקום וכו' (*ibid.*, 79c).

followed them in other respects as well. In fact, their entire argument was in line with the policy originated with Rashbash and pursued by Ẓemaḥ Duran — a policy that parted completely with the strict attitude toward the *forced* convert, adopted by the Franco-German school, and the severe attitude toward the *voluntary* convert advocated by Maimonides. In truth, as far as forced conversion was concerned, it showed greater leniency toward it than that allowed even by Maimonides, as it stopped insisting that the forced convert leave the country of persecution; and as for real and willful conversion, the basic attitude was hardly different. What was the reason for this display of tolerance toward a phenomenon which had always aroused, in Judaism as in other religions, the sharpest rebuke and most intense aversion? The reason, no doubt, lay in the objective. What the new policy was aiming at was to maintain, as far as possible, the last ties between the Marranos and the Jewish people; and since these last ties could be found only in the status of the convert, through the laws applying to him, the extension of the convert's rights was considered vital for the strengthening of the relations between Marranism and the Jewish people. The struggle for the convert was thus in reality a struggle for the Marrano, and the various elements which appeared in this conflict — the strong emphasis upon the *Jewishness* of the convert, as well as of his descendants for many generations; the objection to defining returning Marranos as proselytes, even if they belonged to the fifth generation of converts; the insistence upon the convert's rights in all that refers to levirate marriage — were all manifestations of that basic intent. Yet, while all this was part of an attempt to save Marranism for the Jewish people, what we see in the responsa literature — from the days of Rashbash on — is fundamentally in reverse of the traditional policies towards both the forced and voluntary convert; and the question we should now ask ourselves is to what extent was the new policy accepted by the Jews of Spain, and how far did it conform to *their* views of the Marranos and *their* appraisal of the situation.

We say "their," because what we should first point out in this connection is that both Ibn Danan and the Duran brothers, as well as their father Rashbash, were never residents of Christian Spain. All of them lived in Moslem countries, and their impression of the Marranos was based on theoretical rather than practical grounds; at all events, it was free from the complexities and entanglements which necessarily resulted from actual confrontation with the vexing problem on the scene. As far as reality was concerned, they knew the Marranos primarily through the element which chose to return to Judaism, and not through the main body of the Marranos which preferred to remain in its state of conversion. It is also reasonable to assume that in the case of Ibn Danan, his judgment of the Marranos was influenced by the romantic tales spread about them by the "returners," who obviously stressed the suffering they had endured since the Inquisition was established, and not the actual relationship between them and the Jews in the period *preceding* the Inquisition. The position of the Spanish Jews, however, was necessarily determined by quite different factors — by their concrete contacts with the Marrano camp, by their historic experience of the Marranos' attitude toward Judaism, by their practical evaluation of what conversion did to Spanish Jewry in the preceding generations, and, above all, by close observation of the Marranos and intimate knowledge of their religious thought and practice. These were the factors which evidently shaped the opinion of Spain's Jews about the Marranos.

What this opinion was we can learn from the responsa of those rabbis who were exiled from Spain and whose views can well be considered as reflecting the traditional position toward the Marranos that prevailed in Spain itself. One of these was Jacob Berav who was exiled from Spain at the age of eighteen. By that time, however, he was already an accomplished scholar — indeed, so highly regarded for his learning that he was appointed Rabbi of the important community of Fez.[175] This fact is mentioned here as proof that such a man could be relied upon as having personal knowledge of the actual attitude that prevailed in Spain toward the Marranos. In fact, in one of his responsa dealing with this problem, he distinctly states that "with

---

[175] See E. Grünhut, "Le-Toledot ha-Gaon R. Jacob Berav," in *Ha-Zofeh me-Erez Hagar*, II, Budapest, 1912, pp. 25–33.

regard to the descendants of the first forced converts who assimilated (נטמעו) among the gentiles, some of them for four or five generations, there was a controversy between the rabbis of Spain and the house of Duran. For in the opinion of the Spanish savants those who were already assimilated (נטמעו) among the gentiles must be considered as *complete gentiles*, the reasons being (a) that owing to *their practice of a foreign religion* "their conception and birth were not in holiness," and (b) "since they became assimilated (נטמאו) they also intermarried with gentiles, and hence their offspring could not be considered Jewish."[176] Thus we see here the same evaluation of the Marranos which we find in the questions addressed to Simon Duran[177] — which fact is further indication that these questions represented the view prevalent among the Jews of Spain. It is obvious that according to the Spanish rabbis of the time, it was nonsensical to consider the Marranos as Jews — first, because they were brought up in Christianity from the very beginning of their lives, and second, because intermarriage with gentile women had assumed sufficient proportions among them as to place in doubt the ethnic purity of every single Marrano. In discussing the legal implications of Marranism from a Jewish point of view, Berav, like his predecessors, can do so only within the legal possibilities applicable to *conversion*; and as far as converts are concerned, he rejects the notion of their belonging to the Jewish people and insists on their *gentilehood in every respect*, with the sole exception of marriage and divorce.[178] Accordingly, he maintains that even those Marranos who did not mix with gentile women, and preserved their Jewish identity ethnically, must be considered as gentiles in every respect, except with regard to relations between the sexes, since they practiced a foreign religion and did not escape when they could.[179] As far as levirate marriage is concerned, however, it cannot be applied to the Marranos of this generation. As Berav tells us, this was not merely his own opinion, but "the conclusion reached by *all* the scholars of Castile or *most* of them." He adds that "from some of these

[176] Berav, *Responsa*, Jerusalem, 1958, p. 81a.
[177] Cf. above, pp. 55, 67.
[178] *Ibid.*, 81b.            [179] *Ibid.*, 84a.

rabbis he has instructions to this effect" and, furthermore, that "this was the practice he noticed in the West" (Morocco).[180] In support of his position, Berav quotes a responsum of Rabbi Yehudah Balan (probably Yehudah Bulat, who was a member of the rabbinical court in Constantinople).[181] According to Balan, the point of departure for evaluating the convert should be the view, derivable from a Talmudic statement, that an apostate is a "complete gentile." Therefore, in his opinion, even the marriage of an apostate to a Jewish woman, though formally contracted according to Jewish law, should not be considered valid.[182] If one, however, wants to take the opposite view and side with Maimonides, who held such a marriage to be valid, he must realize, according to Balan, that Maimonides referred only to an apostate who was born in a state of Jewishness, and not to those of the kind we face today, whose parents were already assimilated in gentilehood and died as gentiles, and part of whom intermarried with gentile men and women.[183] What is more, even if they were of unmixed Jewish stock, it would be absurd, according to Balan, to maintain legal relationships with them in matters of marriage after their having been converted for so many generations; if this were the case, he says, all the gentiles should be regarded as Jews, since Esau, the father of Edom and all Christians, was of the same stock as Jacob and, in one Talmudic discussion, was even defined as an "apostate Israelite."[184] Hence, the descendants of the first forced converts must be considered as complete gentiles, to whom the laws of marriage cannot be applied, let alone the law of levirate marriage, or, as he puts it: "The brothers of those descendants of the first *anusim* who come to *proselyte* are not subject to *ḥaliẓah* and levirate marriage."[185] To fortify his position, Balan tells us

---

[180] *Ibid.*, 82ab.

[181] Cf. Asaf (*loc. cit.*, p. 58, note 1) and Zimmels (*op. cit.*, p. 40, note 2).

[182] Berav, *Responsa*, 81b. Balan relies here primarily on the anti-conversional statements in Ḥullin 5a.

[183] *Ibid.*, 81b–82a.

[184] *Ibid.*, 82a; Qiddushin 18a.

[185] Berav, *Responsa*, 82a. Here again, we should note, the term *to proselyte* appears, as it does in the questions addressed to Simon Duran II and in the "opinions" Ibn Danan sought to defeat (see above, note 152).

that this view of his is not an isolated opinion, nor is it a mere
theoretical proposition: "This is also what was agreed upon in
the entire land of Flanders where they allowed the widows of
proselytes who died without issue to remarry without having
been released, according to the law of levirate marriage, by their
apostate brothers."[186]

What we learn from these responsa about Spanish Jewry's
opinion of the Marranos around the time of the establishment of
the Inquisition is of primary importance.[187] The rabbinical
authorities of Spanish Jewry considered the Marranos not as
crypto-Jews, but as gentiles, and, consequently, they considered
the returners not as penitents, but as proselytes. The complete
detachment of the *conversos* from Judaism and their complete
assimilation to the Christian way of life, coupled with their
partial racial intermingling, were for them unquestionable facts.
They seem to have been little impressed by the movement of
"return" that started with the Inquisition, and did not see in
it an indication of a basic change in the attitude toward Judaism
of the Marrano camp as a whole. They evidently saw in the
action of the Marranos who turned to Judaism as to a spiritual
and social refuge — i. e., in those who "proselytized," the manifest attitude only of that minority, which preferred to take this
action, while the body as a whole, they felt, remained unchanged
and preferred to continue in its state of gentilehood, whether
inside or outside Spain.[188]

It is this evaluation of the Marrano group as a whole, as well
as of the return movement among the refugees, that lay at the
root of the bitter controversy that arose in connection with the

---

[186] *Ibid.*

[187] The strong anti-Marrano attitude that prevailed among Spain's Jews is
also reflected in responsa of rabbis who were exiled from Spain in their childhood, like David ibn Avi-Zimra and Joseph Caro. On the question whether
it is permissible to lend a convert money on interest, David ibn Zimra takes
a positive stand, especially with regard to descendants of Jews who converted
generations before. "Had they wanted to return to the fold," he says, "they
could have done so;" hence they must be treated as non-Jews (*Responsa*, IV,
No. 12, ed. Sudylkow, 1836, p. 3b). — On the attitude of Caro see below,
note 192.

[188] Cf. below, appendix B.

issue of levirate marriage. Levirate marriage was in reality the last tie still holding the Marrano group in association with the Jewish community, and the fight over the issue of levirate marriage, which loomed so large after the establishment of the Inquisition — and especially after the expulsion from Spain — was far from being stimulated only, or even primarily, by consideration for the widowed women of returners.[189] What was at the core of this controversy was the old, fundamental question: the recognition or disavowal of the Marranos as members of the Jewish people. The division of opinion that developed in this case originated in two distinct approaches to the Marrano problem — one realistic, the other idealistic. Simon Duran and Ibn Danan took the idealistic view; the Spanish rabbis, however, preferred the realistic approach, based on their conviction that the Marrano camp as a whole was Christianized beyond recovery, and that it was nonsensical to maintain any further the illusion about its latent Jewishness; therefore they were ready, without compunction, to cut off "the last tie."[190]

The struggle against this position, which was revived in 1514 by Jacob ben Ḥaviv,[191] had really little to do with the Spanish Marranos, and certainly was not occasioned by a change of attitude towards *them*. What renewed the controversy was the problem of the *new* camp of Marranos which appeared in Portugal

---

[189] As suggested by Asaf, *loc. cit.*, p. 56.

[190] That they did not only propose this policy, but actually practiced it, we see from the above cited passages about the procedures followed in Morocco and Flanders, and there is no doubt that the decision in favor of the same position taken by R. Elijah Capsali, Chief Rabbi of Turkey (see Binyamin b. Matityahu [Binyamin Zeev], *Responsa*, No. 75), as well as by his successor, Eliyahu Mizraḥi (see his *Responsa*, No. 48, 127b–130b), was adopted under the influence of Spanish-Jewish authorities, whose views of the Marranos could not be doubted. Other non-Spanish rabbinical authorities, like Judah Mintz (*Responsa*, 127a), David Messer Leon (Mizraḥi, *Responsa*, 127a) and David ha-Kohen (*Responsa*, Ostrog, 1834, IX, pp. 27c–31b), who took or *originally* favored the same attitude, must have also been influenced, at least partly, by what they learned about the Marranos from Spanish sources. Joseph Colon, who adhered to the old position (see his *Responsa*, Lemberg, 1798, lxxxv, 36d), seems to have represented at the time only a small minority opinion.

[191] See on this below, appendix A.

after the forced mass conversions of 1497 in that country. It was the problem of Portuguese Jewry, which included myriads of the exiles from Spain, that was before Jacob ben Ḥaviv and those who shared his opinion. In fact, so bitter was the disappointment with Marranism as a whole, so decisive was the lesson taught by history and experience as to the ultimate results of forced conversion, that even when the Spanish exiles in Portugal (and they were the core of Spain's faithful Jewry!) converted under obvious conditions of duress, the Spanish exiles in the East were generally inclined to consider that camp, too, as lost to Judaism.[192] It was only after permission to depart was granted to the Portuguese Marranos in 1507, followed by an influx of "returners" from that country, that the issue of levirate marriage, or, more fundamentally, of regarding or disregarding the Marranos as Jews, was again brought to the fore — no doubt under the protest of the refugees and in consideration of those who were still expected to return. Yet the decision taken in favor of the first alternative[193] was, as indicated, directed, in effect, not *at the Spanish Marranos of the 15th century, but at the Portuguese Marranos of the 16th.* For by that time a new cycle of Marranism had begun which left its marks in the responsa of the period, only to end a century later with the same evaluation of the Portuguese Marranos that we found expressed regarding

[192] *Ibid.* This view was upheld, among others, by Joseph Caro. In one of his utterances on the subject he considers the testimony of all Portugal's Marranos valueless to all intents and purposes since "they have been held to be idolaters and public desecrators of the Sabbath" (ובין שתאמר שלא נמצאו שם עדים כלל או שתאמר שנמצאו שם מאנוסי פורטוגאל — אין כאן קידושין כלל, כי אין עדותן מעלה ומורידה, שהרי הוחזקו לעובדי ע"ז ומחללים שבת בפרהסיא, שהם פסולים לכל עדות שבעולם; *Responsa,* on Even ha-Ezer, V, Mantua, 1730, p. 4d). This is a view identical with the one expressed in the first of the two decisions adopted by the Spanish rabbis of Saloniki (see below, appendix A). The position Caro takes on *anusim* in his code, where he declares them to be *equal to Jews* (see *Shulḥan 'Arukh, Yoreh De'ah,* 119:12), is formally in no contradiction to that stand, since in the latter instance he discusses *real anusim,* who *practice* Jewish law secretly and *cannot* escape from the country of persecution. In dealing with this *theoretical* proposition, Caro could — and, in fact, could not but — follow the traditional rulings on this issue.

[193] See below, appendix A.

their Spanish predecessors when the former were about to complete *their* cycle.[194]

To sum it up, what we gather about the Marranos from the responsa literature can be broadly outlined as follows: the camp of the forced converts of 1391 began to turn away from Judaism already in the first generation. By the end of the second generation, the majority of them had stopped observing Jewish law, while in the middle of the century that majority became so overwhelming that at times it appeared — as we see from the statements of Rashbaẓ and Rashbash — that no more crypto-Jews remained in the Marrano camp. Sizeable migration of Marranos from Spain stopped already in the first generation, and from then on it gradually diminished until it reached the vanishing point. In Spain itself, however, pockets of secret Jews, or at least of practitioners of some Jewish rites, remained in certain *localities*. But these, too, were constantly narrowing in scope and weakening in the intensity of their Jewish devotion, as their practice of Judaism was limited to the performance of *certain* Jewish rites only. While crypto-Judaism was thus dwindling, the process of assimilation, both social and religious, was advancing without letup, so much so that when the Inquisition was established, it was so deep and thorough-going that the Marrano camp as a whole appeared to Spain's Jews as a predominantly gentile camp. In the determination of most of Spain's Jews to define returning Marranos as proselytes, we see how pronounced was their view of them as Christians and strangers to the Jewish people.

We also see the gradual change of the terminology from "forced ones" (אנוסים) to "apostates" (משומדים) and finally to

---

[194] See, for instance, the total denial of the Marranos' Jewishness by the Venetian Rabbi Isaac Gershon and his sharp criticism of Joseph ben Leb for the latter's pro-Marrano stand on the question of levirate marriage (Yom Tov Ẓahalon, *Responsa*, Venice, 1694, No. 148, pp. 123c–124b). See also the castigating attack upon the *anusim* by Jacob Boton in his responsa collection, *'Edut be-Ya'akov*, 72, Saloniki, 1720, p. 222b): ... כי אע"פ שחטא ישראל הוא

הנה זהו במשומד שנולד בקדושה ונשתמד והוא לפנינו ... אך אמנם במשומדים לע"ז כגון אלו האנוסים אשר בספרד פוליה ופורטוגל ובשאר ארצות הגויים ... שהם ואביהם ואבי אביהם כולם נשתקעו בגויות, הורתם ולידתם כולם שלא בקדושה והם כולם ערלי לב וערלי בשר, הרי הם כגויים גמורים חשובי, וגריעי מינייהו לכל דבריהם.

"complete gentiles" (גוים גמורים). From these "gentiles" sprang the movement of "return" shortly after the establishment of the Holy Office. The force of this movement, however, was quickly spent; evidently because it was not, in the main, a product of deep-rooted tendencies and traditions, or of an old, wide-spread underground, but of an *external* force alone, i. e., the Inquisition's impact. That impact, indeed, was capable of harrassing and confusing the minds of many, but revolutionized the religious thinking only of the few. Outsiders like Ibn Danan could see in these few a representative body of the camp as a whole; the Spanish rabbis, however, thought differently; in the "returners" they saw not the typical, but rather the atypical Marranos, not the rule, but the exceptions; and as for the Marrano camp as a whole, they considered it too steeped in the foreign religion and too far advanced in its assimilation for any substantial change to be expected within it; in fact, they gave it up as lost. The historical development of Spanish Marranism in the 16th and 17th centuries has certainly confirmed this opinion.

## III. THE PHILOSOPHIC AND POLEMIC LITERATURE

### 1

The references to the Marranos in the extra-Responsa Hebrew sources emanating from the period under discussion are considerably more complex than those in the Responsa. Yet, they are also more illuminating, for, unlike the latter, they throw light not only on the static, but also the dynamic phases of Marrano history. By way of explanation, the Responsa references to the Marranos deal primarily with facts, not with causes; they describe situations, not developments. We would like to know, however, not only *what* the Marranos were religiously, but also *how* they came to be so and *why*. We would like to know the major urges and motives, the basic views and arguments, the social, intellectual and political forces that moved the Marranos along the historic road they traveled. In brief, we would like to gain a deeper insight into their spiritual life as it changed and evolved in the course of a century.

The documents we are about to investigate help us gain such an insight. They contain views about the *roots of Marranism* and the *causes of its growth and expansion*. We shall see, upon analysis, that these views did not always correspond with reality; but even when we find them wanting in this respect, they are often suggestive of the true development. In addition, the accounts these documents contain of the Marranos' religious *beliefs* and *behavior* also contribute to the same end. Compared with the similar accounts in the Responsa, they are more detailed and incisive, and altogether more instructive. Although they consist solely of generalizations and never refer to individual cases, they should, nevertheless, be considered quite factual. For, written as they were by communal leaders of high moral and intellectual standards, these statements no doubt represent the sum of long experience and conclusions arrived at after much reflection upon what was known to be fact. Above all, they are *all* of Spanish origin, i. e., authored by people who *lived* in Spain, negotiated with Marranos, or observed them at close range. And as they convey both views and feelings, they may well be taken to reflect, on the one hand, the emotional relationships between Jews and Marranos and, on the other, public opinion of Spain's Jewry on Marranism as a socio-religious problem.

These are some of the features of these documents which may largely be counted on their credit side. Of distinct disadvantage to our investigation, however, is a peculiarity they are marked with which must also be considered. We refer to the fact that the literature under review does not, as a rule, discuss the Marranos openly. More clearly, in the overwhelming majority of cases it does not refer to them by their accepted appellation (*marranos*, or rather *anusim* in Hebrew), but designates them by other terms that do not ordinarily signify the Marranos.[1] Quite often it hints at them by cryptic allusions, or treats of them in veiled discussions or remarks that seemingly refer to converts in general, or to conversionist movements in other times and lands. What prompted this practice is not hard to see: fear of the authorities, of both Church and State, and a desire to avoid involving Jews and Marranos in a compromising situation. What we have before us, then, is a self-imposed censorship, and one which was remarkably honored, although its enforcement was left entirely to the writers' conscience and common sense.

[1] The rarity with which the term *anusim* is used in Hebrew writings of Spanish origin — in striking contrast to its frequent occurence in works produced outside of Spain — is already noticeable in the early part of the century, i. e., in the period close to the forced conversions. Among the exceptionally few cases of such use, one may point to Bonafed's remark introducing a letter he had sent to a forced convert: כתב שלחתי לאנוס אחד לפראנגא (see A. Kaminka, "Shirim u-Meliẓot le-ha-Rav Shelomo ben ha-Rav Reuven Bonafed," in *Haẓofeh le-Ḥokhmat Yisrael*, Budapest, xii [1928], p. 34). Even so, the reference here is only to a *member* of the Marrano group. As a designation for the group as a whole, the word is found in the chronicle of Joseph ben Ẓaddiq of Arevalo appended to his *Zekher Ẓaddiq* as the 50th chapter of that work (see A. Neubauer, *Mediaeval Jewish Chronicles*, I, p. 99). The term, however, may have been introduced here *after* the expulsion and *outside* of Spain, as it is by no means certain that the work was completed prior to 1492 (see below, chap. III, note 51).

That this censorship considerably constricted the discussion
of the Marrano issue, and excluded from it matters of prime
value and interest, can indeed hardly be doubted. But it is
also clear that it did not suppress what was regarded as essential
to the problem. As often happens in such cases, those who were
denied full and free expression found ways of communicating
their basic thoughts and feelings to those who shared their
concerns. Between the writer and his audience there developed
a new link, a special system of communication, or a kind of
secret code, by which his message was conveyed and brought
home. Thus, when the Spanish-Jewish author or preacher spoke
of "criminals," or "rebels," or "wicked," or the like, his audience
knew precisely to whom he referred and what these words implied.[2] Similarly, when the discussion turned on conversion *in*

---

[2] Although the use of these appellations for converts stems from
talmudic literature, they were employed there for signifying a variety of
sinners, and not converts exclusively. In the case of רשע this is clearly evidenced
from the various degrees of "wickedness" considered (see, for instance,
Tosefta, Sanh. xiii.3; Rosh ha-Shanah 16b; 'Eruvin 19a) and the various
acts of wickedness listed by Maimonides (*Hilkhot 'Edut*, x, 1–4) which
range from offenses entailing financial retribution to crimes involving
the death penalty (and cf. the definition of רשע in *Tanḥuma* [ed. Buber],
Korah, xxi, *Pesiqta*, ed. Mandelbaum, II, piska 28.2, p. 423, and *Numbers R.*,
Korah, x, which has nothing to do with conversion). The identification of
רשעים with converts, and for that matter with heretics and epicureans (see
below, notes 15, 107), was no doubt grounded upon the fact that all these
latter sinners belonged to the class of the extremely wicked who have no
share in the world to come (Tosefta, Sanh. xiii.1; Sanh. 110b) or rather, who,
because of their great wickedness, are subjected to the eternal tortures
of hell (Tosefta, Sanh. xiii.5; Rosh ha-Shanah 17a; Maimonides, *Hilkh.
Teshuvah*, iii.6: נידונים על גודל רשעם). — The term פושעים (criminals, or rather
rebellious criminals, and more precisely: rebels against God [see Is. 66.24]),
likewise indicated a variety of wrongdoers, belonging, however, to the *basest*
types: they all seemed due for punishment in hell, though in different degrees
of severity (see Tosefta, Sanh. xiii.4–5; Rosh ha-Shanah 17a; 'Eruvin 19a;
Ḥagigah 27a; and see Tosafot, Bava Meẓi'a 58b on חוץ, where the different
opinions expressed in this regard, some of which at least ostensibly contradictory, are coordinated). As such, פושעים served as synonym for רשעים, evidently of similar degrees of sinfulness (see, for instance, 'Eruvin 19a and Sanh.
100b). Its common application in medieval times to converts, especially in
the form exclusively applied to Jews: פושעי ישראל, stemmed probably from the
fact that the "criminals" of Jewish stock who, according to tannaitic sources,

*general*, or on phenomena of conversion in *other times and places*, the audience sensed quite clearly whether the author had really *these* matters in mind, or whether he used them merely as a ruse to express his opinion on the Marrano problem. What was clear, however, to the writer's contemporaries presents a problem of identification for the investigator in our time. The difficulty posed by the extra-Responsa sources, when scrutinized for our special purposes, is therefore a double one. We can establish the material related to the Marranos only after discerning it under the guise of other themes, and we can fully perceive its content and objectives only after determining the meaning of its applied symbols and allusions.

2

Of the extra-Responsa documents of the period, it is the philosophical and polemical writings that ought to have first claim on our attention, as they contain substantial evidence on the Marranos in the earlier years of the century under review. This is also *one* of the reasons why the two groups of writings, so different in many ways, are here combined under the same heading. The other reason is inherent in the fact that both these branches of Hebrew literature were motivated, now more than ever, by a common purpose which, from the standpoint of this inquiry, makes them rather inseparable.

Though originally moved by the same ideal of establishing the supremacy of the Jewish faith, and differing mainly in their

were destined to damnation, included converts, as well as *minim* and Epicureans (see Tosefta, Sanh. xiii.5; Rosh ha-Shanah 17a; Mishnah, Sanh. x.1; and cf. Maimonides, *Hil. Teshuvah*, III, 6, 9), who came to be regarded as converts (see below, notes 15, 107). Also the fact that Yeshu, taken to be the founder of Christianity, was defined as a פושע ישראל (Gittin 57a; according to the unpurged version) may have added stimulus to the spread of that usage. — מורדים, as an appellation for converts, no doubt originated in its synonymity with פושעים in the sense above mentioned, especially since the acts of the latter had been explicitly defined as acts of rebellion (Tosefta, Kippurim, ii.1; Yoma 36b). The medieval identification of מורדים with apostates was fortified in some measure, it may be assumed, by the new meaning now attributed in Christendom to the old Greek translation of the biblical מורד (ἀποστάτης).

specific targets — philosophy hitting at the skeptics from within and polemics attacking the critics from without —, in the course of the 12th–14th centuries philosophy gradually drifted away from polemics in search of speculative aims of its own. The events of 1391, however, changed this course of Jewish philosophy drastically. It made a sharp return to polemics, and resumed its old combative role. As a result, the philosophic and polemic literatures were now again essentially but two arms of the same religious campaign. Both, as we shall see, while differing in means, storve to attain the same end: to check the process of christianization. For what loomed largest to the authors in both fields was the phenomenon of Marranism and large-scale conversion; and this all important fact not only determined the character of the new philosophical works, but changed that of the polemical ones as well.

Of course, the anti-Christian polemic literature which developed in Spain after 1391 was, in many ways, a continuation of similar works that had for centuries been written in Spain and elsewhere. Yet it differed from the latter both in content and direction, and this gave it a place apart in the history of Jewish polemics. Until 1391, Jewish polemical literature was mainly concerned with repelling attacks launched against Judaism on theological grounds, its main task being limited to proving that the claims of its adversaries were unfounded. In the theological conflict that unfolded after the first Crusade and continued for centuries until 1391, the Christians thus assumed the role of aggressors, the Jews of defenders of their traditions, and the battle, one may add, was constantly waged not in Christian, but in Jewish "territory." After 1391, however, the scene of battle radically changed, for Jewish polemical literature then adopted fundamentally different tactics. It passed from the defensive to the offensive, and deeply penetrated the "field" of the enemy. In accord with Christian-conversionist strategy, it now attempted to prove, on the basis of Christian writings, not so much the veracity of Judaism as the falsehood of Christianity. Instead of limiting itself to self-defense, i. e., to re-assertion of the Jewish interpretation of the biblical, talmudic and midrashic statements — which until then formed the main theme of the controversy —, it now concentrated on examining the Christian religious sources, seeking out their weak and vulnerable points, and turning them into the central issue of the discussion. The sources thus examined by the new polemic literature were both ancient and medieval, encompassing the New Testament, the writings of the Church Fathers and those of the later Christian authors. But in particular it delved into the Gospels, dissected and analyzed every part of them, and by means of this analysis tried to demolish the entire theological structure of Christianity.[3]

What were the reasons for these revised tactics of Jewish polemic literature? Whence this onset upon Christianity *as such* which lasted for more than half a century? The answer seems to lie on the surface. When a body of literature is devoted to prov-

---

[3] To be sure, criticisms of Christian dogma are found also in earlier polemical literature, but there they serve merely as supporting arguments in the refutation of Christian biblical interpretations. Jacob ben Reuben, of the 12th century, who devoted a special chapter in his book to disproving Christian doctrine through an analysis of the Gospels (see *Milḥamot ha-Shem*, ed. J. Rosenthal, Jerusalem, 1963, pp. 141–156), hardly forms an exception to this rule, since the chapter referred to is actually an appendix to the work which, as a whole, is devoted to a negation of christological interpretations of the Bible. Even in its limited form, his attack may have been encouraged by the particular climate of opinion which prevailed in southern France, then a center of the Albigensian heresy, where his work was, in all likelihood, composed (see Steinschneider, *Die hebräischen Übersetzungen des Mittelalters*, p. 440; Loeb, "Polémistes chrétiens et juifs en France et en Espagne," in *REJ*, xviii [1889], p. 47; Jacob ben Reuben may have come to France from Spain, as suggested by several scholars, but there is no compelling reason to agree with Rosenthal, "Prolegomena...," in *PAAJR*, xxvi [1957], pp. 128–129, that, after residing temporarily in Gascogne, he settled in Christian Spain, and not in Provence). — Among the Spanish polemicists Moses ha-Kohen of Tordesillas went farthest in his disapprobation of Christianity in his *'Ezer ha-Emunah*, composed in 1379 (see MS. of the National and University Library, Jerusalem, No. 659/353, copied and annotated by A. Posnanski, e. g., pp. 10, 12, 13, 22, 42, 46, 59); but based as they are on philosophical or logical premises, his criticisms of Christian dogma merely accompany his comments on biblical passages used by Christians for theological ends. Nevertheless, the frequency of his theoretical charges against Christianity entitle him to be considered as a forerunner of the new approach.

ing the invalidity of the tenets of a certain religion, its purpose is clearly to destroy *faith* in that religion within the audience to which it addresses itself. What is more, when this literature is religious in essence, it obviously seeks to attract that audience to the religion of its own authors. Thus, the purpose of the anti-Jewish literature, composed by Christians and converts in the Middle Ages, was to undermine faith in Judaism among Jews and prepare the way for their conversion to Christianity. Similarly, the campaign against Christian dogma, now conducted by Jewish polemicists, was designed, first, to undermine faith in Christianity among people who apparently *believed* in it, and, secondly, to steer these people away from Christianity to Judaism. Now, who were the Christians for whom this literature was intended? Surely, not Christians of Spanish stock. Consequently, they were Marranos swayed by Christian doctrine whom the Jewish polemicist tried to save for Judaism.

To appreciate more fully the logic of this conclusion, which is so pertinent to the subject of our discussion, a few more remarks are in order. What we should recall, in the first place, is that the new line of argument described above, constituted a departure, not only in Jewish polemical literature, but also in the entire policy then pursued by the Jews on the religious issue. Practically throughout the medieval period, Jews carefully refrained from campaigning among Christians for the purpose of converting them to Judaism. Such a campaign, they knew, would not only jeopardize the very existence of the Jews within Christendom, but doubtlessly terminate it altogether. Nor, as a rule, did their religious agitation aim at winning back to the Jewish fold voluntary converts to Christianity; for they generally considered the latter abject sinners who had betrayed their faith for non-religious motives, and consequently could not be wooed back to Judaism by religious arguments of any kind.[4] The only task of the Jewish polemicist, as he saw it, was to guard the faithful Jew against the intrusion of doubts that might be stirred in him by the Christian arguments. And to fulfill this

---

[4] For an unqualified expression of this view, see *Sefer Ḥasidim*, ed. Wistinetzki-Freimann, Frankfurt-on-Main, 1924, §1273 (p. 314), §183 (p. 72).

task it was quite sufficient, he believed, to meet the Christian theological arguments by proving the soundness of the Jewish position. Hence, there was no need or purpose in attacking Christianity as such.

The rise of the new polemical literature, however, reveals a situation fundamentally altered. It shows that the polemicists now recognized the emergence of a new type of convert, one who took to Christendom not by force of circumstances, or for reasons other than religious, but *because of his belief in the teachings of Christianity, in their historic truth and religious promise.* To such a convert, or candidate for conversion, it was not sufficient to clarify the Jewish view of what the Bible or the Talmud meant in certain instances. To him, one had to prove the erroneousness of the faith he had adopted or was about to adopt; to him, indeed, one had to expose the absurdity of the conceptions upon which that faith was grounded; and to him, it was thought, such proof and such exposal *could* prove efficacious. For, having adopted the new religion *not* from ulterior motives, but out of honest, though muddled, thinking, his reasoning, it was hoped, could still be corrected. In any case, he was not considered a lost cause, especially in the first stage of his conversion, when the new faith had not yet struck deep roots in his spiritual life. We may safely assume, therefore, that it was to *such* neophytes that the new polemics were directed.

That this was the case, and that the neophytes referred to were socially not of Jewish, but of Marrano origin, is clearly indicated by the first work to represent the new polemical approach. As all available records show, the epistle of Profiat Duran (better known as Efodi), *Al Tehi ka-Avotekha* ("Do Not Be like Thy Fathers"), which ridicules Christian dogma and seeks to reduce it to absurdity, did not serve — at least, in the first stage — to influence Jews, but Marranos — and Marranos only. Originally addressed, probably in 1395,[5] to a forced convert who was persuaded by Christian teachings, the epistle soon became a means of campaigning among the Marrano rank and file. The fact that the authorities ordered it to be burned

5 See below, appendix C.

wherever found among Christians (i. e., Marranos)[6] is sufficient proof to this effect, and it also suggests that this sort of agitation attained some measure of success. Perhaps this success encouraged and induced to further efforts of a similar nature. In any case, the *Epistle* was merely the first step in the Jewish campaign in the new direction. The second step was much more daring. What characterized it, above all, was the abandonment of all camouflage in favor of an outright assault upon Christianity. What is more, this assault was penetrative and far-reaching to an extent never before displayed. While in the *Epistle* Duran's criticism of Christianity is based on general logical grounds and avoids allusion to Christian sources, in his later work, *Kelimat ha-Goyim* ("The Shame of the Gentiles"), he tried to substantiate his contentions by a careful analysis of Christian sacred writings. In fact, Duran here followed the policy pursued by the Christians in their attacks against Judaism, but with other means and opposite objectives. Just as the Christians tried to prove that ancient Jewish literature contains acknowledgments by some of the Sages of the rightness of Christianity, so Duran tried to show that the early Christian writings, and primarily Jesus' sayings, contained an admission of the rightness of Judaism.[7] And, just as the argument employed

---

[6] See Isaac 'Aqrish' introduction to *Iggeret Ogeret . . . (Qovez Vikuḥim,* Breslau, 1844), p. 3 (not paginated). Also, according to the latter, anyone distributing this epistle among Christians was subject to death by fire (*ibid.*). 'Akrish, however, states, that these penalties were introduced after it had been revealed, through Ibn Shem-Tov's commentary, that the *Epistle* was making a mockery of Christianity (*ibid.*). It does not require much reflection, however, to decide that at least this detail is fictional. The Christians, let alone the true converts among them, who included accomplished Hebrew scholars like Paulus of Burgos, did not need sixty years and the help of a Jewish commentator to make this discovery. Essentially, therefore, 'Akrish' story must reflect an older tradition, according to which the *Epistle* had a public impact that repeatedly attracted the attention of the authorities. This is indicated by the fact that they (the "Christians," in 'Akrish' presentation) came to refer to it as *Alteca Boteca* (*ibid.*) and by the severity of the means employed against its distribution (although, it should be added, the punishments *actually* imposed may have differed from those mentioned above).

[7] In Duran's opinion the effectiveness of this method lies in "answering on the basis of the rival's own statements" (להשיב כפי מאמר האומר). See

by the Christians attempted to play upon the Jews' faith in the wisdom and knowledge of their Sages, so must the argument followed by Duran have been aimed at those who recognized, at least to some extent, the authority of Jesus.[8] Thus we come again to the conclusion that the work was meant primarily for the Marranos, and more particularly, for those among them who were *partly* Christianized, or on the verge of complete Christianization.

As we see from Duran's introduction, it was Crescas who urged him to write his second polemical work, and also suggested its basic approach, namely, to devote it to a thorough negation of Christian religious doctrine.[9] This point, too, is of paramount importance. The fact that the official Jewish leader of Aragon found it necessary to instigate such a campaign is in itself sufficient proof that the Christianization of many Marranos was nearing the point of no return. Yet Crescas, it seems, was not entirely satisfied with Duran's accomplishment. What he had in mind, it appears, was a less scholarly work, less cluttered with statements of authorities, and more given to a logical analysis of the Christian principles of faith, or rather to a demonstration of their inacceptability on purely logical grounds. Crescas, in other words, wanted a new version of *Do Not Be like Thy Fathers*, yet one that would not strike at the weaknesses of Christianity by means of satire and subtle allusion, but would expose them for what they were in plain, positive language. Evidently unsatisfied, at least in part, with Duran's work, Crescas went on to write the desired book himself.[10] Thus

*Kelimat ha-Goyim*, ed. A. Posnanski, in *Ha-Zofeh me-Erez Hagar*, Budapest, III (1914), p. 12.

[8] The fact that Duran was simultaneously trying to ruin this authority with respect to Christian doctrine involved no inner contradiction. Fundamentally, his purpose was to show that Christianity was not the creation of Jesus, who considered the Law eternal and immutable, nor in the main even of the Apostles, but rather of the Church Fathers and their successors. While the former were, according to Duran, merely misguided Jews (טועים), the latter were misguiding gentiles (מטעים). See *ibid.*, p. 104; and see also pp. 107, 109, 110, and throughout the work.

[9] *Ibid.*, p. 102.

[10] See below, appendix C.

he produced his *Refutation of Christian Dogma* — a short analysis of Christian beliefs from a strictly logical point of view. There are no references here to authorities, either Jewish or Christian. There are no deviations from the main line of thought, no side remarks and no elaborations. Crescas tries to focus his readers' minds solely upon his basic argument, starting with certain logical premises and examining each dogma in the light of its compatibility or incompatibility with these foundations of reason. That he composed the work in Catalan,[11] and not in Hebrew, is additional and indeed decisive proof that it was aimed at the Marranos. For, although the author thus came dangerously close to publicly exposing his true aims, he thought it vital to place in the hands of the Marranos, to whom the reading of Hebrew books must have become a rarity, a work which could reveal to them what Christianity really was.

All this clearly shows that by 1397, only six years after the great conversion, there was already afoot, among the forced converts, a strong movement toward real Christianization which threatened to dominate that camp. Had this indeed not been the case, the new type of polemic literature would not have made its determined appearance. Having come as the result of careful consideration by the leaders of the Jewish community in Aragon,[12] its frontal attack upon Christianity, with

[11] See the introduction of Joseph ben Shem-Tov to his translation of Ḥasdai's work into Hebrew, *Bittul 'iqqarei ha-Noẓrim*, Saloniki, 1860 (?), p. 2, wherein he states that Crescas "composed this treaty in the language of his country" (אשר חיברו בלשון ארצו). Since the translator was a Castilian Jew and Crescas an Aragonese, it is obvious that in בלשון ארצו he did not refer to Castilian (Spanish), as Graetz (*op. cit.*, VIII, p. 388) and others thought, but to Catalan, which by that time was already the literary language of Aragon.

[12] That Crescas was not alone in planning this campaign is evident from his introductory remark to the *Refutation*: שרים ונכבדים בקשו ממני ויפרצו בי לחבר מאמר וכו' (*Bittul 'Iqqarei ha-Noẓrim*, p. 4). By שרים ונכבדים Crescas referred, of course, to Jewish notables and courtiers, and not to Christian ones, as suggested by Graetz (*op. cit.*, VIII, p. 388). Crescas may have had several reasons for leaving the religious identity of these notables unspecified; in any case, the assumption that Christian laymen urged him to compose a book against Christianity, and that *this* is why he wrote his work "in Spanish" (*ibid.*), must be seen not only as far-fetched in itself, but also entirely dissociated from the historic circumstances.

its brushing aside of the old policy of caution, represented a desperate measure which could be justified only by extreme circumstances. That the situation appeared hazardous or even critical, that Christianity was gaining ground among the Marranos to an extent and at a rate hitherto unseen, we can indeed learn not only by implication, but also by direct evidence. The matter is indicated, as clearly as he could afford, by the author of *The Shame of the Gentiles* himself. In the introduction to this work, Efodi says that he wrote it as a means of defense against the "rebels" who connive against the faith, who "raise ramparts against its walls in order to render it defenseless and open to conquest."[13] What is more, he points out that the situation has assumed catastrophic aspects, that the "tottering hut" of Judaism is being destroyed, that "the leprosy of heresy is upon the foreheads of the people," and that "the staff of wickedness buds and insolence blossoms."[14] These enigmatic and ambiguous terms are obviously meant to conceal the author's aim, for, on the surface, the statement may be interpreted as referring to elements *within* Jewry who deviated from the path of normative Judaism. However, what served as disguise against would be accusers, or as a possible defense against them, would not mislead the discerning reader as to the true meaning of the statement. Duran could obviously not have referred here to *internal* critics of rabbinic Judaism, or to the rationalists of the Averroist brand. He could not have referred to them as the prime movers of the campaign against which his book was directed, because there is nothing in his book against *this* type of critic or innovator within the Jewish fold. As indicated, his entire book is directed against *Christian theological principles only*, and, therefore, the above statements should and can be interpreted as referring to an entirely different element, i. e., to the activist group of converts who conducted an intensive campaign among the Marranos for true acceptance of Christian doctrine.[14a] In fact, the terms "rebels" and "heretics," which

---

[13] *Kelimat ha-Goyim*, p. 102: ‏...המתפרצים והמעמיקים לַסתיר עצה ולשפוך סוללה‎ ‏על חומת התורה האלהית לתת אותה כמלונה במקשה כעיר פרוצה.‎

[14] *Ibid.*: ‏ציץ מטה הרשע פרח הזדון.‎

[14a] The campaign of the apostates among *Jews*, on the other hand, was still conducted along the old lines: it concentrated on proving, through biblical

Duran, as we have seen, used in his introduction, were but appellations for these converts — and this in full accord with their common usage in earlier Hebrew polemic literature[15] —

and midrashic statements, the *messiahship* of Jesus, i. e., his being the realization of the *Jewish* messianic hope, and minimized the discussion of other Christian dogmas or relegated them to the background. That this was their policy also after 1391 and, further, that this was the only approach by which, they believed, a breakthrough could be achieved in the Jewish attitude toward Christianity, is testified by the following words of their leader, Paulus of Burgos: מאמין בתורת מרע"ה, אשר אחד משרשיה הוא ביאת המשיח, ראוי עליו לחקור ה כ ת ו ב והמקובל במשיחנו אם הוא המיועד ... וחקירה זו היא פתח תקוה (L. אשר בה נכנסתי במסורת הברית וזה השער לה' צדיקים יבואו בו Landau, *Das apologetische Schreiben des Josua Lorki an den Abtrünnigen Don Salomon ha-Lewi*, Antwerp, 1906, Hebrew version, p. 19). Such demonstrations, of course, required an answer *of the kind*; accordingly, when the apostates' campaign gained momentum among them, the Jews were not late in offering it (see, e. g., Joseph ben Lavi's *Qodesh ha-Qodashim* [1412], MS. National and University Library, Jerusalem, No. 800). On the strength of the conversionist campaign among the Jews around 1396, the date of Duran's above-cited statements, see below, note 17a. And see above, p. 29, Ribash' remarks on conversionist pressures exerted upon the Marranos.

[15] Regardless of the question of the historic relationship between the *minim* of the Tannaitic sources and the early Christians among the Jews, it is clear that the correct definition of *minim* already presented a problem to the Babylonian Amoraim ('Avodah Zarah 26b), as well as to the talmudic commentators (see, for instance, Rashi's two different definitions of *min* in 'Avodah Zarah 26b and Rosh ha-Shanah 17a). Although *minim*, according to Maimonides (*Hilkhot Teshuvah*, III, 7), indicates essentially holders of wrong opinions about God, and although in Talmudic and Midrashic literature *minim* head the lists of the worst religious criminals (see 'Avodah Zarah 26b; Rosh ha-Shanah 17a; Tosefta, Sanh. 13.5; *Exodus R.*, 19) and represent a class apart from converts and, in fact, more depraved than the latter (see Horayot 11a; *Tanḥuma* [ed. Buber], Korah, addition, 1; *Numbers R.*, addition to Korah, 1), they were also identified as idolaters ('Avodah Zarah 26b: איזהו מין? זה העובד אלילי כוכבים; see also Horayot, 11a; Ḥullin 13a; and cf. Maimonides, *ibid.*), and as such their name (*minim*) had been used, at least since the 12th century, as a designation not only for heretics, but also for converts, and primarily for apostates who espoused their new faith. Thus, Joseph ben Isaac Kimḥi, in his *Sefer ha-Berit*, represents the advocate for Christianity, obviously a convert, as a *min* (see *Milḥemet Ḥovah*, Constantinople, 1710, pp. 19ab, 20b, *et al.*). Also in the account of the disputation between Yeḥiel of Paris and the convert Nicolaus Donin, the latter is described as *the min* (see *Vikuaḥ Rabbenu Yeḥiel mi-Paris*, ed. Grünbaum, Thorn, 1873, p. 1: ונקרא שמו ניקלוש (=ניקולש) המין ימות ויחלש; see also pp. 2, 4, 6, 9). In like

while his allusion to those "who laid deep and secret plans"
with the intention of putting Judaism under a hopeless siege[16]
undoubtedly refers to the group of leading converts, headed by
Paulus of Burgos, who, at that time, had already conceived
elaborate plans for the total destruction of Judaism in Spain,[17]
and simultaneously conducted an energetic campaign for Christianity, especially among the Marranos.[17a] That this group was
not limited to a small minority is suggested by the words רבו
המתפרצים,[18] and that its campaign attained considerable success,
and made the inclination toward Christianity widespread among
the Marranos, is indicated by the above quoted statement that
the "leprosy of heresy is upon the foreheads of the people," that

---

manner, Moses ha-Kohen of Tordesillas uses the same appelation for converts
in his 'Ezer ha-'Emunah (see MS. cited, p. 3).

[16] See above, note 13.

[17] Of the anti-Jewish schemes of Paulus of Burgos in the royal court
of Aragon and the papal court in Avignon, Efodi himself speaks in one of
the concluding paragraphs of his Epistle. See Qovez Vikuḥim, pp. 44–45
(not paginated).

[17a] It appears that in the first two decades after the riots, the conversionist
drive among the Jews slackened and, as far as their Jewish front was concerned,
the apostates now bent their main efforts upon influencing the authorities,
both of Church and State, to enact oppressive legislation against the Jews
(without which, they must have felt, their agitation could achieve only very
limited results). It was only in 1412, after that aim had been attained, that
they intensified their campaign against the Jews to the utmost, without,
however, changing, to any extent, their traditional mode of agitation (see
above, note 14a).

[18] The term המתפרצים as indication for active converts is also found
in earlier polemic literature which Efodi no doubt examined before writing
his own work. Cf. Moses ha-Kohen of Tordesillas, op. cit., introd. (p. 2):
רבו ממירי תורתנו, כל אחד מעיז פניו למרוד ביוצרו, לבו ועיניו . . . המתפרצים איש מפני אדוניו.
Considering its biblical connotations (I Sam. 25.10), the term seemed to
indicate both rebellion against one's master and an attempt to escape from
him, and as such it appeared to befit apostates (in their relation to God
and His people). Similar to this is the title pariẓim used by Isaac Pulgar,
in his 'Ezer ha-Dat, to describe converts, who are also defined by him as
"religious rebels" (מורדי הדת). See 'Ezer ha-Dat, ed. G. S. Belasco, London,
1906, introd. (and cf. above, note 2). And see also the use of the same appellation before Pulgar, e. g., by Isaac ben Joseph Israeli (Yesod 'Olam, II,
Berlin, 1846, p. 36a) and after him by Isaac Abravanel (see below, chap. III,
note 103).

*"the entire people is at strife,"*[19] and that "the staff of wickedness buds and insolence (זדון) blossoms." "Wicked" (רשע) and "insolent" (זד) were also terms by which the active converts came to be commonly designated in medieval Hebrew literature.[20]

This testimony of Profiat Duran, if we read it correctly, as we believe we do, corroborates, and at the same time broadens the information we have gained about the Marranos thus far. It tells us not only that by that time — i. e., in 1396[21] — there were already many Marranos who actually adopted Christianity as a faith, but that the change of their inner religious allegiance was largely the result of a determined campaign conducted by a group of conversionist apostates bent upon bringing to a total end the existence of Judaism and the Jewish people. The reasons for the success of that campaign are not stated by Duran. In any

---

[19] *Kelimat he-Goyim*, p. 103: כי צרעת המינות במצחות האנשים פורחת ... ו י ה י. כ ל  ה ע ם  נ ד ו ן. The word נדון in the latter phrase (borrowed from II Sam. 19.10) means, according to traditional interpretation, *embroiled in arguments and disputations.* This connotation may suggest a great deal about Duran's subject of discussion. To assume that conversionist agitation among Jews had, in 1396, such an effect as to stir the whole people, or large masses thereof, to arguments over the soundness of Christian dogma, is plainly unthinkable. It took a much sharper deterioration of their condition, and a combination of several factors, including a monarchic policy of persecution, to bring masses of Jews to such a state (see on this below, p. 119). On the other hand, it is quite conceivable that the forced converts of 1391, under the incessant pressures of their new surroundings and the constant hammering of Christian preaching, were brought to such a state of perturbation that the issue of Christianity, its theory and practice, was argued in every Marrano home.

[20] Thus, Pulgar (*op. cit.*, p. 3) describes the disputations between converts and Jews as a struggle between "wicked" and "innocent" (לוחמים יחד רשעים ותמימים) and describes the position and arguments of the converts as emanating from the insolence of their heart (זדון לבם). Similarly, Yeḥiel of Paris designates converts by the titles "wicked" (*Vikuaḥ* . . ., pp. 11, 12) and "insolent" (*ibid.*, p. 1: ויהי הנחש למטה זדון ונקרא שמו ניקולאוס המין). See also his remarks on the converts' ultimate punishment: שנאמר ... בכליון ... נידון יהיה ... זה המין [מלאכי נ', י"ט] הנה היום בא בוער כתנור [והיו כל זדים] וכל עושי רשעה לקש ... ואותו היום שישרפו הזדים יהיה מרפא לצדיקים ... ואחר שישרפו יהיו אפר ... שנאמר [מלאכי נ', כ"א] ועסותם ר ש ע י ם (*ibid.*, p. 12). All this is, of course, on the basis of Tosefta, Sanh. 13.1, Rosh ha-Shanah 17a and *Tanḥuma* (the common), Koraḥ, XII, where the term זדים appears as a synonym of מינים (ברכת הזדים).

[21] See below, appendix C, pp. 221–222.

case, it appears quite clear that six years of Marrano life were sufficient to weaken the hold of Judaism upon the forced converts, and further evidence, supplied by the same author, indicates progress in the same direction even at an earlier stage. For, three years before, in 1393, while Duran still speaks about the Marranos *as a whole* as of people who are *"compelled* to violate the Law openly,"[22] he already finds himself impelled to observe that *part* of them display *reluctance to return to Judaism,* or even to practice it secretly, so that it may appear *"as if this part had actually left the fold."*[23] What is more, they seemed to be "happy" in their new religious state, thus giving credence to the pessimistic thought that "their condition will never be remedied."[24] Still believing, nonetheless, in their inner faith in Judaism (כי ה' הוא ית' יודע מצפוני לבם), Duran even then alludes to the need of campaigning among the Marranos and "stirring their hearts to return to God."[25] Also later, in 1396, when Christianization entered a much more advanced phase, he evidently still believed in the possibility of bringing these backsliders back to Judaism, for otherwise, as is clear, he would not have written his book. In any case, what is evident from his introduction to the work is that the situation was now highly aggravated, that, in fact, it was not short of critical, and that what was happening was not merely a *practical* integration into the rival religious life, but also a *theoretical and spiritual* one. In the light of these indications, the statement made by Ribash and discussed above, namely that many of the Marranos, who "first practiced Christianity out of compulsion, later practiced it of their own free will," now assumes a more definite meaning. It means that this *voluntary* practice of Christianity was not only a matter of *convenience,* but also — as must have been the

----

[22] See Duran's letter to En Joseph Abram, published as addendum to *Ma'ase Efod,* ed. J. Friedländer and J. Kohn, Vienna, 1865, p. 195: חלק מזרע אברהם הנאנס לביטול תורתו בנגלה ... אשר עברה עליו גזירת השמדין בגליל הגדול הזה.

[23] *Ibid.:* ראה התרשלות קצתו בתשובתו ... לפי שכבר יֵחָשֵׁב מזה היות החלק ההוא יוצא מכלל העם.

[24] *Ibid.:* כי רעתכי אז תעלוזי ... שמא ח'ו אין להם תקנה.

[25] *Ibid.:* כי עליהם יצדק ... לעורר לבבם לשוב אל ה'.

case with many — one of *faith and conviction*. It was because of this "conviction," this spread of the belief in Christianity as such, that Crescas and Duran found it necessary — nay, essential — regardless of the difficulties and dangers involved[26] — to slash out openly against Christian dogma with every theoretical weapon at their command.

That the new policy provided a tactical instrument in the bitter struggle with the conversionist movement, is evident from the fact that it dominated Jewish polemical literature for at least several decades. This does not mean, however, that it proved at all effective. On the contrary, from the evidences preserved in this literature we may gather that it failed in achieving its aim. In any case, it did not check the tide. When Joseph ben Shem-Tov, the last contributor to these polemics, translated Crescas' treatise into Hebrew (1451), he could summarize the results of the religious struggle only on a note of gloom and defeat. "Our enemies, who are bent upon our destruction," he admits, "have confounded and consumed us all the time;" and they achieved this by their loud, supercilious[26a] protestations that the her-

---

[26] Of the special threat posed for the Jews by any attempt on their part to refute Christianity, Jacob ben Reuben speaks in his introduction to the 11th chapter of his book in which he attacks Christian theological propositions as presented in the Gospels: בשפטנו ( = ) והם שרינו, מה נזכה בשופטינו. ושופטינו, נשמרה מחסום לפינו וללשוננו, למה נמות לעינינו? (*Milḥamot ha-Shem*, p. 141). And further: וממעותו, ומעשר מן (the New Testament) על כן הזכרתי משניאות ספרם המעשר לא גיליתי כי יראתי (*ibid.*). In like manner, Moses ha-Kohen of Tordesillas, the other outstanding critic of Christian theology prior to the period under discussion, expresses his apprehension over the audacious step he took: וכופר) ( = ), ואם כתבתי בו דברים כנגד אמונתם וחברתי זה הספר להתוכח עם כל מין וכופר לזייף ולהכחיש תורתם, והבאתי ראיות מעדותם החדש לקיום תורתנו הקדושה, החכם עיניו בראשו, שישמור פיו ולשונו לשמור מצרות נפשו, כי הם אדונים מושלים עלינו והם דייניו ושופטינו . . . לכן כל משכיל שיענה ישים לבו ועיניו לבל יכשל במאמריו ובמעניו . . . שאם יטיח דברים כנגד תורתם או יבזה אמונתם יקומו עליו ביד רמה להרנו בערמה (*'Ezer ha-Emunah*, MS. cited, p. 3). Similarly Rashbaẓ, in presenting the reasons for the failure of the Jews to offer detailed refutations of Christianity and Islam, points out, outside the "self-evident weakness of their (i. e., the opponents') claims," the danger involved in such refutations (*Qeshet u-Magen*, Livorno, 1790 [?], p. 25b).

[26a] Also *deceitful*, according to Ibn Shem-Tov's own interpretation of the phrase used here: לשון מדברת גדולות. See his Commentary on *Al Tehi Ka-Avotekha*, in *Qoveẓ Vikuḥim*, p. 42 (not paginated).

itage of our fathers was mere falsehood."[27] So the enemy's campaign was described by him as devastating (which is indicated by the words אכלונו הממונו), unmitigated and *constantly* successful (which is manifest from the words כל היום), and its gains were in the field of religious *belief*, as is evident from his reference to the *contents* of the campaign, i. e., the Christian "exposition" of the "Jewish falsehood." Nevertheless, our author evidently assumed that revived, invigorated, anti-Christian polemics might still have a beneficial effect; and hence his efforts in this direction. Yet, at least as far as the Marranos were concerned, it would be unreasonable to suppose that his rather uninspired efforts fared better than the works of his brilliant predecessors. In fact, his polemic writings must be regarded as an oddity, since the course he took, by then already obsolete, apparently was not subsequently pursued. What happened was clear. After decades of inveighing against Christianity *as such*, the Jewish polemicists had to give up these tactics, and, moreover, had to revert to the earlier policy of defending the positions of their own faith. For while they were attacking Christianity in an attempt to bring converts back to Judaism, the "enemy" made deep inroads into the Jewish camp itself.

## 3

To the Jewish scholars of the fifteenth century, it was quite clear that the Jews of Spain fell short of the rest of the Jewish communities in the sincerity of their devotion to Judaism. As they saw it, Spanish Jewry, the greatest Jewish community in the world, had miserably failed in the crucial test which every

---

[27] *Bittul 'Iqqarei ha-Noẓrim*, p. 2: כל היום אכלונו הממונו אויבינו העומדים עלינו לכלותינו בלשון מדברת גדולות אלי כל היום כי שקר נחלו אבותינו. In the passage quoted, the author, no doubt, referred especially to converts, who were often signified by the term אויבים or אויבי ה' on the basis of *Evel Rabbati*, II.10 (see, for instance, *Vikuaḥ Rabbenu Yeḥiel mi-Paris*, p. 4, and Joseph b. Nathan Official, *Sefer Yosef ha-Meqane*, in *Mi-Mizraḥ u-mi-Ma'arav*, ed. Brainin, IV [Berlin, 1899], p. 17, where the term used is עויניו). Also לשון מדברת גדולות was known as typical for the converts' way of disputing with the Jews. See, for instance, *Aḥituv ve-Ẓalmon*: ואם ישאל מין קלה או חמורה, אין איש יודע להשיב כשורה . . . כאשר פיהם רברבן אמלל (= ממלל) (MS. Jewish Theological Seminary of America, No. ENA 1663, p. 1).

Jewish community was faced with at one time or another. Not only could it not be presented as a model of faithfulness to the rest of the Jewish people, but should serve rather as an example of weakness, retreat, and downright betrayal.[28] That such an opinion could arise and prevail was not, however, due to the fact that during the cataclysm of 1391 only a small minority of Spain's Jews chose the alternative of martyrdom. Of course, compared to the Jews of Germany in 1096, or those of England in 1190, Spanish Jewry could not boast of heroic devotion to the Jewish faith. But, after all, *forced* conversion was no crime; it was traditionally tolerated and even recommended; and had the forced converts of 1391 shown zeal and determination in maintaining their Jewishness; had they made efforts to return to Judaism even at the cost of migrating from the country, the above-mentioned view of Spain's Jews could not have been fostered. If it did strike roots and become widespread, it was largely the result of the converts' religious conduct, consisting initially in vacillation and carelessness in matters related to the observance of Jewish law, then in complete abandonment of that law, and finally in assimilation and Christianization. It was this attitude of the forced converts toward Judaism, as it evolved in the course of years, that was partly responsible for the growth of that view about Spanish Jewry as a whole. However, in addition, there was another factor that played an even greater, indeed decisive part, in the same development.

For what must be borne in mind, in this connection, is that, contrary to common notion, the camp of the Marranos was far from consisting only of *forced* converts. It had been basically created in two stages and through *two* processes, manifestly different. The first stage was that of 1391; the second that of 1412–1415 — and the difference between the two in the nature of the conversions was enormous indeed. While most of the converts in the first stage were *forced*, most of the second were *voluntary*, neither physical compulsion nor direct threat of

[28] See Joseph ben Shem Tov, *Kevod Elohim*, Ferrara, 1555, p. 7(2ab); not paginated. — In this, and other not paginated works, the extra-parenthetical figure marks the number of the sheet, the intra-parenthetical one — the number of the leaf.

death having been the cause of their conversion.  We shall later examine some characteristics of the latter class of converts and see how deeply it affected the Marrano camp *qualitatively*.  For the time being we shall merely point out that even *quantitatively* it formed a most impressive force.  So powerful, indeed, was it numerically that the tradition of Spain's Jews, recorded by Jewish chroniclers, considered it to have formed approximately half of the original Marrano population.[29]  In any case, by 1415 voluntary conversion was not a minor current, but one of the two main streams that fed the Marrano group.  And it was this decisive fact, more than anything else, that engendered the opinion referred to above about the "great betrayal" of the Jews of Spain.

That the Spanish scholars who pondered the subject — at least, those of the generation of 1412–1415 — were aware of the fact that the extreme measures, then taken by the authorities against Spanish Jewry, had a share in the development of the conversion movement, can be taken for granted; in fact, it can be demonstrated by ample evidence.[30]  Yet it is also clear that they knew something else: under hardships no smaller and pressures no slighter, Jews in other countries and other times had firmly adhered to their religion.  Whenever oppression led to desertions, these were limited to individuals or small groups, to the weakest, most corrupt and most degenerate elements, as the converts were generally held to be.  On the other hand, whenever *mass* conversion occurred, it always took place at the point of the sword.  Never before, however, had Jewry witnessed a mass movement of *voluntary* conversion in the wake of sheer social or economic distress.  What took place in Spain was, therefore, considered to be a phenomenon unique in Jewish history; and as such, it agitated the minds of many in the involved and the following generations.

In the great perplexity of mind that ensued, the question that loomed largest was: why? What was the reason for that plague of conversion that attacked Spanish Jewry in such an unprec-

[29] See appendix E.
[30] See, for instance, Alami, *Iggeret Musar*, ed. Habermann, Jerusalem, 1946, pp. 39–40; Albo, *Sefer ha-'Iqqarim*, ed. Husik, Philadelphia, 1946, IV (2), pp. 455–456.

edented manner? Since it appeared quite certain that the condition of Spain's Jews in 1412–15 was no worse than that of many other Jewries that had remained faithful under oppressive circumstances, it was obvious that what distinguished them for the worst was not the amount of suffering they endured, but their inability and unwillingness to withstand it. In other words, they were deficient in the crucial qualities by which firmness of faith was measured. The question that presented itself to the generation of 1412, as well as to scholars of later periods, assumed therefore the following form: what was it that undermined the faith of Spain's Jews to the extent that they so readily, and in such large numbers, chose the road of apostasy?

The answers given by the thinkers of the age were all basically the same: it was a spiritual factor that had invaded the Jewish camp and caused the religious downfall. Faith in Judaism had been *shattered* before it was abandoned; and what had shattered that faith, at least in the initial stages, was not Christianity, but the thorough-going, long lasting and corruptive influence of secular philosophy.

Writing in the middle of the 15th century, Joseph ben Shem-Tov, the philosopher, explained the working of this influence, i. e., the relationship between an increased interest in philosophy and a declining appreciation of religion, as follows. Philosophy set before man as his supreme goal the development of his speculative powers and the attainment of knowledge in the highest possible degree. Consequently, the value of religion, *all* religion, was reduced to the very minimum (לא יחשב דת בעיניהם).[31] The devotees of philosophy sought access to those avenues which would best lead them to their main objective, i. e., the *possession of supreme knowledge.* Having found, however, that those avenues were closed to them as Jews, they were prepared to pursue their goal as Christians. And, indeed, since the aim of life, as they saw it, was *not* the perform-

---

[31] *Kevod Elohim*, p. 7(2a). The same attitude is indicated in Joshua Lorki's letter to Paul of Burgos: או שמא השיאך העיון הפילוסופי להפך הקערה על פיה ו ל ח ש ו ב על מחזיקי האמונות כי הבל המה מעשי תעתועים (see L. Landau, *Das apologetische Schreiben des Josua Lorki* etc., Antwerp, 1906, Hebrew section, p. 1).

ance of religious duties, why sacrifice one's life for it? "We see from experience," says Joseph ben Shem-Tov, "that in every state and nation where philosophy was not widespread, many thousands laid down their lives for their faith."[32] But Spanish Jewry was ridden with philosophy, or rather, ill-affected by *some* of its teachings, and this was the root of the catastrophe.

Expressed half a century after the events, the above cited statement of Joseph ben Shem-Tov cannot, of course, be taken as the testimony of an eye-witness. Although his judgment may have been based on a realistic observation of conversion cases in his own time, it might nevertheless have been entirely wrong with regard to the earlier phases of the same phenomenon, i. e., the great conversion movement of 1412–1415. Nor was he the first to assign to philosophy the major blame for the great losses suffered by Spanish Jewry. Indeed, in espousing this view, he himself points out his indebtedness to his father, Shem-Tov ben Shem-Tov.[33] Now the latter *did* live in the period of the great conversion, and consequently we may attach much greater weight to his statement in this connection.

After describing the rise of philosophy among the Jews and the development of heretical ideas as a result, Shem-Tov ben Shem-Tov states that, according to what he noticed, "in all these generations on which philosophy left its mark, those who became absorbed in philosophical investigation denied the essentials of our religion"[34] and finally left Judaism altogether. "And there is no doubt that this (i. e., philosophy and the heresies that grew from it) was the cause of our community's destruction. For the sharp-minded sophists abandoned the hut and broke through its fence [in their desire to pass to the enemy's camp]. And they were followed by the mass of the people to the extent that our bones became dried and our hope [of restoring our strength] was lost."[35]

Thus, according to Shem-Tov ben Shem-Tov, the spearhead

---

[32] *Kevod Elohim*, p. 7(2ab).
[33] *Ibid.*
[34] Shem-Tov b. Shem-Tov, *Sefer ha-Emunot*, Ferrara, 1556, p. 4a.
[35] *Ibid.*

of the conversion movement consisted of the sophists,[36] the students of philosophy, the allegorists and the rationalists, who actually denied the traditional teachings while reading into them the conclusions of Greek thought. He claims, furthermore, that in going over to Christianity they served as an example to the people as a whole. But he fails to explain the influence of these sophists over the mass of the people. It is not clear from his statements whether the people were moved by the sophists' position of leadership or by their ideological campaign. Indefinite and incomplete as it is, his testimony assumes further significance from the fact that it is corroborated by two additional testimonies of unquestionable value. The first testimony is that of Ḥasdai Crescas; the second, that of Solomon Alami.

Writing in 1410, on the eve of the mass conversion, Ḥasdai Crescas notes in his *Or Adonai* the ill effect produced by Maimonidean philosophy, and especially by the ultra-rationalistic interpretations given it by some of its latest commentators. After discussing Maimonides' own failing in basing his premises on Greek philosophy, "albeit his intentions were laudable," he adds that "there arose today slaves who broke away [from their master] and who turned into heresy the words of a living God."[37] They interpret Maimonides' statements as "implying heresy," the very opposite of the master's intent; and those who paid attention to their words, "when they saw how the abomination was purified" by arguments allegedly based upon the Law, could not be saved from confusion, and consequently were hit by panic.[38]

---

[36] Thus we translate here the term המתחכמים which suggests not real wisdom and understanding, but acuteness of mind used for evasion of truth and morality. As a designation of the philosophers in Jewry, the term is also found in the earlier anti-philosophical literature. See, for instance, *Minḥat Qenaot*, Pressburg, 1838, p. 45.

[37] *Or Adonai*, Ferrara, 1556, introd., p. 1(3a), not paginated.

[38] *Ibid.* The expression וכבר דפקתם הבהלה follows of course Maimonides, *The Guide*, introduction, according to Samuel ibn Tibbon's translation (ונשאר במבוכה ובהלה) which means, according to the intent of the author, bewilderment. The Hebrew rendering, however, has the connotation of panic, and it appears that this is the meaning which Crescas wished to convey here.

The charge of heresy now leveled against the philosophical party was, of course, not entirely novel. From the beginning of the 13th century, and for decades thereafter, it formed the battlecry of the orthodox in their determined attempts to root out philosophy from the Jewish camp. Philosophy, however, was not to be defeated, and throughout the 13th and 14th centuries it was, on the contrary, constantly on the advance. To be sure, the charge of heresy against the philosophers was not entirely suspended. It was also heard during the second controversy over the place of philosophy in Judaism, and occasionally even after that.[39] Nevertheless, its effectiveness was reduced, or neutralized by the counter-charges of the philosophers, who stigmatized their opponents in the same manner.[40] Indeed, all the rationalistic interpreters of Maimonides sincerely maintained that it was they who presented the views of pure Judaism in its noblest and highest form. And, in fact, not only Falaquera, Yeda'-yah of Béziers and Gersonides were most faithful and devoted Jews, but also Ibn Caspi, Narboni, and Albalag. As theoreticians they may have been close to Averroes; as Jews, however, they followed tradition and were careful in observing all the command-

[39] Accusations of heresy were levelled at the philosophers during the first controversy over philosophy by Solomon ben Abraham of Montpellier (see *Koveẓ Teshuvot ha-Rambam*, III, p. 4c), Judah Alfacar of Toledo (*ibid.*, pp. 2b, 2d), Meir b. Todros ha-Levi Abulafia (*ibid.*, p. 6d) and their supporters (*ibid.* 17c, 13b); during the second controversy they were less boisterous (see *Minḥat Qenaot*, pp. 32, 105, 106, 119), yet explicitly stated in the Barcelona ban (*ibid.*, p. 153) and in some of the statements issued in its support (see, for instance, *ibid.*, p. 175). Insinuations and assertions about the "heresy" of the philosophers were made also by Moses b. Ḥasdai Taqu in his defense of the notion of the corporeality of God against Saadia and Maimonides (see *Ketav Tamim*, published by R. Kirchheim in *Oẓar Nechmad*, III [1860], pp. 59, 80, 98).

[40] The labeling of the anti-Maimonidean traditionalists as heretics is noticeable especially in the first controversy over Maimonides' philosophical writings. See especially the letters of David Kimḥi and R. Abraham ben Moses, Maimonides' son (*Qoveẓ . . .*, III, p. 1b, on Solomon of Montpellier: כל בעלי האמונה המקולקלת מינין וכופרין; 15b, 19c, 20d: לאחר זקנתו נזרקה בו מינות). The same practice, and the attitude that engendered it, persisted also in later times, deriving support from Maimonides himself (*Guide*, I.6). See, for instance, Pulgar, *'Ezer ha-Dat*, p. 90.

ments.[41] None of their critics could find fault with them as to their actual Jewish behavior. Moreover, it was from the ranks of the philosophers that the most ardent fighters against Christianity emerged. Narboni, Ibn Caspi, and Pulgar may be mentioned among the polemicists of the earlier period who took up the cudgels against the converts,[42] while the greatest anti-Christian disputants and theoreticians who arose in the era under discussion all belonged to the philosophical camp. What, then, was behind Crescas' accusation of "heresy," and the charges voiced in later years to the effect that the "philosophers" were highly responsible for the mass-conversion of 1412–15? May we not conclude that the renewed attack upon philosophy at the beginning of the 15th century was merely a repetition of the previous waves of the early 13th and 14th centuries? May we not assume, indeed, that what is before us is an imaginary conception of what took place, a conception nurtured by the anti-rationalists, who conscientiously, but wrongly, pinned the blame for what had happened upon their historic opponents? In brief, does not the philosophical party serve here as a mere scapegoat for a development with which it had little to do?

However plausible this assumption may appear, it cannot stand examination. In any event, it cannot be substantiated in the case of Crescas. For he was neither a fault-finder of the kind suggested, nor a diehard traditionalist, an adversary of philos-

---

[41] In this respect they did not part from the earlier philosophers whose attitude toward practical Judaism was described by David Kimḥi as devotional, though not non-critical: ואנחנו הם המחזיקים בדת סומכין דברי רז"ל לעזור בלי לב ולב, משכימין ומעריבים בבית אל, עומדים באימה וברעדה כאשר בישראל, מדקדק[ים] [ב]דברי סופרים אשר הדת מורים לא כדברי המורים דורשי ההגדות אלא כמשפט החוקים והעדות, להיותם עם השכל אחוות ולחכמה נרמזות כאשר הורונו קדמונינו הגאונים (*Qoveẓ*, III, p. 3d). Rashbaẓ, in his defense of Gersonides, testifies to this quite clearly: . . . . ובכאן הגיע הדבור ללמד זכות על חכמי אומתנו אשר עלו בידם דעות נכריות כיון שהם שלמים באמונתם נזהרים מעבירות התורה ומתחזקים בקיום המצוות כהוגן (*Ohev Mishpat*, Venice, 1589, p. 15a).

[42] Thus, Ibn Caspi attacks on every suitable occasion Christian biblical interpretations in his commentary on the Prophets (see *Adnei Kesef*, I, London, 1912, e. g., pp. 97, 100–101, 165; and cf. *Tam ha-Kesef*, London, 1913, p. 41). Narboni's attitude toward converts and Christianity is clearly expressed in his *Maamar ha-Beḥira* (see E. Ashkenazi, *Divrei Ḥakhamim*, Metz, 1849, pp. 40–41).

ophy, who would look for an opportunity to revive the old feud. He was, it should be recalled, above all, a philosopher, and one of the highest rank and merit, and was capable of parting with traditional views when these did not agree with his thinking.[43] If he, as a philosopher, came to denounce as "heretical" views of other Jewish philosophers — a thing that, to my knowledge, had never been done before — there must have been an extraordinary situation that provoked him to such action. And that situation was, as he himself indicated, the state of religious panic he had noticed among the people. To be sure, he drew no connecting line between this latter phenomenon and the trend toward conversion. And yet, in view of what happened later, the above-cited statement of Ḥasdai Crescas, may well be seen in a different light and assume historic significance.

This emerges all the more clearly when we carefully consider Crescas' references to his *main* theoretical opponents — i. e., to those whom he singled out for his special criticism and rebuke. Surely these were not Maimonides, whom he still revered as "our master,"[44] and the rest of the renowned Jewish philosophers, whom he classed "among the greatest sages of our people."[45] Of course, in some of the opinions of these thinkers, especially of the commentators of the Averroist brand, Crescas saw the *root* of the evil. In speaking of the evil itself, however, that is, the phenomenon he came to combat, he does not refer to scholars of *former* generations, but to people of his *own time*. He says clearly: "There arose *today* slaves who broke away [from their master], who turn into heresy the words of a living God." He further says that "the arguments of the Greek" (namely, Aristotle), on whom these people rely, "have darkened the eyes of Israel *at this time*."[46] What he refers to, therefore, is a novel

---

[43] On Crescas' deviations from traditional Judaic concepts and his independent view of God, free will and man's final happiness, see J. Guttmann, *Ha-Filosofia shel ha-Yahadut*, Jerusalem, 1953, pp. 207, 217. Of relevant interest are also Baer's remarks on the influence of Christian concepts on Crescas' philosophical theory (see "Sefer Minḥat Qenaot shel Avner mi-Burgos," in *Tarbiẓ*, XI [1940], pp. 205–206).

[44] *Or Adonai*, p. 1(3a): הרב הגדול רבינו.

[45] *Ibid.* (מנדולי חכמינו).

[46] *Ibid.*

phenomenon, a new type of "sophists" who, while relying on the earlier commentators, constitute, nevertheless, a new class. And he points to a state of religious perplexity which obtained as a result of their attitudes. Clearly, the new students of philosophy were of a more radical kind than the earlier followers of Maimonides, and their particular effect, it seems, lay in the fact that they not only drew the most extreme conclusions from some philosophical teachings, but that they also applied these conclusions to the field of practical religion. In any case, Crescas felt, there was something in the air that was new, and sinister, and foreboding; and he feared that this new spirit, unless checked in time, was bound to lead to disaster.

The mass conversion of 1412, which came in the wake of Crescas' criticisms, seemed to indicate that the by then deceased thinker had sensed the danger correctly. There was, it appeared, a direct link between the state of religious confusion, infused by the new sophists, and the mass movement of retreat from Judaism. In any case, Solomon Alami, a rigorous moralist, perhaps the most outstanding in that period, had no doubts about that relationship. According to him, the philosophical movement was the major cause of the religious catastrophe which befell Spanish Jewry. And, as he sees it, its impact upon the great movement of conversion was not an indirect one — i. e., through the state of intellectual confusion it created — but direct, and thorough, and decisive.[47] To be sure, Alami did not single out philosophy as the *only* cause of what had happened. In surveying the spiritual causes of the debacle, he noticed two additional factors which had a share in the tragic development: the casuistic, truth-evading and self-seeking rabbinic scholars, and the power hungry, wily and unprincipled Jewish courtiers.[48] In both these groups, Alami sees definitely destructive forces. Nevertheless, he states categorically that far more harmful, dangerous and destructive was the activity of the sophists, these "stumbling intellectuals," who are "wise in their own eyes" and proudly display their wisdom to others. These are the "heretics," who "make light of the commandments and treat the words of the

47 *Iggeret Musar*, p. 42.
48 *Ibid.*

Sages with contempt."[49] These sinners of the soul are "far worse than the cheats and intriguers of all sort;"[49a] they are even worse than the apostates ("the rebels and the criminals") for "they are not only sinning themselves, but leading others to sin."[50]

Alami points to the process of thought which links philosophy to conversion. The sum total of philosophical thinking, namely, that the commandments were promulgated for the sole purpose of helping man attain intellectual exaltation, and that they are therefore not an "end" but a "means," at once relegates the biblical precepts, the backbone of Judaism, to a mere secondary position. What is more, the conception that man's perfection lies in abstract speculation, and not in action of any other kind, contributed further to the same result and, in consequence, to the degradation of religion. For, if the highest aim of man is to effect the maximum actualization of his potential powers of reasoning, if such actualization cannot be achieved without concentration and peace of mind, and if *this* is what secures man's perfection in this world and whatever measure of after-life he may hope for, why should he exert himself in the performance of the commandments under *all* circumstances and at *all* costs? Surely there is no point at all in laying down his life in their defense, for by destroying himself he will curtail his spiritual advancement and thus vitiate, or at least diminish, his chances for "success." A means is only useful so long as it serves a purpose; when it proves to be a detriment, it should be abandoned. Now, if a person is subjected to harassment and suffering because of his performing the commandments, i. e., of living the life of a Jew, he is obviously deprived of the peace of mind essential for the development of his reasoning capacity, and is thus distracted from his main goal.[51] The inevitable conclusion

---

[49] *Ibid.*, p. 30.

[49a] Thus according to most editions, including that of Jellinek of 1872 (p. 15). Habermann's edition (p. 30), however, has here נבלי (instead of נכלי) בני אדם.

[50] *Ibid.*

[51] *Ibid.*, p. 41–42; and cf. Maimonides, *Guide*, I, 34 (end), wherein undue material distractions are rated among the prime factors preventing man from reaching his spiritual destiny.

of all this is quite obvious. To attain the highest aim as viewed
by philosophy, Judaism may be helpful under *normal* circumstances; in periods of adversity and persecution, however, not
only does it fail to help in this direction, but it proves to be an
obstacle that must be removed.[52]

This is the inherent, undefeatable logic which, as Alami sees
it, leads inevitably from philosophy to conversion. It is true,
Alami admits, that the initiators of this course did not aim at
that result. "Their purpose was to combine philosophy and
religion, to complement religion by philosophy and *vice versa.*"[53]
Their purpose was to give a new "appearance" to the Law, to
augment its honor and increase its prestige.[54] But the outcome
was quite the opposite; they destroyed its grandeur and diminished its stature.[55] For results are determined not only by intentions, but by the logical premises on which the intentions rest.
Consequently, it was out of this school of philosophers that a
group arose which poured contempt on all the religious laws[56] —
the very laws, which, according to their master, are supposed to
serve as instruments for the attainment of their aims. Now,
these people who refute tradition and actually "tear the Law
apart," these vile and villainous persons, whom Alami considers
even more harmful to Jewry than both the Moslems and the
Christians,[57] served as an example to most of the notables of the
community, to its noblemen and leaders.[58] The latter were not
slow to fall in line. The flock, too, was soon affected by the
shepherds,[59] and in due course followed the same path. The

[52] *Ibid.*, p. 42: כי הפורק עולה מעל צוארו והבדל מעדת הגולה להפר ברית האלה יקל.
עולו וינוח מעצב הגלות ורגזו וימצא מנוח לכף רגלו להשיג העיון בשלמותו That
considerations of this kind could lead such a philosopher to the choice of
Christianity as a preferred medium for his advancement is also stated by
Lorki in his letter to Paul of Burgos: ולכן פנית אל היותר נאות מן הדתות להשקט
הגוף וליישוב השכל בלי חרדתה ואימתה ופחד (see L. Landau, *op. cit.*, p. 1).
[53] *Iggeret Musar*, p. 41: חשבו לחבר תורת משה עבד ה' אל היונית ולהשלימם ולהשוותם.
[54] *Ibid.*: הערימו סוד לחדש פני התורה . . . וילבישוה בגדי יונות.
[55] *Ibid.*: ויוליכוה קדורנית וישינוה אחורנית.
[56] *Ibid.*, p. 43.
[57] *Ibid.*
[58] *Ibid.*, p. 44: אחריהם החזיקו בתרמית רוב גדולי הציבור אציליהם נאוניהם ורועיהם.
[59] *Ibid.*, p. 46: ויהיו מאשרי העם הזה מתעים ומאושריו מבולעים.

result? — "Look hard," says Alami, "and you will find that *faith
does no longer exist in the majority of the people.*"[60]

What we have before us, then, is a full affirmation of the
view advanced by Joseph ben Shem-Tov about the theoretical
position of the philosophic party and its resulting attitude toward
Jewish religious practice. But we have here also a confirmation
of what Crescas alludes to regarding the nature of the contemporary radicals. We see that Alami, too, differentiates between
the founders of the rationalistic school in Jewry, whose intent
was positive, albeit misguided, and the latest disciples of the
same school who turned against the very aims of their masters.
Indeed, like Crescas, Alami makes it clear that these disciples
were a new phenomenon in Jewry, a group apart in Jewish
scholasticism, and that it is this group, the product of the age,
which was largely responsible for the religious dissolution that
characterized Spanish Jewry at the time. As he put it, these
"wicked" elements who "with their sharp tongues tear up the
Law, mock at the commandments and refute tradition" appeared
"in *this obscene generation*"[61] — and thus he offers indisputable
support to the interpretation we gave to Crescas' statement,
cited above: "There arose *today* rebels who broke away [from
their master] and turned into heresy the words of a living God."
Yet whereas Crescas concealed rather than revealed the essence
of the heresy which was embodied in the new thinking, Alami
made it abundantly clear.

In light of the foregoing, we can outline the basic differences
between the new radicals and the earlier rationalists. From the
standpoint of religion, these differences appear to have been
centered in the following three areas: the evaluation of Judaism,
the attitude toward the Commandments, the stand toward
Christianity. While all earlier rationalists of whatever school,
including those of the Averroistic trend, held Judaism to embody
the highest truth, honored its precepts and were eager to defend
it, or rather assert its superiority, against rival religions, the new
"sophists" considered Judaism a secondary thought-system, if
not one of dubious value, had little or no use for the Command-

---

[60] *Ibid.*, pp. 45–46: ותראה אם עינים לך לראות כי האמת נעדרת מרוב בני עמנו ואם
תתבונן אליהם אבדה האמונה ונכרתה מפיהם.

[61] *Ibid.*, p. 43: בדור הלזה הנבוה.

ments, and had no real urge to expose Christianity as a faith
inferior to Judaism. In fact, their basic attitude toward all
religion which was one of disrespect or indifference — an attitude
which Joseph ben Shem-Tov so aptly expressed in his terse
statement: לא יֶחְשָׁב דת בעיניהם —, inclined them to treat Christianity "philosophically," that is, tolerantly in a way, as just
another religion, helpful to the masses, but not to the enlightened.[62] What is more, this indifference was often exchanged for
an active, favorable interest in Christianity — not owing to its
spiritual import, but due to the social advantages it could offer.
It was indeed no mere coincidence that we first hear of these
new radicals in the period between 1391 and 1412. Reflecting
"realistically" over the state of Spain's Jews, as such rationalists
usually would, they took a dim view of the future in store for
Jewry, and they began to consider avenues of escape, not excluding that of Christianity.[63] In all likelihood, it was this very
consideration that pushed them to their extreme theoretical
position, as it was a means of justifying the unpopular step they
had already contemplated from time to time. Their theory,
then, which in itself was an outgrowth of Averroistic thinking,

---

[62] Clear confirmation of these contentions is offered also by Solomon Bonafed
who attributed the weakness of the faith in Judaism (אזלת יד האמונה),
which he noticed during the Tortosa disputation, to the prosecution of that
line of logic. Maintaining, says Bonafed, that the Law is helpful only to the
masses who are educated to believe in tradition, the intellectual aristocracy
(חסידי הדור) regards philosophy as the only means leading to man's spiritual
perfection, which is the ultimate "human success" (A. Kaminka, Shirim
u-Meliẓot le . . . Bonafed, in Haẓofeh le-Ḥokhmat Yisrael, XII [1928], p. 40).
Bonafed also points out the conclusions derived from these assumptions:
if salvation of the soul lies in the study of philosophy, Revelation and
the giving of the Law in Sinai were really of no consequence (ואם ישע
נפשות עם ספריו [של אריסטו], לחינם בא בסיני יה וְנָה!). Thus, according to Bonafed,
the groundwork was laid for the destruction of the faith in Judaism.

[63] This, too, may be gathered from Bonafed's presentation of the various
stages of the retreat from Judaism: ורבים מבני הגולה נטיו רגליהם באפס תקוה
ויביאו עצות נכריות לעקור שרשי הדת (ibid.). The employment of "foreign ideas"
(i. e., the philosophical conceptions) for the purpose of disqualifying the
principles of the faith was, then, a direct consequence of the prevailing despair
concerning the future of Jewry. In other words, these "ideas" were speculative
ruses used to justify the desire to convert — a desire which Bonafed noticed
to have possessed even many of those assembled in Tortosa (בראותי בעת
הויכוח כי היה שמה רוח רבים ונכבדים להמיר; ibid., p. 39).

was actually developed and brought to the fore out of inner drives and external pressures, as an escapist device and as an alibi for conversion.[63a]

That these radicals contended with their opponents, that they argued for their views and tried to justify their position, is attested to by the sources.[64] But these discussions were conducted, as it appears, only orally, and not by means of the written word. This fact, which gave rise to the assumption that such a group did not actually exist, or did not exert substantial influence,[65] is not surprising at all. For it is one thing to discuss subversive thoughts orally, perhaps in mere defense of one's behavior, and quite another to commit them to writing. To present a systematic exposition of a theory that would reduce Jewish religion, and religion as such, to a virtual status of superstition; to advocate, on the same ground, the negation of all precepts, of all laws and customs that were considered sacred, would mean to stamp the writer *officially* as a heretic, and thus subject him to the most serious consequences. That a ban would be placed on such an author and his writings was a foregone conclusion; for no Jewish community, however enlightened, would tolerate such a man in its midst. Thus, so long as the critic did not make up his mind to depart from Judaism completely, he would obviously not dare campaign in writing for

---

[63a] These remarks, and some made earlier (p. 100 f.), suggest of course that the opinion of the above-mentioned critics about the general role of philosophy in Jewry can, at best, be considered one-sided. As we see it, the mainstream of Jewish philosophy led, in most cases, to the bolstering of Jewish faith rather than to skepticism and denial and, when an anti-religious current developed, the latter was usually subdued by it or, at least, kept in bounds. The critics referred to arrived at their conclusions because they had in mind only *such a current* and, alarmed by its sudden rise, identified it with the movement as a whole. Yet, even at that time philosophy could stir not only *doubts* in Judaism, but also inspire *zeal* for it, as is evident from the polemical literature of that period which combats Christianity with philosophical concepts. The subject was recently touched upon by J. M. Millás-Vallicrosa, "Aspectos Filosóficos de la Polémica Judaica en Tiempos de Hasday Crescas," in *H. A. Wolfson Jubilee Volume*, II, Jerusalem, 1965, pp. 568–574.

[64] *Sefer ha-Emunot*, p. 4b (כבר התוכחתי עם קצת המפולפלים מהם ומצאתים על דעת זה); *Iggeret Musar*, p. 43; *Or Adonai*, p. 1(3a).

[65] See H. H. Ben-Sasson, in *Zion* (Jerusalem), xxvi (1961), No. 1, p. 60.

his ideas. Yet, if he *did* decide to convert, he would be even less likely to do so. For a written denial of *all* religion would certainly be a document hard to erase, dangerous to convert as well as to Jew. In fact, the notoriety it would assuredly gain might hamper the latter's integration in Christendom, or even bar his "rescue" via conversion altogether. Considering, therefore, both the background and motives of the propagators of the new ideas, their failure to put their thoughts in writing can well be explained.[66]

We have thus established the existence, identity and character of the new religious critics. The question which now remains to be answered, and the one which is of greater significance, is to what extent, if any, these critics were responsible for the mass-conversion of 1412–1415. Even if we assume what stands to reason, namely, that the majority of the "sophists" converted, it is also clear that the majority of the converts were by no means "sophists." Obviously, the radicals were few in number, as philosophers have always been; and philosophical thinking could not be shared by the multitude, then perhaps less than ever. Yet our sources insist that there was a solid tie between this element and the mass conversion; that, in fact, the "sophists" served as the spearhead of the conversion movement as a whole.[67] If so, what was the nature of that tie? And in what way did they serve as a spearhead? Surely it would be unreasonable to assume that the mere example of the sophists' action changed a deeply religious people into a mob of renegades and deserters.

[66] That the trail of heretical movements in the Middle Ages can often be traced only by the records of their opponents, and not by the writings of their protagonists, has been noticed also beyond the Jewish scene. Accordingly, James H. Todd writes: "The twelfth and thirteenth centuries were sufficiently prolific of sects and heresies. But most of them expired in the same intellectual twilight that saw their birth, and have not left to posterity any written memorials of their doctrine" (*The Waldensian Manuscripts Preserved in the Library of Trinity College, Dublin*, London and Cambridge, 1865, p. 93). Even regarding the Albigenses, the most powerful of all "heretical" sects to emerge in Europe prior to the Reformation, it is extremely doubtful whether they produced any doctrinal writings throughout the period of their growth and consolidation (the 12th century) and much beyond that (see *ibid.*, pp. 94–97, 100, 101–104, 113).

[67] *Sefer ha-Emunot*, p. 4a; *Iggeret Musar*, pp. 44, 46; and see above, notes 58, 59.

The fact that many of the leading "sophists" belonged to the high-ranking aristocracy would not add much substance to that assumption; for, after all, there were many leading Jews who remained steadfast in their faith, and the people could look up to *them* as to shining examples of proper conduct. Obviously, if the "sophists" wielded such a vast and decisive influence, as some of our sources ascribe to them, there must have been a spiritual link between them and large segments of the people. Only if we fail to find such a link, or rather become convinced of its absence, shall we be entitled to conclude that the authors of our sources, while correct in defining both the "sophists' " views and the nature of the influence they exerted in *some* quarters, saw nevertheless, in their dismay of what had happened, the facts completely out of focus, and wrongly put upon their opponents the blame for the misfortune that befell Spanish Jewry as a whole. In brief: was there, or was there not, a causal relationship between the group of the new radicals and the *mass* conversion — and if there was, in what was it expressed?

4

In order to answer this question correctly, we should first try to denote the doctrinal area in which the change in religious opinion was initially felt. More clearly, we should establish the fundamental beliefs which were most deeply affected in the course of the transformation and which, when shattered, endangered the stability of the whole complex structure of faith and tradition. Once, it seems to us, this is ascertained, we can properly determine what really took place and which factors played a part in the development under review.

Our sources give us sufficient clues to clarify this matter. We shall first turn our attention again to Shem-Tov ben Shem-Tov. In presenting the reasoning of the philosophers which, as he sees it, infected the entire people, he refers, among other things, to a line of thought which has a particular bearing on our discussion. Here is what he has to tell us:

"For having reached the conclusion that there is no divine judgment and no accounting for good and evil, and that the elite of the people may receive the affluence [of the active intelligence] only after thorough and deep reflection over all things, one is obviously free [to follow his chosen course] and will [indeed] arrive at the goal of his aspiration when he is in a state of freedom, and not in a state of bondage while professing faith in God, the Most High."[68]

What the statement conveys is quite clear. The super-intellectuals, whose highest aim was to attain a state of undisturbed speculation, believed they would be more likely to achieve their aim in the life of freedom which Christianity offered than in the life of servitude and misery offered by Judaism. This is the same argument which, as we have seen, was presented by Alami.[69] But Shem-Tov adds another important element which Alami seems to have overlooked in his discussion of the philosophers, but which he mentions, as we shall see, elsewhere in his work. The rationalists also had reached the conclusion that there was no divine judgment and no accounting for good or evil — and that this applied to every person regardless of his adherence to Judaism or not. Hence there was no need to suffer for Judaism or for the fulfillment of its numerous commandments; in fact, there was no reason why, in pursuing his aims, one should not abandon Judaism altogether. Suffering for the sake of Judaism, as we have seen, could merely stand in the way of the attainment of one's aims, even when these were purely spiritual; now by denying the existence of Reward and Punishment, the last deterrent was removed. The identification with Judaism and the bearing of its heavy burden did not now make any sense at all.

Could such a theory of Providence, and of Reward and Punishment associated with it, become a matter of common belief among the ordinary Spanish Jew in the Middle Ages? To understand what occurred in the evolution of the mass attitude, and how it was affected by the philosophical thinking, we must differentiate between the purely philosophical elements of that thinking and those that touched upon religion. Of course, the idea about the development of the intellect to the

---

[68] *Sefer ha-Emunot*, p. 4ab.
[69] See above, pp. 104–105.

point of its association with the Active Intelligence was certainly not one that could spread among the masses. But a view denying Reward and Punishment, and decrying the folly of those who believe in it, and thereby lose opportunities to improve their life, *could* gain credence in certain circumstances. That this view actually spread mong the people in the period under discussion is, first of all, attested by Crescas.

Crescas admits that he has no ready explanation for the suffering of the just and the prosperity of the wicked.[70] It is obviously in line of righteousness and equity that the gravity of retribution match the gravity of sin. Yet this desired balance between crime and punishment is seen neither *within* Israel, nor in Israel's lot as compared with that of the nations.[71] We must give up any attempt, Crescas conceded, to find the reason for this seeming discrepancy, for the ways of God are beyond our comprehension and He alone knows the purpose of His deeds. Consequently, we should be satisfied in believing that in the final account there will be a full and exact equation, or, more simply: "We [must] have faith in the justice of the Judge."[72]

Yet Crescas knows that he cannot stop at this point, and despite his admission of inability to interpret the moral order of the world, he nevertheless tries to lift the curtain from the apparently impenetrable mystery. While giving the reason for this attempt, he offers us information pertinent to our inquiry — more precisely, on the prevailing view of Providence among the Spanish Jews in the first decade of the 15th century. *"For in this time of ours,"* says Crescas, *"many of the common people* (עמי הארץ) *are endeavoring to show the faultiness of this conception,"* viz., that justice reigns in the world or that His judgment should be accepted as right under all and any circumstances. They arrived at this conclusion, he adds, by comparing the sufferings of the two exiles of the Jewish people and by weighing them against the initial sins that were supposedly their cause.[73] What they found, admits Crescas, is indeed puzzling

---

[70] *Or Adonai*, III, viii, 2, p. 28(4a).

[71] *Ibid.*

[72] *Ibid.*: כי הוא היודע תכלית רצונו ונאמן עלינו הדיין.

[73] *Ibid.*: אמנם לְמָה שבזמננו זה רבים מעמי הארץ מתחזקים להפוש על הדעת הזה לשערם בהקש הגל[וי]ות ולהעריכם אל העוונות הקודמים הגורמים אותם.

and may give room for perplexity. The crimes that brought about the first exile — idolatry, incest and murder on a large scale[73a] — were incomparably heavier than those that preceded the second, and yet the first exile was much shorter than the present one (70 years as against more than 1,300!) and by far less burdensome.[74] As a solution to the problem, Crescas advances the theory that, in reality, there was no second exile at all; that what is considered as a second exile is really a continuation of the first, and therefore the suffering of this exile, too, must be attributed to the crimes committed during the period of the First Temple.[75] Though skillfully avoiding both horns of the dilemma, the solution, Crescas felt, could hardly silence the grave doubts then widely raised concerning the belief in Providence. In attempting to stop the dangerous gap in faith, he advanced, therefore, alternative answers, too;[76] but by doing so he highlighted his fundamental admission of inability to offer a foolproof explanation, and thus left the whole problem in a state of obscurity, only partly relieved by inadequate light.

While Crescas was thus trying to meet the objections raised by the common people on this issue, his main effort was, nevertheless, directed to refute the views on Providence held by the Averroists, i. e., to demonstrate the *possibility* of Providence as traditionally upheld by Jews. This in itself suggests that he attached much importance to the influence wielded by the radicals in this instance, and that he saw in their circles the main source of the spreading heresy. In any case, the six major principles of faith — God's omniscience, providence, omnipotence, prophecy, free-will, and the final end — in which he sees the core of Jewish religion, are all grouped around this issue. The matter becomes increasingly apparent when we consider the whole structure of Crescas' theory, which is based on the relationship between God, the Commander, and man, the commanded.[77] The first three of his six articles of faith relate to the working of Providence in its divine aspects, while the re-

[73a] See Yoma 9b.
[74] *Or Adonai*, III, viii, 2, p. 28 (4a).
[75] *Ibid.*, p. 28(4b).
[76] *Ibid.*, p. 29(1a).
[77] See *Or Adonai*, II (introduction), p. 9(4a).

maining three refer to its human phase. How is God's providence, i. e., His observation of all beings — possible? This can be explained by His omniscience. How can He execute His will in all beings in the course of their evolution and throughout all their vicissitudes? This is explained by His omnipotence.[78] How does God make known His will to man, warn him against wrongdoings and guide him in the right path? This is explained by the principle of prophecy which is the main medium for this purpose. How is man capable of receiving these instructions, of choosing right from wrong? This is explained by the principle of free will. Finally, what is the ultimate purpose of Providence and its media — prophecy and the mechanism of free will? The purpose is to lift man's spirit to a state wherein he can eternally cleave to God. Thus we see that it is around the belief in Providence that Crescas built his entire philosophical system.[79]

Whatever the reasons that Crescas advanced to fortify his theoretical position, and whatever the place this position occupies in the history of speculative thought, the historic root of the theory he developed must be sought in the skepticism con-

---

[78] The inseparability of these three principles from the standpoint of the belief in Providence, was pointed out, among others, by Profiat Duran: וזהו מה שהגיע קצת רשעיהם וסכליהם שיחסו זה [כלומר, הסתלקות ההשגחה] אם להעדר הידיעה ממנו יתברך אם לְאָותו וקוצר ידו מהושיע (see his letter of lamentation over the death of Don Abraham Isaac ha-Levi of Gerona, written in 1393, in Ma'ase Efod, p. 193).

[79] A comparison between Crescas' Or Adonai and Simon Duran's Ohev Mishpat (1405) brings this out even more patently. In the latter work, Duran shows how Providence and its manifestation in the world are inseparably connected with God's Omniscience (ed. Venice, 1589, 10a), His Omnipotence (19b), Prophecy (7a, 28 ff.) and Free Will (10a). In addition to Providence itself, it is precisely these four conceptions that Crescas recognized as beliefs meriting the status of dogmas, adding to them only the Final End as an element giving, in his opinion, more meaning and a higher purpose to the divine order. The fact that he excluded the Existence of God (coupled with His unity and noncorporeality) from the list of dogmas and elevated it to a status of a super-dogma, as the "foundation of all religious principles," was in full agreement with this approach, no less than was the fact that he relegated all other articles of faith, enumerated by Maimonides as well as by Duran (ibid., p. 7a), to a position of merely "true faiths." All this makes it indubitably clear that Crescas' theory of dogmas is a Providence-centered system.

cerning the existence of Providence which was then assuming, as he felt, alarming proportions. It was in 1410, on the eve of the great conversion, that Crescas completed his philosophical work. Five years later, in 1415, after the great waves of conversion had passed, we hear Alami offer us the same testimony in even clearer and more emphatic terms: "*For the deniers of Providence are now numerous among the mass of the uneducated* (עם הארץ) *and few are those who believe in the reward and punishment of the soul.*"[80] So the validity of Providence and of Reward and Punishment was denied not only by a small group of Averroists, radicals, and super-intellectuals, but also by the rank and file of the people, by the '*am-ha-arez*, the same element of which Crescas spoke, i. e., those who are usually the backbone of religion and of unaffected, unsophisticated faith. Thus, denial of Providence and Reward and Punishment now took the form of a *popular* attitude, and only *few* were those, as Alami tells us, who stuck to the traditional position — namely, to faith in Judaism as a religion and to the worthwhileness of suffering on its behalf. This is clear and direct evidence as to the importance that the Providence issue attained at that stage; but equally important is the indirect evidence which we draw from the philosophical literature of the time.

Never before in the history of Jewish thought did the Jewish religious thinkers exert such efforts in establishing the principle of Providence. The Maimonidean conception of Providence had served, of course, as a target for the attack of the traditionalists since the beginning of the 13th century. Yet not until the period under consideration did it form a central issue. In the first controversy over the Maimonidean philosophy, the discussion revolved mainly around Maimonides' conception of God. In the second controversy it revolved around the allegorical interpretation of the Bible.[81] Now Providence formed the central

---

[80] *Iggeret Musar*, p. 46: הן רבים עתה עם־הארץ הכופרים בהשגחה . . . ומתי מספר הם המאמינים בשכר הנשמות ועונשם.

[81] Although other issues were also raised, especially by Abba Mari of Lunel who repeatedly attempted to present Providence and Creation as the main points of division between the philosophers and the traditionalists (see *Minḥat Qenaot*, Pressburg, 1838, pp. 11–19, his introduction to the

theme. We have already seen how this is reflected in the philosophical theory of Crescas, and how the six articles of Judaism
enumerated by him all hinged on Providence as on a pivot.
Duran, who reduced the number of the major articles of faith
to three, Providence being, of course, one of them,[81a] deemed it
necessary to write a special book on this subject in an attempt
to demonstrate the validity of the principle.[82] Likewise Albo,
who followed in Duran's footsteps, devoted the final and greatest
part of his work to proving the working of Providence in the
world. This, too, is the major aim of Shem-Tov ben Shem-Tov,
the qabbalist thinker, who, believing the answers of these
philosophers to be far from satisfactory, since they could not
truly explain to the skeptic how Reward and Punishment were
effected, set out, in his *Sefer ha-Emunot*, to establish this principle
through another medium — the theory of metempsychosis.[83]
Thus we see that all major philosophical works written in that
crucial period concentrate more than ever before on establishing
the principle of Providence, and its concommitant idea of Reward and Punishment. The fact that the philosophers found
so great a need to argue the issue in philosophical terms, is
indicative of where they saw the root of the evil. They sought
to re-establish the disavowed truth, first of all in philosophical

20th letter, p. 60, and the 7th chapter of his *Sefer ha-Yareah, ibid.*, p. 127),
they hardly elicited any reaction. The course of the controversy was determined
by Rashba who centered his attack upon the rationalists' allegorical interpretation of the Bible (see *ibid.*, pp. 31, 48, 50, 51, 52, 54, 59, 61, 69, 70,
72, 74, 77, 89, 114, 120).

[81a] More precisely, Reward and Punishment, which of course postulates the
existence of Providence. And see, for instance, Albo, *'Iqqarim*, III, chap. XII.4,
p. 110, and IV (I), introd., pp. 1–2, on the relationship between the two concepts.

[82] See *Ohev Mishpat*, Venice, 1589, in which he declares that "the
inquiry into the problem of Providence is more incumbent upon us than
all other inquiries related to the Law" (p. 15b). Indicative of the real motive
behind this declaration is his fight against the Averroistic view of Providence
(*ibid.*, p. 24b ff.).

[83] Providence is presented as a major issue already in the introduction
to *Sefer ha-Emunot* (pp. 1b, 4a), but especially in sections 1, 3 and 4
of chapter 1.

circles, because it was here that they found the origin of the heretical conception. What is more, it was in these intellectual circles that they saw a veritable drive in its behalf, or rather a source of *general* contamination. Surely, the fact that the "sophists" did not present their views in carefully written treatises may have somewhat diminished the force of their argument. But that their influence was there, and deeply felt, is best demonstrated by the elaborate works composed to counteract it.

That it could spread so swiftly and penetrate so deeply into the consciousness of the devout and ordinarily faithful, was, however, the result of social, rather than intellectual conditions. By this we mean especially two factors that came to the fore after 1391: (a) the miserable status to which the Jews were reduced in Castile and Àragon, and (b) the marked social and economic advancement which characterized the position of the Marranos. The concrete evidence Jews had daily before them indicated that *faithfulness to Judaism did not pay*. For while they who remained true to their heritage became more and more downtrodden and subjugated, often deprived of even the barest necessities, the Marranos, who became more and more "sinful," showing clear signs of complete assimilation, increasingly enjoyed affluence and prestige. *It is this striking contrast, more than anything else, which was responsible for undermining in the minds of many their faith in Providence, and it was this situation which attuned many to the arguments of the intellectual cynics.*

Albo, in one of his discussions of the matter, testifies to this quite clearly. Commenting on Psalm 73, which deals with a phenomenon enigmatic to all believers: the adversity of the righteous and the happiness of the wicked, he asserts that it is the prosperity, wealth and honor of the wicked which tempt one to worship a foreign religion.[84] Even when one knows the reason for the good enjoyed by the wicked, the suffering which is the lot of the righteous is sufficient to torment one's heart.[85] Albo interprets the Psalm to mean that whatever apparent evil be-

[84] *Sefer ha-'Iqqarim*, IV(i), chap 13.26, p. 125.
[85] *Ibid.*, chap. 14.6, p. 137.

falls the latter, it is, in truth, for their own good; and yet, he admits, this lesson can hardly capture the mind. "The continual peace and tranquility of the wicked, which the righteous constantly see before their eyes, fills their hearts with sorrow and envy, and they return to their homes depressed and crushed. They imbibe the spirit of disbelief and are led to deny Providence. They say: how does God know? Is there knowledge in the Most High?"[86] Finally, since they see, on the one hand, that they who shun sin, who keep their hands clean, are constantly afflicted and endure suffering without end, and, on the other, that the wicked are always at ease and constantly rise in wealth and honor, they are led to the conclusion that it is vain to serve God, and it is vain to cleanse one's heart. And the Psalmist concludes: "If it were my purpose to elaborate upon these doubts, *I would have left the fold of the righteous and betrayed the generation of thy children.*"[87]

It is, then, the ruin of faith in Providence which leads one to the great betrayal, according to what Albo tells us, and it is the agonizing sight of the contrast between the fate of the "just" and that of the "wicked" which leads to the destruction of that faith. He thus corroborates our assumption on both scores: the religious faith in Judaism was undermined primarily through the weakening of the belief in Providence, and the belief in Providence was deeply shaken by the striking, overwhelming evidence to the contrary, offered by the hapless condition of the faithful as against the prosperity of those who left the fold. For there is no question in my mind that, in referring to the "wicked," Albo meant in this instance the conversionist camp, or at least those of them who willingly abandoned Judaism and were advanced on the road of assimilation. This emerges from the whole contents of the discussion.[88] But even if he refers here to the

---

[86] *Ibid.,* chap. 14.4, pp. 134–135.

[87] *Ibid.,* chap. 14.5, p. 135; I must deviate here from Husik's translation which, in this instance, is erroneous and misses the whole point of Albo's statement.

[88] The description of the physical and moral characteristics of the "wicked" as given by Albo (*ibid.,* IV [1], chap. 14.2–3, pp. 133–134) also fits the converts, the rich city dwellers, more than any other conceivable group. From the standpoint of the external features (fatness and fairness of complexion), it might

"wicked" in the broader sense, it was no doubt the contrast between the condition of the converts and that of the Jews, and the impact it had upon Jewish thinking, that stood before his eyes and led him to his conclusions. To the frustration and dismay caused by the facts, Albo adds the psychological effect wielded by the mockery of the faithful by the "wicked." "For this is the way of the wicked — to scorn the man who trusts in God."[89] This scorn had an especially demoralizing impact upon the Jews of Spain under the circumstances in which they found themselves at the time, and Albo, in a search for the causes of the "betrayal," could not fail to point this out. As for the condition of Spain's Jews, Albo considers it wretched beyond description. "We have been reduced," he says, "to the last degree of misery and shame."[90] "We are like a sick man near death whom everybody has given up."[91] In fact, "we are accounted like dead."[92] Albo wrote these wrods after the great conversion of 1412–1415. But the situation, no doubt, was so seen by most Jews already prior to 1412. It looked dark, and grim, and hopeless in the extreme, with no quarters to turn for help. When, in this situation, the campaigning convert derided the Jewish belief in divine "justice," or rather the bright future the observant Jews expected as reward for their faithfulness, his mockery appeared to have a decisive effect. We have a sample of this scornful approach in a convert's agitation piece from that time — a Hebrew letter of Franciscus de Sant Jordi. In it the convert *ridicules* the hope of the Jews for salvation or a better future;[93] and it is

possibly apply also to the higher Spanish clergy, but these — in contrast to the lower clergy and mendicant friars — did not distinguish themselves as enemies of the Jews. — On the arrogance (גאוה) of the conversos also speaks Abravanel (*Mashmi'a Yeshu'ah*, Lemberg, 1871, p. 160).

[89] *Sefer ha-'Iqqarim*, IV (2), chap. 46.7, p. 44.

[90] *Ibid.*, chap. 50.3, p. 475.

[91] *Ibid.*, chap. 45.9, p. 448.

[92] *Ibid.*, chap. 50.4, p. 476.

[93] See *Qovez Vikuḥim*, p. 25a (not paginated). The scoffing of the convert at the Jewish messianic faith is expressed in the following questions: התחיינה העצמות היבשות? ברול עשות — כארז בלבנון ישגא? הירוצון בסלע פסח וחולה יחדיו וכצבאים על ההרים? — On the identification of Astruc Rimoch, the author of the letter under discussion, with Franciscus de Sant Jordi, see Baer, *Die Juden im christlichen Spanien*, I, pp. 808–809.

illuminating that, in addition, he harps upon the *contrast between the misery of the Jews and the happy lot of the converts.*[94] Thus he offers full corroboration of Albo's dual contention.

What we gather from the foregoing is, therefore, as follows: first, there *was* a spiritual link between the theories of the "sophists" and the movement of conversion; this was their *denial of Reward and Punishment, Resurrection and Providence,* which was indeed the *basis* of their attitude toward the commandments, and toward religion as such. To be sure, the intricate philosophical content of their views was grasped only by a minority. But their conclusion, sifted through many channels, reached even the least educated. It penetrated their minds and sank there deeply, because it seemed to lend credence to what was suggested by the grim lessons of life. It furthermore offered a logical explanation of the facts they witnessed daily, as well as of those of history as they knew them, and what followed in their inner religious thinking was a matter of course. The inevitable result was summarized by Alami in what was perhaps his most telling statement: *Look around and see, there is no longer faith among the majority of the people!"*[95]

What we have, then, before us is a breakdown of faith, a religious crisis of the first order; and that this crisis was instrumental in leading to conversion cannot be doubted. In saying this, we do not lose sight of the persecutions then launched against the Jews of Spain as a contributory factor in that development. Of course, there was an element of duress also in the conversions of the second decade of the 15th century. But the difference between the converts of 1391 and those of 1412–1415 was, nevertheless, decisive. While the former were a product of an external cause (fear of being murdered by a riotous mob), the latter were a product of both external and internal

---

[94] Thus, he points out that while the converts attained social success and a life of wealth and luxury, the strength of the Jews was being sapped in a life of squalor and hard labor: הגבורים שעלו מן הרחצה . . . (i. e., the baptized converts) כלם אנשים [אשר] בחצריהם ובטירותם שנהבים וקופים ותוכיים . . . ונפשך. The emaciated Jew also admits, according to this agitator: יבשה בעבודה קשה. ונהפך לשדי כעצמות ונידים (*ibid.*).

[95] See above, p. 106.

causes (oppression and shattered religious convictions). Inevitably, the conclusion suggests itself that the influx of the new converts into the Marrano camp had a disastrous moral effect upon the Jewish element within it. The very fact that most of Spain's Jews were now in the Christian orbit, and that the voluntary converts now constituted the majority of the Marranos, made clandestine Jewish life, and further resistance to assimilation, appear more futile than ever before. On the other hand, and quite apart from the general demoralization which the new mass conversion must have caused among the crypto-Jews, the new converts could not possibly form a source of recruits to the Jewish underground. For crypto-Judaism, it should be recalled, was a by-product of *forced*, not *voluntary* conversion; and even if we assume that many of the *new* converts — and for that matter, even most or all of them — adopted Christianity merely formally and insincerely, they would still be unlikely to offer sustenance to the underground and lead the life of Jews secretly themselves. For to do so would mean not only to endanger their newly won safety and freedom, but also to risk repetition of the persecution from which they fled in such panic. *And of this they were incapable.* The essential prerequisites for such a course — *an unshaken faith and resolution to guard it* — were obviously missing in their case. Indeed, *why would they do for Judaism as Christians what they had failed to do for it as Jews?*

5

Our inquiries into the philosophic and polemic Hebrew literature have thus far yielded us two major conclusions: first, that the forced converts of 1391 were subjected to an increasing and rapid Christianization — not only in behavior, but also in *belief* (which explains the efforts of the Jewish polemists to invalidate Christian dogma), and second, that the converts of 1412–1415 went over to Christianity with a broken faith in Judaism, or with no faith in Judaism at all. From these conclusions, we have gathered by deduction the course followed by Marranism *after* the "second decade," and to *this* extent we relied here on what may be regarded as *indirect* evidence. Does the philosophic and polemic literature also offer us *direct* evidence on the developments in the later period? Since we now reenter the realm of elusive language, deliberately vague, curtailed, or symbolic, our answer must necessarily be guarded and reserved. We find no additional statements in this literature that refer to the Marranos (or to "those who left the fold") in a clear and open manner. We do find in it, however, a number of assertions, views and data concerning "heretics," converts and conversionist agitation which, in our opinion, can be safely construed as referring to the Marrano camp, or to parts thereof. However veiled, ambiguous and incomplete, these statements reflect views and conditions that offer some answer to the question posed above.

Such allusions to the Marranos are noticeable, first of all, in Albo's discussion of the question of compulsion in the fourth part of his *Sefer ha-'Iqqarim* (1428). According to Albo, acts done under fear of suffering cannot all be classed as acts of compulsion. It all depends on the nature of the acts. "If the act is such that it does not justify the suffering of great pain on its account, it may be classed, when committed under the fear of such pain, as an act of compulsion." If, however, avoidance of such an act merits the endurance of any pain in the world, its performance, despite this, must be considered an act of choice. "Hence a person deserves reproach if he does not suffer great or extraordinary pain rather than lift his hand to strike his father or *rebel against his King or God.*"[96]

It is significant that Albo also avoids discussing the *alternative of certain death*. The reason is, as we see it, that the converts of the second decade were not confronted, on the whole, with such an alternative. What took place was a series of hardships — social, economic, and also physical —, stemming from the legal administrative measures then introduced against Spain's Jews,[97] and it stands to reason that many of the new converts

---

[96] *Sefer ha-'Iqqarim*, IV (1), chap. 27.3–4, pp. 259, 260.

[97] On the anti-Jewish policy pursued by the government of Castile since 1408 and by that of Aragon since 1412, see Baer, *Toledot ha-Yehudim bi-Sefarad ha-Noẓrit*, pp. 323–325. On the anti-Jewish legislation of the

*originally* pointed to these hardships as the sole cause of their conversion. Although such reasons could in no way afford a legitimate excuse for conversion, it appears that they were generally accepted as valid, so that these converts, too, were commonly regarded as *anusim* (forced ones). In rejecting this excuse, and in trying to prove that the conversion was voluntary rather than forced, Albo is obviously seeking to determine not a legal, but a psychological issue, and in doing so he is also considering the post-conversion period, which is our main interest at the moment. For Albo introduces an additional criterion to determine whether an act is compulsory or not. This criterion consists of the *attitude toward the act after the acute crisis has passed*. If the act is not regretted after the crisis, it must be classed as voluntary, "though at the beginning it involved some compulsion"; if it *is* regretted, it should be regarded as compulsory. To clarify what he means by this, Albo illustrates his rule by an example from common experience — the casting of a cargo overboard during a stormy sea voyage. The act was done under compulsory conditions, and yet from choice and after clear deliberation, which is proven by the fact that it was never regretted and, in fact, always re-justified.[98] The same criterion applies to sin. "If one duly regrets a transgression he has committed and *does not desire its continuance*, he shows thereby that the act was not absolutely voluntary and that, if he had been left to his simple will *in its present determination*, he would not have done it."[99] "Due regret," then, must be measured, according to Albo, not only by a man's attitude toward the completed act, but also toward its repetition in the future, by his determination never to do it again "should he find himself in the same position."[100] The proof of this determination is offered by one's behavior, when one is actually confronted with the possibility of committing the same transgression again, and yet "avoids it

period, and the related literature, see id., *Die Juden im christlichen Spanien*, II, §375 (pp. 263–272); I, § 483 (pp. 788–789), § 485 (pp. 790–791).

[98] *Sefer ha-'Iqqarim*, IV (1), chap. 27.5, pp. 260–261.

[99] *Ibid.*, chap. 27.8, p. 263.

[100] *Ibid.*, chap. 27.6, p. 262.

knowingly, willingly and of his own free choice because he assumes that this thing is evil in the eyes of God."[101] "This is
real repentance which makes the act appear as if it was done by
error and without understanding."[102] Consequently, if there is
no such regret, demonstrated by actual conduct, the transgression
must be viewed as *deliberate and voluntary* and, like any such
transgression, it involves a measure of heresy — i. e., denial of
the existence of God or the operation of Providence in the
world.[103] A deliberate sinner like this, who persists in his evil
doings, belongs, therefore, to the category of the "heretics,"
who must be regarded as *excluded from the fold of Israel and the
seed of His faithful,* and hence are destined to eternal damnation,
which they duly and fully deserve.[104]

All this no doubt reflects Albo's attitude toward the Marranos,
an attitude which, in turn, may well represent his reaction to
Marrano religious leanings as revealed in daily life. What impressed him most negatively, we may conclude, was not the
failure of the Marranos to effect or even seek actual return to
Judaism ("complete penance"), but their consistent disregard
and violation of the commandments in a manner typical of
genuine renegades. Aware as he was of the circumstances of the
conversion of 1412–15, and convinced that, in the first place,
most of these conversions were voluntary, the conduct of the
Marranos could not mean to Albo — as it did to Ribash, who
witnessed truly forced conversions — a *change* from the original
position of *anusim* to that of *apostates.*[105] To him it was merely
a *continuance* of the same outrage, a repetition of the crime
originally perpetrated, and conclusive proof that the conversion
was not forced but voluntary, a product of a final, calculated
decision to throw off the heavy burden of Judaism (the casting
of the cargo into the sea). Of course, the realistic background of
Albo's conclusions is nowhere stated by him openly. However,
it is suggested to us by his views, and it is the only possible
setting which can reasonably explain them, not as abstract
speculations (which they could hardly be), but as theories evolved

---

[101] *Ibid.*, chap. 27.8, p. 264.                    [102] *Ibid.*
[103] *Ibid.*, chap. 28.4, pp. 267–268.
[104] *Ibid.*, IV (2), chap. 38.6, p. 378.            [105] See above, pp. 29-30.

to meet a concrete problem rooted in an agonizing situation. As we see it, by his theory of compulsion, Albo was trying to do away with the notion that must have still been prevalent about the Marranos, at least about those of the second mass conversion, according to which they were *forced* converts. That he regarded this notion dangerous no less than false, as leading to religious confusion and distortion, is quite understandable in view of his conviction that the salvation of Judaism in his time lay in a clear-cut definition and differentiation. In fact, Albo may represent an early trend in Spanish Jewry to consider the unrepenting Marranos as completely cut off from the people of Israel, not only religiously but also ethnically,[106] and hence meriting no special consideration, but solely the severity due to "haters of God."[106a]

The main mark of difference between the *haters* of God, i. e., the converts, and His *lovers*, i. e., the Jews, lies, according to Albo, in the attitude toward the commandments.[106b] But these "haters" were not comprised of Epicureans[107] only. For many

[106] This seems to be implied in the terms he employs to indicate this exclusion: שהם יוצאים מכלל ישראל ומכלל זר ע אוהבי השם (*Sefer ha-'Iqqarim*, IV [2], chap. 38.6, p. 378).

[106a] *Ibid.*

[106b] His supposedly commonplace repeated emphasis upon the keeping of the commandments by the "lovers of God" and the refrainment from such action by His enemies (והבלתי שומרים מצוותיו ... שונאי ה' והבלתי שומרי מצוותיו ... אוהבי השם ושומרי מצוותיו, *ibid.*), bears this out clearly.

[107] Epicurean, according to Albo, is one who denies the existence of God and believes in the accidental formation of the world (see *ibid.*, I, chap. 10.3–4, pp. 98–99; II, chap. 13.5, p. 74; III, chap. 26.3, p. 247). The concept was no doubt borrowed from Simon Duran (*Magen Avot*, Leipzig, 1855, 2b; *Ohev-Mishpat*, X, Venice, 1589, 15b–16a), who, in turn, deduced it, it appears, from Maimonides' definition of the אפיקורוס in *The Guide* (III.2, where, however, the Epicurean's main trait is the denial of Providence and the divine order of the world). Obviously, such views cannot be ascribed to a Christian or to a true convert to Christianity. Also Maimonides' other definition of the Epicurean (*Hil. Teshuvah*, III, 8) can in no way apply to a Christian as it entails distinctly anti-Christian doctrines (such as denial of prophecy and divine instruction to man). In medieval Hebrew literature, however, *Epicurean* often served as synonym for *apostate*, and particularly for one who embraced and preached the dogmas of Christianity (see, for instance, Lipmann-Mühlhausen's *Sefer Niẓẓaḥon*, Amsterdam, 1822, p. 472; Joseph ben Nathan

of them, we gather from Albo, ignore the commandments not due to lack of faith, but due to the excessive value they attach to faith in itself. More clearly, they maintain that the command-ments were "temporary," i. e., given for a limited time, that that time has already passed, and that they were now replaced by pure faith which is the essence and purpose of the divine instruction. This is of course Christian doctrine and there can be no doubt that Albo referred here to the spread of Christianity among the Jews. In fact, the Christian conversionist campaign, by stressing the idea of the abolition of the Law — so intimately connected with the idea of Jesus' Messiahship, which was the springboard of the conversionist efforts among the Jews[107a] — attracted, according to Albo, so many Jews to Christianity ("entrapped" and "harassed" them, in his language) that it actually threatened Judaism with extinction.[107b] It is clear, then,

---

Official, *loc. cit.*, p. 17; Solomon ben Simon Duran, *Milḥemet Miẓvah*, Leipzig, 1856, p. 3). The usage seems to have rested on the more common concept of the Epicurean which was rooted in Talmudic opinion. Thus, according to Maimonides' summation (i. e., his *third* definition of אפיקורוס), *Epicurean* is one who "scorns at the Law and its students" (*Comm.* on Sanh. X.1; fol-lowing Sanh. 99ab), and, consequently, who denies the Law altogether (*Hil. Sheḥitah*, IV, 14), or impugns its flawlessness and immutability (*Hil. Melakhim*, XI, 3). Especially the last of these formulations pointed to the identification of the *Epicurean* with the apostate to Christianity (cf. *Qodesh Qodashim*, MS. cited, p. 7). Also the description of Yeshu (Jesus) as one who "mocks at the words of the Sages" (Gittin 57a; and see above, note 2) may have been a factor in that identification.

[107a] See above, note 14a.

[107b] See '*Iqqarim*, III, chap. 21.2, p. 193: ולומר . . . והבא לפרש ולשנות את התורה שאיסור החזיר היה זמניי או נאמר על יצר הרע וכיוצא בזה, ושעיקר כל התורה תלוי באמונת הלב ולא במעשי המצוות . . . אל זה רמז המשורר באמרו כרו לי זדים שיחות אשר לא כתורתך [תהלים, קי"ט, פ"ה], ובאר שהשיחות הם שאומרים כי כל מצוותיך אמונה בלבד ושכבר עבר זמנם ושאין צורך למעשה המצוות כלל, ובזה השקר רדפוני [שם, שם, פ"ו], ועל כן עזרני [ה'] כי אני צריך לעזרתך, שאם לא כן כמעט כילוני בארץ [שם, שם, פ"ז] On זדים as an appelation for converts, who may be referred here, too, as they were the main agitators for Christianity among the Jews, see above, note 20. — On the argument concerning the eating of pork, see Lorki's allegations in his treatise against the Jews (Latin version, Zürich, 1552; lib. I, cap. 9) and in the minutes of the Tortosa Disputation (Antonio Pacios López, *La Disputa de Tortosa*, II, Madrid-Barcelona, 1957, pp. 262, 372); and cf. Joseph ben Lavi's reply to Lorki in *Qodesh Qodashim*, MS. cited, p. 30).

that in his statements analyzed above (about those who threw away the cargo in the storm), Albo aimed mainly at those Marranos (both the so-called "forced" and voluntary converts) who forsook their people in times of trouble not because of belief in Christianity (which they lacked), but because of the weakness of their devotion to Judaism (which they shared due to latent or manifest heresy). Albo, however, had very much in mind the *true* converts to Christianity, too, and indeed his polemic and educational effort was directed toward the prevention of *real* apostasy, no less than it was bent upon defeating the trend which led to desertion through skepticism or "denial."

A similar manifestation of this trend, and added proof that Albo's remarks referred to the Marranos, is offered by another polemical discourse, written, in all likelihood, at approximately the same time. I refer to the work known as *Aḥituv ve-Ẓalmon*, whose author, Matityahu, has generally been identified as Matityahu ha-Yiẓhari, who, like Albo, was one of the spokesmen of the Jews of Aragon in the Tortosa disputation (1413–1414). In answering criticisms raised by converts concerning the Jewish prayer against the *minim* (i. e., apostates), the author makes the following statement: "As for apostates, what is meant by this designation are those who apostatized from the Jewish faith both under compulsion and out of error of mind."[108] It is clear, then, that this author places *all* the Marranos, of whatever past tendency and background, in the category of apostates — a striking attitude which is further emphasized in the following revealing passage: "They [the apostates] cannot hope to exonerate themselves [probably on the Day of Judgment] by claiming, 'We were *forced* to convert' or 'We acted out of wrong judgment', and therefore 'We committed no sin.' There is no hope of forgiveness for them until they repent and abandon the way of the heretics, those who halt between two opinions, who throw off the yoke of the commandments and publicly declare that there is no divine Providence in the world, who do not fear God and, in fact, deny

---

[108] *Aḥituv ve-Ẓalmon*, MS. cited, p. 16: ולמשומדים הוא ר"ל אותם שנשתמדו מן האמ[ו]נה הן על כרחם הן מחמת טעות רוחם.

Him, or express false notions about Him. They *deserve* the curse that they be destroyed at once."[108a]

The moral and intellectual characteristics of the converts, as given herein, coincide entirely with the features of the converts who went over to Christianity in 1412–1415. They disregard the commandments, they deny the rule of Providence, or even the very existence of God. These were also, as we have seen, the traits of the voluntary converts — the "haters of God" as described by Albo in the passages quoted above. What is more, our author sees no room for differentiation between voluntary converts (those who converted out of erroneous beliefs) and forced converts (*anusim*); for the latter discarded the yoke of the commandments in no lesser measure than the former and, on top of this, embraced their "heretical" beliefs. The camp of the Marranos is thus conceived as uniform both in spirit and conduct. Hence none of them can seek excuses in "compulsion" and all of them deserve to be destroyed — a wish which no Jewish author would harbor for real *anusim*.

In the apology he offers for this wish, the author reveals the deep gulf of enmity separating the Jews from the Marranos. The prayer of the Jews that "the converts and all the enemies of Thy people, the house of Israel, should be quickly cut off," is, in his opinion, fully justified. "One should not be censured when he prays to God, who saw his sufferings at the hands of his enemies, that he destroy these foes" and rid him of his tormentors. "This is quite apart from the fact that the same people are also enemies of God;" but the two enmities are of course corelated. Just as scripture (Ps. 83.3–4) says: "For *Thine* enemies, O God, are in an uproar . . . they secretly plot against Thy *people*."[109]

If *Aḥituv ve-Ẓalmon* was indeed written by Matityahu ha-Yiẓhari, as suggested, the author had occasion to experience personally the connivance and "plotting" of the converts. What

---

[108a] *Ibid.* אין להם תקוה לומר אנוסים היינו או שוגגים אנו ועבירה בדבר אין לנו עד שיחזרו בתשובה וישובו (ל) [מ][דרך] מינים אותם שפושעים על שתי(ם) הסעפ[י]ם והפורקי[ם] עולם ואומרים שאין השגחות אלהות בעולם ואחרי יראת השם לא ילכו (?) כחשו בהשם ואומרים לא הוא. ראויים הם לקלל שיאבדו כרגע.

[109] *Aḥituv ve-Ẓalmon*, MS. cited, p. 16b.

is more, his description of the apostates' beliefs and opinions
may well represent his own impressions of the views then current
among the converts of 1412–1415. To be sure, the identification
of apostates with "heretics," as well as with "Epicureans" and
"skeptics," was not a novel phenomenon among Jews; it dates,
as we have indicated, from Talmudic times,[109a] and was also
noticeable in the Middle Ages.[110] Yet this was not the *dominant*
opinion about converts, and to the extent that it was upheld in
medieval Jewry, it was usually related to *some* of the converts,
and by no means to all of them. Indeed, according to the
dominant opinion, apostasy was the product of the "evil inclination," that is, of passion for earthly good — in other words,
it was motivated primarily by material, not spiritual considerations. But the author of *Aḥituv ve-Ẓalmon* ignores all this.
What he sees is only their "errors of mind," i. e., their believing
in false theories, in the views of the "sophists" as described
above, and thus it appears that his conclusions were shaped not
so much by the prevailing tradition as by his own observations
and reflections. Now, to what extent these observations were
correct, and more notably, in what measure they justified his
generalizations, is of course difficult to determine. For he undoubtedly knew the views of many converts *when they were still
in the fold of Jewry*, and this may have strongly influenced his
judgment. In any case, what he says here should not lead us to
assume that by the end of the twenties — or the thirties, at the
latest — the approximate date of the above-quoted statements[111]

---

[109a] See above, notes 15, 107.

[110] *Ibid.* — Furthermore, *minim* (converts), according to Lipmann-Mühlhausen, signifies those who *halt between two opinions* (*Sefer Niẓẓaḥon*, p. 426),
i. e. who hesitate between the religion of the Jews and that of the gentiles —
a description identical with that of apostates in *Aḥituv ve-Ẓalmon* (see above,
p. 127).

[111] Since the author speaks in the above cited passage (p. 127) about apostates
who could claim that *they* had been forced to convert, he obviously referred to converts of the *first* generation. By the end of the thirties, however,
more than 25 years passed since the second great conversion, and about
50 years since the first. It is therefore not likely that the work was written
after that date (and cf. Schirmann, *Ha-Shirah ha-Ivrit bi-Sefarad u-bi-Provence*,
II, Tel-Aviv, 1956, pp. 648–649).

— all of the Marranos were skeptics and Epicureans and that there were no substantial number of real Christians among them. The whole polemic literature against Christianity *per se*, which appeared shortly after 1391, is a direct denial of this assumption. But further such denials, and more conclusive ones, are supplied by the polemic literature that developed since the twenties of that century.

We shall first consider the testimony included in the treatise against Christianity (and partly against Islam) which was composed by Simon Duran in 1425 (*Magen Avot* — "In Defense of the Fathers"*). In this treatise, after presenting his criticisms of the Christian dogmas of the Trinity and Incarnation, Duran makes a brief statement which bears significantly upon the theme of our discussion. He explains to us that he found it necessary to "refute these Christian conceptions at length" since "*it is a long time that many have been becoming adherents of these principles.*"[112] Now, whom did Duran mean by these adherents? Surely he could not have in mind people who were at that time in the Jewish camp. For Jews who believed in the Trinity and Incarnation in the form they were conceived and propagated by Christians, were no longer Jews but full-fledged Christians, and would undoubtedly convert before long. Then, even if there were such Jews, they could have constituted only small esoteric circles; but Duran speaks here of large numbers and of a process that continued for a long time.

It is clear, then, that Duran referred to converts, or rather to a movement of real Christianization that had originated long before the date of his writing and reached at his time such wide proportions that it called, as he felt, for a renewed campaign against it, based on more detailed and more effective arguments than those heretofore employed. It must remain questionable, however, whether, in speaking of this movement, Duran was thinking of a development in the *Marrano* camp, or in Spanish *Jewry*, or in both groups together. If his statement referred

---

* An introduction (parts I–III) to a commentary on Avot (part IV). The polemical arguments appear in the 2nd and partly the 1st part.

[112] *Qeshet u-Magen*, p. 27a (omission from *Magen Avot* I): והארכנו לסתור דברים אלו לפי שנמשכו אחריהם רבים זמן רב.

to the Marranos, it tells us, in effect, that many of the Marranos who had been forced converts, or voluntary ones but still Jews at heart, or at least antagonistic or indifferent to Christianity, became in the course of time Christians in the full sense, that is, *ideological*, and not merely *formal* converts. In that case, we would have here an important testimony confirming the conclusions we reached earlier regarding the prevalence of true Christians among the Marranos. However, if the statement refers to Jews, or rather to original converts from Judaism, it would substantiate this contention regarding the Marranos in no less forceful a manner. For it would mean that the Marrano group had steadily absorbed an influx of true Christians who, in due time, must have formed a substantial number. What is more, in this case we would be entitled, it seems to us, to the following afortiori deduction: if the Christian campaign made such inroads among Jews, who were constantly under the influence of their Jewish teaching and environment, how much greater must have been its effect upon the Marranos, who were more exposed to Christian influence, ignorant for the most part of Jewish counter argumentation, and practically cut off from Jewish society. We may therefore safely conclude that by 1425, the date of the above quoted statement from Duran, the number of *convinced* Christians among the Marranos must have been large indeed.

While Duran in his above mentioned treatise may have directed his arguments at Marranos, or at Jews expected to campaign among them, another polemic work, clearly aimed at Jews, also leads us to the same conclusions regarding Marrano Christianization. This is Ḥayyim ibn Musa's *Magen va-Romaḥ* ("Shield and Dagger"), a refutation of the christological interpretations of the Bible, composed in 1456. In the introduction to his work, this levelheaded author tells us, in a matter-of-fact style, that "the ignorants who do not know the ways of disputation *are persuaded by the Christians, and especially by the converts*"[113] whose conversionist writings evidently enjoyed wide circulation among Jews. It is noteworthy that among the

---

[113] *Magen va-Romaḥ*, MS. National and University Library, Jerusalem, No. 787, introd., p. 1.

converts he considered influential, he mentions not only contemporary apostates, or rather apostates who were active in
the first half of the century, like Paulus of Burgos, Jerónimo
de Santa Fe and Franciscus de Sant Jordi, but also agitators
who lived centuries before, beginning with Petrus Alphonsi of
Huesca, whose writings marked the inception of conversionist
literature produced by Jewish converts in the Middle Ages.[114]
The fact that old works were in vogue as new ones shows not
only the *breadth*, but also the *depth* of the campaign, which
indeed is also suggested by the fact that Hayyim ibn Musa,
a most thrifty author,[115] found it necessary to write, in reply to
this literature, several polemical tracts in addition to his *Shield
and Dagger*.[115a] As he put it, he wrote the latter book so that the
"Jew would not be overwhelmed when he saw their (i. e., the
converts') proofs drawn from the Bible, Talmud and Midrash
and deemed these proofs to be strong, while in reality they are
weak."[116] So ibn Musa had noticed that the arguments of the
converts were considered "strong," that they were even "overwhelming," and that they had actually "persuaded" the "ignorants" to go over to Christianity. By "*the ignorants*," Ibn Musa
did not refer, of course, to *all* of the unlearned among the Jews
(who in Spain, as in most countries, were in the majority).
He must have referred to a *part* of these; but even so, his formulation indicates that the number of those "persuaded" was not
insignificant. The upshot of all this is that, up to the middle
of the 15th century, Spanish Jewry kept supplying converts by
*persuasion*, and the constant flow of such converts to the Marrano
camp not only augmented its Christianized segment, but also
must have served to further weaken and demoralize whatever
Jewish force still remained in it.

We are now in a position to summarize what we gathered

---

[114] *Ibid.* On the identification of some of the converts mentioned by Ibn
Musa, see Steinschneider, in Kayserling's *Homilet. u. liter. Beiblatt als Anhang
zur Bibliothek jüd. Kanzelredner*, I (1870), p. 35, and id., *Polemische und apologetische Literatur in arabischer Sprache*, Leipzig, 1877, p. 366.
[115] Zacuto, *Sefer Juchassin*, ed. Filipowski, p. 229.
[115a] *Magen va-Romah*, MS. cited, p. 2.
[116] *Ibid.*

from the polemic and philosopnic literature concerning Marranism in the period ensuing the second great conversion — say,
between 1415–1455. In broad outline, what we see of Marrano
life represents the following picture. The camp of the converts
after 1415 consists of former *anusim* who turned renegades, of
voluntary apostates whose outlook was "heretical," and of convinced Christians whose number was large and was steadily
increased by newcomers from without. The numerical relationship at this time between the "heretical" and the fully Christianized Marranos is a matter that must be left to conjecture;
but whatever this relationship, it is quite clear that both segments are estranged from Judaism and disregard or violate the
commandments. Indicative of this estrangement is the mutual
enmity which characterizes the relations between Jews and
Marranos, and perhaps also the intermarriage of Marranos with
Christians, which is suggested by one document.[117] If we add
to this that crypto-Jewish life is rarely alluded to in this literature,[118] we may conclude that, all in all, it confirms what we

[117] We refer to the qabbalistic work, *Sefer ha-Qana*, which contains the
statement: והיו היהודים משתמדים לקנות להם מלכות וממשלה והיו נושאין להם נשים נכריות
(ed. Porizk, 1776, p. 16a). Although the author discusses here a hypothetical
case in relation to Babylonian Jewry, the statement may well reflect Spanish
conditions, as suggested by Graetz, (*op. cit.*, VIII, Note 8, p. 451).

[118] Such an allusion may perhaps be found in Abraham Bibago's introduction
to his *Derekh Emunah* in which he explains the reasons for writing his book.
One of the reasons, it seems, was the need to acquaint the crypto-Jews with
the essentials of Judaism: למען ירושלים ועמה היולדת גולה וסורה
(perhaps a hint to those who were detached from the fold; cf. Is. 49.21, Jer.
17.13) בין תנור וכירים בירכתים (possibly an allusion to the hideouts and
remote corners into which crypto-Judaism was forced) לקחה מאת ה' כפלים,
אחד המרבה ואחד הממעיט (perhaps not in the study of the Law, as in Berakhot 5b,
but in the performance of the commandments) ובלבד שיכוון לבו
לשמים . . . חשכו הרואות בארובות בארץ תלאובות . . . בנויים אין תורה,
בשצף קצף שם פחדו פחד בלילות, אין רועה ואין מקיץ
מציץ מחרכי התבונה, אין פוצה פה ומצפצף, להיות צל על
היונה ראשם בשוק אצל פנה העיר (*Derekh Emunah*, Constantinople,
1521, p. 2b). An allusion to the Marranos may also be found in the following
cryptic statement in the same introduction: למען (ל) מוג לב טהור, לא
קרא ולא שנה יום לשנה . . . למען זאת ועוד סבות אחרות לא יכילם ספר ולשון
אף לחשון שמתי נפשי בכפי ואקלענה בתוך קלע העיון התורני.

have gleaned from the Responsa about the sharp decline of Judaism in the Marrano camp. But its contribution is not limited to this. It points to the causes of that decline (the religious crisis in Jewry; the conversionist agitation), it shows us the inner trends in Marranism (Epicureans, semi-Christians, and Christians in the full sense) and hints at the relations between Jews and Marranos, not only on a religious, but also on a social level. What emerged from all this, in clear perspective, is that not only the ritual practices of Judaism, but also real faith in it and yearning therefor, if they did not yet abandon the Marrano camp completely, were definitely on their way out. We shall now see whether the last chapter of our study, summarizing our findings in another group of sources, will allow these conclusions to stand.

## IV. The Homiletic and Exegetic Literature

While the polemic and philosophical literature helps us understand the origins of the conversion movement and the intellectual climate in which it arose and developed, especially in
the period around 1412–15, the homiletic and exegetic literature
of the century offers us valuable information with regard to the
religious position of the Marranos in the period around the
establishment of the Inquisition. It picks up the thread at its
other end, and therein lies its particular contribution.

The problems that had beset the Hebrew authors in Spain in
the previous two generations continued to trouble the minds of
the Jewish thinkers from the sixties to the very end of the
century. The flow of converts from Judaism to Christianity
seems to have subsided from the end of the late fifties, as may
be gathered from the lull in the polemical literature, that is, in
the efforts to prove the erroneousness of the interpretations
applied by the converts to Biblical and Talmudic passages.
These efforts were resumed in full vigor only toward the end of
the century, when conversion to Christianity again became
widespread as a result of the expulsion and the consequent
suffering.

Also, the attitude toward philosophy changed considerably in
that period. Although severe attacks upon the rationalists,
coupled with general denunciations of philosophy, stifled philosophical creativity for decades, the study of philosophy was
never rooted out, and in the second half of the 15th century we
notice a slow but gradual recovery of philosophical learning.
This is shown by the works of Joseph ben Shem-Tov, Abraham
Bibago, Shem-Tov ben Joseph, Abraham Shalom and others, all
of whom were again trying to build a bridge between Judaism
and philosophy.[1] This general change of attitude, however, was

[1] Thus Joseph ben Shem-Tov, while maintaining that a Jew is in no
need of philosophy to attain "divine," ethical perfection, claimed that
philosophy is essential for the attainment of "human," speculative excellence,

135

paralleled by a renewed upsurge of Averroistic learning and opinion.[2] Several thinkers, who recalled the lessons of the past, saw in this trend new threats to Jewish existence in Spain.[3] They also seemed to observe, at the same time, a reduction in the zeal for Jewish faith and learning, a phenomenon which they

and suggested to permit philosophical learning under the strictures advocated by Adret (*Kevod Elohim*, p. 7[2b]). Abraham Bibago, who likewise stressed the overall superiority and priority of the Law, nevertheless defended secular learning on the ground of its general helpfulness to mankind, and agreed to prohibit only such investigations as are related to foreign theology (*Derekh Emunah*, pp. 46b–47a). Shem-Tov ben Joseph went a step further when he declared that the study of both the Law and philosophy is essential for human perfection and that, lacking either of them, one cannot attain true happiness (*Derashot ha-Torah*, Venice, 1547, p. 64). The realignment of Judaism and Philosophy was accomplished even by thinkers like Shalom and Arama who violently attacked Greek thought (see Shalom, *Neveh Shalom*, introd., last two pages [without pagination]; Arama, *Ḥazut Qasha*, ed. Pollak, Warsaw, 1884, p. 21b f., 23ab, 24; '*Aqedat Yizḥaq*, III, pp. 113b–114). What they sought to establish was a philosophy that would be truly Jewish, or that would be, according to earlier scholastic doctrine, completely subservient to the principles of Jewish faith (see *ibid.*, IV, p. 14a).

[2] See Ibn Musa's letter to his son, published by D. Kaufmann, in *Beth Talmud*, ed. I. H. Weiss, II (1882), pp. 117–118, and especially Arama, *Ḥazut Qasha*, pp. 38–40, 46–47a. In their struggle against the growing Averroistic tendencies, and in their effort to establish a philosophy of Judaism, the above mentioned thinkers (see preceding note) now placed special emphasis upon the creation *ex nihilo* doctrine (see *Neveh Shalom*, chap. I, p. 116; *Derekh Emunah*, pp. 4cd, 74c, and especially II.3, pp. 86b–89c; '*Aqedah*, I, chap. 4, pp. 64–67). In fact, of the two major issues which, according to Abba Mari (*Minḥat Qenaot*, p. 127), divided the traditionalists from the rationalists — Providence and Creation —, the latter occupies, in the last third of the century, the position occupied by the former in the first. It is significant that, in revising the dogmas of Judaism as formulated by Duran and Albo, Shalom introduces only one change: he replaces Reward and Punishment with Creation (*Neveh Shalom*, X, p. 188a), while Arama, in *his* list of dogmas, places creation *ex nihilo* in the second place, immediately after the Existence of God, and *before* God's Omniscience, Providence, and Omnipotence, i. e., the dogmatic trio which is concerned with Providence (see above, note 78). In evaluating Creation as the foremost Judaic doctrine, Joseph Jabeẓ (*Yesod ha-Emunah*, Lemberg, 1865, p. 15; *Or ha-Ḥayim*, Amsterdam, p. 7a) and Isaac Abravanel (see especially *Mif'alot Elohim*, Venice, 1592, pp. 3b–33c, 58b–93c, and *Shamayim Ḥadashim*, Rödelheim, 1828, pp. 1a–12b) obviously followed in the footsteps of these thinkers.

[3] See Arama, *Ḥazut Qasha*, p. 47a.

attributed to the influence of philosophy.[4] If these developments, they feared, were allowed to run their course, Spanish Jewry might well lose its great historic battle for survival. Any social or political crisis could reproduce the results of 1412.

Above all, what loomed large in the eyes of these thinkers was the constantly expanding Marrano camp, which in numbers, as in wealth and prestige, had far outstripped the Jewish population. The very existence of this camp considerably facilitated the passage to Christianity and thus presented a perpetual threat that had to be systematically fought off. The pull of Marranism, to be sure, was considerably reduced after the middle of the century, especially in the 60's and 70's, by the struggle between the Old and New Christians, which assumed the proportions of a civil war. Yet the danger presented by Marranism to Judaism was by no means considered eliminated, and the lure of the Marrano status in the economic, social, and political life of Spain was still strong enough to be seriously reckoned with. A new evaluation, analysis, and probe of the whole conversion problem seemed, therefore, again to be the order of the day.

The task was performed by Isaac Arama, who, more than anyone else in his time, spoke for his generation in this matter. Moved by the same major aim that inspired almost all medieval Jewish thinkers — to establish the over-all superiority of Judaism — he set out to offset the twin challenge and influence of philosophy and Christianity. It is in his campaign against these two factors that he makes many statements which throw light on the religious position of the Marranos, on the views that the Jews of Spain held of them, and consequently on the relations between the Jewish and the Marrano camps.

What intrigued and puzzled him most in Marranism — and to this he reverted again and again — was the very possibility that Judaism could be forsaken and replaced by the worship of foreign deities. While preceding writers saw in the Spanish conversions a deviation from the path of the earlier generations who were ready to lay down their lives for their faith, Arama saw in the Spanish "betrayal" merely a *recurrence* of the phenomenon

[4] *Ibid.*

of desertion which typifies Jewish history throughout. Not only, he claimed, had this phenomenon been common to all the countries of the Diaspora, but it was current in Israel when it lived in its own country and under its own government. Already the prophet Jeremiah was mystified by the strange and unexampled behavior of a people who, privileged to serve the true God, abandoned the "source of living water," and chose instead to "hew broken cisterns," which could not hold water at all.[5] As Arama sees it, the root of the tendency lies in man's nature, in the conflict between his material and spiritual interests, and conversion simply testifies to the great power exercised over man by his bodily passions, which are aimed at satisfying his material needs. Translated into plain, everyday terms, the above simply means that conversion must be attributed to the desire for fortune and the accumulation of property. Indeed, "these are the mighty gods," Arama cries out scornfully — "on whom they (the converts) rely and by the sanctity of whose name they deny the Lord in heaven, abandon His Law, and leave it deserted and beshamed in a corner."[6] In thus stating the cause of conversion, Arama no doubt followed the traditional attitude which prevailed in Jewry for generations. Yet, this is not the complete answer which he offers to the question.

For we notice that elsewhere Arama distinguishes between *two* kinds of sinners: one who is moved to sin by his evil *will*, and the other who comes to sin by way of his evil *thought*. According to Arama, the second kind of sinner is incomparably worse.[7] While the first one chooses the path of sin because of the strength of his material passions and his inability to resist them, the second does not wish to resist sin at all. He chooses it as a sagaciously preferred course, objectively better than that of the Law, and thus he represents not mere lewdness, but full fledged treachery and rebellion.[8] Yet from this, it does not follow that this type of sinner is free from the influence of material passions. On the contrary, such passions appear in him in great force, even greater than in the sinner of the first type.[9] At the same time, says Arama, the latter himself is not completely free from an

5 *'Aqedat Yizhaq*, IV, 195–196.
7 *Ibid.*; *ibid.*, p. 90ab.
9 *Ibid.*, II, p. 90ab.
6 *Ibid.*, II, p. 164a.
8 *Ibid.*, IV, 198a.

element of heresy.[10] The difference between the groups lies really in the fact that while for the first type the *inclination* toward evil is the origin of their heretical thoughts, for the other their heretical thoughts give free reign to their evil inclinations. In both groups, then, heresy and appetite play a part in the actual perpetration of evil.

With this yardstick Arama sets out to evaluate all forms of heresy, desertion and conversion that appeared in Jewry. Considering the above, it is quite apparent why the skeptics and Averroists within Jewry should have formed his first target. And, indeed, it is in them that he saw the main root of the conversion impulse. Having described their major tenets — denial of God's omnipotence and prescience, as well as Providence, both universal and individual — Arama states his view of them, or rather of the role they played in Jewry, in the following critical terms. As he puts it, "these are the hypocrites[10a] who bite the people, who are *hated by the divine Law and are its enemies, who narrow its domain and broaden that of its competitor, who expel from it its finest sons more than all those who committed the sin of worshipping all kinds of foreign deities* . . . These are the people whose power was always felt throughout the generations, and it is they who brought upon us the great calamity of *having the sons exiled from their fathers' homes.*"[11]

This strong attack by Arama upon the Epicuraen and rationalistic thinkers as responsible, more than any other factor — even more than the activist, campaigning converts — for the calamity of voluntary conversion, cannot be taken, of course, as decisive evidence for the actual causes of conversion in Spain in the first stages of the movement toward desertion. Nevertheless, the vehemence with which he speaks of the "philosophers" suggests that the matter was not for Arama a merely theoretical issue. What was said above about Joseph ben Shem-Tov might well apply to him, too: conversion cases he saw in his own time may have considerably influenced his judgment regarding the historic relationship between the conversion movement and Averroistic

[10] *Ibid.*, II, p. 60b; III, 115a.

[10a] צבועים, which should perhaps be translated here as vipers (see Rashi and Radak on I Sam. 13.18).

[11] *Ibid.*, II, p. 159ab; see also *Ḥazut Qasha*, pp. 22–25.

thought. Yet the similarity between his assertions and those of earlier writers is so close that literary influence cannot be ruled out either. To the extent, therefore, that it referred to *earlier* generations, his above-cited view, we may conclude, merely echoed the opinions of his predecessors, especially of Alami.[12] Consequently, one cannot regard these statements as descriptive of the intellectual origins of Marranism — or of its spiritual attitudes in the seventies, although one is inclined to arrive at the conclusion that the philosophic-Averroistic circles in Jewry kept on supplying converts, though in small numbers, even in Arama's times.[13]

We may get clearer insight into the Marrano situation in Arama's own time from his discussion of several other phenomena peculiar to conversion. We have noticed that one of the two major groups into which Arama divided the "sinners" (i. e., the converts) was the one that consisted of those transgressors who were attracted to sin by temptation.[14] That they, too, are "wicked" goes without saying, for they committed the wanton act of following a foreign God with full knowledge of the meaning of their deed, and, as we have seen, there was, according to Arama, also an element of heresy in their action from the start.[15] And yet, there is a difference between them and the "specula-

[12] See above, pp. 103–104.

[13] Accordingly, in discussing the relationship between secular learning and the abandonment of Judaism, Bibago, in his defense of the former, states that the fact that some people, who engaged in foreign learning, foresook Judaism and became evil and sinful (רעים וחטאים) should not be held against secular learning, for such people are numerically insignificant (בטלים במיעוטם). See *Derekh Emunah*, p. 47d. This may be taken as indication of the general weakness of the conversion movement in the '60s — a weakness which is also attested by other sources (see, for instance, below, appendix D., p. 227). Elsewhere, Arama himself states that the Jewish Averroists of his time do not convert (see *Ḥazut Qasha*, p. 43a).

[14] See above, p. 138

[15] That these people, too, were, according to Arama, at least to some extent heretical when they parted with Judaism, is also evident from what he says about them in connection with his view of the truthfulness of the Law. He says: "Since the truth is so self evident, there is no one among us who will doubt it, *except that breed of men who choose licentiousness and prefer to leave the fold for the sake of satisfying their passions*" (*'Aqedat Yizḥaq*, V, p. 26b). Arama, then, maintains that not only the Epicurean, but also the appetitive convert *doubts the veracity of Jewish teachings*.

tionists" in one very important respect. While the latter cannot be considered capable of repentance, the former can; and the reasoning behind this is quite obvious. One who sins out of weakness of character, though aware of his sins, is beset by remorse, and may, under changed circumstances, repent. There is still an element of probity in him. One, however, who sins with full conviction that he committed no evil, suffers no pangs of conscience, and sin thus becomes part of his nature. Hence such a sinner, unless reformed — and this, as is evident, may happen only rarely — must expect total and utter destruction — i. e., the fate which divine justice holds in store for him.[15a]

Penitents can come, then, primarily out of those who converted because of "earthly" considerations. But what are the chances for such a return when measured in realistic terms? Arama ponders the process of estrangement which took place in the Marrano group. What led those who originally committed the sin of conversion out of fear of death, or who went over to Christianity under the impact of material passions, but who, in their hearts, believed in Judaism, to such deep immersion in the foreign way of life? How could they become so totally estranged from both their former faith and people? As Arama sees it, the estrangement is inherent in the nature of the criminal. Just as the "righteous" person keeps coming nearer to God, so the "wicked" one keeps withdrawing from Him. He constantly stumbles into sin and is hindered from returning to the right path.[16] And Arama adds the significant words: "All the more so now when *almost all of them* (רובי רובם) ... *have excluded from their direction the approach to the God of Israel ... nay, have*

---

[15a] The presentation of Arama's views here is based on my conclusion that the two classes of "deliberate sinners," discussed in 'Aquedah, V, 242a, 243a (where the second class is subdivided into two groups), are identical with those referred to by him in ibid., II, 90–91 (and cf. ibid., 82ab, 90b), IV, 198a, and other places.

[16] According to Arama, the "end" of a course for those who persist in it is usually determined by the very direction of the course, and so the road of wickedness ends in extreme wickedness and consequently in extreme punishment: דרך רשעים ... להביא אותם אל תכלית האבדון ואין אומר השב, ment: דרך רשעים תאבד מאליו ותפסק, וישארו ההולכים בו אובדים ונדחים ממנו יתברך לעולם (ibid., V, p. 163a).

*turned their back upon Him; and in this condition they accelerate their pace and increase their effort in running away from Him until they are as far from Him as one can go."* [17]

Arama, then, sees the Marranos of his time, to the exclusion of only a minor fraction, as having turned their back on the God of Israel, as being bent in quite the opposite direction (i. e., that of Christianization) and as being lost in assimilation beyond recall. That he had abandoned any hope for the "return" of this multitude is further evidenced — and, in fact, emphasized — by his analysis of the psychological factors involved. As he sees it, this persistence in sinning, that constant withdrawal from the right course, is inherent in the nature of the criminal; it is determined both by his blindness and stubbornness. The process of his ever sinking deeper in sin is, therefore, automatic, and in most cases irreversible. Arama thus offers support for the conclusion we arrived at earlier in this inquiry, namely, that in the seventies, that is, in the decade preceding the Inquisition, the overwhelming majority of the Marranos were Christianized, that they had no desire or intention to return to Judaism, and consequently did not practice Judaism secretly.

As for the fraction he excluded from this category, Arama, as it seems, did not refer here only to the crypto-Jews who performed Jewish rites (on his attitude toward these, see below[18]), but also to others among the Marranos whose assimilation was not yet thorough and who, although not adhering to Judaism in practice, still harbored some longing for it. It is these latter, together with the crypto-Jews, who, in his eyes, formed the "exception," the small minority that had not yet taken the road of no return. In any case, it was owing to this minority, it appears, that he did not consider the door of salvation closed to *all* Marranos. Now, salvation, or return, can be accomplished by repentance which, in turn, may be induced by any of the following three stimulants: self-awakening, instruction and punish-

---

[17] *Ibid., ibid.*: ומה גם עתה בהיות רובי רובם מכוונים ברוע בחירתם לסור מני דרך ולנטוש מני אורח, משביתים ממגמת פניהם הקריבה אל קדוש ישראל... אבל פנו אליו עורף ולא פנים, ובאותו מצב ממהרים תנועתם ומתאמצים במרוצתם עד שיתרחקו תכלית הריחוק.

[18] P. 146.

ment (the latter always coming in the wake of sin).[19] Which of these agents would operate and prove effective in the repentance of the converts? Of course, had they realized the enormous advantages of repentance, had they known that in this, and this alone, lay their chance for salvation, they would have needed no other stimulus; for "it would behoove them to build ladders in order to ascend to heaven, if it were necessary to wrest it from there."[20] So much the more "should they have boarded ships and crossed the sea lanes in order to attain this purpose."[21] For although it is *difficult* to accomplish the "return," it is not *impossible*, and "everything feasible should be done in order to get out of the prison."[22] Yet, it seems that Arama does not class the converts, who *do* show signs of repentance, among those who truly know what repentance means. Their repentance belongs to the third category, that which is induced by the punishment of sin, and as long as it is motivated by *this* consideration, it is not a voluntary but a forced repentance, which is no repentance at all.[23]

Commenting on Jeremiah 3.2–25, Arama claims that the prophet inveighs against those who "return" under severe pressure only, under the impact of the evils that befell them when they attached themselves to foreign worship. This is why the prophet said: "If you return, O Israel . . . return unto *Me*, etc." (4:1), thereby meaning, "if you wish to come back to God through real repentance — then return to *Me*, that is, for the sake of My name and honor, *out of sheer conviction that you sinned against Me*, that you are *duty bound* to return and seek my forgiveness, and not for the sake of your own benefit."[24] And again,

[19] '*Aqedat Yiẓḥaq*, V, pp. 163b–164ab.

[20] *Ibid.*, *ibid.*, p. 172a.

[21] *Ibid.*          [22] *Ibid.*

[23] Arama considers this sort of repentance false (תשובה מזויפת; *ibid.*, II, p. 42a). Elsewhere, however, he defines it as defective (תשובה פחותה וחסרה; *ibid.*, IV, p. 198b), or as "the lowest of all forms of penance" (הפחותה בדרכי התשובה; *ibid.*, V, p. 164b). In any case, it is obvious to Arama that this kind of repentance does not truly cleanse the sinner's soul ("the crime is not blotted out"); in other words, the penitent remains inherently a sinner — at least to some extent (see *ibid.*, IV, p. 198b).

[24] *Ibid.*, II, p. 42a.

"If you remove your abominations, do so for My sake and not because of the evils that befell you as a result," *while actually you still adhere to the old opinions.*[25] "Only then will you swear by the name of God in truth," and your repentance will not be false.[26] That any other kind of repentance is usually false is also proven by experience.

For it is the habit of the people who are sinners by nature to *dislike* the life of the "just"; in fact, it fills them with sadness and sorrow. Therefore, "having been forced by suffering to walk for some time in the path of righteousness, as soon as the whip of the oppressor is removed, they return to their mischief."[27] It is possible, adds Arama, that the statement in Isaiah 6.10: *Make the heart of this people fat and make their ears heavy and shut their eyes,* etc., "also refers to the same phenomenon, as was indicated by Maimonides.[28] "For since the returners do not come back in honesty and fidelity, it behooves them to have their hearts fattened and their senses dulled, so that they may not sense the punishment destined for them, in order that they do not return as *a result of fear,* while their hearts are still longing for the patterns of sin, until they receive their punishment in its full measure. This is why it is said there: "Until when, O God?" And the answer is: "Until the cities become desolate."[29]

If this passage refers to the Marranos, as we believe it does, it is clear that, according to Arama, most of the "returners" came back to Judaism not as the result of predilection for it, but of the fears that haunted them while in Christendom. In other words, what the Marranos *really* wanted was to *remain* in their state of conversion. Their real preference was not for Judaism, but for the alien way of life; and while they were supposedly "repenting" and "returning," their hearts still longed for the pattern of sin. It is only *when their cities became desolate,* when their punishment became extreme, that they began to realize what this path involved. Prior to that, however, they were immersed in their foreign worship, they were blind to the threatening signs of catastrophe: "their hearts became fattened

[25] *Ibid., ibid.*　　[26] *Ibid., ibid.*　　[27] *Ibid., ibid.,* p. 114a.

[28] *Ibid.,* II, 42a; V, p. 164b, and see Maimonides, *Hilkhot Teshuvah,* VI.3.

[29] *'Aqedat Yiẓḥaq,* II, p. 42a; see Isa. 6.11.

and their senses dulled," so that they did not sense the approaching punishment.

When were these words written? The verse cited as indication of the punishment assured to the persistent sinners — "until the cities became desolate" — brings to mind the fate of the Marrano cities, especially in Andalusia, that were abandoned as a result of the Inquisition's persecutions. But this is not the only possible interpretation of this passage. Marrano communities were severely hit, and actually destroyed, after the great outbursts of 1473, which particularly ravaged the Marrano communities in Cordova and Jaen. Arama may well have written the above statement under the impact of these events. Also his above quoted remarks on the vacillation of the wicked between sin and repentance may have been influenced by Marrano reaction to the repeated massacres they were subjected to since 1449. In all likelihood, each massacre resulted in a certain ideological crisis, which affected *some* among the Marranos. Perhaps as a result, a few returned to Judaism or at least joined the ranks of the Jewish underground.[30] If, however, we accept Arama's above-quoted words as related to this situation, the return was neither wholehearted nor durable. As soon as the storm quieted down, the "penitents" reverted to their old way of life, abandoning any further thought of returning to Judaism which they inwardly disliked ("it only filled them with sadness and sorrow"). Consequently, Arama does not expect many among the Marranos ultimately to return to Judaism. It is only extreme punishment in the fullest measure, a disaster of the first magnitude, that will move them to *real* return, but even then, be believed, this would affect only a *small minority* among them. This, too, is indicated by the words of the prophet: "And if there be yet a *tenth* in it, it will be subjected to a *further purge*" or, as the Hebrew word used here may allude to: to "a purge by *fire*."[30a]

Whether we have here a direct reference to the autos-da-fé of the Inquisition, or whether the similarity is merely incidental,

[30] A similar process has been noticed in the dominions of the Almohades where apostatized Jews, descendants of forced converts, returned to Judaism under the impact of persecution. See A. S. Halkin, "Le-Toledot ha-Shemad bimei ha-Almuwaḥḥadin," in *The Joshua Starr Memorial Volume*, New York, 1953, p. 106.

[30a] *'Aqedat Yiẓḥaq*, V, p. 164ab; see Isa. 6.13.

so that actually we have here a *prognostication*, is really immaterial for our purpose. For already in the seventies there was
room for an acute observer to draw correct conclusions about the
future of Marranism and the chances of a Marrano return to
Judaism. As we have seen, Arama considered these chances to
be limited only to a small fraction of the Marranos, as he was
convinced that the overwhelming majority of them had advanced
too far on the road of assimilation and *did not want to return to
their former faith*. If this was not the condition at the time of
the Inquistion, it certainly was so on the eve of its establishment.

Such, then, was Arama's view of the character and future of
the Marrano camp as a whole (of those whom he signified by
רובי רובם). What was his view of the small minority which still
clung to Judaism secretly? The answer is included in several
passages which touch upon the issue involved. According to
Arama, the dual life led by such groups was aimed at deriving a
double benefit: one from the open enjoyment of the foreign life,
and the other from the clandestine attachment to Judaism. As
Arama puts it: "Some of the criminals of Israel (קצת פושעי ישראל)
thought that it would be profitable for them to hold on to such
practices (namely, to worship God *and* the foreign deities).
They should realize the faultiness of this reasoning. God will
not tolerate the shame of such worship, for He is a Holy God,
jealous and vengeful, and will not forgive this crime of yours,
albeit you worship Him."[31]

This passage clearly reveals Arama's stand toward the surviving
Jewish or semi-Jewish element within the Marrano group. What
we see here is no appreciation whatsoever of their secret attachment to Judaism, but bitter and unqualified castigation of their
shameful attitude toward divine worship. Adherence to Judaism
is based, according to him, on *two* fundamental requirements: the
one is to serve God sincerely, the other — *not* to serve any other
deity.[32] To assume that both forms of worship can be combined
by the same people is to posit the impossible. In fact, "God
cannot be served by one who serves another deity,"[33] and hence

[31] *'Aqedat Yiẓḥaq*, V, p. 30a.
[32] *Ibid., ibid.*, also p. 30b (אנכי ולא יהיה לך).
[33] *Ibid., ibid.*, p. 30a (כי הוא בלתי נעבד ממי יעובד זולתו).

the very assumption of faithfulness to Judaism while professing such a dual allegiance is grounded in error.

Yet Arama goes on to make an additional statement which is highly revealing. He asserts that this duplicity will, in any case, result in complete assimilation. The vacillation — this "halting between two opinions" — cannot go on endlessly. "By the dictates of your very nature you will be compelled to choose between one of the two sides, *and it is known beyond any doubt that you will finally abandon God [completely] and worship [only] a foreign deity.*"[34] On the basis of Marrano history or his own observations, Arama, then, indicates quite clearly that the Jewish underground has no future in Marranism. It gradually dwindles through assimilation, and is thus bound to disappear altogether.

We have thus seen Arama's attitude toward the three groups among the Marranos: the outright converts, the crypto-Jews and the repentants. We noticed that it is negative in all cases, and that he sees no future for Marranism and no return from it, beyond that of a small minority. Yet, besides his *view* of Marranism, and his religio-ideological position toward it, there is the important question of his feelings toward the group. Now these are clearly reflected in several of his statements, and first of all in his discussion of those elements who seek to induce Israel to abandon the true faith. Whether they are outside or still inside the fold, active solicitors of apostasy or merely passive exemplars of it, individuals or whole communities, they should be treated, according to Arama, in the same manner: with open and unrestrained hostility. "It is of these renegades that the Psalmist said: I shall hate those who hate you, O God. I shall hate them with an extreme hatred."[34a] This is not the kind of hatred one feels for the enemy of his friend or master. It is a hatred of the kind one manifests toward his *own* enemies, and this is what the enemies of God become, just as the Psalmist indeed indicated: "for they became *My* enemies."[35]

---

[34] *Ibid., ibid.*

[34a] Psalms 139.21–22. And cf. Tosefta (ed. Lieberman), Shabbat, xiii.5.

[35] *'Aqedat Yiẓḥaq*, V, pp. 77–78. And see above, chap. II, note 27, on the term אויבי ה' which Arama uses here to describe solicitors for conversion.

This intense enmity for the renegades in no way excludes family relations.  Having in mind the numerous family involvements among Jews and Marranos throughout Spain and the many conversions that took place as a result, Arama, in his comment on Deuteronomy 13.7 which deals with the "seduction of thy brother," stresses the fact that the inducement by one's relative for conversion is all the more effective because of one's "natural inclination" to follow the advice of close relations.[36] Hence the special danger such a relative represents, and hence the order: "Do not hearken unto him and do not pity him" which means, according to Arama, that in such cases one should not follow his natural inclination and allow himself to be swayed by blood relationship, but one should rather become the inducer's mortal enemy *against* his natural inclination.  "For no love or pity nor any other humane quality should stand in the way of *His* awe and worship."[37]  This was also the position of the Sages. "For where the violation of God's honor (חלול השם) is involved, and where a grave danger looms to the soul, the *right measure is to show cruelty to God's enemies*."[38]  Actually, explains Arama, the term is here misused, for "cruel is he who shows *pity* for the wicked," while he who treats them with the severity due them is acting in accordance with the "true compassion," which is that of God himself.[39]

These statements are certainly revealing.  Of course, their core is to be found in earlier Jewish literature, both halakhic and philosophical, and they reflect the general attitude toward the apostate, then dominant also in Christianity and Islam. And yet they betray an intensity of feeling which clearly transcends the speculative position.  Arama, as we see it, here gives vent to emotions which were current in his time.  And these emotions of unquenchable hostility are also evident in his discussion of the "wicked's" fate.

For the wicked will pay for their sins, and they will pay for them, first of all, in *this* world.  Arama is not impressed with the

[36] *'Aqedat Yiẓḥaq*, V, p. 77b.
[37] *Ibid.*, *ibid.*: כי אין אהבה ורחמנות ולא שום מידה אנושית עומדת לפני יראתו ועבודתו.
[38] *Ibid.*, *ibid.*, p. 78a.
[39] *Ibid.*

achievements of the Marranos, and he already knows that their success is ephemeral. The growth of the wicked, including their "flowering," resembles, in his eyes, that of grass in the field; it withers before long. As it is said in Ecclesiastes 8.13: "It shall not be well with the wicked, neither shall he prolong his days."[40] And even if they achieve some success, it is only as a prerequisite for their eternal destruction. *For the enemies of God will be torn apart and dispersed*, just as Job said: "For the company of the godless shall be desolate" (15.34).[41] On the other hand, the "just" will enjoy success in this world. They will reach old age and spend it in happiness.[42]

Whether the passages referred to were written after the establishment of the Inquisition, or, which is more likely, after the riots and pogroms against the Marranos in 1467 and 1473, it is clear that they date from the pre-expulsion period. For Arama can still compare favorably the condition of the Jews (the "just") with that of the Marranos (the "wicked"). This evaluation, moreover, reflects the changes which, in the course of the century, were wrought both in the Jewish and the Marrano camps. While the position of the Jews, since 1419, has much improved, that of the Marranos, since 1449, has greatly deteriorated and, in fact, became precarious. The wheels of Providence had certainly turned, and the Jewish preacher could now use what he saw to prove the existence of divine justice. In the later parts of this book, and especially in the fifth, which was probably written, or edited, during the eighties, we find a number of passages alluding to the Inquisition and the punishment the Marranos took from its hands.[43] And in all these allusions, as

---

[40] *Ibid.*, II, p. 84b.

[41] *Ibid.*

[42] *Ibid.*, II, pp. 84b–85a.

[43] Among the passages which, in all likelihood, were written under the impact of the Inquisition, the following is of special interest: "God's medium for punishment is death by fire, and this is a proper and fitting punishment for those who were informed by God through fire [on Mount Sinai] that he alone was God and that they should have no other God" (*ibid.*, V, p. 200b). While it is most probable that, when writing these words, the author had in mind the autos-da-fé, they should not be taken as justification of the Inquisition *sub specie humanitatis*. Although he viewed the Marranos

well as in the direct references, we see no sign of compassion for the Marranos.[44] Of course, had the massacres and persecutions produced a change of heart in the group as a whole, Arama, we may assume, would have taken a different attitude. But evidently since no such thing took place, his original deep-rooted animosity was now only fortified through added severity, justified by the Marranos' latest behavior. What they get, he thought, was only fitting for such hardened criminals — in fact, it is much below what they really deserve. Thus, he assures us that the punishment taken by the Marranos (the "criminals of Israel") in *this* world is trivial in comparison with the real punishment which awaits them in the world to come. What awaits them there is total doom, following long and inconceivable agonies. It is about these criminals that the Sages said (Rosh ha-Shanah 17a) that their body is to be consumed and their soul burned and that they have no share in the world to come.[45] One, therefore, should not be misled into thinking that *such criminals may pay their penalty and after that have a share in the world to come.*[46] The statement in the Mishna (San. X.1): "All of Israel have a share in the world to come," in no way refers to them. For if the author of that statement meant to say that *all* of Israel, the "just" and the "wicked," will have a share in the world to come, he would subscribe to a clearly grave injustice (עָוֶל נָמוּר), since this would mean that the reward of the just would be equal to that of the wicked; hence, he could not have meant this.

as "criminals" and their fate as a divine punishment for their crimes, he surely did not identify himself with the Inquisition, in whose functionaries he saw merely instruments of God's wrath, employed for purposes entirely different from those that motivated their actions. And see below, note 44.

[44] This attitude is highlighted in · Arama's comments on the case of the messengers of King Ahaziah to Elijah who were consumed by fire because they refused to listen to the word of God (II Kings 1.9–12). This happened repeatedly until the remaining group realized their sin and were saved from annihilation. Thus the only choice left the "wicked rebels" is between consumption by fire and swift and real repentance, one which is effected with a whole heart and not as a mere means to avoid destruction (*ibid., ibid.*, p. 201ab).

[45] Cf. Tosefta, Sanh. 13.4.

[46] *'Aqedat Yiẓḥaq*, III, p. 173a.

On the other hand, the assumption that the author meant to say that *every one who belongs to Israel is just*, and consequently is assured of a share in the world to come, is also impossible to accept. For reality refutes this assumption. In fact, the original thesis is denied by the statement in the same *mishna* which enumerates those who will *not* have a share in the world to come, and these are all from the children of Israel. Hence, the real meaning of the statement, and the novelty it represents, lies in the thought that *no one can be defined as Israelite except he who is just*; "just" and "Israel" are synonymous terms. For every Israelite, according to his essence, is *bound* to be just, and consequently is bound to have a share in the world to come. However, those people who refuse to follow the Law and perform its commandments, *are not Israelites except in name only*.[47]

This statement is of special importance. It argues the propriety of introducing a sharp division between the two types of Israelites, the treacherous and the faithful, and it meant to uproot any thought of their basic equality which may have been suggested by the procedures of levirate marriage, which was still recognized for the Marranos.[48] It was in line with the policy of separation, of emphasizing the cleavage between the groups, rather than their common elements, which we have noticed among Spain's rabbis in the Responsa.[49] Above all, it was a statement which no doubt expressed the *actual* relationship between Jews and Marranos and the feeling of animosity that prevailed between the groups. Yes, they are both called Israel. But there are Israelites in the flesh and Israelites in the spirit.

[47] *Ibid., ibid.*, p. 55b.

[48] In this connection, I should remark that nothing definite can be gathered about his attitude toward the Marranos from his accession to, and justification of the old rule that a Jewess, to be divorced from a convert, must get from him a divorce in full accordance with Jewish law (*ibid.*, V, p. 131a). The opinion expressed here, it should be noted, refers to a convert who was *raised as a Jew*, and not to one *born in gentilehood* as were practically all the Marranos (on the different attitudes toward these categories of converts, see above, p. 71, and below, p. 215). Of greater interest is the hypothetical argument he advances *against* that time-honored law, as it indicates that Arama, although deciding in its favor, had been beset by doubts about its propriety.

[49] See above, pp. 69–72.

The real Israelites are the latter. They are the *just*; the others are the *wicked*.

This fundamental difference between the Jews and the Marranos, which spelled the exclusion of the latter from the camp of Israel, is further brought to relief in other passages. As we have seen, Arama does include the Marranos within the system of divine justice which applies to Israel — but this does not mean communion with the Jewish people, but rather separation from it. For it means, above all, punishment for betrayal, for *leaving the fold*, and joining other peoples and other religions. As for the question of reunification, it remained, as we have seen, a possibility for Arama, depending on the kind of repentance performed. But even with reference to this issue, there is sufficient evidence to the effect that he did not agree to compromise his position by considering the returners as actual Jews. The following passage is the most revealing in that respect.

Discussing the "return" of the worshippers of foreign deities, Arama, in accord with his previously stated views, believes that it will come only at the end of a long process of suffering and, indeed, at the very peak of the agony. Only after they have gone through the crucible of the exile, and have been cleansed by the great torrents of persecution, will their uncircumcised hearts yield. They will then be covered with shame for leaving God ("the source of living water") and for following the foreign deities of the gentiles ("the broken cisterns") in which they found neither use nor help. "And after *they have been* ashamed to lift their faces to God, for abandoning Him in their pursuit of mirages, *they will find forgiveness nowhere but in the house of His servants and the performers of His will.* Then will they recognize God's justice, as manifested through His generosity in Israel, and admit their guilt in betraying Him and wooing the foreign governments each according to his own strength, while now they will have no remedy or restitution except by returning to Him and by taking shelter under His wings as *proselytes of righteousness.*"[50]

---

[50] *'Aqedat Yiẓḥaq*, V, p. 198b.

This far-reaching, telling statement falls in with the rest of Arama's views as herein presented. In fact, it complements them. Since the Marranos are not regarded by him as true Israelites, they cannot automatically become so merely by a change of heart. It is the actual "return" that will alter their status; and then it will be equal to that of gentiles who turn to Judaism as to the true religion. In all this Arama no doubt reflects the general attitude of Spain's Jews who regarded the Marranos as gentiles and the "returners" as proselytes.[51]

Having pointed out, as it seems to us, the basic features of Arama's views on the Marranos, we may summarize them as follows: Arama considered the overwhelming majority of the Marranos as religious culprits who rejected their former faith and detached themselves from it to *the very extreme*. The fate which they suffered was just punishment for their crimes, and the Jews should not bemoan it. In fact, they should consider the Marranos their enemies, because they are enemies of God. The prospect of their "return" he held limited to a small minority, and even for these he considered it likely only after extremely severe persecutions. Those who 'returned' in his time, however,

---

[51] In addition to what was said above (pp. 61–71) on this matter, I should add that Joseph of Arevalo, while discussing the Marranos (see above, chap. III, note 1), refers the reader to the "end" of his book, where he promises to present Rashi's comment on Zechariah 13.9, and seemingly also his own remarks on it. None of this is to be found there (which, incidentally, gives rise to speculation that the extant text is incomplete), but Rashi's comment, which our chronicler saw applicable to the Marrano situation, can of course be examined independently. It reads as follows: "Some of the *proselytes from among the gentiles* will suffer from the hands of the idolaters the tribulations to be afflicted during the messianic travail ... and *through this they will be tested whether they are true proselytes; for many of them will first relapse and join Gog* (the enemy of Israel)." It appears, then, that the penitent Marranos were considered by Joseph of Arevalo as "*proselytes from among the gentiles*" and in the punishment they took from the hands of the Inquisition he saw a test to determine whether they were *true* proselytes or not. Those who maintained their Jewishness in defiance of the Inquisition, and surely those who died as Jews at the stake, evidently demonstrated their sincerity, while those "who relapsed and joined Gog," i. e., who confessed their "Judaic crimes" and were reaccepted by the Church, or who died at the stake as Christians, were false proselytes and must be still considered gentiles.

did so in many cases — as far as he could gather — not willingly, but out of fear, because they saw no other alternative. Hence they cannot be considered true "returners". Only those among them who "return" in earnest, out of free choice and purity of heart, should be accepted wholeheartedly, but even so they should be thought of as *gentiles who were proselytized*. In all these statements about the Marranos, Arama alludes to them in various terms: the "criminals;" the "wicked;" the "rebels;" "those who left the fold." Nowhere does he use the term *anusim*— not even in the cardinal passage in which he summarized the activities of the Inquisition and which, indeed, is the most transparent of all his discussions of the Marranos. To this passage we shall now turn.

Referring to Deut. 28.64, Arama states that he considers it very likely that "the words of the prophecy allude to those thousands and myriads of Jews in this Diaspora who changed their religion as a result of the persecutions. It is of those who left the fold that the prophecy said: 'And among those nations shalt thou have no repose, etc., and thy life shall hang in doubt before thee.' *For although they assimilated among those nations entirely*, they will find no peace among them; for they, the nations, will always revile and beshame them, plot against them, and *accuse them falsely in matters of faith*. Indeed, they will always suspect them as Judaizers and subject them to tremendous dangers, as was the case throughout this period of innovations, and especially in our own time, when the smokes [of the autos de fe] are rising toward the sky in all the kingdoms of Spain and the Islands of the Sea.[51a] A third of them has been consumed

---

[51a] Several points related to the translation should be noted. Arama writes:
על אלו המחליפים שטחם אמר: ובנוים ההם לא תרניע וגו' . . . והיו חייך תלויים לך וגו'. כי אף על פי שנתערבו בגויים ההמה לנמרי לא ימצא[ו] ביניהם מרנוע ומנוח לכף רגלם, כי הם [הגויים] יחרפו ויבזו אותם תמיד ויחשבו עליהם מחשבות ועלילות מפאת דתם, ותמיד הם חשודים בעיניהם למתיהדים ומנלגלים עליהם סכנות עצומות כמו שהיה בכל המשך זמן אלו החידושים, ומה עתה בזמננו זה אשר עלה עשן השמימה בכל מלכויות ספרד ובאיי הים (*'Aqedat Yiẓḥaq*, V, pp. 149b–150a).
In the words המחליפים שיטתם the reference is not to *formal* conversion, but to a *fundamental change of view* (cf. Rashi, 'Eruvin 99a, on מוחלפת השיטה), or more clearly to *ideological* apostasy (and note the formulation in the introduction to this passage (*ibid.*, p. 149b): שהחליפו שיטתם והמירו דתם, which shows that

by fire, a third runs here and there to hide, and the rest of them live in great fear and extraordinary weakness, caused by the terror which was struck in their hearts and by what they see with their eyes."[52]

This passage offers overhwelming support to our earlier exposition. It is clear from it that, according to Arama, the Marrano group as a whole was *thoroughly assimilated*, or, as he put it, "asimilated entirely," which is an even more extreme formulation than the one quoted earlier to the same effect, namely, that *almost all of the Marranos were removed from Judaism as far as one can be.*[53] Consequently, Arama sees in the claims of the Inquisition no substance, but a sheer expression of hostility. It is a kind of obsession with the Christians to hate the Marranos, plot against them and accuse them in matters of religion, but *these charges are false*, and are merely part of the divine scheme to subject the Marranos to such punishment.[54] Also significant is Arama's

the expression under consideration is not just a synonym for conversion. — נתערבו בגוים should be rendered *assimilated*, as is clearly suggested by the biblical verses from which this expression derives (Esra 9.2; Ps. 106.35, on the basis of Judges 3.5–6), except that Arama does not refer here to *ethnic* fusion, of which the above-mentioned verses speak (this is excluded by his use of the word לגמרי), but of *complete* assimilation in the social and cultural sense (including of course the religious one), which erased all other distinctions between the New and the Old Christians. — The expression ויחשבו עליהם מחשבות follows Jer. 11.19 and Dan. 11.25, where it alludes to crimes hatched against *innocent* people or to conspiracies contrived for *ulterior* motives. — מפאת דתם (=מצד or מחמת דתם) refers to the Marranos' religion at the time, i. e. Christianity (as correctly understood by H. J. Pollak; see *'Aqedah*, V, p. 149, note 2).

[52] *'Aqedat Yiẓḥaq*, p. 150a. — Also Joseph of Arevalo, in his aforecited remark about the Marranos (see above, p. 153, note 51), seems to evaluate the number of the Marranos who were subjected to the extreme punishment by the Inquisition, as a third of their total (והבאתי את השלישית באש; see *Medieval Jewish Chronicles*, I, p. 99). Since it is difficult to believe that neither he nor Arama knew that the actual number of victims was much smaller, their statements, in reality, may only suggest their expectation that, in conformity with Zechariah's prophecy (Zech. 13.9), about a third of the Marranos would be destroyed.

[53] See above, pp. 141–142.

[54] It is remarkable that although the above statement of Arama was already noticed by Graetz (*Geschichte*, VIII, 4th ed., p. 317) and others, its tremendous

account of the effect of the Inquisition: fate has split the Marranos into three approximately equal parts, and of these one is that of the escapees, of those who flee their homes in search of a refuge. It would appear that this was an occasion for Arama to indicate the impact of the Inquisition upon the fugitives also from a religious point of view. There is no allusion, however, to their disappointment with Christianity, nor a word about a movement of return.

Of course, Arama may have deliberately avoided touching upon the subject of "return" when he discussed the Marranos in such an undisguised manner;[54a] but his general presentation of their religious position in this and other passages of his writings, as well as his statements regarding the paucity of the returners, would certainly not call for a basic change in his summarized picture of the Marranos' condition. Had the Jewish underground been large and impressive, Arama would not have found it possible to present the Marrano group to the Hebrew reader as "entirely assimilated," nor would he describe the charges of the Inquisition as concocted and wholly malicious. Similarly, had the religious impact of the Inquisition been such as to stir many of them to "return," he would not have divided the Marranos solely into three categories of wretched victims, without mentioning the one group with the redeeming features of faith, hope and salvation. Arama knew, of course, of the "return" movement

significance for the issue before us — its testimony concerning (a) the measure of Marrano assimilation and (b) the nature of the Inquisition's activity — has completely passed unnoticed.

[54a] This is especially likely if we assume that Arama's work was completed in Spain. His work, however, and particularly the last part, i. e., the commentary on Deut., may have been revised or supplemented after the Expulsion, i. e., in Naples. In any case, the passage referred to could have hardly been written — at least, in its available form — before 1490; for, speaking of the autos de fe of the Inquisition, he says that "their smoke went up in all the kingdoms of Spain and in the islands of the sea" (אשר עלה עשן השמימה בכל מלכויות ספרד ובאיי הים). In the "islands of the sea" the reference could be only to Sicily and the Balearic Islands in which the Inquisition was established respectively in 1487 and 1488 and where the first autos de fe were held in 1487 (in Sicily) and 1489 (in Majorca). See H. C. Lea, *The Inquisition in the Spanish Dependencies*, New York, 1922, p. 2, and id., *A History of the Inquisition of Spain*, I, New York, 1922, p. 267.

that sprang from the Inquisition. But he evidently considered it so weak and inconclusive as to have no significance in the general situation. Arama then offers us full confirmation of the conclusions about the Marranos we have drawn thus far.


2


The homiletic works with which we shall now deal were all composed *after* Arama had written his *'Akedah*. In addition, save for one, they were all produced, not only after the Spanish, but after the Portuguese expulsion, when the whole lesson of conversion and exile seemed to have been fully clarified. Isaac Caro, a Castilian rabbi who was invited to Portugal, probably in the eighties, to instruct students in the Law, and who later, probably in 1497, was forced to flee Portugal, in the wake of the anti-Jewish persecutions, was among those who witnessed the end of the 15th century drama of both Jewish and Marrano life in Spain. His homiletic commentary on the Pentateuch, which includes his thoughts on the conversion problem, was written, when he was already in Turkey.[55] His veiled references to the Spanish Marranos, most of whom were descendants of converts for generations, are no doubt mixed with remarks on the conversions of his *own* time, just as his references to the latter were no doubt influenced by his view of the Marranos. When Caro, therefore, speaks of conversion in general, we may take his view as an indication of his position on the Marranos as well.

Caro is unique, first of all, in his very attitude toward *forced* conversion. To him, worship of a foreign god is a capital sin, whether it is done out of will or out of compulsion — for *"compulsion is also will."*[56] It is the *preference of conversion to the right deed that makes the so-called forced conversion voluntary*, and the right deed under the circumstances, the only right deed, is sanctification of the Name. For sanctification, to Caro, is not only the better course, which one should follow when the

---

[55] *Toledot Yizḥaq*, Amsterdam, 1708, introduction.
[56] *Ibid.*, p. 118b.

alternative is death, but it is the *only* course which the faithful *must* follow if he is to abide by the divine rules. Hence, whether conversion is effected willully or forcibly (בהכרח או ברצון), it is seen by Caro as the same transgression (עוון גדול).[57] Clearly, Maimonides' position in favor of forced conversion, at least when the whole community is threatened with extinction, is completely rejected by him; and in this, as we shall see, he was no exception. Advocacy of sanctification as the only right course was common to practically *all* Spanish savants after the expulsions from Spain and Portugal. Not only do they fail to recommend, in any measure, conversion under the threat of death, but they actually reject it totally and unreservedly, and, in fact, denounce it as a voluntary act. The above statement of Caro ("compulsion is also will") conclusively summarizes their view on the subject; and it means that forced conversion was in their eyes an act indicating a criminal inclination of the same nature revealed in conversion by choice.

Such a view, which was a departure from tradition, evolved under the impact of the grim historic lesson taught by the developments in Spain. This much one can say with certainty. By the turn of the century, it was quite clear that forced conversion resulted in an estrangement no less complete than that caused by apostasy, and the prevailing view in Spanish Jewry, based on their observation of the conduct of the forced converts, as well as of their progeny for several generations, was that this outcome was due not to outside pressures, but to intrinsic tendencies and inclinations. What held the forced convert back in Spain? What brought him, or his offspring, constantly closer to Christianity, and finally to a full acceptance of it? His own evil will, of course; and it was the seed of the same will which had driven him to deny his faith in the first place. This conception leads Caro to reject any excuse for conversion based on external circumstances. As he sees it, *all* conversions may be interpreted as results of pressure, of compulsion, and all converts are placed by him in the category of arch-criminals, including those whose "hearts are devoted to

[57] *Ibid.*

Heaven" (to employ an expression often used in the Responsa by rabbis who were lenient toward crypto-Jews).

Accordingly, when referring to this type of convert, which he must have seen among the Marranos as among the neophytes of his time, Caro states, in a comment on Deut. 29.18: "There are many people who say that they wish to convert since *they cannot withstand so much suffering* and who intend to worship a foreign deity while in their hearts they would serve God."[58] Since "the principles of the Mosaic religion are in their hearts," they delude themselves in believing that they will enjoy peace and suffer no divine punishment. What these people intend to do is to hold on to two religions or, more precisely, to add the religion of the Gentiles, which is the "satisfying" one, i. e., that satisfies man's worldly desires, to "our religion" which is the "thirsty" one, i. e., that prevents man from yielding to his passions and leaves him "thirsty" for their fulfillment. "Such a man, then, follows two laws: the divine law which is in his heart, and the law of the Gentiles which he honors in practice. Now it might occur to some that God will forgive such a man since he believes in the articles of the true faith. This is why Scriptures say: *"God will refuse to forgive him."*[59]

This complete rejection of "suffering" as an extenuating circumstance for the sin of conversion meant, of course, a negation of the whole concept of *anusiut* and denial of the right for *any* of the Marranos to be considered and called *anusim*, a title which, *de facto*, was attached in Spain not only to the forced converts of 1391, but also to those of 1412. "Suffering," after all, did signify a form of compulsion, at least to many. But Caro, under the influence of the Spanish experience and his strictly negative opinion of the Marranos, takes a different view of "suffering." In fact, he sees no difference between the convert out of suffering and the renegade out of greed and lust. Avoidance of suffering and pursuit of pleasure are to him merely two expressions of man's desire for sensual happiness, and thus they are placed by

[58] *Ibid.*, p. 131a.
[59] *Ibid.*

him, as motivations for conversion, on the same level — and precisely for the same reason.

But Caro's attitude toward this type of convert is even more fully revealed in the following. Perhaps under the influence of antecedent literature, as well as under the influence of current evidence, Caro sees two basic reasons for conversion, and correspondingly two major types of converts. One type consists of those who *deny* the principle of Providence and that of Reward and Punishment which is associated with it. The other is comprised of those who *know* full-well that the thirteen articles of faith represent the truth, but who sin because of their inflamed passions. Both types are indicated in the warning stated in Deut. 29.17–19. The first type is the one against whom the prophecy inveighs: "In case there is within you *a root of poison and bitterness*," by "root" alluding to the principles of one's religion. This type of convert is so described because he denies the "roots" (the principles) of the divine faith and substitutes for them his own poisonous beliefs. The second type is referred to in the words: "In case there is among you a man or a woman *whose heart turns today from the Lord thy God*." Here the allusion is to those who turn away from God because of *the inclination of their heart*, who are attracted by what they see among the gentiles — their success in great enterprises and amassment of fortunes — and thus, because of their passion for wealth, they become worshippers of a foreign deity. Now, this kind of convert, who takes the path of conversion because of his passion for material gain, may intend to stay in his state of conversion only temporarily. This is why, referring to him, the prophecy uses the word "today," alluding to his concealed thought: "Today that I am devoid of riches, I shall serve a foreign deity, but later, when I acquire wealth, I shall return to worship God." He persuades himself that he will suffer no harm, for he attributes his sin to his evil inclination, namely, to a material passion which *compels* him to sin. And he believes that because he is thus compelled, while actually he is not a denier of the Law, God will forgive him. It is against this type of sinner, namely, the one who, in his heart, does not deny any principle, that the Law says: *"God will refuse to forgive him.*" For because he believes that he actually did not sin (on the assumption that he was *compelled* to his action), the wrath and vengeance of God will fall upon him with the greatest severity. He will be subjected to all the curses enumerated in the Law, and, furthermore, God will wipe out his name from under heaven. The other type of convert, on the other hand, will suffer all the punishments implied in all the curses, but his name will not be wiped out."[60]

Caro thus reverses the traditional attitude toward the two types of converts — the one who denies the principles of faith and the one who follows his evil inclination. The crime of the latter is *greater* than that of the former, and therefore his punishment will be heavier. As we shall see, this reversal may have been influenced by a current socio-religious development, but, at least formally and theoretically, it is justified on the ground that sin should be measured by the damage it entails, and the damage which follows from the action of the second type is far greater than that resulting from the first one. "For he who denies the principles of faith will not be followed by the people, for everyone will say, 'he is an agnostic.' But he who does *not* deny the principles will mislead many in following his path, because his example will stir the temptations of others for wealth and material welfare."[61] In this evaluation of the public harm resulting from each of these types of *conversos* — Caro again seems to differ with the accepted notions, for earlier authorities held firmly to the opinion that it was the "denier" who was far more dangerous than the "libertine," since it is he who, by his instruction, leads many to sin.

It would be impossible to gauge the historic contents of these statements without determining the phenomena to which they referred. Caro is the first among the authors reviewed here who wrote his works after the expulsions from Spain and Portugal, and, as indicated, we must bear in mind the possibility that, in his discussion of conversion, he refers not to Spanish Marranism in its crystalized form prior to the establishment

---

[60] *Ibid.*, p. 129b.
[61] *Ibid.*

of the Inquisition, but to the new phenomena of conversion
in Spain and Portugal. As far as the last quoted passage is
concerned, however, the question can be decided by internal
evidence, that is, by relating the contents of the statement
to contemporary conditions as we know them from other sources.
Now, those who converted *after* the Spanish expulsion, both
in Portugal and in Spain, did not, on the whole, do so because
of a desire for wealth. In Spain Marranism was no longer
an attraction, and everyone knew that the Marranos' wealth
was but a factor attracting punishment by the Inquisition.
Those who converted there in 1492 did so primarily to avoid the
expulsion, the wandering and homelessness, which they feared
most. The rich who converted did so, in all likelihood, also with
a view to protecting their wealth; but this is something different
from envy of the rich, which is described as the motive by Caro.
Nor does the economic condition of Spanish Jewry in the two
or three decades preceding the expulsion suggest conversion
for material reasons,[62] and certainly not in any considerable
degree as may be gathered from Caro. Even if the relative
wealth of the Marranos was greater than that of the Jews,
that alone could not serve as inducement for conversion, when
the economic position of the Jews was satisfactory and the
political position of the Marranos was so shaky.[63] The envy
of the gentiles' wealth — or, for that matter, of the converts' —
which Caro refers to in his statement, is therefore a phenomenon
which can hardly be associated either with the conversions
that followed the expulsion or with the situation directly preceding it. We must, therefore, conclude that the above remarks

[62] On the satisfactory economic condition of Spain's Jews in the
period preceding the Expulsion, we have the testimony of Don Isaac
Abravanel who estimates the total wealth of Spain's Jewry at the time at
more than 30 million gold ducats (*Ma'yenei ha-Yeshu'ah*, 1647, introduction,
p. 7b).

[63] Besides, as we have stated (see above, p. 140), we have no records
indicating a conversion trend in the seventies, and judging by all other
indications, we may rather conclude that, by that time, the conversion
movement had subsided, or was reduced to insignificance (and see above,
p. 140, note 13, and below, note 64a).

of Caro merely reflect the opinions prevalent among the Jews about the original motive of the Marranos' deflection. This view was nurtured by three factors: first, the age-old, deep rooted, opinion in Jewry that Jews leave the fold for ulterior, and mostly material motives; second, the commonly accepted notion since the beginning of the century which rightly associated the great conversion of the second decade with economic hardships, although these, as we have seen, were not the *only* reason; and third, the general affluence of the Marrano society, in which hostile popular opinion, usually substituting effect for cause, saw *the* reason for the conversion. The logic operating in such deductions can be briefly summarized as follows: "Many of the Marranos are extremely rich; hence they converted for attaining this richess; furthermore, it is for the same reason that they keep on in their state of conversion." This was the logic, as it appears to us, that underlay Caro's statements on the general relationship between "wealth" and "conversion," and the same logic, it seems, was also applied in his statement on the convert, who allegedly went over to Christianity "temporarily," until he amassed "wealth and fortune." This, in all probability, reflects the position of the crypto-Jews who must have excused themselves for their continued stay in Spain by their inadequate economic condition, and assured their detractors that, as soon as they amassed capital sufficient for settlement overseas, they would leave both Spain and Christianity. Here, too no doubt, we have the substitution of result for cause. The motive presented by such Marranos for their stay in Christendom was seen also as the motive leading to their initial change of faith.

But something else of relevant importance can be gathered from this statement. We have seen that, like Caro, Arama divided the renegades into two basic groups: the materialists and the speculationists; yet, when he attacked the Marranos generally, he pointed only to their materialism (their love of wealth) as the one God to which they *all* bowed.[63a] This, of course, could suggest that the "speculationist" type was not conspicuous among the Marranos in that period, and this, in turn, might

[63a] See above, p. 138.

mean that the Averroistic element, which was so pronounced
in Jewry during the second mass-conversion, and in the Marrano
camp as a whole after 1415, had greatly diminished in the
course of time. Nevertheless, since materialism was regarded
as one of the common signs of Averroism, and hence symptomatic
of the Averroistic convert no less than of the "appetitive"
one, no conclusive proof could be drawn from that statement.
Caro, however, tips the balance of the argument in favor of
the presumption above referred to. For had the "heretics" and
"agnostics" been numerous among the Marranos, had the
Averroists been a common type among them, even if merely in
the important upper classes, Caro would *not* have said that
this kind of convert had no following at all.[63b] Consequently,
what the statement conveys, as far as the *conversos* are concerned, is that the Averroistic segment among them had been
dissipated, or rather become insignificant.[64] This conclusion,
far from surprising, is in full accord with the general course of

[63b] Support for this deduction may be derived from the view of Providence
which Abravanel attributes to the *conversos'* ancestors, a view not at all com-
patible with the Averroistic concept (see below, pp. 181–182), and by his
presentation of the main reasons for conversion wherein "heretical" opinions
are not even mentioned (see below, p. 179). Regardless of the historic value of
these statements, they suggest that, in the 1480's, Averroism was not upheld
among the Marranos to a considerable extent.

[64] Baer, who had noticed and stressed Averroistic influences upon the conversions of 1412–1415, seems, nevertheless, to have limited these influences to
the intellectual and aristocratic circles, for he believes that, after the conversions, the "masses" retained their Jewish convictions for generations,
while the "upper and intellectual circles" remained Averroists and nihilists —
also for generations to come (*Toledot ha-Yehudim bi-Sefarad ha-Noẓrit*, p. 380).
As for the religious attitude of the "masses," the results of our inquiry thus
far, as we have seen, widely differed from Baer's views. And, as far as Averroism is concerned, we maintain that, while during the conversions of 1412–
1415, its influence, as we have shown, extended far *beyond* the above circles,
which were indeed its main supporters, in Christendom it was reduced to such
an extent that it could no longer serve as a mark of identification for any social
group (aristocracy *or* intellectuals). I must relegate to another place the discussion of the Christian sources upon which Baer seems to have relied in this
instance. But in trying to prove his point, he also uses one (!) Hebrew source
(dating from the 70's or the 80's of the 15th century), and that *does* belong to the
realm of this discussion. According to him (*ibid.*, pp. 371–372), Arama stated
that the intellectuals among the Jews did not differ, in their Averroistic

things. There was hardly any room for Averroism *per se* in the Spanish Christian society of the 15th century; it was neither tolerated nor expounded.[64a] And ideas without advocacy and propagation are bound to peter out.

It eventuates, then, that, according to Caro, most of the converts were originally materialists, subject to their lusts, and moral weaklings, and this, fundamentally, is also his view of the crypto-Jews among them of all sorts. Just as his attitude is extremely negative toward those who had *never parted with Judaism inwardly*, but actually kept living as Christians, so is he radically critical of those who *had been or become devoted to Christianity*, but then admitted to the truthfulness of Judaism, without changing their mode of life. Such a man believes that the troubles that befell him were a result of the fact that "God was not within him," and thus he assumes that "if he serves God in his heart and the foreign deity with his hands," he does no evil and deserves no punishment. He is, however, utterly mistaken. For it is about him that it was stated: "And I will surely conceal my face on that day for all the evil which he shall have wrought."[64b]

---

attitudes, from the intellectual among the converts; hence, the Marrano intellectuals were Averroistic. But the statement on which he relies does not say this at all. What Arama says is that "those people [i. e., the Jewish intellectuals] have followed, in this respect, our enemies and believe that the Law has already lost its sense and has no more real power of jurisdiction, *as is the view of all people who have left the fold* (*Ḥazut Qasha*, p. 43a). Arama, then, makes no distinction between intellectuals and non-intellectuals, between "aristocracy" and "masses," but simply states that in the eyes of *all* converts Jewish Law has no longer any sense and has lost its practical validity. Thus, if anything can be gathered from this statement, it is that *all* Marranos, of whatever social layer, had, in Arama's times, no regard for Judaism, a conclusion which rather denies Baer's other supposition that the *masses* of the Marranos (in contrast to the aristocracy) remained Jews at heart (and see also what I wrote on this in my *Don Isaac Abravanel*, p. 275, note 25).

[64a] Significantly, among the reasons which Isaac Arama gives for the refusal of the Jewish Averroists in his own time to go over to Christianity, is their awareness, according to him, of the fact that, *unlike in Jewry*, in Christendom they would be unable to propagate their theories, for the "other nations would not tolerate their views and words, or even an infinitesimal part thereof" (*Ḥazut Qasha*, p. 43a).

[64b] Deut. 31.16–18.

"The "concealment" of the "face" is repeated in the prophecy (הַסְתֵּר אַסְתִּיר) to indicate that this kind of sinner will undergo a double punishment, first, for his idolatry in mind and deed, and second, for his idolatry in deed only.[65] The second punishment will be more severe, since, according to Caro, the second stage of his behavior is more harmful, as his example is more likely to influence others.[65a] Thus he actually joins the category of those who converted to, or remained with Christianity for material reasons only.

We can safely assume that the reference here is to Marranos who, under the impact of the Inquisition, admitted their error in clinging to Christianity, but did not dare to return to Judaism and continued to behave religiously as Christians. Caro does not see in such a changed view any "return" or even a repentance. On the contrary, in accordance with his basic view of religious crime, he classes such a Marrano among the worst of criminals, for his example, suggesting a compromise solution, might actually dissuade others from a real "return." It would perhaps not be too far-fetched to assume that Caro saw in this type of "returner" — i. e., the "theoretical" and "platonic" one — a serious obstacle to the return movement. And it was perhaps this very phenomenon that led him to evaluate conversion — or rather, its two basic types — in a manner quite opposed to the traditional one. For what clearly counted most heavily for Caro were not the Marranos' *beliefs*, but their *performance*, and it is mainly on *this* basis that he judged them. Although his statements on the question, save for the last quoted, deal with the initial converts, and not with their descendants, near or remote, they nevertheless suggest that he doubted, or even denied, the Christian sincerity of most Marranos. But what he did not deny or question, but rather emphasized time and again, was their detachment from the Jewish way of life and their systematic performance of Christian ceremonial. The fact that he nowhere mentions, or even alludes, to secret or partial performance of Jewish rites, is, of course, also indicative of his conviction

---

[65] *Toledot Yiẓḥaq*, p. 131a.
[65a] *Ibid.*

that crypto-Jewishness was insignificant numerically and that, whatever the Marranos' real beliefs, all of them except for a tiny minority practiced the religion of the gentiles.

The fate that befell the Spanish Marranos is part and parcel of the divine punishment which was promised in the Law. "When the prophet said: '. . . and you [when in exile] shall serve other Gods . . . and become an astonishment, a proverb and a byword' (Deut. 28.36–37), he seems to have referred to what the gentiles say: 'These people did not convert because they believed in our religion, but because they were afraid that we might kill them. Actually, they observe neither our religion nor theirs.' And this is what was meant by *becoming a proverb and a byword*."[66] This is quite a different view from the one we have noticed about the "halters between two opinions," which indicated the inner wavering of the converts and was common, in all likelihood, among *Jews* in the period following the second great conversion. What Caro represents here, as he himself says, was an opinion current among *Christians*, and according to this, the Marranos did not waver either in belief or in action; they simply practiced no religion at all. This was certainly not the view of the Inquisition which maintained that, at least, a large segment of the Marranos practiced Judaism secretly. This was a view that originated *prior* to the Inquisition in Christian circles hostile to the Marranos, but was still upheld even in the nineties — among others, by some of the Inquisition's supporters.[67] Elsewhere we shall discuss the remarkable co-existence of such conflicting views about the Marranos among their enemies. At the moment we shall merely point out that, in presenting the view quoted above, Caro in no way subscribes to it. For while he does not seem to object to the assertion that the Marranos did not practice Judaism, he does object to the notion that they did not practice Christianity; and he expresses his own opinion very clearly via the verse he cites

[66] *Ibid.*, p. 127a.

[67] See, for instance, *El Alboraique*, in N. López Martínez, *Los judaizantes Castellanos*, p. 301; and see also Bernáldez, *Historia de los Reyes Católicos*, chap. XLIII, in *Crónicas de los Reyes de Castilla*, III, Madrid, 1953, p. 599a.

from Deuteronomy: *and you shall serve other Gods*. What he says, in effect, is that although the Marranos *do* practice a foreign religion ("serve other Gods"), this fact is not being recognized by the gentiles who loudly deny it, albeit they admit that the Marranos do not observe Judaism any longer. To judge from Caro's statement, the root of this denial was not observation of the bare facts, but the Christians' disbelief in the sincerity of the conversions that were motivated, as they claimed, by fear alone. Obviously, this is one of the complex punishments or "curses" to which the converts are subjected, and it is by no means the worst of them all.

Caro did not see any "return" except that which was effected under *heavy* punishment. He evidently believed that none of the Marranos who in his time sought refuge in Judaism would have ever done so were it not for the Inquisition. It is the suffering they had endured that stirred their hearts to repentance; and although such repentance was defective, he recommended that this consideration be overlooked and the returners be admitted to the fold.[68] As for the rest of the Marranos, who did not "return" at all, he regarded them "cut off from the tribes of Israel," destined for a terrible fate in this world and for total destruction

[68] *Toledot Yiẓḥaq*, p. 118b. Any other reference to repentance of the Marranos can hardly be found in this book. His discussion of repentance on p. 130ab clearly relates to the faithful Jews, and not to the converts. But when he speaks there of the true and full repentance to God under the impact of the punishment meted out to others (כשרואה שבאים עונשים על אחרים; p. 130 a), he may well refer by the "others" to the Marranos. It is to these "others" that he applies the statement of Zephaniah (3.6): "I have destroyed *goyim*. Their strongholds became desolate; their streets were laid waste, so that none passed by"; the word גוים might be taken by him to mean here not *nations*, but *gentiles*, by which he could allude to the Marranos whose desolate cities were a known fact, and served as an admonition to many Jews to avoid sinful thoughts concerning their faith. In like manner, his reference in this instance to the biblical verse (Deut. 30.7–8), "And God will put all these curses upon your [i. e. Israel's] enemies and haters who persecuted you, and you will repent and listen to God's voice" (*ibid.*, p. 130b), may have alluded to the Marranos, about whom he had already said that the full brunt of the curses enumerated in Deuteronomy would be directed against them (*ibid.*, p. 129b) and whom he had described as enemies of the Jewish people and persecutors of the Jewish faith.

in the world to come.[69] Thus, he gives expression to the feeling of "separation," of the distinctiveness of the Marranos both in faith and destiny, which was prevalent among Spain's Jews at the time.

Caro's views are partly echoed in the homiletic writings of the mystic Abraham Saba, a Spanish exile who first found refuge in Portugal and later escaped from there to Turkey.[70] Like Caro, Saba emphasized the duty to sanctify the Name, and like Caro, he found no extenuating circumstance that might justify conversion. But in Saba's writings this attitude is brought to sharper relief and, in fact, raised to the position of an Article of Faith. There is no sign here of the flexibility with which the rabbis treated the rule: "Let him be killed, and not transgress" (namely, not convert); nor of the advice given by Maimonides to convert under duress and then escape. Saba's position is definite and one sided. One should give his life, and not convert; one should suffer imprisonmnet, hunger, and torture — and not convert. In fact, to undergo the death of a martyr is, in his opinion, no torture, but the attainmnet of real peace through complete union with God.[71] This is what the Law meant when it said: "And teach them to your sons." For *this* is the lesson which you should teach them: "that they should die for the sanctification of His Name." This is what was meant in the statement: "and you will speak of these things while sitting at your home, when walking on the road, when you lie down, and when you get up." In all these places and times, you should talk of this alone, i. e., "prepare them to die for the sake of the Name."[72]

This adamant, uncompromising position on the issue of sanctification is in itself indicative of Saba's attitude toward the Marranos. But it becomes explicit in some of his statements which we shall consider forthwith. According to Saba, the crime of the convert consists in three sinful acts: first, in following

[69] *Ibid.*, p. 129b.
[70] On Saba see N. S. Libowitz, *R. Avraham Saba u-Sefaraw*, New York, 1936, and Alexander Marx' remarks, *ibid.*, pp. 39–40.
[71] *Ẓeror ha-Mor*, Warsaw, 1879, p. 15ab.
[72] *Ibid.*, p. 16a; and cf. Deut. 11.19.

foreign gods; second, in abandoning God; and third, in violating the Covenant. It is obvious that Saba lists these crimes according to their importance, for he says: "Had they abandoned God . . . but not followed the gods of the foreign lands, they would not have committed such a terrible evil, and God would have forgiven them."[73] But "since they committed that major sin, God will have no mercy upon them. Indeed, the verse says quite clearly: 'I shall conceal my face from them for all the evil that they have done, since they followed foreign gods'."[74]

Is there no remedy for these criminals? With all his hatred for converts of all kinds, Saba does not shut the door of salvation to the Marranos completely, but neither does he throw it wide open. True and complete repentance for the triple crime they committed is the only means by which they may hope to evoke God's mercy, but certainly nothing less than that. If a convert, in the midst of his tribulations, recognizes his sin in abandoning faith in God, but remains, de facto, in his former position; in other words, if the true faith is rekindled in his heart merely as a tenable theory, but is not accompanied by detachment from foreign worship and full-fledged performance of Jewish law, his repentance is not complete. Furthermore, even if he recognizes all the facets of his crime, confesses all of them and performs full penance "during the calamity," such repentance cannot be taken as sincere, for it was inspired by fear and suffering, not by a free development of his thinking.[75] The chances are that once the troubles are over, such penitents will revert to their evil ways.[76] Thus we see that Saba, who shared Caro's attitude toward the "theoretical," passive "returners," took a more severe position than the latter toward the *active* "returners."

---

[73] *Zeror ha-Mor*, p. 19a; cf. 66b.

[74] *Ibid.*, p. 59a. While those who sanctify God's name are assured, according to Saba, beatitude in the world to come (*ibid.*, p. 42a), those who follow the opposite path should better realize in advance the consequences. "If you do not want to worship God out of love," says Saba, "worship Him out of fear, for He is a jealous God who will not forgive the sin of conversion and who will wipe you off the face of the earth" (*ibid.*, p. 16a).

[75] *Ibid.*

[76] *Ibid.* ואולי אחרי שיצאו מן הצרה ישובו לקלקולם.

Obviously, he had no faith at all in the sincerity of the Marranos who returned to Judaism during their persecution by the Inquisition.

But there is another idea in Saba's writings which further displays the same attitude toward the Marranos and his view as to the probability of their "return." As he saw it, the converts had plenty of opportunities to repent before the final day of reckoning, but since they did not *want* to return, and held on to their evil ways, *"they will fall among the falling,"* and from this fall they will not arise. This is what was meant in the verse: "They will stumble at the time of the reckoning." For if they stumble *before* the day of reckoning, they may learn their lesson, repent and arise. However, if they stumble *at* the time of the reckoning, they cannot possibly arise, for there is no time left them for doing true penance. This is what was meant by the words *"the one who falls will fall,"* for there are sinners who are *essentially* "fallers," who refuse to "return" because of that, and who will therefore keep "falling" to their very end.[77]

In other words, if there was a chance for the Marranos to develop true repentance, it was not in the last stages of the punishment. Between the earlier, less severe punishments which they experienced from time to time, they had plenty of opportunities to reconsider their situation, repent, and return to God, but those who failed to use those opportunities, whose minds were not changed by the earlier travails (the "little stumblings"), cannot be trusted now in the day of wrath. It is now too late for them to achieve a state in which real repentance can develop. There are no longer interim periods between persecutions; nor would such people take advantage of such periods, for experience has shown that they are "fallers" by nature. Therefore, their fate is sealed.

Of course, Saba in all this may have intended to offer an answer to the obvious question that skeptics or cynics might have addressed to the faithful in those days. Why does not God help even those Marranos who, in their state of suffering and

[77] *Ibid.*, p. 37a.

torment, return to God and cry out to Him for help? But even if such an answer is implied here, what his thinking unmistakably reflects is an unusual coldness and aloofness toward the Marranos. And such an attitude, in the heyday of the Inquisition, can be explained only by the complete estrangement which had taken place between the Marranos and the Jews, by the widespread belief that the former wanted to remain Christians and that their return to Judaism could not be taken seriously. Not only does Saba see nothing good in the Marranos even at their stage of "return," but like a severe judge he keeps on enumerating all their crimes, one by one, and although theoretically he leaves them a narrow avenue to salvation, he actually closes to them every door of hope. Having refused to sanctify the Name or flee the country; having not only forsaken God, but worshipped a foreign deity; having persisted along their evil path throughout the long period of their conversion; having never considered repentance and "return" before the final day of wrath; having even now, in the last stage of their judgment, returned in but small numbers, and in some cases merely in thought and not in actual deed, their repentance cannot be judged to be true, and the extreme, relentless punishment due them cannot be witheld. Their cries to God from the midst of their tribulation cannot be heard now, for their crime was too heavy — in deed and in thought — and God's attitude toward such criminals *manifesting that kind of repentance* was clearly foretold: "*I shall conceal my face from thee.*"

Even more radical in his negative attitude toward the Marranos than Saba, is Joel ibn Shuaib, also a Spanish rabbi (of Aragonese origin) who lived in Navarre throughout the eighties, and possibly also in the nineties.[78] As far as Ibn Shuaib is concerned, the Marranos, or all those who abandoned the Jewish faith, are "wicked," while those who adhere to it are the "just" and the "righteous."[79] The main cause for conversion, as he sees it, is despair of Jewish redemption, the belief that the exile was

---

[78] His commentary on Psalms, in which this attitude is reflected, was written in 1489. See Steinschneider, *Cat. libr. hebr. in Bibl. Bodl.*, col. 1400, No. 5838.

[79] *Nora Tehilot*, Salonici, 1568, p. 155a.

destined to continue until the total extinction of Israel, and that God has abandoned His people totally and forever.[80] Such thoughts are considered by Ibn Shuaib not only sinful, but also vicious, and, in his opinion, the basic wickedness of the deserters is evinced in their attitude both toward God and His people. To prove their view about God's relationship with Israel, they entangled themselves in false arguments, for they hate the truth and the representatives of truth, and hence their animosity for the people of Israel.[81] Indeed, as far as Ibn Shuaib is concerned, the Marranos are worse than the Gentiles, "for their wickedness is greater in our eyes than that of the latter,"[82] and hence, their unusual punishment, which is commensurate with their crime. Their purpose was to escape the Jewish lot, the sufferings of the exile; but their sufferings will be tenfold greater. They wanted to free themselves from the yoke of exile, to take part in the lives of the nations among whom they settled, and therefore they segregated themselves from Israel; God will indeed segregate them from all the tribes of Israel, just as the smoke is separated from the fire.[83] Moreover, while Israel is compared to pure fire, and the converts to black smoke, the latter's punishment and ultimate fate will be effected by media related to these similes. They wanted to escape the "fire" of Israel; they will be punished by a consuming fire (i. e., the autos de fe of the Inquisition).[84] But their destruction is not meant to be physical only. It is to be absolute (אבדה החלטית), both in this world and the world to come.[85] Just as the smoke disappears into nothingness, so will they be wiped out completely. They believed that Israel was destined to eternal exile, to unremitting suffering and doom, but doom was ordained only for these criminals. When the time of redemption comes, they will have no share in it.[86] If they try to join Israel then, they will not be accepted. "God will reject them with both hands."[87]

[80] *Ibid.*, p. 155a; see also p. 158a.
[81] *Ibid.*, pp. 154–155.
[82] *Ibid.*, p. 155a (לְמָה . . . שרשעם נחשב בעינינו יותר מרשעת הגוים).
[83] *Ibid.*, p. 158a.
[84] *Ibid.*, p. 155a.     [85] *Ibid.*
[86] *Ibid.*, p. 158a.     [87] *Ibid.*, p. 155a.

It is difficult to find a stronger expression of hatred than that indicated here, except in the writings of Ibn Shuaib himself. For, he says, since "the wickedness of these people is greater in our eyes than that of the Gentiles," their fate should be a cause of great rejoicing.[88] To those who tried to restrain that happiness in keeping with the biblical maxim — "When your enemy falls, do not rejoice"[89] — he advocates the abolition of all restraint. The expression found in Psalms 68.4 that the "righteous will rejoice in the happiness" (ישישו בשמחה) came to indicate, in his opinion, that the righteous will have the right to be happy over the happiness caused by the fall of the wicked. "For there is a difference between being happy over something and being happy over happiness."[90] Indeed, this should be a joy without reservation, a joy not mingled with any worry over the violation of the precept above referred to: "When your enemy falls, do not rejoice." Thus the suffering of the Marranos in the days of the Inquisition evokes nothing in the heart of Ibn Shuaib, except a feeling of joy over the downfall of the "enemy," who now received what was due him. What happened to them arouses in him only the satisfaction engendered by the victory of the right cause. Indeed, what happened was the balancing of the scales of justice which was ordained and predicted long before, and the fulfillment of the prediction only proved to him the worth-whileness of the suffering on behalf of the Jewish faith. Those who left the fold "kicked" at these sufferings; now they know what real torment means.[91] No thought of mercy, toleration, or compassion appears to enter the mind of this author for the Marranos or for any part of them. He seems to brush completely aside the possibility of the repentance of a broken heart. The only future he can foresee for them is to rot forever in the "prison of the exile."[92] They chose to live in the "parched wasteland" of the gentiles; never will they get out from it. When redemption comes, they will naturally

[88] *Ibid.*
[89] Prov. 24.17.
[90] *Nora Tehilot*, p. 155a.
[91] *Ibid.*, p. 198a.
[92] *Ibid.*

like to join the redeemed, but "God will reject them with both hands."[93]

To be sure, Ibn Shuaib's attitude may have been influenced by the quality or quantity of the "return" movement in *his* time; but there must have been much more to it than the effect of the new phenomena. Only deep-rooted antagonism between the Jews and the Marranos could make a man of piety like this utter such words as above cited against those who formerly belonged to his people; and only a complete abandonment of Judaism by the Marranos, only Christianization and assimilation, coupled with a hostile treatment of Jews, typical of apostates at all times, could create such a feeling. The gulf between the two camps was evidently so deep, and so wide, that in the eyes of Ibn Shuaib it could not be bridged in any foreseeable future.

The general feeling of happiness over the "fall" of the Marranos, over the divine lesson they got for their betrayal, is also shared and fully justified by another remarkable preacher of that time, Joseph Jabeẓ from Portugal. Like ibn Shuaib, he, too, was trying to do away with the biblical admonition not to rejoice over the fall of one's enemy. In his opinion, that admonition was meant for *gentile* enemies, for cases like Haman, who plotted the destruction of the Jewish people, but it has no bearing on the case of converts. In the former instances, it was animosity between man and his fellow man; but the converts are enemies of a different sort. They are, first of all and primarily, the enemies of God, and only because of that are they *our* enemies as well: "For Thy haters, God, shall I hate, and with Thy rebels shall I quarrel."[94] This is why it was prescribed that even upon the death of a convert who is the nearest relative of one of the faithful, the latter should not bemoan his death, but on the contrary, be happy over it. "When the wicked are lost," says the Book of Proverbs, "it is a cause for rejoicing."[94a] And it is about such cases that the proverbialist also said: "The righteous will see their fall and rejoice."[95]

[93] *Ibid.*    [94] Ps. 139.21.
[94a] Prov. 11.10.
[95] Prov. 29.16; Jabeẓ, *Magen Avot*, Leipzig, 1855, p. 72b.

Jabeẓ sees in his time the fulfillment of the prophecy in Deut. 32.35: *"For vengeance and retribution is mine, for the day of disaster is near."* "How could the prophecy define as near," he asks, "something that was removed from its time approximately 3,000 years?" Jabeẓ therefore interprets the word "near" as meaning "near to understanding."[96] Indeed, it is in the nature of the divine order of the universe that God will rise and His enemies will disperse. By "enemies" here again are meant those who worship foreign deities, i. e., the Marranos, who were now subjected to God's wrath and vengeance. And there will be no relief for them. The wicked will be eliminated in the presence of God just as darkness disappears in the presence of light.[97] None of them will escape punishment, for the punitive measures will not be directed against the group as a whole, but against its individuals, one by one.[98] The existence of the "wicked" as a group will be tolerated so long as it contains potentially "righteous" (i. e., "returners") who may emerge from its midst. Once this potential is exhausted, their destruction will be immediate and complete.[99]

---

[96] *Ḥasdei Adonai*, New York, 1934, p. 45.

[97] *Ibid.*, p. 46.

[98] *Ibid.*, p. 52.

[99] *Ibid.*, pp. 50–51. The passage in *Ḥasdei Adonai*, pp. 57–59, in which Jabeẓ discusses the various forms of Jewish reaction to decrees of compulsory conversion, should not be taken as an expression of opinion about the Spanish Marranos generally, but rather about the *recent converts in Portugal in 1493–1497*, as well as those who converted in Spain to avoid expulsion (in 1492), or who, after experiencing the hardships of exile, returned to that country and converted. In the opening of this discussion, Jabeẓ says clearly: בדורו של שמד, שראינו בעינינו ובאזנינו שמענו רבים ונכבדים יראי שמים אשר יצאו מן הכלל (*ibid.*, p. 57), which indicates that the phenomena therein considered belonged to his own time. This is also evident from his remark on the martyrs (*ibid.*), among whom he mentions R. Simon Mimi, the Rabbi of Lisbon, who died as a sanctifier of the Name in 1497 (which, incidentally, proves that the publisher's statement, suggesting that the sermons in *Ḥasdei Adonai* were held in the "second year after the expulsion from Spain" [*ibid.*, p. 17], is erroneous). Further, we arrive at the same conclusion by what Jabeẓ tells us about the three kinds of converts that appeared in the "generation of *shemad*": those who hastened to convert; those who converted unwillingly and *returned*; and those who, although converted unwillingly,

## 3

Our survey of the homiletic and exegetic literature has now come to its last phase, i. e., the examination of the views on and attitude toward the Marranos of Don Isaac Abravanel. Having been, more than any of the authors quoted, personally familiar with the Marrano society; having been, as a Spanish courtier, closely associated with the Marrano aristocracy, his statements on the Marranos are of special significance, as they surely represent, at least to some measure, not only the voice of public opinion, but also his own impressions and observations. Yet the advantage is paralleled by a shortcoming which should not be overlooked. It is the influence of Abravanel's historic and messianic theories which dominated his general outlook. It affected his treatment of every subject related to the fate and future of Jewry, that of the Marranos forming no exception, but rather a typical example. Thus, while the statement of his contemporaries, above quoted, can be taken on the whole as indicating or representing the dominant public opinion of Spanish Jewry, those of Abravanel reflect, at least partly, his *own* opinion only. What is implied here is, of course, not an assumption that the view of the majority should necessarily be preferred to that of a minority, or even an individual. It is rather that public opinion, unless swayed by consistent, purposeful agitation, may well be based on the cumulative

later preferred to live as Christians (*ibid.*, pp. 58–59). That the first two types could fit into the *shemad* that took place in *his* time is quite obvious. But also the third group belonged — and could belong only — to the recent converts. His very formulation: "converts under coercion who later, in the course of time, assimilated willingly" (אנשים הומרו בהכרח ואחר־כך נטמעו ברצונם ברוב הזמן) shows that Jabeẓ referred here to converts of the *first generation*, and not to *descendants* of converts. Once we realize that the statement was made at least six or seven years after the Spanish expulsion and the first conversion wave in Portugal (1493), possibly even a few years after the expulsion from the latter country, his remark that these forced converts assimilated "in the course of time" (ברוב הזמן) is quite understandable. Six or seven years was a sufficient time to bring about a radical change in the attitude of some of the new converts, as it was for many of those who converted in 1391 (see above, pp. 87, 91–93).

effect of impressions and experiences shared by many, and, therefore, proven as sound and reliable as any testimony can be. On the other hand, statements made not by a mere observer, but by a dogmatic philosopher of history, are likely to be bent, colored and shaped to accomodate his particular philosophy. This is what we must guard against in Abravanel.

Indeed, his discussions on the Marranos reflect two streaks of attitudes, one in accord with Jewish public opinion, showing what the Marranos really were, or at least were generally held to be, and one in harmony with his theoretical proposition, indicating what he *wanted* the Marranos to be or, at least, to become in the near future. Strongly inclined toward a nationalistic outlook, Abravanel placed racial origin and historic relationship as factors determining national association even above religious fidelity. Accordingly, he was moved to consider the Marranos, who were bound to Jewry by both fate and origin, as belonging to the Jewish people. This does not mean, however, that he regarded them as Jews in every respect save the religious. Quite to the contrary, he stressed their belonging to a group apart in more ways than one. For besides the affinities that pulled the Marranos toward the historic orbit of the Jewish people, there were, as he saw it, several factors that made for separation between them and the rest of Jewry. In fact, Abravanel points out the deep gulf which runs across the whole of the Jewish people and divides it into two distinct parts, differentiated from each other like black from white. What rends these parts asunder, according to Abravanel, is not the faith or faithlessness by which they are identified, but qualities belonging to mentality and character which constitute the basic makeup of the nation. True, all Jews belong to the same stock; yet there are two types of this stock which are distinguished from each other like light from darkness.

Against the honesty and untrammeled loyalty of the one element, there stands the deceitfulness and disloyalty of the other, and hence the different names by which the Jewish people was designated at different times: *Jacob*, which etymologically alludes to cheating, signifies "that sect of the criminals of Israel who departed from the communion of the Law," while *Israel*, suggesting courage to fight for one's convictions, and *Yeshurun*, meaning honesty, signify that part of the people which represents the "real Jews" (*yehudim gemurim*).[100] The idea had already been suggested by Bibago,[101] but Abravanel brings it into sharper focus and clearly identifies the "Jacobites" with the Marranos and the "Israelites" with the faithful Jews.

These "Jacobites," these unfaithful ones, comprise according to Abravanel, the Marrano camp as a whole. We shall later see that Abravanel mentions an element of the Marranos that "performed some of the commandments secretly," but in discussing the group as a whole he couples "apostates" and "forced ones," recognizing no difference between them in terms of crimes committed or punishment deserved.[102] The "criminals of Israel," according to Abravanel, consist of "those who left the fold (community of religion) and assimilated with the gentiles, either forcibly, at the point of the sword, or lured by temptations, or in other manners."[103] The terms "apostates" and "anusim," which Abravanel repeatedly uses in one breath, seem to be employed as synonyms or, at most, as indications of the *original* position of the converts who consisted of these kinds, the "willful" and the "forced" ones. Yet as far as the Marranos of *his* time were concerned, it is clear that he placed

---

[100] Comm. on Isaiah, 44.1 and 44.21, Jerusalem, 1956, p. 213a and p. 215b.

[101] According to the latter, the names "Jacob" and "Israel" denote two distinct approaches to the divine teachings: "Jacob" represents that of questioning and investigation, "Israel" that of implicit faith (see *Ze Yenaḥamenu*, Constantinople, 1522, chap. II, p. 3d). According to Bibago, however, the former approach is legitimate and commendable, provided it is held within bounds (see above, p. 136, note 1).

[102] Comm. on Ezek., 20.33, pp. 520b, 521b.

[103] Comm. on Isa., Introd., p. 7b. פושעי ישראל is the term by which Abravanel commonly signifies the Marranos. Other terms used by him to define the whole group, parts of it, or members thereof are: אויבי ה' (Comm. on Isa., 1.24, p. 24a), רשעים (Comm. on Hos., 2, p. 228b), בוגדים (*ibid.*), רשעי ישראל (Comm. on Isa., 30.1, p. 169), מורדים (Comm. on Hos., 2, p. 228a; Comm. on Amos, p. 253d), פריצים (*Yeshu'ot Meshiḥo*, Königsberg, 1861, pp. 5a, 16b), האנשים הפושעים (*ibid.*, pp. 5a, 16b), אפיקורסים (*ibid.*, pp. 5a, 16b), פוקרים (*ibid.*, p. 5a), ארורים (*ibid.*), ממזרים (*ibid.*, p. 4b). Almost all of these terms were appellations for converts commonly used in medieval rabbinic and polemic literature.

them all in precisely the same category — evidently because
of the similar course ultimately followed by both groups. As
he saw it, the treacherous "Jacobite" quality has permeated
the Marranos of all origins, so that what he had before him
were the "sons of the wicked," those who were already "born
in gentilehood, and had no conception of Judaism and its
teachings" (שלא טעמו טעם תורה ונולדו בגייתם).[104]

This definition, however, was not an exhaustive one. For
besides the formal and ceremonial position, there was an inner,
emotional attitude that Abravanel detected among the Marranos
toward Israel and its faith. This was an attitude of deep hostility
toward Judaism which turned their departure from the Jewish
faith into an act of war — *perpetual* war — against Judaism
and the Jewish people. That this animosity, as Abravanel
saw it, was shared by all Marranos, or the overwhelming majority
of them, is evident from his statements about the "returners"
he saw or expected to see among them. In enumerating the
advantages to be gained by these "returners" upon their re-
embracing Judaism, Abravanel lists the following two contrasts
which are of especial importance to our discussion: "When they
were Jews," he says, "they performed the commandments, and
*now in their gentilehood, they do nothing of the sort. When they were
Jews, they were lovers of God*; now, in their gentilehood, *they are
enemies of God and deserters of His Law*."[105] Thus, we have here,
besides the clear-cut pronouncement that *the Marranos performed
none of the commandments*, amplifying the statements already
cited to this effect, also the very important declaration that
the Marranos were *enemies of God*, an appellation used for
outright apostates and converts distinguished by their Jew
baiting. Indeed, the same appellation is employed by Abravanel
for describing converts like Lorki, who, in their vicious campaign
against Judaism, "stormed the gates" of the Jewish camp.[106]

[104] Comm. on Isa. 44.5, p. 213a.
[105] *Ibid.*, p. 212ab: פושעי־ישראל שיצאו מכלל הדת אבותיהם ואבות אבותיהם
והם נולדו בגיות . . . משוללים ומרוחקים משש מעלות שהיו להם בהיותם בקרב ישראל . . .
[המעלה] השנית: ממעשה המצוות שהיו עושים ביהדותם . . . ועתה בגיותם ל א י ע ש ו ד ב ר
מ ז ה ; השלישית: שהם היו אוהבי ה' ביהדותם ועתה בגיותם היו א ו י ב י הש״י ועוזבי תורתו.
[106] *Yeshu'ot Meshiḥo*, p. 16b.

In other words, the general attitudes of the Marranos toward Judaism were identical, in his eyes, with that of their campaigning leaders, those "cursed criminals" who sought to "destroy" Jewry and wipe out its name from under the heavens.[107]

But Abravanel has something else to say on this particular matter. The campaign against Judaism by the converts, he avers, was not only an expression of hostility. It was also part of the converts' effort to show themselves "imbued with the new faith as real gentiles of Christian origin."[108] Now this endeavor to "appear as gentiles" was not made merely for external appearances. It was also part of an inner desire to *be* like the gentiles, and it was common not only to the arch Jew-baiters, but to the group as a whole. This point which Abravanel suggests repeatedly, is clearly expressed in the most significant statement he made concerning the Marranos.

We refer to Abravanel's commentary on Ezekiel 20.32–37 — a prophecy which he interprets as relating to the Marranos, their present condition and final destiny. There are several sections discernible in this commentary, and because of their special importance to our thesis, we shall fully present here the content of each.

Already in the opening of the first section, Abravanel states that the Marranos of all kinds, whatever their conversionist background and origin, *"intended to be like the rest of the gentiles,"*[109] and he proceeds to explain the purpose and logic that animated this intention. The purpose was to escape divine supervision and be relieved from the duty of keeping the Law. Consequently, they thought, they would escape the punishment ordained for the violators of that Law, the punishment which is actualized in the woeful lot of Israel in exile. On the other hand, by sharing the practices of the gentiles, they hoped to share their fate, too. Like the other worshippers of foreign deities, they thought, they would not be governed by divine providence, whose rigor was responsible for their calamity, but rather be subjected to

[107] *Yeshuʿot Meshiḥo*, introd., p. 4b–5a.
[108] *Ibid.*, p. 4b.
[109] Comm. on Ezek., 20.32, p. 519b.

the chances of fortune and to the fate decreed by the heavenly
bodies. In brief, they would no longer be the people of God,
the flock given to His care, and no longer be referred to by the
name of Israel. They wanted to be gentiles, plain and simple,
and expected to reap success in their activities as all gentile
nations do.[110]

Abravanel thus offers us decisive testimony not only as to the
condition of the Marranos, but also as to their *intentions*, their
inner attitude, which is so important for our thesis. Accodring
to him, the conversos *wanted to be gentiles*, or negatively speaking,
*refused to be Jews*, or to be associated with Jewry in any manner.
This is a far-reaching statement of fact, which Abravanel would
not have made unless he was certain of its veracity. As for
the *explanation* of this fact, that is, the *reasoning* of the converts
as he presents it, this is another matter. However logical and
plausible it might have appeared to him, it can hardly be
considered the *real* reason, and our sources from the period
of the mass conversion do not support it in any degree. What
we gather from these sources is, as we have seen, that the *denial*
of providence, both individual and collective, prompted the
conversion of many a Jew. Nowhere do we find them stating
or suggesting that *faith* in Providence, especially as limited to the
Jewish people, was a basic or related cause of conversion.[111]

[110] *Ibid.*; and cf., *Mashmi'a Yeshu'ah*, Lemberg, 1871, pp. 99–100.

[111] The idea may have originated with Arama, who suggested it
as an escapist conception favored by a fraction of the deserters. Arama
speaks here of יחידים, who did not deny Providence completely, but believed that the curses indicated in the Law applied only to those who held
on to the Law, even though in a limited measure. They assumed, therefore,
that by abandoning the Law *completely* they would free themselves from the
curses intended only for the partial violators of the Covenant. On the other
hand, these people believed that, having been associated with the *people*
of Israel, they would *benefit from the good promised Israel by Providence*
(*'Aqedat Yizḥaq*, V, p. 159b). Abravanel changes Arama's idea. In the first
place he applies it clearly to the *entire* Marrano group, and second, he attributes to the Marranos the conception that by removing themselves from
the sphere of the law, as well as of the Jewish people, they freed themselves from *the rule of Providence* with respect to both its curses and bless-
ings. According to him, it was their preference to be under the rule of the
heavenly bodies.

Thus what we have before us is an explanation proposed by Abravanel to suit his philosophy of history and his campaign of chastisement among the Marranos. By asserting that the Marranos miscalculated their course in their attempt to escape the sphere of Providence, and by pointing to the horrid results of that failure, Abravanel could illustrate his historiosophic view that Jewish history, and the fate of every Jew, was not man-made, or a plaything of nature's forces, but determined by God, His will and His justice. What is more, he could prove that while Providence, in the stricter sense, is limited to Jews only, the concept of Jewishness is not at all limited to religious behavior or religious faith, but to ethnic origin and historical association. Hence, no Marrano, however heretic, however idolatrous or assimilated, can ever escape the grip of Providence, or more precisely, of divine law and the judgment it assures one according to his conduct.[112]

Yet, in addition, the same theory served Abravanel as a rebuttal of the position taken by many who, under the impact of the expulsion and its aftermath, were prone to deny the existence of Providence and thereby justify conversion to Christianity or Islam. The additional lesson Abravanel sought to convey here was, accordingly, as follows: instead of being led to the denial of Providence by the suffering of the supposedly righteous Jews, one should rather be led to its reaffirmation by the greater suffering of the undoubtedly criminal Marranos. Thus, by using the Marrano example, he sought to stem the escapist aspirations which became rampant among the Jews of his time.

This becomes overwhelmingly clear in his further comments on Ezekiel's prophecy, which appeared to him to bear out this conception. It was indeed largely owing to these comments that his generation came to see in the following verses the consummate expression of its fate:

> That which comes into your mind shall not come to pass,
> In that you say: We shall be as the nations,

---

[112] See *Mashmi'a Yeshu'ah*, p. 101: אַף עַל פִּי שֶׁעָבְדוּ עֲבוֹדָה זָרָה לֹא יָצְאוּ מֵהַשְׁגָּחַת הַשֵּׁם יִתְבָּרַךְ וּמִסֵּדֶר הַנְהָגָתוֹ, וְלֹא יוּכַל אֶחָד מִצָּאנוֹ וְעִם מַרְעִיתוֹ לִהְיוֹת מֵעַם אַחֵר, לֹא יַחֲלִיפֵנוּ וְלֹא יָמִיר אוֹתוֹ הַזְּמַן טוֹב בְּרַע אוֹ רַע בְּטוֹב.

As the families of the countries, to serve wood and stone.
As I live, said the Lord,
With a mighty hand, and with an outstretched arm,
And with fury poured out,
Shall I be King over you.[112a]

As Abravanel sees it, the prophet alludes here to the different forms of divine treatment accorded to the various segments of the Jewish people in the Diaspora. By "mighty hand" he alludes to His rule over the faithful Jews who live in the realms of Christendom; by "outstretched arm" he refers to His rule over the Jews who live in the lands of the Moslems, while by "fury poured out" he indicates his treatment of the apostates and forced converts (המשומדים והאנוסים) who left the fold of our religion.[113] The latter were singled out for the *harshest treatment* because of the greatest severity of their crime — the total change of religion. Thus, the prophecy alludes to the fact that "although they and their descendants after them *endeavored to be like complete gentiles*, they did not achieve this aim. For the native peoples of the lands will always call them Jews, mark them as Israelites *against their will* (בעל כרחם), consider them as Jews and *falsely accuse them of Judaizing in secret* (ויעלילו עליהם שהם מתיהדים בסתר). [Indeed,] they will burn them for this in fire, all of which is indicated in the saying 'with a fury poured out'."[114]

Barring its mystic theological associations, the statement constitutes a historic document, and one of extraordinary significance. What it tells us is that the Marranos, who embarked upon the course of assimilation, sought to detach themselves so completely from Judaism, and attach themselves to thoroughly to other nations, that they would no longer be associated even with the name of Israel, and that this was no outcome of chance development, but, on the contrary, of a clearly conceived

---

[112a] Ez. 20.32–33.

[113] Comm. on Ezek. 20.32, p. 520a.

[114] *Ibid.*: אף על פי שישתדלו הם וזרעם אחריהם להיות כנויים
נמורים הנה לא יהיה כן, כי תמיד יקראו אותם משפחות הארצות יהודים ובשם ישראל
יכנו[ם] בעל כרחם ויחשבו אותם ליהודים ויעלילו עליהם שהם מתיהדים
בסתר ובאש שרוף ישרפו אותם על זה.

program, pursued systematically for generations, from the first, original, converts to their latest descendants. Moreover, it tells us that this was not a program embarked upon unwillingly, or under the external pressure of circumstance, but rather out of the Marranos' free will and, in fact, with their full determination, as is indicated by the word "endeavored" which is used here to describe the Marranos' action. Indeed, the only element of regret or unwillingness that appeared in this action, Abravanel adds, was connected not with the attempt itself, but with the failure of the Marranos to achieve their goal. It was free will, not coercion, that moved the Marranos away from Judaism, but it was coercion, not free will, that brought home to them the realization that they were regarded as Israelites after all. Thus, as the irony of history would have it, they who so systematically abandoned all practices of Jewish religion, are now *maligned* that they perform Judaism in secret. They who made every effort to assimilate, so that their relationship with Israel be forgotten, are constantly regarded as Jews and so designated to their great vexation and dismay. As Abravanel saw it, the assimilation of the Marranos into the Christian society would never be accomplished. This has been proven by the Inquisition. Christian society forces them out of its midst by means of fire and sword, "with fury poured out."

But Abravanel makes here another important statement which indicates the extent of the Marranos' assimilation, as well as the nature of the Inquisition's persecution. He says: "And since [the prophet foresaw that] they *would assimilate with the gentiles and intermarry with them and spread within their countries*, he said, and I shall take you out from the midst of the nations."[115] On top of the *religious* assimilation of the Marranos, that is, their failure to carry out the commandments and their worship of foreign deities, their fusion with the gentiles was also expressed socially, ethnically and geographically. The reference to the Marranos' intermixture with the gentiles is to be found in the word יתערבו בגויים which indicates, in its Hebrew connotation,

---

[115] *Ibid.*:  ולפי שהם יתערבו בגויים ויתחתנו בהם ויפוצו
באִרצותם, אמר: והוצאתי אתכם מן העמים.

that they appeared to be blended with the gentile society; their ethnic assimilation is expressed by the statement, "they intermarried with them," which offers another testimony to the effect that intermarriage between Marranos and Old Christians was much more widespread than what may be gathered from the Responsa of some non-Spanish rabbis;[116] and the geographic interspersion is alluded to in the words "they *dispersed* within their countries."[116a] It appears that instead of the close settlement which was generally practiced by the Jews in the Middle Ages, both for purposes of defense and other communal needs, religious and educational, the tendency noticed among the Marranos was to detach themselves more and more from the Marrano community and live *"dispersed* among the gentiles."  This tendency, however, did not eliminate, especially in the big cities, the main Marrano groupings which remained identifiable as distinct social bodies, but it must have been quite apparent, particularly among the upper crust of the Marranos, where intermarraiage must also have been more common.  Here again Abravanel sees the contrast between the aims and policies of the Marranos and their actual historic fate.  For while assimilation was many-sided and *deep-rooted*, so that the Marranos appeared to become part and parcel of the nations amongst whom they lived, they were nevertheless *uprooted* from their midst in a manner as thorough as was their assimilation.  Indeed, the development

---

[116] Intermarriage of Marranos with gentiles is repeatedly presented by Abravanel as a typical phenomenon of Marrano life.  See his *Comm. on Deut.* 30.1 (p. 9c): שיקבצם מכל העמים להיותם מעורבים בהם ומתחתנים בהם . . .; and see also *Mashmi'a Yeshu'ah* — for instance, p. 100 (שהם התערבו בגוים ויתחתנו בהם).  Furthermore, in his attempt to attract the Marranos to Judaism, Abravanel assures them that, when they part with Christianity, they will not have to leave behind "the children they have begotten from the daughters of the gentiles" (הבנים אשר יולידו מבנות הגוים).  The repetition of this assurance by Abravanel, undoubtedly for the sake of emphasis, suggests its importance for a large number of Marranos.  As a matter of fact, these assurances appear to have been directed to the Marrano group as a whole.  See *ibid.*, p. 13.

[116a] The matter is further indicated by Abravanel in the following statement: אמנם על הכת הב' מאשר יצאו מכלל הדת מפני אנסם . . . אמר [רב' ל', ג'] שיקבצם במקום שהיו מפוזרים ומפורדים בהם [בגויים] ומתחתנים עמהם (*ibid.*, p. 12).

appeared to him so strange and inexplicable by the ordinary course of events that only a supernatural intervention could suggest its rationale.

According to Abravanel's conception of history, all supposedly natural historic developments, the links in the chains of cause and effect, were actually supernaturally ordered or manipulated by divine will.[117] On the other hand, God's plans for mankind are so executed as to *appear* in most cases not as miracles, but as parts of a natural, causal development. The eradication of the Marranos from among the nations, inherently opposed to all logical expectations, was carried out, by God's will, through man's psychological chains of reaction. God set and triggered the mechanism of supernatural intervention, and the rest was an inevitable process, part of ordinary natural history. In pondering the mysterious fate of the Marranos, Abravanel was searching for that moment in which the hand of God was manifested, for that miraculous, divine act which started this new, fantastic course. And as he saw it, the "miracle" was manifested through a spiritual phenomenon which appeared within the Marrano group; and this phenomenon, plus the development that ensued, is described by him as follows: "For in the end of days, the prophet foresaw, *God would awaken* in the hearts of the Marranos (*anusim* and *meshumadim* [i. e., apostates]) a desire to return to Him *and perform some of the commandments secretly*; This would rouse the gentiles to persecute them and falsely accuse them: 'You are judaizers, and do not carry out the laws of the gentiles.'[118] Then, in a burst of wrath and cruelty, the gentiles would burn them by the thousands, as we have seen with our own eyes in this our own time in the kingdoms of Spain. In turn, these actions of the gentiles would stir the Marranos (*anusim*) to flee their countries of residence, get out from the midst of the Christians and save their lives by migrating to distant lands. Thus their gathering from the lands of their dispersion would be a result of compulsion and

[117] On Abravanel's conception of history, see my *Don Isaac Abravanel*, pp. 130–149.

[118] Comm. on Ezek., 20.32–37, p. 520b: ‏להעליל עליהם לאמור: אתם מתיהדים ואתם לאמור‎ . . .
‏ואת דתי הגוים אינכם עושים, וישרפו אותם לאלפים ולמאות באכזריות חמה ושטף אף.‎

fear of death. God's rule over them would be manifested through the fury poured out over them."[119]

This statement which, like the previous one, is replete with historic evidence, must be carefully scrutinized. It should be noticed, in the first place, that the "awakening" among the Marranos to "return to God" was a new, sudden development that took place at the "end of days." Their pro-Jewish element at the time of the Inquisition was, then, according to Abravanel, not an established, traditional phenomenon dating from the early periods of the conversions, but something new that appeared at the "end of days," that is, according to his eschatological conception, *in his own generation*.[119a] In other words, it appeared *after the old Jewish underground had died out to all intents and purposes*. This is why it is here that he saw the workings of God's hand, the historic miracle. For at the very time that Judaism among the Marranos seemed to be extinguished and covered with ashes, flickers of the old fire suddenly appeared, with the power to cause a huge conflagration.

By "conflagration" is meant here, however, not the spread of Judaism, but the outburst of anti-Marrano hatred to an extent and with a force unimagined before. The acts of the few Marranos who leaned toward Judaism led the gentiles to accuse the entire group as consisting of Judaizers and violators of the Christian laws. This is why here, too, Abravanel uses the word להעליל ("accuse falsely") to describe the Christian charges against them. For these charges were not pressed against the few, perhaps the isolated crypto-Jews, but against many thousands of Marranos — in fact, against all of them — and to this extent they were groundless and libelous.[120] Furthermore: just as Abravanel said, as we have noticed, that the conversos "endeavored to be like real gentiles" and that the name Israelite was foisted

---

[119] *Ibid.*

[119a] See my *Don Isaac Abravanel*, pp. 216–226.

[120] Abravanel brands the charges of the Inquisition against the Marranos as false also in a third place: עוד ראינו שהתעוללו הגויים כנגד האנוסים, היוצאים מהדת, בזמננו זה באמרם שלא היו שומרים דתם כראוי והיו דנים אותם לשרפה למאות ולאלפים (*Comm. on Isaiah*, 43.6. The word התעוללו must, of course, be interpreted in light of Psalms 141.4: שהתעולל עלילות ברשע. It fits the full meaning of *'alila*, which is a false accusation concocted with a vicious intent.

upon them, so he claims that their flight from their native lands, their emergence from among the Christians, and consequently their return to God resulted from "compulsion and fear of death," i. e. were an outcome of the Inquisition's terrors. *No element of their own free will was involved in this crucial development.* It was only through the "fury poured out" that God's rule was again established over these gentilized Jews.

Thus, this remarkable statement of Abravanel offers direct confirmation of our thesis that the trend toward Judaism among the Marranos, noticeable after the establishment of the Inquisition, was not the product of an underground movement which was merely forced to the surface by the Inquisition, but rather the product of the Inquisition itself; it was a fundamentally new phenomenon without roots in the past or even in concealed Jewish feelings, and entirely an outgrowth of external pressures. The Marranos, catapulted out of Christendom, were a kind of "forced converts" in reverse. Just as their forefathers had *joined* Christianity unwillingly and solely under the fear of death, they now *left* it unwillingly and solely under the same fear. Their re-embracing of Judaism at this stage was really not a matter of choice, but rather of choicelessness, the result of the absence of any other — or at least preferred — alternative.

Abravanel, who views the Marranos' return in a manner we may term "realistic," is thus in accord with the other Spanish sages whose views on this issue were cited above. Like the latter, he, too, sees the "returners" as "penitents out of fear," but his attitude toward them is quite different. That this attitude was dictated by practical considerations can hardly be doubted; in any case, it should be pointed out, it was in line with his views. Since both the punishment and the return of the Marranos were, as he saw it, part of God's plan, there could be no room for objection to their "return." For they returned in the only way they could possibly do so; therefore, even though they turned to Judaism only under the impact of suffering and terror, once they came back to God, they were entitled to His pity and forgiveness.[121] What is more, they must be rated among

---

[121] Comm. on Ezek., 20.32–37, p. 520b; the same view of repentance out of suffering is expressed in Comm. on Isa., 30.18, p. 157a.

the most faithful and righteous, for they share with the latter
an equal chance to live to the very day of Redemption and
*enter the promised land.*[122]

Abravanel thus parts company with the harsher critics, like
Ibn Shuaib, who denied the Marranos a share in the Redemption
and saw them as cut off from the Jewish people forever. "In the
future Redemption," says Abravanel, "there will return to God all
the criminals of Israel who left the fold and assimilated among the
nations, either forcibly, at the point of the sword, or *through
temptation* and in other ways. In the end of days they will regret
their deeds and return to the God of their Fathers."[123] The
religio-national philosophy of Abravanel, no less than the
developments he witnessed in his time, led him to believe in
the ultimate reunification of the New Christians with the Jewish
people. Consequently, he also believed in their ultimate equaliza-
tion with the faithful Jews.

And yet, there is a passage in Abravanel's writings which shows
that he could not ignore the prevailing view in the matter and
could not help differentiating between Jews and "returners,"
if not in terms of religious association, at least in other fundamentals. We refer to the consideration of the Marranos as
"gentiles" and of the returners as "proselytes," a consideration
which, as we have seen, was common among Spain's Jews

---

[122] *Ibid.*, 43.6, pp. 206b–207a.

[123] *Ibid.*, introd., p. 7a. The same idea is also expressed in *Mashmi'a Yeshu'ah*,
p. 13 (ובא: הנביא כמאמר הדת, מכלל ליוצאים וגם יעקב זרע לכל תהיה העתידה הגאולה
מפשעם וידאנו שישובו ישראל פושעי הם פשע שבי כי . . . ביעקב פשע ולשבי גואל (לציון,
and see also *ibid.*, pp. 48, 97. The all-inclusive generalization — זרע לכל
הכלל מן ליוצאים וגם יעקב — must nevertheless be considered as an extreme
expression which was modified by Abravanel himself to mean: all the
Marranos except the die-hard rebels, who will not change their ways
even under the heaviest punishment. These "wicked of Israel" will not live
to enter the "land of God," for they will be wiped out during the wanderings
and travails that will precede the coming of the Messiah (*ibid.*, pp. 42, 67
[המשיח וחבלי הטלטול בזמן יכלו ה' אויבי], 68, 100, 101, 160). What is more,
Abravanel assures these rebels that, at the time of the Resurrection, they
will be brought back to life only to be subjected to the eternal torment of
hell (*ibid.*, pp. 74–75). These repeated announcements about the frightful
punishments awaiting the Marranos who will persist in their Christian
way of life may have also been intended to serve as inducements for the latter
to hasten their return to the fold.

in the period under review. Of course, Abravanel, who so often stressed the racial selectivity of the Jewish people, and who repeatedly found it necessary to point to the racial intermingling of the Marranos with the gentiles, could not make light of this issue. His strong ethno-nationalistic feeling must have rebelled against the recognition of returning Marranos, whose Jewish origin could be often questioned, as ordinary "penitents" and not as "proselytes." But this feeling conflicted with his other concept that all attempts of assimilation were futile, that none of "God's flock" could become a member of another people, and that either those who were led astray, or their descendants, however remote, "would be returned to the herd from which they were taken."[124] This is, he comments, why the prophet said "and I shall take you *out* from amidst the nations."[125] It is God who brings the Marranos back to Israel; He knows who belongs to His flock; and thus the very fact of the "return" proves, in a way, the ethnic Jewishness of the returners.[126] True, Isaiah spoke of "proselytes" at the time of the redemption, but the Sages have already clearly established that proselytes would not be accepted in the days of the Messiah. Hence, he averred, "what was meant by proselytes were the criminals of Israel whose fathers and forefathers left the fold of religion and who themselves were born in gentilehood and returned to God. These are the proselytes of righteousness who will attach themselves to Israel at the time of the redemption."[127]

Abravanel thus gives a left-handed endorsement to the persistent claims of his contemporaries that the "returners" should be regarded as *proselytes*. True, in his basic presentation of the reasons by which he justifies this appelation, he cautiously avoids mentioning the ethnic argument. All he indicates in this connection is that, while the Marranos should be considered members of the Jewish people, they may nevertheless be called

---

[124] Comm. on Ezek., 20.32–37, 520b; and cf., *Mashmi'a Yeshu'ah*, p. 44a.

[125] Comm. on Ezek., 20.33.

[126] Cf. *Mashmi'a Yeshu'ah*, p. 74: ואמר שמאותם בני ישראל שיביאו מהארצות הרחוקות שהיו מעורבים בגוים ונשקעו בתוכם גם מהם יקח להיות כהנים ולויים ולא יחושו אם נמכרו לעבדים ונעשו גוים על צד האונס. ואמנם איך ידע זה אין ספק שיהיה ברוח הקודש.

[127] Comm. on Isa., 44.5, pp. 212–212b.

"proselytes" because they were immersed in "gentilehood" for generations — "gentilehood" meaning here a state of non-Jewishness from a religious point of view. Yet, in the final phase of the discussion he repeatedly hints at another development which is related to the same issue: "The offspring of the Marranos who are assimilated among the gentiles (נטבעו בגויים) will cause, by their return, the proselytization of many gentiles."[128] Does Abravanel, in speaking here of "gentiles," refer to Christians of pure gentile stock? In this case, however, he would contradict his own position regarding the inacceptability of "proselytes" at the time of redemption. Possibly he refers here to those Marranos whose fathers were Jewish and mothers gentile, and yet were equally presecuted by the Inquisition and could find refuge only in Judaism and the Jewish people. The term נטבעו, suggesting *ethnic fusion*, which he uses on this occasion, offers some support to such an assumption; and, as we have seen, Abravanel advocated the acceptance of the sons of Marranos born to gentile mothers.[129] In any case, his description of the Marranos as "born in gentilehood" and as deserving, upon their return, the title of "proselytes," although they had sprung from Jewish stock, further supports his general position that the Marrano camp as a whole was an assimilated camp and that only under the hammer blows of the Inquisition, part of it was "awakened" to return to God.

This is Abravanel's basic view of the Marrano group as a whole and, as we have seen, it generally accords with the dominant opinion expressed in the works of other Spanish Jews of his generation. What is more, the statements on the subject which we have culled from his writings amplify and fortify that opinion, since in several aspects they are more elaborate and far-reaching than those made by contemporary Jewish authors.

There are, however, passages in Abravanel's writings which, at least on their face value, do not tally with the above views. They contain expressions about the Marranos which give us the impression of a different type of convert, or at least modify the image we have gained thus far in one or two important aspects.

---

[128] *Ibid.*, p. 213b.
[129] See *Mashmi'a Yeshu'ah*, pp. 12–13; cf. above, p. 188, note 123.

For the sake of both correctness and completeness, these isolated statements of Abravanel, apparently contradicting the bulk of his pronouncements, must be reconciled or explained away, in any case, they cannot be overlooked.

Of these apparently "contradictory" statements, the one to be examined first is included in his commentary on Ezekiel 5.7–9 — a prophecy whose beginning is somewhat obscure, although its general contents is quite clear. It runs as follows: "*Because your rabble* [*is worse*] *than the nations* (יען המנכם מן הגויים)[130] that are around you; because you have neither walked in my statutes, nor kept my ordinances, nor have you acted in accordance with the ordinances of the nations that are around you; therefore, said the Lord, I shall rise against you and punish you severely in the sight of the nations. I will do within you that which I have not done, and the like of which I will not do any more, because of all your abominations."

In commenting upon this harshest of prophecies, Abravanel expresses his belief that "Ezekiel prophesied here about the Jews who left the fold of religion at the time of the persecutions as well as about their offspring who today are called *anusim* (forced ones) and who do not keep the ordinances of God, his laws and instructions" because they "fear the Gentiles may kill them" for this as "heretics and Epicureans," and likewise do not perform the laws of the Gentiles because they do not believe in the religion of the latter.[131] It is of this that it is said here: '*because your rabble is worse than the Gentiles.*' What is meant here is that, contrary to the times of happiness in which you were the choice of all nations, you now made yourselves rabblelike and vile people more than any of the nations which are round about you; and since, having left the religion, *you have not followed the laws which I decreed, either those whose motivations can be established by our reason, or those whose motives are unknown to us*, and, on the other hand, although you have made yourselves part of the nations of the land, you did not observe the laws of those nations, and therefore you are considered heretics and Epicureans

---

[130] The translation is according to Abravanel's interpretation. See below, the following paragraph.

[131] Comm. on Ezek., 5.7, p. 475a.

and disbelievers in both religions—i.e., in the teachings of God and
of the gentiles as well—therefore, said the Lord, I shall rise against
thee, etc." [132]

What should be pointed out, in the first place, is the inconsistency apparent in this statement. On the one hand, it is stated
that the Marranos did not observe Jewish law out of fear of the
Gentiles, implying that they actually believed in the Jewish
religion but dared not follow it in practice because of fear;
on the other hand, however, they are rated as heretics and
Epicureans and, more particularly, disbelievers in *both* religions,
*in Judaism as well as in Christianity.* The inconsistency may
perhaps be resolved by the assumption that, according to
Abravanel, *real* faith should be paralleled by performance, and
since the appropriate parallel was missing, the Marranos must
be judged as faithless and heretics, even though their failure
to observe Jewish law was apparently prompted by fear alone.
The same applies to their attitude toward Christianity; here,
too, their faith must be judged by their performance; and it is in
the claim that they ignore the "laws of the gentiles" because
they do not believe in their religion, that the problematic side
of the statement is contained. For it contradicts other passages
of Abravanel wherein he clearly and emphatically states that the
Marranos *did* worship a foreign deity, did their best to follow the
gentile's religious pattern, and even tried to outdo the Christians
in their devotion to Christianity and opposition to Judaism.

This contradiction can possibly be resolved if we assume that
the observation referred to relates not to the *entire* Marrano group,
but to a certain element within it, and this assumption gains
some plausibility from the fact that Abravanel, in this instance,
uses the term "anusim" — to be sure, with an obvious indication
on his part that the term is a misfit (אלה הנקראים אנוסים),
and yet, without alignment to the term *meshumadim* (apostates)
as he usually does when discussing the Marranos. Now, if
he did refer only to those who were still considered *anusim*
(forced converts), we could draw the conclusion that crypto-
Judaism in his time assumed a completely "platonic" character,

132 *Ibid.*

devoid of any practice of Jewish law, while its inward attitude toward Christianity was expressed in avoiding Christian ceremonial whenever possible. If this assumption is correct, we must conclude that Abravanel saw the Marrano camp as composed basically of *two* elements, *devout* and *fictitious* Christians — i. e., of *apostates* (משומדים) and *anusim*; but even so, it must be emphasized that he did not consider the latter element as devoted to Judaism either, that he considered them "heretics and Epicureans and disbelievers" in Judaism no less than in Christianity, and, above all, that he stressed their detachment from Jewish law, their failure to perform *any* of the commandments (note his emphasis: *"neither the commandments whose reasons are clear to us, nor those whose motives are unknown"*). All this represents, of course, a drastic repudiation of the assumption that the Marranos contained an underground so devoted to Judaism that it secretly and persistently practiced Jewish law at the risk of property, freedom, and life itself.

Yet it is of course also possible, and seemingly more likely, that what we have here is a *fleeting reflection about the Marrano group as a whole.* We have noticed that the same view of the Marranos is found in Isaac Caro, wherein it is presented as an opinion commonly held among gentiles.[132a] Thus, what we have before us is a view of Christian origin, which Abravanel, like Caro, may have adopted temporarily. And we say "temporarily," because the statement forms an exception and an incoherency in Abravanel's dominant view of the Marranos, as repeatedly expressed and as presented above.

Whatever the correct answer to the above query, attention must be called also to another "exception" which discusses the Marranos in the same vein. Referring to the prediction of the Amora Isaac Napaḥa in San. 97a — to wit., that "The son of David (i. e., the Messiah) will not come until the entire Kingdom is afflicted with heresy"[133] — Abravanel says that the word "heresy" mentioned therein alludes to the position of the Jews who left the fold under "compulsion" and "abandoned God." "Since they were Epicureanized and not integrated in

[132a] See above, p. 167.
[133] Cf. Sotah, ix.15.

any religion (ולפי שנתפקרו ולא נטבעו בשום דת), the Sages, in discussing them, "employed the term heresy." However, the
words "the *entire* kingdom" indicate that the statement may
revolve upon the gentile world, or upon the "wicked kingdom" in particular. It may indeed refer to Rome (Christendom) in as much as it foretells the "appearance of many heretics within their faith, as we see with our own eyes this very
day in the Kingdom of Spain, where the heretics and Epicureans
are numerous in all its lands and where they are burned for heresy
by the thousands." "Also," adds Abravanel, "all the priests
and bishops of Rome (i. e., Christendom) in our time are addicted
to avarice and bribery and do not care about the prohibitions
of their religion, for heresy has shone upon their foreheads."[134]

This statement throws some light on the question before us from
a different angle. To be sure, here, too, the Marranos are designated as "heretics" to both Judaism and Christianity. Yet as
far as their "heresy" toward the former is concerned, it is not
expressed merely in disregard of the commandments, as may be
gathered from the previous statement, but also in *an ideological
attitude which negates the fundamentals of the Jewish faith.* All
this is indicated by the word נתפקרו which, although we have
rendered it by "Epicureanized," really does not refer here to
Epicureanism, but to the specific medley of views and attitudes
which had typified Jewish apostates at all times.[134a] As for the
"Christian" heresy of the Marranos, Abravanel's view of it may
be gathered from his remark: לא נטבעו בשום דת, which may mean

---

[134] See *Yeshu'ot Meshiḥo*, p. 34a; cf. *Ma'yenei ha-Yeshu'ah*, XII.6 (ed. 1647,
p. 87b).

[134a] This is amply evidenced by Abravanel's use of this word. Thus he
describes Joshua Lorki, leader of the conversionists, as ראש הפוקרים (*Yeshuot
Meshiho*, introd. p. 5a). Needless to say, Lorki propagated not Epicurean, but
Christian views, yet from a Jewish standpoint he misinterpreted the Law and
the meaning of the prophecies, and thus could be defined as a "heretic" (מ' י ן).
That the verb פקר, as employed by Abravanel, implied not only a practical,
but also a theoretical attitude can be further proven by other quotations, as
for instance, the following: . . . [עם ה.הגדות הזרות" על המשיח שבתלמוד ובמדרש]
עמהם אויבי ה' פריצי עמנו ה מ ת פ ק ר י ם שות שתו השערה ובהתוכחם עם חכמי ישראל זה לנו
ימים, ומהם עשו האנשים הפושעים כוונים לפסילי אלהיהם ותערועי אמונותיהם, כמו שבאו
זכרונותיהם משלי אפר ב ס פ ר י פ י ק ו ר י ה ם אשר חיברו (*ibid.*, p. 16b).

that the Marranos were not "immersed" in Christianity, or were not truly "saturated" or "imbued" with it. Perhaps he thought that this fact was responsible for their alleged failure to abide by the "laws of the nations," of which he spoke in the afore-cited statement,[134b] without telling us, however, which laws he had in mind. On the other hand, in his reference to the "priests of Rome," whom he also regards as "heretics," Abravanel does specify *some* laws which were transgressed by the former; but these laws, while certainly Christian, clearly belong to the general moral code. May we gather from the association of the Marranos with the "priests of Rome," that the laws violated by them were likewise *moral*, or at least partly moral as well? If this was the view held by Abravanel, he may have echoed here the Christian anti-Marrano campaign, which stressed the depravity of the *conversos*, as well as prevailing *Jewish* opinion about the basic immorality of all converts. But this, of course, could not at all be tantamount to the "heresy" attributed to the Marranos by the Inquisition.[134c]

Yet even more problematic than the above statements seems to be another reference to the Marranos (again: והם הנקראים היום אצלנו אנוסים) in his *Announcer of Salvation*, where they are described as "violators of the laws, intermingled with the gentiles, followers of their practices,"[135] and yet Jewish in their inward faith.[136] Considered in itself, this statement suggests that

---

[134b] See above, p. 193.

[134c] It must of course be realized that when Abravanel speaks, in this as well as in the afore-cited statement (see above, pp. 191–192), of "heretics and Epicureans" in *Christendom*, he refers to religious offenders different from those who were signified by the same appellations in *Jewry*. The apostate from Judaism and the Judaizer represented, in effect, *antagonistic* "heresies," while the *Epicurean* Marrano, when seen from a Christian standpoint (perhaps, according to Abravanel's definition [*Rosh Amanah*, Königsberg, 1861, p. 30b], as a denier of God, and thus *more* radical than the Averroist), may have similarly been at variance with the Jewish *poker* (who did not deny God or even Providence; see above, note 134a). In keeping with common practice, however, Abravanel may have used here the term אפיקורסים as a mere synonym of מינים, without attaching to it any special import. And cf. above, p. 125, note 107.

[135] *Mashmi'a Yeshu'ah*, p. 11.

[136] *Ibid*.

Abravanel discusses here the group of *real anusim* within the
larger body of the Marranos, especially since he emphasizes
that their foreign practices are a result of coercion (והם במעשיהם
הנָכרים אשר יעשו אנוסים ומוכרחים), while "their good deeds are
performed secretly."[137] Further references to the *anusim* in
the same work, however, seem to identify them with the Marrano
body as a whole;[138] but the contents of these additional statements
is so contradictory to the above quoted that we must conclude
that Abravanel again expressed here a tentative opinion, most
favorable to the Marranos from the Jewish standpoint, or else,
was loosely employing the same term (*anusim*) for different
components of the Marrano group. In any case, in the additional
statements about the "second sect," Abravanel no longer
describes them as secret Jews whose "heart is confirmed in
the faith in God," but as people whose heart must be
"circumcised," who follow the practices of the gentiles not out
of compulsion, but of intention, who intermarried with the
gentiles and were "born upon their knees," so much so that
at least many of their offspring have lost track of their Jewish
lineage.[139] What is more, according to these statements, the
Marranos were comprised by the following three segments:
those who returned *inwardly* only, and would not perform the
commandments out of fear; those who would return after further
punishment and wandering from land to land (in the "desert of the
nations"); and those who will never return. The latter are the
real "criminals and rebels," the "enemies of God," who are
destined to destruction in the "wilderness" of the gentiles

---

[137] *Ibid.*

[138] *Ibid.*, pp. 12, 13.

[139] *Ibid.*, p. 12: ורמז עוד באמרו ומל ה' אלהיך וגו' על כת פושעי ישראל
האנוסים שזכרתי, שעם היות שיולדו על ברכי הגוים וילמדו
ממעשיהם, הנה הש"י ימול לבבם הערל וגם ערלת בשרם. The statement,
which reflects Abravanel's hopes for the ultimate return of the Marranos,
incidentally testifies also to the "validity" of the charge, hurled against the
latter by their denouncers, that circumcision was common practice among
them. And see also Abravanel's remark on the *conversos* in his Comm. on
Ezekiel 20.37 (p. 521a): ולא יהיו עוד ערלי לב וערלי בשר כאשר הם בין הגויים, and
especially (*ibid.*): . . . ולפי שהאנוסים בהתערבם בגויים היו כל בניהם וזרעם ערלים.

and to eternal damnation in the world to come.[140] Now, this tripple division is indicated by Abravanel so clearly and so frequently that one is led to conclude that his first statement about the "second sect" may have referred not to a secret underground of long standing, but to the first of these three groups, i. e. to those who had returned under the impact of the Inquisition — returned in thought, but not in deed.[141] That such returners were believed to exist we have noticed also in Caro's writings.[142] Yet Abravanel may have momentarily been enthused, or carried away by the hope that these returners represented *most* of the Marranos, and thus he equated them with the group as a whole, while further observations cooled down this enthusiasm and forced him to take a more realistic view of the Marranos' condition.

For it is quite clear that Abravanel struggled with his conception of the Marranos. His Jewish upbringing and rooted attitude toward converts made him lend an ear to the charge that the New Christians were not sincere Christians; but what he saw before him was a group *immersed in gentilhood for generations, detached from Judaism and performing Christian rites*. What then were the Marranos or most of them: *believers* in Christianity or *disbelievers*? Despite his basic inclination toward the latter view, he could not in all honesty accept it. And, therefore, in trying to eliminate the conflict between what he *saw* from the Jewish side and what he *heard* from the Christian side with regard to the Marrano attitude toward Christianity, he made, on one occasion, a statement which represented a compromise between the conflicting assumptions. The Inquisition, he said in one place in his writings, burned in its autos de fe "those of the Marranos who *believed* in their religion (Christianity) as well as those who did *not* believe in it."[143]

---

[140] *Ibid.*, pp. 66, 100.

[141] *Ibid.*, p. 12: שהיתה תשובתם בלב, אבל לא היו עושים מעשה המצוות מפחד האויבים; and similarly: כי תהיה תשובתם בלב לא בפה כי לא יוכלו לפרסם תשובתם ואמונתם (*Comm. on Deuteronomy*, 30.1, p. 9c).

[142] See above, pp. 165–166.

[143] *Ma'yenei ha-Yeshu'ah*, p. 87a: והמאמינים בהם בדתם כמו הבלתי מאמינים אלו ואלו נשרפים.

One, however, should not take this to represent his final position on this issue. Indeed, a later statement on the subject may be found in his commentary on Hosea,[144] and here we see him not only refraining from expressing any view on the Marranos' attitude toward Christianity, but also ascribing the notion of their faithlessness to that religion exclusively to Christian sources,[145] thus confirming our supposition that his other pronouncement, wherein he offered support to that notion, merely echoed Christian opinion. Abravanel was, of course, fully aware of the hatred for the Marranos entertained by the Old Christians, and while he did not attribute the charge of the Marranos' disbelief in Christianity to sheer malice, the very fact that he declared it to be of Christian origin, withholding any additional comment, may well mean that, at that stage of his writing, he was not prepared to vouch for its truthfulness even to a limited degree. What is more, his entire statement about the Marranos, from which the above reference is drawn, suggests a tendency on his part to dismiss that accusation as a calculated excuse for inflicting vengeance. For the Marranos, as depicted in this statement, are not only *disbelievers* in God, i. e. in the religion of Israel, but apparently *believers* in the gentile way of life, including their religion, which they adopted out of choice.[146] Accordingly, he speaks of them as all-out as-

---

[144] Commentary on Latter Prophets, Amsterdam, 1641, p. 228b (On Hos. 2.16). While his *Wells of Salvation* (cited above, p. 199, n. 143) was completed in January 1497 (see my *Don Isaac Abravanel*, 1998[5], p. 77), he probably began to write his commentary on Hosea in August 1498 (see *ibid.*, p. 286, n. 62). His commentary on the Minor Prophets was completed on August 23, 1499 (see Gregorio Ruiz, *Don Isaac Abravanel y su comentario al libro de Amos*, 1984, p. 246).

[145] *Ibid.*: ומי שאינו מאמין בו [באלהי ישראל] והולך לאומות העולם הם הורגין אותו כאשר עושים היום בכל מקומות בני אדום לאשר יצאו מכלל דתינו, שהורגין אותם באמרם שהם בלתי מאמינים בדתם. Note that Abravanel does not say here that the Christians kill the converts *because* they do not believe in their religion, but "*claiming* that they do not believe in it."

[146] According to Abravanel, already the ancestors of the Marranos, i. e., the original converts, although stirred to conversion by the hardships of the exile (מפני חרבות ומפני כובד מלחמה ומפני צרת העמים), were capable of implementing this desire only because of their inner religious transformation (*ibid.*): they lost faith in the God of Israel (and consequently in the future of the Jewish people) and developed faith in the future of the Nations (and consequently

similationists (who "made up their minds to be like the gentiles")
and, more precisely, as irredeemable culprits (who were determined to practice the foreign religion), applying to them the
verse in Proverbs (2.22): For "the wicked will be cut off from
the land and the traitors uprooted from its midst,"[147] as well as
the verse in Hosea (7.8) on assimilationist Israel (ואפרים בעמים
הוא יתבולל), in which he sees a forecast of the Inquisition's
persecution: and they will be exposed to fire "like a cake not
turned."[148] "Wicked" and "traitors" are, of course, the real
converts who passed from their people's camp to that of its
enemy, without remorse or compassion for their former brethren,
and whose fate — their being charred like an unturned cake —
is the proper punishment ordained for such renegades. But
what should be further noted at this point is that Abravanel
speaks here not only of the Marranos generally, but more
specifically of the victims of the Inquisition. And so, according
to him, all these victims, all those who met their death at the
autos de fe, were outright traitors to their ancestral faith, and
not Jewish martyrs, not devotees of Judaism, not secret performers
of Jewish law. There is not a hint or an allusion to anything
of the kind.

in the essentials of their religion). To be sure, Abravanel does not say here
explicitly that the converts actually believed in Christianity, or harbored
some measure of faith in it, but his whole argument implies this conclusion
or, at least, suggests that he was very close to it.

[147] The precise words used here by Abravanel are: כי יֵעָרוּ רשעים מן הארץ
ובוגדים יסחו ממנה (ibid.) — a formulation which combines Proverbs 2.22 with
Job 38.13.

[148] Abravanel presents here his opinions via an original, though forced,
interpretation of a passage in Pesiqta (V.20; ed. Buber, Lyck, 1868, p. 49b;
and cf. Yalqut Shim'oni, on Hosea, 518, which, as Buber has pointed out
[introd. to Pesiqta, p. XLI], appears to have been the version used by
Abravanel). — Indicative of the length he was ready to go to in order to
prove his point in this matter is the fact that, apart from seeing references
to the converts in the words "wicked," "traitors" and "assimilationists," he
found such references also in the words יסחו and עֻנָה which appear respectively
in the above verses. As he sees it, these latter words allude to סיחון and עוֹג,
or rather to the "Desert of Siḥon and Og," which, according to his
interpretation of the Pesiqta, symbolizes the religious orbit of the gentiles,
and for that matter of the converts.

This, then, is Abravanel's last word on the Marranos and the Marrano problem. That it essentially contains, in its narrow compass, some basic elements of his views on Marranism, as shown by analysis of previous statements, is quite apparent; and from this standpoint it represents no novelty. However, it brings into sharper focus his negative evaluation of the group as a whole, and particularly its stand toward Judaism. As for its stand toward Christianity *as such*, Abravanel, as we have seen, even at this stage, despite the far-reaching implications derivable, limits himself to the stating of some observable facts (the practice of Christianity by the Marranos, Christian opinion of that practice), and cautiously avoids making clear-cut pronouncements of a more speculative nature. This caution of his must, of course, be paralleled by proper circumspection on our part when we come to finalize our exposition of his opinions. With this reservation in mind, and taking into consideration all the partial retreats of Abravanel from what is markedly his main line of thought, we can, nevertheless, summarize his view of Marranism in no uncertain terms. What we can say definitely is that, while his position on the Christian faith of the Marranos may have been divided or indefinite to the very end, and while he may have had occasional qualms about their inner attitude toward Judaism, several things appeared to him as certain in all his reflections about the Marranos: *their deep assimilation in the Christian way of life, leading, in part, to ethnic fusion, their governing desire to be like the gentiles and, above all, their complete detachment from, and disregard for Jewish law.* Not only does he repeat this emphatically, but he distinctly charges the Inquisition with falsification in presenting the mass of the Marranos as "Judaizers." To the extent that there were "judaizers" and returners," they had become so, he claimed, through the persecution by the Inquisition. Yet, despite the new movement of "return," his basic view of the Marranos remained unchanged; and this is clearly indicated also in the terms he used to describe them generally: "the criminals of Israel," the "wicked," the "rebels," the "rabble," "enemies of God," "worse than gentiles," and "vile people" — appelations which had been traditonally employed by Jews to describe apostates. Indeed, as we have seen, he uses the term "apostates," too, as a designation for the group as a whole, just as he uses the terms "heretics" and "Epicureans," which also often served as synonyms for apostates, for defining the entire Marrano body. And, while he is not overjoyed over their fall as were others of his contemporaries, the woeful fate of the Marranos does not seem to evoke in him any special feelings of sympathy either. The fact that he can point out triumphantly — when discussing the Marrano tragedy — only God's stern justice,[149] is clear proof that Abravanel voiced here the overall attitude of Spanish Jewry — an attitude crystalized for generations by experience, and sustained by a conviction of the Marranos' animosity toward, and estrangement from, everything Jewish. Despite his occasional wavering, therefore, on the question of the Marrano's faith in Christianity, Abravanel offers us the most telling testimony on their religious stand in the crucial conflict that then engulfed Spain.

[149] See above, note 123, and see also *Mashmi'a Yeshu'ah*, pp. 74–75, 100–101, 107.

## V. Conclusions

In view of the proofs adduced in the foregoing concerning the religious development of Marranism, can we still uphold the widespread notion, so prevalent in the histories related to the subject, that "most of the *conversos* were Jews, in faith and in deed"?

As we see it, the answer to this question must be in the negative.

For what has been gathered from the sources examined about the decline of Judaism among the Marranos — from the first signs of decay to virtual dissolution; what has been noticed about their leanings toward Christianity since the *early* days of their conversionist life (Ribash: they follow the laws of the gentiles *willingly*); what has been observed about the state of mind that typified the converts of 1412, their failing faith in Judaism and their faltering morale; what has been shown of the far-reaching gains made by the massive campaign of conversion, incessantly conducted for over half a century among both Marranos and Jews; what has been remarked about the assimilationist philosophy that guided the Marranos socially and religiously, and the actual attainments of this assimilation by the time the Inquisition was established (note the expressions: נטמעו, נשקעו, נטבעו, (התערבו בגויים לגמרי); what has been indicated about the upbringing of the *conversos* in a strictly gentile way of life and about the products of that education from the second generation on (Rashbash: the Marranos *believe* in the teachings of apostasy, i. e. in Christian dogma[150]); what has been revealed about the pent up animosity felt by the Marranos for Jews and Judaism, and the counter-hatred, no less consuming, which was felt by the Jews for the Marranos; and, finally, what has been ascertained about the reaction of the Jews to the excesses of the Inquisition, their lack of sympathy for the hard-pressed *conversos*

---

[150] And see below, Appendix D, pp. 228–229, on the thorough Christian education of the converts' children.

and their irrepressible joy over their "fall" — all this shows, beyond a reasonable doubt, that the New Christians, at the beginning of the eighties, were *not* Jews, in practice or in spirit, but assimilated to the core, Christianized and anti-Jewish.

Assimilation, Christianization and anti-Jewishness were indeed the foremost symptoms of Marranism, or rather of its *dominant* type, i. e., the element which, by its words and actions, generated the *prevailing* view of the Marranos in the literature examined. Moreover, these were the main *features* of the group, determining its image as it emerges from our sources, and as such they cannot be overlooked in any attempt to *describe* the Marranos, or assess them religiously. If, however, on the basis of these characteristics, we also attempt to *define* the Marranos, or signify them by a single designation, our task becomes somewhat more complex — although, we should add, the choice seems to oscillate between two terms only.

It was on this point, as we have seen, that controversy developed between the defenders of the Marranos, who were non-Spanish Jews, and their attackers, who were of Spanish origin. The former saw the Marranos, of the time of the Inquisition, as *ordinary* apostates, or even as apostates of a preferred class, their apostasy having been rooted, as claimed, in compulsory conversion. Consequently, these apologists for the Marranos could attribute to them the characteristics which Jews have traditionally associated with apostasy — most notably, that of religious insincerity, commonly interpreted as disbelief in Christianity and hidden conviction of the rightness of Judaism. The denouncers of the Marranos did not share this view. They considered the latter as *extraordinary* apostates by virtue of their apostasy for several generations, and therefore were prone to divest the Marranos of the aforementioned characteristic. Between these two attitudes stood Abravanel who, being a unique combination as he was of a stark realist and a messianic visionary, tried to combine both attitudes, but actually fluctuated from one to another. Thus, while he repeatedly appears to us as the castigator of the Marranos, he occasionally also becomes their defender. Predominantly, however, as we have seen, he remains "Spanish" in his attitude.

In view of this controversy, we should ask ourselves how *we* should define the Marranos. Which of the two evaluations should be preferred, or rather, which of them, as we see it, is closer to historical truth? Surely, it appears, we must align ourselves with the *Spanish* authorities of the time — not only because they were on the scene, and their opinion must therefore be considered more reliable, but also because of the rest of the evidence we possess about the Marranos. Admittedly, the third of the major traits mentioned, i. e., the Marranos' anti-Jewishness, can also be attributed to ordinary apostates. Similarly, Christianization, in theory and in practice, could be assumed in apostates of the every-day sort. But as far as assimilation is concerned, especially that thorough and far-reaching assimilation attributed by our sources to the Marranos, coupled as it was by total *ignorance* of, and complete *alienation* from, everything Jewish — that could *not* be attributed to *ordinary* apostates, i. e., typical of the first generation. Such assimilation could be attained only after several generations of life "within the nations"; and, indeed, it was precisely because of *this* that "all the scholars of Castile, or most of them," as Berav tells us, defined the Marranos as "gentiles" and their "returners" as "proselytes."

Yet, while the common acceptance of this view by Spanish Jewry[151] offers in itself a clear cut evidence to the depth and breadth of Marrano assimilation, and while it suggests that also ethnically this assimilation was of no mean dimensions, we cannot, nevertheless, regard that appraisal as reflecting the situation accurately. In all probability, the Marranos were not precisely as seen by either their Spanish critics or their non-Spanish advocates. For while it appears that, at the outset of the Inquisition, they had long passed the stage of *ordinary* apostasy, it is also clear that they had not yet reached that of *complete* gentilehood. Had they been *fully* gentilized, it is obvious, they would not have been further identified as *New* Chris-

---

[151] How widely this view was held is also indicated by Abravanel, who says tersely: The Marranos are "assimilated with the gentiles, *and are considered as such*" (הם מעורבים בהם [בנויים] ונחשבים כמוהם). See Comm. on Deut. 30.1, p. 9c.

tians, and no counter-reaction would have set in to block their advancement toward total fusion. Similarly, had they been wholly relieved of their burdensome apostatic legacy, they would no longer have displayed that particular Jewish complex to which our sources since the eighties still allude. In brief, if we are to define the Marranos as they were on the eve of the Inquisition's founding, we shall probably be close to truth if we see them as passing the final stage of transformation from a still *partly* apostatic into a *post*-apostatic state and from partial gentilehood into a complete one.

Having thus arrived at the conclusion that the Marranos, in general, were *semi-gentilized*, there is hardly any need to consider further the strength of the Judaic element among them. Surely a segment of secret Jews survived, in semi-dormant fashion, up to the days of the Inquisition; and, shortly before the establishment of the latter, it may have even been "revived" or strengthened by some sort of "awakening." But this "movement," if it can be so called, was clearly so feeble and so ineffectual, that in the questions addressed in the 1480's to the rabbis Simon Duran and Ibn Danan, the *pre*-Inquisitional "awakening" is completely disregarded, and only one "awakening" is spoken of — that which began after the establishment of the Inquisition. What emerges from all this is that the pro-Jewish element among the Marranos, consisting as it did of "platonic" Jews as well as of performers of "some precepts," belonged to the very fringes of the camp, while the broad current of the Marrano force moved incessantly forward toward its desired goals without sharing in any Judaizing effort. In fact, if there was a religious process still astir among the Marranos, it was not of *Judaization* but of *dejudaization* — and this to the very limit.

But if that was the case, the persecution of the Marranos launched by the Inquisition could not have been aimed at removing a religious menace, or at stifling a growing heresy. Plain logic so dictates, and this is, indeed, what the sources confirm. Both luminaries of the age, Arama and Abravanel, tell us in clear and vigorous language that the charges of the Inquisition regarding the Judaizing of the Marranos lacked any substance whatsoever, that they were libelous fabrications (both use the word להעליל) maliciously concocted for the sole purpose of bringing about their ruin.

This brings our evidence to its summit, as well as to its conclusion. For as to the rest, i. e., the *reasons* for the hostility manifested in the Inquisition's actions, our sources suggest no answer that we may consider historical. All they offer us is the theological interpretation, namely, that this hostility was a product of God's will, of his preordained plan, a punishment for the Marranos' betrayal, and the like. We shall get a clearer insight into the motives of the persecution when we turn to the non-Hebrew sources of the period. But a *hint* of its causes may also be found in the following address of the Jewish people to God, as formulated by Isaac Arama:

"You, God, know, and You are my witness, that in all the evils they have perpetrated against me, and in all the acts of vengeance they have wrought upon me, *their sole intent was to annihilate and destroy me not because of my sins, but because of what I am.*"[152]

Perhaps what Arama said about the Jews could be extended to the Marranos.

---

[152] *Commentary on Lamentations* (appended to *'Aqedat Yiẓhaq*, V), p. 17a.

APPENDICES

# A

## THE SALONIKI RABBINICAL DECISIONS ON
## THE MARRANOS

Two decisions adopted by the rabbis of Saloniki between 1499 and 1514 concerning the personal status of the Marranos, and particularly concerning that of the Marranos of Portugal, throw considerable light on the views then prevalent among the Jews of Spain about the Spanish Marranos and the Marrano problem in general.

According to the first of these decisions, all marriages contracted by Marranos in Portugal after the conversion of 1497 were null and void from a Jewish standpoint, since by that time there were no longer people in that country who could qualify as witnesses under Jewish law. Consequently, any woman who was involved in such a marriage was free to marry any Jew who was legally in a position to become her spouse; and, if her Marrano husband died without issue, she was under no marital obligation to his brother (Moses Ḥagiz, *Leqeṭ ha-Qemaḥ*, Hamburg, 1711, pp. 113d–114a). According to another version of this decision (Samuel de Medina, *Responsa*, on Even ha-'Ezer, No. 10), the ruling referred also to the Marranos of Castile; and insofar as Castile was concerned, such regulations would entail no problem. As we have seen, already Rashbaẓ considered marriages contracted between Marranos not in the presence of Jewish witnesses (or at least when Jews did not live in the town in which the marriage took place) valueless from a Jewish point of view; therefore, the disqualification of all Marrano marriages in Spain after the expulsion of 1492, when no Jews were left in that country, would be quite in line with this policy. What surprises us in the above decision, however, is its being directed also, or even primarily, to the *Portuguese* Marranos, i. e., to those who only "yesterday" went over to Christianity under apparently intolerable conditions of duress. Ordinarily we would assume that these Marranos, most of whom were *Spanish* exiles, who had preferred homelessness and destitution to conversion, should have been trusted to behave secretly as Jews, and as such they

211

should have been accredited with all the rights of Jews, including that of serving as witnesses, as Rashi and Ribash and Rashbaẓ maintained. Instead, the attitude displayed toward them is one of negation only, and the decision even goes as far as to declare that *none* of them can be regarded as a legitimate witness *in any respect, or for any purpose* (ואין שם עדים כשרים בשום צד; Ḥagiz, *ibid.*, p. 114a). This is, to say the least, an extreme position, and one marked by its severity. What lay behind it?

That the decision brought relief to many women who escaped without their husbands from the land of persecution, as is suggested by Asaf (*loc. cit.*, p. 56), can be taken for granted, especially since contact with the Marranos in Portugal, as in Spain, became over the years increasingly difficult. Nevertheless, it cannot be assumed that this was the *main* reason for the stand taken by the rabbis of Saloniki. Expediency could explain certain leniencies in the treatment of borderline cases, but not a radical change of accepted procedure in such a grave matter; and, indeed, such a change *would* have been involved in the decision under discussion, had the rabbis of Saloniki sincerely believed that the Marrano population of Portugal included a large crypto-Jewish element. It seems to us, therefore, that the answer lies in the assumption that the rabbis of Saloniki did *not* believe this to have been the case; more clearly, that, in their judgment, the converted Portuguese Jewry, or at least its overwhelming majority, did *not* consist of *forced* converts (אנוסים), but of apostates (משומדים), plain and simple. How and why was such a view established, quite in opposition to the general opinion formed of that group in later times, we shall now try to explain.

Several factors may have been responsible. To begin with, the conversion of Portugal's Jews was not occasioned, as the conversion of 1391, by the *direct threat of death*. From Portuguese sources (see M. Kayserling, *Geschichte der Juden in Portugal*, Berlin, 1867, p. 133, note 1) we know that, when the Jews of Portugal were confronted, in 1497, with the alternatives of conversion or exile, about 20,000 persons were assembled in Lisbon for the purpose of being deported from the country. But Portuguese Jewry at the time was supposed to have consisted of a much larger number! Zacuto (*Sefer Juḥasin*, ed. Filipowski,

p. 227a) tells us that more than 120,000 Jews came to Portugal in 1492, after the expulsion from Spain; and to this large number we should add the native Jewish population of Portugal, which was not insignificant. What happened to this mass of people? Assuming that about half of Spain's exiles in Portugal left the country in 1493 (see E. Capsali, *Excerpts from D'Bei Eliyahu*, Padua, 1869, p. 76),[1] and granted that the losses Portuguese Jewry had suffered through the forced conversion of the children were not inconsiderable, it is still evident that most of the remaining body did not appear in Lisbon on the day fixed for departure. The inescapable conclusion, therefore, is that the majority of Portugal's Jews preferred conversion to exile. Whether the reasons for this choice were materialistic or psychological (lack of stamina again to experience exile), or whether the minds of many were made up in its favor by their refusal to part forever with their children (the converted ones),[2] it is clear that these converts could not qualify in the eyes of the rabbis as *anusim*, since the essential prerequisite for such qualification — an overwhelming fear of immediate death (see Perfet, *Responsa*, No. 11, p. 3b) — was missing in their cases; therefore, they had to be regarded as apostates. As for the remaining 20,000, most of whom were also converted when the right for departure was suddenly denied them, it is difficult to gauge from the different sources (see Graetz, VIII [4th ed.], note 14, pp. 484–487) both the scope and determination of the resistance offered by this group to conversion. It appears, however, that while a small minority heroically and unyieldingly resisted to the end, the majority broke down after encountering the first hardships, and this despite the fact that the alternative now offered to conversion

---

[1] Since Capsali's narration of what happened to the Jews in Portugal in 1492–1497 is both detailed and cohesive, and since it is basically substantiated by other sources, the various figures he quotes in this connection (*Excerpts from D'Bei Eliyahu*, ed. Lattes, Padua, 1869, pp. 74–76), which fall well into line with the rest of his story, must also be considered based on good authority and, in any case, more reliable than those cited by Bernáldez in his obviously curtailed and tendentious account (*Historia de los Reyes Católicos*, cap. cxiii).

[2] Capsali (*op. cit.*, p. 85) speaks of "countless" conversions that took place on that account (cf. also *ibid.*, p. 74).

was, as it appears, not death, but imprisonment. Thus, at least technically, these converts, too, could hardly qualify in the eyes of the rabbis as truly forced converts. Yet, if we consider the sufferings and hardships to which the Jews of Portugal were subjected in 1493–1497, and the fact that many of the remaining group were, after all, *dragged* to the baptismal font; on top of this, if we consider the fact that many of these *did* practice Judaism secretly, we cannot explain the above cited decision, denying the Jewish faithfulness of *all* the Marranos of Portugal, unless we bring into account another factor: the strong anti-Marrano sentiment that prevailed among Spain's Jews — this and their deep-rooted conviction that forced conversion leads to real conversion, unless the convert hastens to escape from the land of religious coercion.

In 1499 the Marranos of Portugal were officially prohibited from leaving the country, and thus the view *could* have been fostered among the Spanish exiles in the East that Portuguese Marranism was a lost case. The decision referred to was probably taken a few years after the conversion, when Marrano migration from Portugal came to a standstill, and when a great deal of damaging evidence was gathered, from the reports arriving from that country, about the religious behavior of the Marranos (this is indicated in Jacob ben Ḥaviv's statement [see his responsum, *loc. cit.*, p. 123b]: והלא מט"ו שנים עד היום בקרוב התחילו ימי השמד והאונס כי רבים מבני עמנו הביאם הכרח אונס גוף וממון להראות עצמם משומדים גמורים כופרים בעיקר ובתורת משה בפרהסיא). Then, unexpectedly, things radically changed. The massacre of the Marranos in Lisbon in 1506 and the royal decree of 1507, permitting Marranos to depart from the country, brought in their wake the renewal of Marrano migration from Portugal and a new stream of "re-turners" to the East. Under the impact of these developments the second Saloniki decision was adopted (in January, 1514), according to which a childless widow was bound under the levirate law to her husband's brother, even if the latter was a convert who lived in the land of persecution.

It is quite evident that this decision presented a change both of attitude and position on the part of Saloniki's rabbis, and it is also clear that it was, in large measure, the result of remonstrances made by the escapees, who considered themselves forced converts, against their being treated as gentiles or apostates. Nevertheless, for the reasons above mentioned, most rabbis could not see their way clear to granting Portugal's Marranos a status of forced converts, and the discussion of their particular case inevitably soon revolved upon the old question of the *real* convert's rights under the law of levirate marriage. Jacob ben Haviv who now took the lead in the struggle on behalf of the Marranos, and clearly favored their recognition as forced converts, went as far as to claim that even Marranos' descendants, however remote, should be treated as Jews with respect to that law (*loc. cit.*). Nevertheless, the decision of 1514, which was based on this view, related only to the Marranos of Portugal, and not to the conversos of Spain.[3] Insofar as the Spanish Marranos were concerned, Spain's Jews persisted in evaluating them as gentiles and in their determination to treat them as such. The isolated cases of "returners" (if there were such) from the many who converted on the eve of the Expulsion could not alter this radical attitude, which by then was widespread and dominant.

---

[3] One ought at this point again to refer to Jacob ben Haviv's aforecited statement that "many of our people" began to behave like "real apostates some fifteen years ago" — that is, two or three years following the Portuguese forced conversion of 1497.

# B

## The Destinations of the Fugitives from the Inquisition

S. Asaf, in his "Anusei Sefarad u-Portugal be-Sifrut ha-Teshuvot," in *Zion*, Jerusalem, V, 1932–33, pp. 44–45, states that the "large majority" of the Marranos who left Spain did so with the view of returning to Judaism. I can find no support for this statement in the sources, whether of Jewish or of Christian origin; and, if we carefully consider what the sources tell us about the *destinations* of those Marranos, we can reach only a conclusion to the contrary.

It appears to us quite evident that most of the Marranos who left Spain turned not to Moslem, but to Christian countries, where they could *not* return to Judaism. This is obvious even from Bernáldez' statement about the initial wave of fugitives from the Inquisition: "vinieron mas de ocho mil almas a Mairena, y Marchena, y los Palacios . . . y de estos fueron muchos á pasar á tierra de moros, allende é aquende, á ser judíos como lo eran; é otros se fueron á Portugal, é otros á Roma" (*Historia de los Reyes Católicos*, xliv, in *Crónicas de los Reyes de Castilla*, III, Madrid, 1953, p. 601a). Bernáldez, the arch-enemy of the Marranos, would have gleefully pointed out that the *majority* of the first escapees fled to Moslem countries to live openly as Jews, had this been the case. His use, instead, of the indefinite word "many" is, to my mind, sufficient indication that only a minority of the refugees turned to the lands of the Moors. Similarly, his mention of these lands first in order among the Marranos' countries of refuge need not be taken, in our opinion, as indication of their importance as havens, but should rather be attributed to Bernáldez' bias against the Marranos and his insatiable desire to besmirch them.

Other reports about the flight of the Marranos, found in contemporary sources, only substantiate this contention. Thus

Pulgar records, significantly, that "muchos de los de aquel linage (i. e., the Marranos), temiendo aquellas execuciones, desampararon sus casas e bienes, e se fueron al reyno de Portugal, e a tierra de Italia, e a Francia, e a otros reynos" (*Crónica de los Reyes Católicos*, Madrid, 1943, I, p. 336). We see, then, that Pulgar, in contrast to Bernáldez, *does not even mention the Moslem lands explicitly*, evidently because they were known to have attracted only a small minority of refugees. To be sure, it may be argued that Pulgar might have deliberately omitted their mention because, as a Marrano, he sought to minimize, or even suppress damaging evidence against his own kind; but such an argument can be safely discarded with reference to the *main* issue. Had the Moslem countries served as refuge for a *majority* of the escapees, or even for a large number of them, Pulgar, living under the searchlights of the Inquisition and being cautious and careful as he was, would not have dared avoid mentioning them, if not *first*, at least *last* in order. Indeed, the very fact that, being what he was, he *could* avoid mentioning the Moslem lands in this instance, or even be evasive about them, is rather *proof* of their relative insignificance as havens for the refugees.

In addition, we have the account of Lucio Marineo Sículo who, although not violently anti-Marrano as Bernáldez, was certainly not pro-Marrano either. He writes: "Y muchos otros judíos, temiendo esta justicia y sabiendo sus maldades, dejaron sus casas con muchos bienes, y a España, y fueron huyendo, de ellos a Portugal, otros a Navarra, muchos a Italia y algunos a Francia y a otras partes, a donde pensaban estar seguros" (*Vida y hechos de los reyes Católicos*, Madrid, 1943, p. 72). So Marineo, too, does not mention the Moslem lands among the Marranos' countries of refuge; and, judging by his general presentation, we can also see that Pulgar listed these countries in the order of their true importance as asylums. Thus, he corroborates Pulgar's statement on *two* accounts. What is more, as we have seen, Marineo, like Bernáldez, and in full accord with the Inquisition's thesis, defines the fugitives as [secret] Jews, and the mention of the Moslem countries among their havens would of course have offered support to his contention; yet, he found it impossible to do so. Why? — There can be only one answer: the number of

Marranos who fled to those countries was relatively too small to matter.

Finally, we may consider some additional data known about Marrano migrations to these countries. From the evidence offered by Isaac Abravanel (*Comm. on Ezekiel*, 20.32 [*Comm. on the Latter Prophets*, Jerusalem, 1956, p. 521b]), it is clear that, of all Moslem domains, Turkey was the main haven for Spain's "returners," while the Arab-speaking countries of North Africa absorbed only a minority of them (קצתם בארץ ישמעאל ורובם בארצות התוגרמים).[1] We have no statistical information by which we may establish the size of either the "majority" or the "minority," the only definite figure known to us being that given by Obadiah of Bertinoro for the Marrano community in Egypt (fifty families in 1488).[2] Lacking such data for the Barbary States, we may nevertheless safely assume that, Morocco, due to its proximity to Spain, and no doubt also Algeria, attracted considerably larger numbers, the totality of which, however, could be gauged only

---

[1] From Abravanel's formulation here, it may appear as if *all* the Marrano escapees from Spain settled in Turkey and North Africa. Obviously, however, Abravanel referred only to the "returners," as is evident from another, almost identical passage in which he discusses the fugitives from the Inquisition. והבטיחם הנביא שהחסידים מהם ימלטו מידם; וכן היה, שברחו לארץ ישמעאל ולארץ התוגר ושבו בתשובה (*Comm. on Isaiah*, 43.6 [*Comm. on the Latter Prophets*, p. 206b]). That Abravanel was fully aware that, apart from these "returners," there were many Marrano fugitives who refused to "return," is evident from his repeated remarks about the "rebels" (המורדים) who were destined, according to him, to die during their wanderings ("from nation to nation and from one state to another" — מגוי אל גוי וממלכה אל עם אחר), without sharing in the forthcoming redemption: בקיבוץ הגלויות וטלטולם ימותו המורדים והפושעים המחזיקים ברשעתם ולא שבו אל השם . . . מארץ מגוריהם אוציא אותם ואל אדמת ישראל לא יבואו (*Mashmia' Yeshu'ah*, p. 44a). The countries of wandering of these "criminals" were, of course, the countries of Christendom, and thus, in all likelihood, Abravanel believed that, as long as the Marranos stayed in those countries, they could not be considered "saved" from the hands of the Inquisition (note his formulation: ומפני זה יתעוררו לבות האנוסים . . . לנוס ולברוח מארצות מגוריהם מקרב הנוצרים ללכת למרחקי ארץ ל[ה]מלט על נפשם (*Comm. on Ezekiel*, 20.32 [*Comm. on the Latter Prophets*, p. 520b]).

[2] *Ha-Massa le-Ereẓ Yisrael bishnat 247–248*, Berlin, 1922, p. 28: ויש במצרים היום כחמשים בעלי בתים מן האנוסים אשר היו בספרד . . . ורובם עניים אשר עזבו את בתיהם ואת עשרם ואת אבותיהם. ואבות אבותיהם היו שומרים את דתי הגוים, והם באו לחסות תחת כנפי השכינה.

if we had some tenable conception of what the Turkish "major-ity" was. Yet as for Turkey, all we can go by, in terms of con-crete statistics, is a statement left us by the German Stephan Gerlach, preacher of the Emperor's Embassy in Constantinople, according to whom there were, in 1575, over 10,000 Jews in the Turkish capital who had been Christian converts.[3] If we add to this the less definite computation, based on the same source, namely, that an even larger number of such Jews lived in the rest of the country,[4] we may conclude that the number of ex-converts in Turkey consisted of some 25,000–30,000 souls. This is a rather impressive figure. However, if we recall that this figure re-fers to conditions existing some ninety years (or three generations!) after the establishment of the Inquisition; if we further recall that, for most of the period, Turkey was a haven not only for Spain's Marranos, but also for the Marranos of Portugal, especially after 1506 (see above, p. 214), and even more so after 1536, i. e. after the establishment of the Inquisition in that country;[5] if, in addition, we bear in mind the fact that Turkey served also as an asylum for many of the Neophytes who were ousted from Apulia (1515), we must conclude that Spain's Marrano refugees, from the first two decades of the Inquisition, could not possibly constitute more than a third of the total indicated by Gerlach. Furthermore, if we consider the contemporary Responsa dealing with Marrano questions in the East, we notice that most of the cases mentioned refer to Portuguese Marranos, some to *anusim* from Apulia, and only a few to Spanish *anusim* (including those who converted in 1492). Thus we are led to the conclusion that the "returners" from Spain's veteran Marrano community must

[3] Stephan Gerlach (the older), *Tage-Buch*, Frankfurt-on-Main, 1674, p. 90b.

[4] S. Rosanes (*Divrei Yemei Yisrael be-Togarmah*, I, Tel-Aviv, 1930, p. 314) also quotes Gerlach to the effect that other Marranos settled in other Turkish cities and that "the number of those who came to Saloniki was larger than those who came to the capital." I have not found this additional citation in Gerlach's *Tage-Buch*, but the evaluation, though it seems to belong to Rosanes, may, nevertheless, be taken as correct.

[5] See, for instance, A. Herculano, *History of the Origin and Establishment of the Inquisition in Portugal*, translated by J. C. Branner, Stanford University, California, 1926, p. 529.

have formed in the total referred to even a smaller portion than the one suggested above, so that, in all likelihood, it comprised no more than several thousand souls.

On the Jews of Granada and North Africa, the sudden appearance of Marrano groups seeking re-embracement of Judaism, followed as they were by similar cases, must have made a strong impression — indeed, one of a new and promising movement —, even if the total of these "returners" amounted to a few hundred families only. But to the Jews of Spain, who were fully aware of the massive proportions of the Marrano camp, as well as of what Pulgar and Marineo knew regarding the whereabouts of the Marrano fugitives, the number of the returners to the fold — especially after all the *conversos* had endured from the hands of the Inquisition — appeared extremely small and disappointing. Hence, their different evaluation of that movement, and another reason for the differences of opinion between them and rabbis like Simon Duran II and Ibn Danan on other aspects of the Marrano problem.

# C

## THE DATES OF COMPOSITION OF EFODI'S
## POLEMICAL WORKS

Adolf Posnanski, in his notes to *Kelimat ha-Goyim*, states several times that Efodi, in his work, refers to Crescas' *Tratado*[1] (*Ha-Zofeh me-Erez Hagar*, III [1914], pp. 103, 149, 171) which, according to him, had been completed a short time before Efodi wrote his *Kelima*. The date of the *Tratado*'s composition is given by Posnanski, in reliance on Graetz, as 1396 (*ibid.*, p. 103, note 6). This is also the view of J. Friedländer and J. Kohn in their introduction to *Ma'aseh Efod*, Vienna, 1865, German part, p. 8. They, too, mention Graetz as the basis for their statement, but see further support for their view in one of the remarks which Duran, in *ha-Kelima*, addressed to Crescas: אך אמרתי אם יבוא המאמר הזה ליד מי שלא הרגילו השיג בהשגותיך אולי יאירו עיניו במעט הדבש הזה, meaning that Duran's study might enlighten those who would not grasp the profound arguments supposedly expressed in Crescas' *Tratado*. However, the above statement of Efodi, as quoted by Friedländer and Kohn, simply represents a corrupt version. The correct form appears in Posnanski's edition (*Ha-Zofeh me-Erez Hagar*, IV, 1915, p. 123): אם יבוא המאמר הזה ליד מי שלא הרגיל כהרגלך ולא השיג כהשגתך, which obviously means that *for Crescas* there would be no novelty in Efodi's work and that it was intended for those who did not have Crescas' experience in polemics, or his breadth of knowledge and wisdom.

As a matter of fact, nowhere in his work does Efodi allude to Crescas' Treatise against Christianity. On the contrary, from the very remarks in which Posnanski sees such allusion, it is

---

[1] His treatise, *The Refutation of the Christian Articles of Faith* (see above, pp. 86–87).

quite clear that Efodi speaks about some writing on the subject
which Crescas was then *expected* to do. Thus, he says, using
the future tense, יען ידעתי כי...תוסי ף בו דברים (*ibid.*, III, p.
103). Accordingly, the same tense (and not the continuous
present) is used on page 17: ואתה ... ת כ ה   ארס לשונם בהבל
פיך...וברוח שפתיך ת מ י ת רשע. Also the reference on p. 149
ואין הכוונה להשיב עליהם בזה כי אתה, תפארת הרבנים, כביר כח להקהות
את שיניהם בכיוצא בזה) indicates what Crescas *could* do, and what
he was *expected* to do, not what he actually did. What is more,
the reference by Posnanski, as well as by Friedländer and Kohn,
to Graetz (and, in their wake, also by J. Rosenthal, *Areshet*, II,
164), is in itself based upon error. It is true that in the eighth
volume of his history (3rd ed., p. 86) Graetz states that the
*Tratado* was composed around 1396, but this may well have been
a typographical error. For, in his note on Crescas (*ibid.*, p. 403),
where Graetz gives the *reasons* for his suggested date, it appears
quite clear that the work, in his opinion, was written not in 1396,
but rather around 1398 or, more likely, in 1397, as is stated by
Graetz himself. Crescas' work was thus written not *before*, but
*after* that of Efodi.

It appears that Crescas expected Duran's book to be a carefully conceived refutation of Christianity — a refutation to be
edited by him (Crescas), and perhaps sanctioned by the leadership of the Jewish community of Aragon with little regard to
authorship. Crescas no doubt indicated to Duran that he might
suggest a few additions of his own. This is evident from Duran's
statement: יען ידעתי ברוב חכמתך וברוחב לבבך וגובה שכלך תוסיף בו
דברים כפי פלפוליך (*Ha-Ẓofeh*, III [1914], p. 103). In addition,
Crescas expected Efodi to produce a short treatise, easy to read
and distribute, and thus more useful for propaganda purposes.
This, too, is indicated in Efodi's own words: ואכתוב מעט כַנרצה
אליך (*ibid.*, p. 103). His work, however, turned out to be not
what Crescas had in mind, which fact led the latter to write
the *Tratado*. Hence the radical difference in contents and approach between Crescas' and Efodi's works.

Similarly, Friedländer, Kohn and Posnanski probably err in
suggesting the year 1396 as the date of the composition of
Duran's Epistle (see *Ma'aseh Efod*, German part, p. 7; *Ha-Ẓofeh*,

IV, p. 128; and p. 45, note 28), and this again on the basis of
Graetz, VIII³, p. 399. Now, Graetz' calculations are grounded
on a statement found in one of the versions of the Epistle,
according to which there had elapsed from the death of Jesus
to the writing of the Epistle אלף וש"ס שנה, and on Efodi's statement in the *Kelima* that, according to Christian tradition,
Jesus lived about thirty years (*ibid.*). Graetz read אלף וש"ס
(1360) to mean אלף שס"ו (1366), for had he read the figure as it
apparently means (1360 years), the addition of 30 years of Jesus'
life would bring him to the year 1390, which could not possibly
be the correct date (the Epistle having obviously been composed after the riots of 1391). There is no need, however, for
this involved and forced calculation. In the first place, Duran
does not refer to 1360 years (after Jesus' death) *exactly*. He
says ס ב י ב אלף וש"ס שנה (it is *about* 1360 years). That may
easily mean a year or two beyond 1360. Second, Duran states that,
according to Christian tradition, Jesus lived not thirty years,
but "*about* thirty years," or rather "thirty-two and a half"
(וימי ישו היו לפי מה שאמור ומפורסם ביניהם סביב שלושים שנה או שלושים
ושתים וחצי; see *Ha-Zofeh*, IV, 1914, p. 116, and see *ibid.*, Posnanski's
note 5), while in his own opinion, too, Jesus died not necessarily
at the age of thirty, but possibly at the age of 31 (*ibid.*). Considering all this, it is quite obvious that the year 1396 was not
indicated in the Epistle, and that, if we go merely by the above-
mentioned clues, it could be composed in any of the preceding
years from 1391 on.

There is another item in the Epistle which we should consider
in this connection. The Epistle states that Paul of Burgos, while
in Avignon (in the court of the anti-Pope), intended to calumniate
the Jews, but was prevented from carrying out his plan by the
Cardinal of Pamplona and other lords.[2] Baer says that the Cardinal of Pamplona was Pedro de Luna, who later became anti-Pope
Benedict XIII (*Toledot*, 2nd ed., p. 317; Engl. transl., II, p. 155).[3]

[2] "Al Tĕhi Ka-avotekha," in *Qovez Vikkuhim*, Breslau, 1844, p. 48 (not
paginated).

[3] And this opinion was also accepted by F. Cantera Burgos; see his *Alvar
García de Santa María*, 1952, p. 320.

Since Pedro de Luna was elected Pope on September 28, 1394 (and crowned on October 11 of that year), the events referred to must have occurred while he was still Cardinal, and thus we have, if Baer's identification is correct, a *terminus ad quem* for the composition of the Epistle. Baer's identification, however, is erroneous; for Pedro de Luna was not known as the Cardinal of Pamplona, but as the Cardinal of Aragon. Both by birth and family relationship he was Aragonese, not Navarrene. Nor was his formal title in any way connected with the city of Pamplona; he was cardinal deacon of Santa Maria in Cosmedin (the famous church in Rome). By the "Cardinal of Pamplona" in the Epistle, Duran no doubt meant Martín de Zalva, who was born in Pamplona, served there as bishop, and, while occupying this ecclesiastic office, was created Cardinal in 1390 (by Clement VII). Martín de Zalva, furthermore, was a determined follower of the schismatic party, and as such he became, and remained until his death (Oct. 28, 1403), a most faithful friend of Benedict XIII.[4]

The mention of the Cardinal of Pamplona in the Epistle, therefore, cannot in itself substantially aid in establishing the date of its composition. There are, however, other data in the Epistle referring to the convert's stay in Avignon which may be of assistance in our search. According to the Epistle, Paul of Burgos was enjoying high prestige at the papal court; and the Pope, as well as his entire Curia (וכל הכנסיה שלו), considered him worthy of being appointed as bishop or even created cardinal.[4a] Now, one may assume, of course, that Paul of Burgos visited Avignon shortly after his conversion[5]—say, on his way to the University of Paris, in which he enrolled as a student of theology (October,

---

[4] On his influential position in the College of Cardinals prior to the election of Benedict XIII, see Sebastián Puig y Puig, *Pedro de Luna*, Barcelona, 1920, p. 29. And see also J. R. Serra, "El Cardenal Zalba," in *Hispania*, Madrid, IV (1944), pp. 211-243.

[4a] *Ibid.*, p. 48.

[5] He was converted not in 1390, as his first biographer Santotis claimed (see Paulus de Sancta Maria's *Scrutinium Scripturarum*, Burgos, 1591, p. 24b), but on July 21, 1391, as Baer has rightly construed (*Toledot*, pp. 309, 530, n. 38) on the basis of Graetz' remarks (*Geschichte*, VIII, p. 78, n. 2).

1391),[6] or during some interval in his student career.[7] One may further assume that the astute neophyte came well recommended to the Pope, and owing to this, and his impressive personality,[8] was treated on that visit with a great deal of respect. Yet these assumptions are not in full harmony with some expressions in the Epistle. In the first place, it is unlikely that a recent convert to Christianity, who was still a student of Christian theology, or perhaps only about to become such a student, would be considered by the Pope for high position in the Church hierarchy. It is still less likely that such a man would be *known* to the whole Court and, furthermore, be so esteemed by its members as to be generally regarded as qualified to assume high positions in the Church. In addition, we have no indication from any source that Paul of Burgos visited Avignon during the reign of Clement VII. On the other hand, we know that Pedro de Luna, shortly after becoming Pope Benedict XIII, invited Paul of Burgos to come to Avignon and serve there as his special aide.[9] We also know that Paul accepted the invitation, arrived at Avignon toward the end of 1394, or at the beginning of 1395, and stayed there for four years (until the beginning of 1399),[10] performing political and administrative functions of vital importance to the anti-Papal Church. If the aforesaid references in the Epistle are related to *that* period, the otherwise rather baffling expressions appear quite understandable. For at that time Paul of Burgos was a *power* in Avignon; he did enjoy high prestige, *was* known to the whole court, and could have been considered by the Pope and others as candidate for high Church offices. From the terms used in the Epistle to describe his standing, and the regard with which he was treated, we may gather, indeed, that what is indicated is not

---

[6] See Luciano Serrano, *Los Conversos Don Pablo de Santa María y Don Alfonso de Cartagena*, Madrid, 1942, p. 27. And cf. Cantera, *op. cit.*, p. 307.

[7] It ended in 1394 when he graduated from the University as Doctor of Theology. See Serrano, *op. cit.*, p. 29.

[8] Judging, at least, by the testimony of Bonet Bonjorn (a forced convert to Christianity who fell under Paul's influence), according to the version of the Epistle published in P. M. Heilpern's *Even Bohan*, II, Frankfurt-on-Main, 1846, p. 24: ואמרת שנברא בצלם המשיח ודמותו.

[9] See Serrano, *op. cit.*, p. 31.

[10] *ibid.*, and p. 33.

mere courtesy, or even deference to an important visitor, but *the honor consistently rendered to the occupant of a highly influential position.*[11] For all these reasons it appears most probable that the Epistle was written in that period—that is, after October 11, 1394.

It could not, however, have been written too long after that date. For between the appearance of Duran's Epistle and that of Hasdai Crescas' *Refutation of Christian Dogma* (which occurred not later than 1397),[12] Duran completed his *Shame of the Gentiles*, a sizeable study whose preparation must have taken a considerable time. We thus arrive at the conclusion that the Epistle was composed possibly in 1394, probably in 1395, and the *Shame of the Gentiles*, in all probability, in 1396.

---

[11] *Qoveẓ Vikkuḥim,* p. 47: ואשר עוד כתבת והפלנת והגדלת בספ[ו]ר כל כבודו
ואת יקר תפארת גדולתו.
[12] See Graetz, VIII, note 2, p. 392.

# D

## THE BOOK OF COMPLAINTS

Among the works produced within the time-range of the Inquisition — more precisely, about a decade before its establishment — a Hebrew booklet known as *Sefer Alilot Devarim* (published in *Oẓar Nechmad*, IV [1860], pp. 179–195), is unique, among other things, in the views and information it contains about the Marranos. Completed in the spring of 1468, as is indicated in a manuscript once owned by Kirchheim (see Graetz, VIII [4th ed.], p. 456, note 1), its author chose to hide under the pseudonym of "Palmon b. Peleth of the Fameless" and, in addition, to conceal his thoughts under the cloak of an enigmatic style, which often requires much decoding.[1] No wonder that the work was soon accompanied by a commentary, composed by one Joseph ben Meshulam, a pseudonym for another, or perhaps the same author, as some have suggested with good logic (*ibid.*; and also, p. 457). The reason for this double or triple masquerade was, of course, the author's fear not only lest his identity be exposed, but also lest his views emerge so patently that they could not, should the necessity arise, be defended by the ambiguity of their formulation. Isaac Samuel Reggio, who was the first to publish a portion of this work (*Iggerot Yashar*, I, 1834, pp. 122–132), suggested that the author sought thus to guard himself against persecution by orthodox zealots among the

---

[1] The name "Palmon ben Peleth of the Fameless" is of course an allusion to On ben Peleth, one of the rebels who gathered around Korah and were all "men of renown" (Num. 16.1–2). Like the rebels of old, the author, too, criticised the official leadership of the people, and just as their complaints were groundless, so were ostensibly also his; hence the title of the book, עלילות דברים, i.e., false charges. Both the pseudonym and the title suggest that originally the author here intended to use the figurative-ironic form of writing (which he later abandoned) as another means of covering up both his identity and attitude.

Jews (*ibid.*, p. 123). There may be merit in Reggio's explanation, since the work contains extremely sharp attacks upon the leadership of orthodox Jewry, and the author, who belonged to the rationalistic school, which constituted but a small minority in the community, may well have feared the vengeance of the public he had so grievously offended. Yet despite the fact that it may appear from what he says that the rationalists were persecuted, and that a ban was actually practiced on Maimonides' *Guide* (*Oẓar Nechmad*, IV, p. 185), we know, nevertheless, from other sources, that the study of philosophy, though attacked, was not suppressed, and that besides those scholars who used philosophy for the purpose of strengthening the Jewish heritage (and our author should be counted among them), there were others who belonged to the radical Averroists, as we can clearly gather from Arama (*Ḥazut Qasha*, ed. Pollak, p. 22a). What is more, criticisms against official Judaism for its negative attitude toward philosophical learning were levelled also by other writers at that time (Bibago, *Derekh Emunah*, Constantinople, 1521, 94b); nor was our author alone in his denunciations of what he considered as obscurantism, casuistry, and spiritless or even nonsensical ceremonialism. Such denunciations were voiced, after all, also by men like Alami (*Iggeret Musar*, p. 42) and the qabbalistic author of *Sefer ha-Qanah* (p. 122d). Nevertheless, the fact that this all-out attack upon hallowed religious beliefs and procedures now came not from a pious moralist or a mystic, as was the case with the authors just mentioned, but from a philosophical rationalist who, at that time, could easily be suspected of heterodoxy, plus the particular atmosphere that may have prevailed in his locality (whose identity is unknown to us), may have led the author to exercise extra caution. Reggio, as we suggested, seems therefore to have a point in his explanation of the author's secretiveness. Yet, there was another reason, more apparent and less questionable, that prompted the author to anonymity and disguise.

We refer to the author's statements on the Marranos, and especially on those whom he expected to "return" — a subject which in *no* way could be discussed openly. Although these statements comprise a relatively small fraction of the work, the author would obviously not consider omitting them, as they form integral parts of both its opening and its conclusion and are directly related to the main thesis. The fact that Reggio, Schor (*He-Chalutz*, I, p. 158), Graetz and others did not notice this relationship, and also ignored the historic import of these statements, is, to some extent, understandable: they were fascinated by the author's intellectual approach, in which they saw kinship to the ideas of Enlightenment, and it was therefore natural that they focused their attention on *this* part of the work. As we see it, however, the sections on the Marranos merit careful consideration — first, as essential parts of the work as a whole, and second, as documents containing valuable information about the Marranos and the conversion movement in the author's time.

Let us first examine the introductory passages. After referring to the enormities from which Spain's Jews suffered during the period of massacre, persecution and mass conversion (and to this we shall return later), the author poses the cardinal question that troubled, as we have indicated, many Jews in his century: what was the reason, or rather the justification, for the unprecedented calamity? With all the known facts brought into account, the matter still appeared inexplicable. As the author puts it, the faithful Jews of Spain could in no way see how *they* could be made to blame for what had happened. They knew of no crime in their midst that could justify such a punishment. Nor could they accept the argument that their suffering was due to their ancestors' evil deeds. "If our forefathers, who were exiled, sinned — why are *we* to blame?" (*Ozar Nechmad*, IV, p. 180). In any case, they pointed out, since the beginning of the dispersion, the three capital crimes of idolatry, incest and murder, which were allegedly responsible for the exile, have been practically unknown among the Jews. And since they, the Jews of Spain and the rest of the diaspora, were cleansed so long ago of those sins, why should they still be subjected to their consequences? What is more, their devotion to the Law was greater than that of their forefathers even at the height of the latter's faithfulness; for they are meticulous in observing the commandments, persevere in the study of the Law, and

abound in prayer and fasting; and yet, whereas their forefathers, in the periods of their faithfulness, enjoyed prosperity
and peace in their own land, they, their progeny, whose behavior
is impeccable, are subjected to ever increasing misery. Not
only does God fail to answer their prayers, but "the more we
turn to Him, the more he turns away from us" (*ibid.*). Why?
What was the reason for this great discrepancy between the
deed and the aftermath? — In all this we hear an echo of the
doubts raised concerning the working of Providence which we
have already noticed in earlier writers.

But our author here makes a few additional statements which
reveal to us something of the state of Marranism and that of
the conversion movement in his own time. In presenting the
argument of the contemporary Jew, who is so sure of his righteousness, the author does not fail to take into account something
which is to the disadvantage of the faithful: the fact that Jews
went on converting to Christianity. Was not *this*, he asks, proof
of the sinfulness of the community and justification for its
suffering? The God-fearing Jew, however, finds no difficulty in
rejecting this assumption. In the *paucity* of the instances of
conversion among Jews, and in the *attitude* of Jews toward the
converts, he rather sees a point in his favor. What he says in
this connection is as follows:

"And if 'one of a city and two of a family'[2] convert, they are
excluded from the fold and are ousted from our community,
and even among these, I did not find 'one in a thousand'[3] who
worshipped a foreign deity out of a desire to betray his faith;
they did so out of their inability to suffer the heavy yoke of
the exile; it is their tongue which expressed lies, but their mind
is free of evil" (*ibid.*).

Graetz believed that this passage referred to the Marrano
camp as a whole, and thus used it as proof in his argument
for the Spanish provenance of the work. Yet, although Graetz'
position on the origin of the work merits, in our opinion, unreserved support, it cannot be derived from the above-cited

[2] Jer. 3.14.
[3] Eccl. 7.28.

passage whose meaning he misconstrued. What the author wished to demonstrate here was the faithfulness to Judaism of the Jews in *his* time, and as proof he points out, first, the paucity of the conversions; second, the way the Jews treated the converts; and thirdly, that, save for isolated cases, one could not find even among these few converts true apostates in spirit. Our author could not possibly refer in the above passage to the Marrano camp as a whole, since this camp, as he well knew, consisted of *vast numbers* of *conversos* (not of "one of a city and two of a family"), and the only thing we can learn from this passage is that the conversion movement in the sixties was already reduced to the point of insignificance. Consequently, when he discusses the attitude of *"these"* converts to Judaism, he does not refer, as Graetz thought, to the attitude prevailing in the Marrano body as a whole.[4] In addition, most of the Marranos in his time consisted not of *recent* converts, but of the progeny of Jews who were converted to Christianity two or three generations before, and indeed, about these descendants, i. e., the *sons* of converts, the author, as we shall see, has quite a different view. Then, again, when he speaks of those who "are taken forcibly before they can differentiate between good and evil" (cf. Isaiah, 7.16), he does not refer to the forced conversions of 1391, as Graetz suggests, but to the *children of converts in his time* who were converted at their parents behest, and who grew up "without knowing what Jews are" and "become inadvertently our enemies" (*ibid.*). What we *can* gather from this about the Marranos *generally* may be deduced from the author's view, undoubtedly based on observation, that *those who were converted in their childhood, let alone those who were born as Christians* — and in the sixties the latter were, as we have indicated, the overwhelming majority of the Marranos — *did not know anything about Jews and Judaism and behaved as enemies of the Jewish people.* This is the same view that we noticed in Rashbash as well as in Abravanel.

---

[4] Graetz seems to have been misled by the expression אחד מאלף (see above, note 3) which he believed conveyed what it means literally (or more or less so), while actually it is used here merely as an idiom indicating a tiny fraction.

Actually there is no clear mention in this work of the forced conversion of 1391, although the massacre of that year is referred to in the opening section in the following statement: ויכו ביהודים אויביהם מכת חרב והרג ואבדן, ויעשו ביהודים כרצונם ואין מידם מציל (ibid., p. 179). On the other hand, when in the course of his description of the historic trials of Spanish Jewry, the author says: "and when the days of life among the thorns became long, the light-weighted converted," he undoubtedly alludes to the conversion movement of 1412 which followed a period of suffering and misery ("life among the thorns"). He defined those who converted as of slight significance, and he characterized their life under Christianity as a "success" (ואל כל אשר יפנה ירשיע). Their sons and daughters already act as gentiles, consider themselves as belonging to another nation (בנינו ובנותינו נתונים לעם אחר, ibid.), and some of them even became priests, monks and agitators for Christianity (ומורה ... מהם יקחו לכהנים ולנביאי פסיליהם מעלים על ראשיהם, ibid., p. 180). In fighting the Christians or the converts publicly and in the courts, the Jews stand no chance; and "the more their enemies get on in years, the more they become powerful and successful, and this serves them as proof that there is no God in our midst" (ibid.). The author thus attests to the complete assimilation of the second and third generation of the conversos and to the effect of the contrast between the "weakness" of the Jews and the "power" of their opponents upon the psychological and theological position of the "enemy," and especially upon the development of the conviction that Providence has abandoned Israel. In all this our author confirms what we have learned from other sources.

Nevertheless, while he sees the Marranos on the whole as detached from Israel and estranged from it, the author has not lost hope of their ultimate return to their source. In fact, he reaches the paradoxical conclusion that it is through these future "returners" that the renaissance of the Jewish faith, which, he thought, was badly needed, may come to pass. The following passage, which is remarkable in many ways, conveys this thought clearly:

"And perhaps our distant brothers (אחינו הרחוקים) who left the fold and went over to the religion of the Trinity (אשר יצאו לשלישי),

[or more precisely, perhaps] their sons *who will come after them* (i. e., not in the immediate future), and *your offspring of whom you thought that they were destined to spoliation* (namely, those Jews who were converted in their childhood and became true, or even fanatic Christians) will be moved or compelled in the course of time (יְלָחֲצוּ באחרית הימים), by the very fact of their origin and ancestry (מעיקר שרשם לתולדותם), to look back upon the rock from which they were hewn, to observe the ways of truth (יביטו ארחות תוֹמָה), and once they "awaken," they will be astonished at their ignorance; they will examine, with open eyes, both religions (יפקחו עיניהם על שני הסעפים; an allusion to I Kings, 18.21), they will soon see what their present place of worship (namely their religion, Christianity) truly represents; they will leave that place so that the triple thread (another allusion to the religion of the Trinity) will soon be ruptured, for it does not represent a lasting tie that one can uphold with real sincerity (כי אין בו קשר של קיימא לקיימו בתום לבבם), and they will emerge cleansed from the "bathing" (הרחצה; an allusion to baptism), sevenfold purged of all prejudice (דעה קדומה), purified from the defilement of the announcements (הפרסומים; their denunciations of Judaism, or their declarations of faith in Christianity), as well as from the transgressions in deed (violations of the commandments, and perhaps actions against Jews); they will now resemble clean new tablets on which a human script will be engraved, while the tablets themselves will be divine, as will be the contents of the engraved words. In fact, only *such* will be the contents (containing none of the superstitious beliefs which the author attributed to his Jewish contemporaries); they will walk in the path of righteousness, and will not show favoritism in judgment; truth will be their sole guide, and so single-mindedly will they follow the path of truth that they will find it neither possible nor justifiable to deviate from it; they will seek the God who is above us and will reach out to His dwelling (namely, return to Judaism, which will this time be an enlightened, refined and purified Judaism, in keeping with the author's conception of it). He will be their God and they will be His people, great in numbers (indicating the large number of the Marranos, in contrast to the paucity of the Jews), some of them ordinary people (המונים) and some learned and wise (חכמים ונבונים), and from them will be chosen the priests and the Levites (namely, the leaders of the people); they will defend Judaism against its detractors (המה יריבו בָּרָבִים). They will be the spokesmen of Jewry (המה ידברו במדברים), and they will expel the snakes from among the people" (*ibid.*, p. 195).

It is clear that the author, who was deeply dissatisfied with the spiritual and communal leadership of the Jews (hence his biting criticism against the Rabbis), dreamt of a new leadership for the Jewish people that would be drawn from the camp of the Marranos. Once they returned to Judaism, he hoped, they would grasp it in its *true* meaning, and not in the distorted, corrupt form it assumed, as he was sure, in the minds of the formalists. They will necessarily arrive at such a "*pure*" Judaism, for their joining it will come as a result of *study and examination,* and not of following custom and tradition blindly. Also, the author hoped that the returning Marranos, whose upper class was trained in the humanistic sciences, and especially in logic and rhetoric, and who included so many eloquent speakers, statesmen and men of affairs, would supply Jewry not only with the intellectual force that would bring about its spiritual rejuvenation, but also with the proper communal leadership that would appropriately represent it before Christendom and effectively defend it against its foes.

The author's general view of the Marranos is further indicated in another passage, which suggests a highly original approach. "*For as a slave was Joseph sold, because his brethren did not want him to rule over them, but he came out of prison to become king.* Pharaoh schemed (נרעץ) to subject the children of Israel to hard labor, for he feared lest they become numerous—but they became numerous just the same. What the passage conveys is quite clear. Just as Joseph emerged from prison to dominion, so the Jews, *via* the Marrano element, emerged from the prison and slavery of the exile to leadership over the gentiles (an indication of the decisive political power of the Marranos in the days of Enrique IV[5]), and just as Pharaoh, who

[5] Even three decades later, when they were plagued by the Inquisition, Abravanel could still write similarly: ולא אמר [הנביא] בהם [באותם שיצאו מן הכלל]

planned to destroy the Jewish people by first reducing its numbers to the very minimum, failed in his attempt, and the Jews, under his subjugation, became exceedingly numerous, so did the enemies of the Jewish people in Spain (especially the Church) fail in achieving their aims. They hoped to diminish the number of the Jews by conversion, and finally to wipe them out as a people, but actually it was within Christendom itself that *their numbers increased beyond all normal measures,* and since they will ultimately return to Jewry, the Jewish people will thus increase, rather than diminish, in quantity. The author does not see in the prestige and power of the Marranos, or in their great numerical strength, a cause for jealousy or dismay, as was the habitual attitude of the Jews, but rather a cause for pride and elation. Paradoxically, he believed, Jewry was bound ultimately to *gain* rather than *lose* by the mass conversion. It was the will of God to have a part of Jewry go through the agony of conversion, in order to come out of it enriched intellectually and enforced materially.

"And this salvation is not wondrous (לא נפלאת היא), and not far off and not in heaven (namely, should not be considered miraculous). It is part of man's spirit, imbued in him by God, to yearn for ancestral origin (לחשוק במחצבים—the rock from which he was hewn). Nor is it something new; it happened many times before. And we have received indications to this effect (וכאלה שמועות) from the remote corners of the land (מכנף האדץ), and I need but say: it is a secret, it is a secret (רזי לי, רזי לי)" [*ibid.*].

The author's hopes for a rejuvenation of Judaism through the rejudaized Marrano camp were thus based on rumors he heard about a movement of "self-examination" or "return to Judaism" among the Marranos. The movement must have

---

שביה ועבדות . . . שהם יצאו מכלל השביה והגלות והם כיתר העמים בכבוד ובמעלה, לא בשבי (And the prophet did not attribute captivity and slavery to those who left the fold . . . for they were excluded from the body of the captives and exiles and, like the other nations, enjoy *honor and high status*), *Mashmi'a Yeshu'ah,* p. 12. Also: [והם] בעושר ובכבוד ובמעלה בגויי הארץ וגדולים ושרים בערים זה שנים רבת (they enjoy wealth, honor and high status like the nations of the land, and have been [among the] leaders of the cities since many years ago), *Comm. on Deuteronomy,* 28.49, p. 6d.

originated somewhere on the border of the country; in all likelihood in Seville, which was then at "the end of the land," and
its activity was necessarily shrouded in secrecy. This is why
the author chose to write in such an enigmatic style and even
alluded to the need for secrecy by saying "רזי לי, רזי לי".

What caused the appearance of such a clandestine group,
when the entire Marrano body was either well on its way toward
total assimilation or, in fact, actually assimilated? The clue to
the right answer is given by the date of the composition of the
*Book of Complaints*: 1468. The crucial event in Marrano life
that took place shortly before that date was the outburst of
the populace against the Marranos in Toledo, in July-August
1467, and we may assume that it was this event that provoked
the emergence of the group. It was inevitable that the massacre
and the accompanying campaign, which was incessantly calling
for their total destruction, cause *some* of the Marranos to wonder
about their fate and, as a result, to look back upon their origin,
the religion of their ancestry, and then, after inquiring into the
essence of Judaism, to become convinced of its superiority over
Christianity. Our author's claim that the new movement was
stirred by feelings of *ethnic* belonging is no doubt a reflection of
the reaction of some Marranos to the hostile agitation conducted by the Old Christians against their corrupt Jewish stock.
Such an agitation in itself was bound to rouse in some of them
a revulsion toward the former drive for assimilation and an urge
to look back with pride and longing to the people from which
they stemmed and within which, if they joined it, they would
not be discriminated against.

This was the beginning of the Neo-Crypto-Judaism, of the
"movement of awakening," of which, as we have noticed,
Abravanel also spoke. The group involved must have been very
small, and perhaps limited merely to espousers of a "theoretical
Judaism," and hence the fire of criticism it drew from writers
like Caro (see above, pp. 167–168). Our author, however, placed
great hopes in its development. "It is not beyond its power to
succeed and establish itself," he believed, "for this is a sect
dedicated to this purpose." Surely, the sources we have examined indicate that these hopes were not justified; the group

remained extremely limited in scope and was in no way able to affect the broad current of Marrano life. But it was sufficient to give the Marrano-mongers *another* excuse for their agitation, and enable them to intensify their hue and cry about the threat of "Judaization." The movement which was a *new* phenomenon, not rooted in a long-standing Jewish underground, but which sprang, as we have suggested, out of persecution, was partly responsible for only one development: it helped bring about a far greater persecution — that of the Inquisition.

# E

## THE NUMBER OF THE MARRANOS IN SPAIN

What was the number of the Marranos at the time of the establishment of the Inquisition? The question is obviously of general importance, since it touches upon the general history of Spain in which the Marranos played a notable part; and it is of special significance to this investigation, since it is only by the total number of the Marranos that the strength of the crypto-Jewish element can be correctly gauged. Though modern historiography was concerned with this problem, it did not come up with clear answers. What we have before us in the scholarly writings, either of Jewish or of Spanish origin, is a number of indefinite and conflicting statements, rarely accompanied by any evidence from the sources.

According to Baer, the number of the conversos amounted to "tens of thousands" (*Toledot ha-Yehudim bi-Sefarad ha-Noẓrit*, 1959, p. 365), from which it appears that their total numerical strength was not greater, and possibly smaller, than that of the Jews. This view agrees with Baer's general estimate of the limited number of Spain's Jews in the 14th century. Several considerations, however, have led us to believe that this view is erroneous and that the number of Spain's Jews in the 14th century was much larger than what Baer assumed.[1] If that was the case, there is, at least, a theoretical possibility that the Marranos constituted a much larger group; but a possibility is, of course, not an actuality.

Certain conclusions could possibly be reached about the number of the New Christians at the end of the 15th century, if we could ascertain the number of Jews who went over to Christianity at the end of the 14th century, i. e., in 1391, and later during the second wave of conversion in 1412–1415. The

[1] See Graetz's fundamentally solid arguments on this matter in *Geschichte der Juden*, VIII (4th ed.), 10th addendum, pp. 459–466.

question is whether we possess adequate information to arrive at some conclusions to this effect.

"It is very difficult," says Amador de los Ríos, "to reduce to a figure that could be considered truly historical, the number of Jews who, in one sense or another, departed from the bosom of Judaism" (*Historia de los Judíos de España y Portugal*, II, p. 445, note). According to what he had gathered from various works, he could compute the losses suffered by Spanish Jewry as a result of the attacks of 1391 at about 250,000 souls, including 200,000 converts in Castile and Aragon. "All these figures, however," says Amador, "appear to us extremely exaggerated, even if they include those who left the country through emigration to Portugal and Granada" (*ibid.*). Why these figures were considered by him as exaggerated, and, one should add, even "extremely" so, the Spanish historian does not tell us.[2]

Let us now see what the sources hold for us. Zacuto, whom we have already quoted on the subject, tells us that in the year 1391, i. e., during the great riots, "more than 4,000 Jews" were converted (*Juchassin*, ed. Filipowski, p. 225a), while in 1412, during the campaign of Vicente Ferrer, more than 200,000 embraced Christianity (*ibid.*, p. 225b). As for the first figure, it obviously stands in no relation to the dimensions of the catastrophe of 1391 and to what is recorded by contemporary authors. Thus we know from Ḥasdai Crescas' letter to the Jews of Avignon (published as supplement to *Shevet Yehuda*, ed. Wiener, Hannover, 1855, Hebrew section, p. 128) that the number of

---

[2] It should be noted, however, that Amador's calculations were, to begin with, grounded in error. An assertion by I. Bédarride (*Les juifs en France, en Italie et en Espagne*, Paris, 1859, p. 273) that 100,000 Jews converted in Aragon during the riots of 1391 was believed by Amador to be based on *Shevet Yehudah* (see his *Historia . . .*, II, p. 403, note 1, and p. 445, note 1), while the latter work contains no such information, nor does Bédarride rely on it in this instance (see Bédarride, *op. cit.*, p. 533, note 92). As this historian indicates, his source is Llorente. The latter, however, does not speak of 100,000 converts in *Aragon*, but of "more than 100,000 Jewish *families*, that is, perhaps, a million persons" that "renounced the Law of Moses" *throughout Spain* during the riots of 1391 and shortly thereafter. See his *Histoire critique de l'Inquisition d'Espagne*, I, Paris, 1818, p. 141. Llorente offers no source for this statement.

converts in Seville alone exceeded 4,000 by far. "There were six or seven thousand Jewish households in Seville," says Crescas. Of these, he points out, "many were killed" by the rioters, some of the children were sold as slaves to the Moslems, *"but the majority converted"* (*ibid.*). Baer (*Die Juden im christlichen Spanien*, II, p. 233) rejects Ḥasdai's statement on the number of Jews in Seville as inconceivable. But can it be assumed that a man like Crescas, the leader of Aragonese Jewry, would not know the approximate number of Jews in one of the greatest Jewish communities in Spain? Or is it likely that he who considered it his duty to care for the safety of the Jews in Aragon, would not seek and obtain reliable information about what took place during the riots in other parts of Spain? Indeed as a Jewish leader and courtier, he must have had access to reliable information, and therefore we must consider his statements on this subject as highly authoritative. What is more, to the extent that the Spanish chroniclers deal with the riots in Seville, they confirm — at least, in part — what Crescas tells us. Thus Ayala (*Crónica del rey Don Enrique tercero de Castilla*, año primero, 1391, chap. xx, Madrid, 1953, p. 177) states that "most of the Jews who lived there [in Seville] were turned Christians and many of these were killed." These are precisely the words used by Crescas except that Ayala gives no figures. But Zuñiga, the historian of Seville, lists the losses by death from the massacre in that city at "more than 4,000" — a number which could constitute a "minority" of Seville's Jews if the total consisted of 6–7,000 households (or 30,000–35,000 souls[3]), as recorded by Crescas. All this leads us to the conclusion that the number

---

[3] According to some statisticians, however, the average number of persons per family was 4.5 (see Manuel Colmeiro, *Historia de la Economía Política de España*, Madrid, 1965 [first ed. 1863], I, pp. 298-299), while others raise it to 6, and even 7 in the largest cities (*ibid.*, p. 299, n.11). If we follow the lower estimate, however, the total indicated should be reduced by some 10%. The figure cited does not appear implausible if we recall that Jews were among the first settlers of Seville after the reconquest in 1248, and that by the end of the 14th century Seville was the foremost commercial center of Castile. Perhaps the first reliable figure for Seville's total population is the one offered by the census of 1587: more than 120,000 inhabitants, no doubt representing an increment in the population since 1391; see Tomás González, *Censo de la Población de las Provincias . . . de Castilla* etc., Madrid, 1829, p. 334.

of Jews converted in 1391 in the city of Seville alone amounted to approximately 25,000.

The other definite figure supplied by Crescas is in regard to Valencia. In this community, says he, some 250 Jews were killed during the riots, only a few escaped the fury, while the rest, the "majority" of the community, consisting of some 1,000 households, went over to Christianity. In this instance, too, Baer considers the figure cited by Crescas as highly exaggerated (*Toledot*, p. 116), and here again we see no basis for Baer's contention. That Crescas did not know the size of the Jewish community of Valencia, which was in the sphere of his communal responsibility, is even less likely than in the case of Seville. On top of this, Crescas' report with regard to Valencia is likewise confirmed by the Christian sources. Thus, Escolano, the official chronicler of Valencia, states, no doubt on good authority, that the number of converts during the riots amounted to "more than 7,000 souls" (*Decada primera de la Historia de* . . . *Valencia*, 1610, I, lib. V, cap. x, col. 958) which is more or less identical with the figure of 1,000 households given by Crescas. Hence, the conversion toll in only two out of the numerous cities hit by the riots amounted to tens of thousands of souls; and consequently the figure of 200,000 converts for the whole of Spain does not seem exaggerated, as it appeared to Amador. As a matter of fact, earlier editions of Zacuto's *Juchassin*, do have the figure of 200,000 instead of 4,000 found in the Filipowski edition. The discrepancy was already noticed by Graetz who, while realizing that the figure of 4,000 must certainly be erroneous, could nevertheless not vouch for the authenticity of the earlier version. As we shall see, the correctness of this version can be fully established.

Accordingly, Zacuto gives us this same figure of 200,000 for both the conversion of 1391 and 1412. We have seen that for 1391, this figure is not incompatible with what we find in contemporary sources.[4] As for 1412, however, we have no such

[4] These include the important statement of Reuben ben Nissim Gerundi, testifying that during the riots of 1391, about 140,000 Jews converted (see Hershman, *op. cit.*, pp. 194–195). Gerundi's figure is, to be sure, substantially lower than Zacuto's. But in September 1391 (the date of the above statement), the author may not have possessed all relevant information and, in any case,

corroboration. Among the testimonies available for that year, of special interest is that of Mariana, according to whom some 35,000 Jews were converted to Christianity under the influence of Vicente Ferrer (*Historia General de España*, lib. XIX; ed. Madrid, 1950, p. 48b). This figure is of course much smaller than that cited by Zacuto.[5] But the discrepancy between Mariana and Zacuto may be reconciled; for the latter, under the heading of 1412, included not only those who were converted by the Dominican friar, but also those who were converted for other reasons, especially under the impact of the governmental persecutions then unleashed against the Jews of Castile and Aragon. This is really what his statement says: "In the year 1412 there was a great *shemad* . . . in Aragon and in Castile, by the Christian preacher fray Vicente *and* by the King of Aragon, Don Fernando, *and* by Doña[sa] Catalina, the Queen of Castile, during which more than 200,000 Jews were converted" (*Juchassin*, p. 225b). Nevertheless, while Mariana's statement does not contradict that of Zacuto, it does not confirm it either. To what extent, then, can we consider the latter's claim authentic?

The question cannot be answered definitely as we do not know the sources from which Zacuto derived this information. However, his assertions for 1412, as well as those for 1391, are considerably fortified by the fact that two coeval Hebrew chronicles offer us the identical information. One of these is *Sefer ha-Qabbala* of Abraham ben Solomon of Torrutiel, written in 1510, and the other is *Zekher Ẓaddiq* of Joseph ben Ẓaddiq of Arevalo, written in 1487.[5b] While using practically the same formulation as Zacuto in this instance, both these chroniclers fixed the number of converts at more than 200,000 for each of the conversion waves of 1391 and 1412 (A. Neubauer, *Mediaeval Jewish Chronicles*, I, Oxford, 1887, pp. 98, 110). Whether the two later chroniclers (Abraham of Torrutiel and Zacuto) followed here Joseph of

could not take into account those who left Judaism *in the wake of the riots* and, consequently, were also regarded as converts of "1391."

[5] And still smaller is the number given by Usque: 15,000 souls. See his *Consolaçam ás tribulaçoens de Israel*, Ferrara, 1553, III, chap. 21, p. 188b (Eng. translation by Martin A. Cohen, *Consolation for the Tribulations of Israel*, Philadelphia, 1965, p. 194).

[5a] This (דונה and not זונה) may have well been the original reading.

[5b] See, however, on this date, above, chap. III, note 52.

Arevalo, or whether the three of them relied on some earlier source, cannot now be ascertained. It is doubtful, however, that the source followed dated from the *beginning* of the 15th century. The round and equal figures (more than 200,000) cited for each of the two years, 1391 and 1412, do not suggest factual, historic exactitude, but rather a tradition that was prevalent among Spain's Jews, according to which the number of converts in the period of the great conversions (1391–1415) exceeded a total of 400,000, of whom about half were converted by force and half voluntarily. What is of further importance is the fact that our three chroncilers accepted this tradition unqualifiedly, for it serves to reveal the scope of the Marrano population in *their* time. It shows that the size of that population, which was undoubtedly known to them, was *at least* in the neighborhood of the figures they quoted. Otherwise, these figures would have made no sense to them, and consequently would not have been acceptable.

It is clear, therefore, that about the time the Inquisition was established, the Marrano population numbered not *tens* of thousands, as suggested by Baer, but *hundreds* of thousands. The question is only how many such hundreds. Fortunately, we can be assisted here by a testimony offered by Isaac Abravanel. Surprisingly, this testimony has been overlooked or, at least, not referred to by any of the scholars who have dealt with this problem. Yet it not only offers much support to the statements of Zacuto, Abraham of Torrutiel and Joseph of Arevalo, cited above, but also serves as a definitive clue for determining the number of the Marranos toward the end of the 15th century.

The testimony referred to is found in Abravanel's commentary on Daniel (1497). There, while discussing the converts from Judaism and their ruthless persecution by the Inquisition, Abravanel states that *the number of those subjected to that persecution was larger than that of those who left Egypt* (*Ma'yenei ha-Yeshu'ah*, XII, 6; ed. 1647, p. 87a). Now "the number of those who left Egypt" was not a flowery expression for Abravanel, but a concrete figure. He may have thought of the number 600,000, which usually comes to mind when this phrase is quoted; and, if this was the case, we could say that, according to Abravanel, the number of the Marranos in his time was between 600–700 thousand. On the other hand, Abravanel may have had in mind a much larger figure, based on his *own* conception of the "number of those who left Egypt." This conception is indicated in his Commentary on the Pentateuch.

Referring to the biblical statement which specifies that the exodus from Egypt comprised "about six hundred thousand men on foot besides the children" (Ex. 12.37), Abravanel says that by "600,000 men were meant only those capable of going to battle," while the phrase 'besides the children' alluded not merely to the children, but to everyone who was below military age (i. e., below twenty), or above it, i. e. the elderly people of over fifty who, from a military standpoint, "were classed as 'children'."[6] Abravanel, then, believed that the figure mentioned in the verse he commented upon did not represent the *entire* manhood of יוצאי מצרים as is commonly maintained, but only a majority of it, while the terms employed (גברים and טף) refer to the entire male population of the Exodus. This, in all likelihood, was estimated by Abravanel at 900,000 to 1,000,000, assuming that he calculated those designated as "children" according to population standards of the Middle Ages (when children and people over fifty were subjected to a high rate of mortality).

The size of the Marrano population of Spain at the time of the establishment of the Inquisition was, then, according to Abravanel, somewhere between a minimum of about 600,000 and a maximum of 1,000,000.[7] The question now is which of these estimates is the correct one or, at least, which of them should be preferred. The answer can be given by examining both in the light of further relevant information.

To begin with, we should compare our latter deductions to what we gathered from the contemporary Hebrew chronicles. These, as we have seen, preserved a tradition concerning the scope of the mass conversions which, thus far, has remained unrefuted. Assuming, then, that the original Marrano camp consisted of over 400,000 — or up to 450,000 — souls, it would mean,

---

[6] *Comm. on Pentateuch* (Exodus), Warsaw, 1862, p. 22a.

[7] Of course, if the *female* population was included, the number suggested was twice as large, and this would mean that the Spanish Marranos were, according to Abravanel, 1,800,000–2,000,000 strong. Such a figure, however, is unacceptable, as it would be quite inconsistent with the other available data. See below, pp. 246–248.

if the *second* deduction is accepted, that, in the course of three generations, the number of the Marranos was no less than doubled by natural increase. Such an increase, although not impossible, is most unlikely for the Middle Ages. On the other hand, if the *first* deduction is considered, the natural increase involved would amount to only 50–55% of the total, and such an increase, although also high, is not at all unlikely or improbable, especially in view of the indications we have about the unusual growth of the Marrano population (see above, p. 232). Nor is it necessarily incompatible with the general size of the Spanish people. The 15th century saw also a general increase of the Spanish population, so that at the end of the 15th century it numbered, in both Castile and Aragon, 9,250,000 (according to the Castilian census taken in 1482 by Alonso de Quintanilla, the Contador Mayor of the Catholic Kings, and other reliable sources for the Aragonese provinces[8]). This means that the Marrano population at the time of the establishment of the Spanish Inquisition constituted about 7%, and together with the Jewish community, less than 10% of the total population of Spain — an estimate which would be entirely in accord with the number of Spain's Jews in the 14th century, and their percentage in the general population, as keenly suggested by Graetz.[9] Moreover, there are additional reasons that lead us to consider the smaller of the two figures we have derived from Abravanel as more likely to agree with the historic facts.

The first of these reasons is implied in the conclusion we gather from a remark left us by Zurita concerning a part of the Marrano population. The remark was made in relation to a summary, presented in Diego de Valera's *Crónica de los Reyes Católicos*, of the Inquisition's activities in the archbishopric of Seville. At the end of the 40th chapter of this chronicle, it is stated that "up to the year 1520, there were burned in Seville and its archbishopric more than four thousand persons, and more than thirty thousand were reconciled, not counting the

[8] See Tomás González, *op. cit.*, pp. 94, 137, and Agustín de Blas, *Origen, Progresos y Límites de la Población* . . ., Madrid, 1833, pp. 152–153. And cf. Conrad Haebler, *Prosperidad y Decadencia Económica de España durante el Siglo XVI*, 1899, pp. 13–14.

[9] See *Geschichte*, VIII (4th ed.), p. 464.

others in other cities and kingdoms" (*Crónica . . .*, ed. Juan de M. Carriazo, Madrid, 1927, p. 124). On this passage, obviously an interpolation, since Diego de Valera died in 1488 (see *ibid.*, p. LXXI), Zurita, who owned a manuscript of the *Crónica*, left us a marginal note, in which he remarked as follows: "This chronicler does not know what he is talking about. For among those condemned by the Inquisition as judaized heretics, whether living or dead or absentees, *were more than one hundred thousand only in this archbishopric of Seville*, including those reconciled for the said crime" (*ibid.*, p. 124, note 1).[10] Zurita, who was not only a cautious historian, but also a high functionary of the Inquisition, must have certainly made this statement on good authority; and the vehemence, with which he rejects the summary he criticized, shows that he had no doubt about the matter. Thus, while his statement may serve as basis for evaluating the number of the Inquisition's victims, it can also serve as clue for determining the number of Marranos in Seville and, via Seville, in the whole of Spain.

What can be said in connection with the above is that, although the Inquisitorial net no doubt engulfed the entire Marrano camp, there must have remained *some* Marranos who were not involved in the reconciliations and punishments. On the other hand, we have noticed that Zurita's account includes also the heretics who were condemned by the Inquisition after their death, and by this he refers of course mostly to Marranos who died *prior* to 1481. Bearing both these circumstances in mind,[11] and considering the fact that the period involved covered about a generation and a half, we may estimate the Marrano population of the archbishopric — without incurring, we believe, a gross error —

[10] "Este coronista no sabe lo que dize porque entre bibos y muertos y ausentes condenados por eréticos judaizados fueron mas de cient myll personas solamente en este arçobispado de Sevilla con los reconciliados por el dicho delito."

[11] On the prosecution of the dead, see Lea, *A History of the Inquisition of Spain*, III, New York, 1907, pp. 81–84. Concerning the limits in which the condemnations of the dead may be taken into account when one assesses the Marrano population, see below, p. 266, note 32. And see also below, p. 267, on the source of Zurita's estimate.

at about 70,000. If we deduct from this figure the number added by natural increase in the course of three generations (according to the rate considered above), the remainder of 45,000 would constitute the original Marrano population in the archbishopric, and at the same time would represent about a ninth (or a tenth) of the original Marrano camp in Spain.[12] The entire Marrano community of the archbishopric in the *early period of the Inquisition*, according to what we gathered from Zurita, also formed about a ninth (or a tenth) of the total Marrano population, according to our *first* deduction from Abravanel.

There is another source dating from the same period which leads to the same conclusion. I refer to the report submitted in 1506 by the Venetian ambassador to Castile, Vincenzo Quirini, to the senate of the Republic.[13] The statement it contains concerning the Marranos was already noticed by Graetz,[14] who correctly sensed its value, but, unaware of some of the aforementioned data, could not make full use of it. Now, according to Quirini, the Marranos of his time were estimated to constitute one third of the townsmen and merchants in Castile and other provinces of Spain (si giudica in Castiglia ed in altre provincie di Spagna il térzo esser Marrani; un terzo dico di coloro che sono cittadini e mercanti). If we apply this information to the figures we derived from Abravanel, we see that it too can be easily harmonized with our *first* deduction, but not with the *second*. Multiplying by three each of the figures deduced would give us, respectively, a general urban population for Spain of 1,800,000–2,100,000 and 2,700,000–3,000,000. While an urban population

---

[12] This conclusion is not incongruous with the number of conversions (about 25,000) that took place in Seville in 1391 (see above, p. 238). While additional several thousands of conversions may have later occurred in the *city* of Seville, the balance may have come from localities in the archbishopric both in 1391 and the succeeding period. That this *could* have been the case is suggested by the fact that the general population of only 15 such localities, in which Jews were *known* to have lived in the 14th and 15th centuries, exceeded 100,000, of which about a half belonged to the three cities: Carmona, Ecija and Jerez de la Frontera (see Tomás González, *op. cit.*, pp. 335–337).

[13] Eugenio Albèri, *Relazioni degli Ambasciatori Veneti al senato*, Serie Iª. — Vol. I°., Florence, 1859, p. 29.

[14] *Geschichte*, VIII, p. 464.

of the latter size would constitute some 29–32% of the total, which is far above the averages considered likely for that period, an urban population of the former size would constitute only 19–22% of the total which falls within the range of these averages. True, this is also above the "minimum" of 16.5%, which was used by Graetz in his computation, but it is perhaps more fitting for Spain, where numerous small settlements were defined as *villas*, owned charters or privileges and served as dwelling places, first, for Jewish and later for Marrano communities. Thus, in view of all the above data and considerations, we arrive at the conclusion that the Marrano population of Spain in the 1480's was 600,000–650,000 strong.

But, if this was the Marranos' total number, the quantity of the "returners" which amounted, as we have seen, to a few thousand souls only, perhaps to a maximum of 6,000–7,000 within the first two decades of the Inquisition, constituted no more than approximately 1% of the total. And, if this was their number *after* the establishment of the Inquisition, we can gather the weakness of crypto-Judaism prior to its establishment. Inexorably we are thus again led to the conclusion that the Inquisition was *not* established to wipe out a powerful and dangerous Jewish heresy, as its campaign and activity may suggest, and as its advocates so staunchly maintain, but for reasons altogether different.

POST SCRIPTUM TO SECOND EDITION

## THE MARRANOS' COUNTRIES OF REFUGE

In addition to the evidence adduced in Appendix B regarding the destinations of the fugitives from the Inquisition, it is worthwhile to cite a testimony of Palencia which bears directly upon the same topic. Describing the impact of the Cordova riots (1473) and their aftermath upon the Marranos of Seville, Palencia tells us that most of the latter decided to "flee from those inhumane lands."[1] According to Palencia, the Sevillian Marranos considered only two places *in* Spain that might serve as shelters from the hatred that threatened them. These were Gibraltar and Niebla.[2] Gibraltar had been assigned by the Duke of Medina Sidonia as haven for the Cordovan refugees;[3] and Niebla, adjacent to the territory of Seville, was a stronghold of the same Duke who, at least since 1465, was regarded by the Marranos as a staunch friend.[4] Other Marranos, however, rejected these and, we may suppose, similar solutions as being, in their opinion, far from satisfactory; and, therefore, as Palencia tells us, "many decided" to leave Spain altogether and "go to Flanders or Italy."[5]

What we gather from this document is that, after the riots of 1473, the Marranos of Seville realized full well the hopelessness of their situation. More specifically, they felt certain that in Spain they could live thenceforth only under strong armed protection and in some outlying places. Yet, even when they arrived at this far-reaching conclusion, all that Palencia can tell us in this connection is that many of them decided to leave Spain, but not to leave Christendom. If some of them did harbor such thoughts, and consequently planned to settle in a Moslem country, their number must have been too small to leave an imprint

[1] *Crónica de Enrique IV* (transl. by Paz y Melia), III, p. 133.
[2] *ibid., ibid.*
[3] *ibid.*, pp. 132–133 and 229–233.
[4] See "Los 'Anales' de Garci Sánchez," published by J. de M. Carriazo in *Anales de la Universidad Hispalense*, Seville, año XIV (1953), p. 53 (item 239).
[5] *Crónica de Enrique IV*, III, pp. 133–134.

in public life, and thus be noticed by the chronicler. This, we should add, is all the more striking in view of Seville's closeness to Granada, and its relative proximity to other Moslem countries such as Morocco and Algiers.[6]

There is no doubt that what Palencia here reports are no mere moods and inclinations, but resolutions supported by some tangible evidence—that is, by *actual movements of migration* which, however limited, testified to the concreteness of the tendencies he described. This concreteness, moreover, is also attested by the reasons he offers for the decision of those Marranos who opted to leave Spain at that time. As he puts it, these reasons were (1) "to save at least the lives of their wives and children, and (2) avoid the mark of infamy which awaited them in Spain if they were to become a tribe apart in the towns" by living in places which would soon be known as the "precincts or colonies of the conversos."[7]

Apart from the danger to their lives, then, the Marranos who resolved to leave the country were haunted by the vision of their future life in Spain, if indeed they had chosen to remain there. They felt that the alternative offered for emigration—concentrating in such places as Gibraltar or Niebla—would inevitably

[6] While persistently and heatedly arguing against the plan of turning Gibraltar into a Marrano refuge, some counsellors of the Duke of Medina Sidonia, master of Gibraltar at the time, tried to present the Marrano Gibraltar project as a clever Jewish scheme for an ulterior purpose. They claimed that the Marranos "have preferably chosen that outermost maritime town [allegedly for their settlement], so that many of them could more freely pass from there to Egypt and Jerusalem, the city beloved by all Hebrews from antiquity" (*Crónica de Enrique IV*, III, p. 230). Whatever the origin of this claim or prediction (no doubt produced when other arguments failed), it was soon to be denied by the facts. For after the Marranos had settled in Gibraltar, no such migration to the East took place (had it occurred, Palencia, in line with his policy, would not have failed to report it). On the other hand, we are informed that the Sevillian Marrano group which settled in Gibraltar with the Cordovan fugitives, and comprised several thousand souls, made no use whatever of that "outermost" location for transferring itself to Jerusalem. When they decided to leave Gibraltar (after having quarrelled with the Cordovans), they "returned"—as Palencia tells us—to "their old homes," i.e., to Seville (*ibid*, pp. 233–234).

[7] *ibid.*, p. 134.

render their settlements notorious as "precincts or colonies of conversos," and thus help stigmatize them as "a tribe apart"— a thing which they could not tolerate.[8] Obviously, the wish of these Marranos was not to be grouped in special communities, which would help them retain their social identity and safeguard their own way of life—if indeed they had such—but rather to intermingle with the rest of the population and become "unmarked" and unnoticeable. This, however, is a wish typical of Jewish assimilationists in all places and at all times.

One may argue that the reasoning indicated suggests, in the main, opposition to ostracism. No doubt it does. But had these Marranos been *secret Jews*, they would not have minded too much being considered a "tribe apart," and would doubtlessly have realized that, *by their very way of life*—i.e., as crypto-Jews, they were eventually *bound* to be so considered anywhere else in Christendom. Their belief that they could be *fully* accepted in other Christian societies outside Spain shows that they considered themselves as Christian, and hoped to be so considered by others under less prejudicial conditions. In any case, the choice of *exclusively* Christian countries for Marrano immigration purposes, plus the telling fact that no religious motive is mentioned among their incentives for leaving Spain,[9] reveals the weakness of the Jewish element in their midst in the early 1470s. Surely Jewish

---

[8] One should not ignore, of course, the probability that, of all Christian countries, Italy and Flanders were chosen as havens and areas of resettlement for economic reasons as well. As is known, Italian (especially Genovese) and Flemish merchants were constantly active in Seville, and the Marranos, involved in trade with those countries, developed considerable ties with them (on the relations between the Marranos and the Genovese colony in Seville, see Claudio Guillén, "Un Padrón de Conversos Sevillanos (1510)," in *Bulletin Hispanique*, 1963, pp. 53–54). If Palencia does not mention the economic motive in this connection, it is, we assume, because he came to believe that the questions then uppermost in the Marranos' minds were those of security and their equality as Christian citizens. Italy and Flanders may have been deemed best suited also for the solution of these problems.

[9] And see above, pp. 57–58, concerning the rarity of Marrano migrants to North Africa in the decades preceding the establishment of the Inquisition.

interests, longings and aspirations played no major role in the Marranos' considerations when they charted the future courses of their lives.

And this relates to Seville — a city which, according to the advocates of the Inquisition, as well as the believers in Marrano Jewishness, was the "most powerful" center of crypto-Judaism in Spain.

THE NUMBER OF MARRANOS IN SEVILLE IN THE 1480s

Discussing the Marranos in the 13th volume of his *A Social and Religious History of the Jews*, and touching, among other things, upon the question of their numbers, Professor S. W. Baron says that, in assessing the size of the Marrano community in Spain on the eve of the founding of the Spanish Inquisition, I relied on the "exaggerated assertions of a few Jewish and non-Jewish writers." Accordingly, he states that the figure I suggested for the total Marrano population at the time (i.e., 600,000-700,000) "appears much too high even for the period after 1492," just as my "estimate of 25,000 Jews converted in 1391 in the city of Seville alone[1] does not square with other known estimates, such as those of a maximum total population of 35,000 for Seville and of 7,000,000 for Spain as a whole." Also, Professor Baron maintains that my reference to Seville's population in 1587, which he likewise denotes as "doubtless exaggerated," proves nothing for the earlier period, since the 16th century was one of a "general urban expansion," and Seville, in particular, experienced "fast growth as an emporium of trade for both the Atlantic and the Mediterranean worlds" (see *ibid.*, p. 337, note 4).

The author of the *Social and Religious History of the Jews* undoubtedly deserves the deep reverence of all scholars for the unsurpassed erudition and markedly sound judgment which he displays with such abundance throughout his gigantic work. It is therefore of special interest to note that, in his assessment of the numbers of the Spanish Marranos, he has considerably moved away from the position taken by the well-known historian of the Jews in Christian Spain, Professor Y. F. Baer.[2] The question,

---

[1] Based primarily on Crescas' "Letter to the Jews of Avignon," and partly on Christian sources (see above, p. 237).

[2] Unlike Baer (see above, p. 235), Baron evidently believes that the number of the Marranos ran into hundreds (not tens) of thousands. His estimate that the "sum total of Jewish conversions" in 1391–1412 "may indeed have reached 200,000," may be augmented by taking into account the natural increase of

however, is whether, on this issue, further removal from that position is not necessary for a closer approach to historical truth.

To be sure, as we see it, the sources used in our computation comprise not "a few," but a rather substantial number of documents (a dozen, to be exact). But apart from the quantitative aspect of the evidence, there are its qualitative values to consider (such as the credibility of its authors, or its concurrence with other testimonies); and these, we maintain, are not negligible at all. Judged by the latter criteria, in any case, the statement of Ḥasdai Crescas on Seville[3] cannot, in our opinion, be easily disposed of as a highly exaggerated assertion. In addition to what was said above (pp. 240, 241) about Crescas' general reliability, it should be pointed out that his estimates are moderate and indicate a great deal of caution on his part. Thus, while Zurita, who was by no means an exaggerator, gives for the converts in Valencia in 1391 the figure of 11,000 (see his *Anales de Aragon*, lib. x, capit. 47 [ed. Saragossa, 1668, col. 400cd],[4] and Escolano (who had access to the city's archives), a figure of 7,000,[5] Crescas tells us that the Jewish Community of Valencia comprised, prior to the riots, some 1,000 families—that is, about 5,000 souls (including, *beside the would be converts*, those who were later killed, and others who escaped). Similarly, while an elegy by a Jewish contemporary about the disaster of 1391[6] tells us that of the community of Cordova, "*none* remained who did not convert," Crescas merely says that "in Cordova, too, *many* were converted" (*loc. cit.*, p. 129). Also, the agreement between the data he offers and those recorded in Christian sources is not limited to what we indicated above, but covers additional details, such as

the Marranos for three generations. See *A Social and Religious History of the Jews*, X, p. 172, and especially p. 375 (note 2 to Chapter XLV), where Baron comes close to accepting Zacuto's figure for 1391.

[3] i.e., on the number of the Jews in that city prior to the riots of 1391; see above, p. 240.

[4] From Zurita's formulation (y ay memorias en que parece que se bautizaron *onze mil*) one may gather that he was not certain about this figure. The fact that he considered it acceptable, however, must have been in some relation to the population structure of Valencia in his own time.

[5] See above, p. 241.

[6] Cited by D. S. Sassoon, in *JQR*, XXI (1930), p. 105.

the number of the victims in Valencia,[7] Majorca,[8] Barcelona, and the whole course of the disorders in the latter city.[9] Since Crescas' testimony on all other points is factual and verifiable, it is difficult to single out his statement on Seville—the most important item in his account—as essentially distorted and far from the truth.

Crescas evidently knew for certain neither the number of the Jews killed in Seville, nor that of the forced converts in that city. He refrained, therefore, from giving figures on these matters and resorted instead to such expressions as "the majority was converted" (see above, p. 240) which, he was sure, represented the truth. Nevertheless, to indicate the scope of the catastrophe, he gave, as *one* which he considered safe, the figure related to the Jewish population in Seville.[10] It is an estimate, to be sure; but this estimate, so we judge, speaks *for*, rather than *against*, Crescas' reliability on this point.

[7] Crescas' estimate, "about 250" (*loc. cit.*, p. 129), is confirmed by (a) the report about the riots included in the *Libre de Actes* of the City Council of Valencia, dated July 9, 1390 [= 1391] (published by Amador de los Rios, *Historia de los Judíos de España y Portugal*, II, pp. 595–598), which speaks of "several hundreds of Jews killed in that attack" (*ibid.*, p. 598; and see also, *Boletín de la Academia de la Historia*, Madrid [indicated below: *BAH*], VIII [1886], p. 392), and (b) a letter from Valencia, dated July 10, 1391 (drawn from the archives of the Count of Faura), which gives the number of the Jews killed as 230 (published by Francisco Danvila, in *BAH*, VIII [1886], p. 392).

[8] The figure quoted by Crescas for the killed in Majorca, "about 300" (*loc. cit.*, p. 129), is identical with the one offered by a Christian source (see J. Lorenzo Villanueva, *Viaje literario á las iglesias de España*, XXI, p. 224).

[9] See the Latin document published by Fidel Fita, in *BAH*, XVI (1890), 433–435, about the riots in Barcelona. Noteworthy in both accounts, among other things, is the reportedly negative attitude of the authorities toward the rioters (see *ibid.*, 433–434, and Crescas, *ibid.*). The figure of "about 250" given by Crescas for the Jews killed in the Jewish quarter of Barcelona (beside those who were killed in the Castle) falls within the scope of the total of some 400 indicated by the Latin document. The latter, nevertheless, says that about 100 Jews were killed on the first day of the outbreaks, while Crescas' aforecited figure may likewise refer to the victims of the first day. If there is a discrepancy at this point, however, it need not, as Fita correctly argued, be ascribed to Crescas' error (see *loc. cit.*, p. 444).

[10] Actually, he gave two figures: 6,000–7,000 families. See above, p. 240. Crescas' caution is all the more understandable in view of the occasionally

In their attempt to disqualify the figures cited, Loeb and Baer proposed revised readings which, in our opinion, can in no way be upheld. Loeb presents Crescas' statement as if it read 6,000-7,000 *souls*, not *families* (and he considers even this figure exaggerated).[11] Baer suggests that the "4,000 killed," repeatedly mentioned in the Christian documents, is actually a distortion of "4,000 converts."[12] More changes, however, will have to be made to accommodate the sources to the theory.

For whatever the objective value of Crescas' evidence, there can be no mistake as to its intent. When relating the fate that befell Seville's Jewry, Crescas was certain that he was referring to what was probably the largest community in Castile and the whole of Spain, and not one of the size of Valencia, for instance. Nor was he, it seems, alone in this conviction. The author of the elegy published by Schirmann calls it הגברת בת אשבילייא ("the lady of Seville") and שרה ורבת עם (the "leading and populous" community).[13] Also, Crescas, in his above-mentioned letter, describes that community as רבתי עם ("populous");[14] and these epithets, incidentally, are, in both sources, applied to Seville alone. As for the reports of Christian origin concerning the victims in Seville—again, disregarding the measure of their validity—, they distinctly differentiate between "killed" and "converted," and therefore we see no basis for the assumption that an error occurred here of the kind visualized by Baer.[15] Crescas,

drastic fluctuations to which the number of Seville's population was subject, such as those resulting from the plague of 1383. See on this below, note 22.

[11] See his study "Le nombre de juifs de Castile et d'Espagne au moyen âge," in *REJ*, XIV, p. 171. Loeb's argument that Crescas may have been ill-informed because he was "far" from Seville (*ibid.*) is not applicable for a community of Seville's reputation. Seville, in addition, was in constant relations with the Catalonian cities—at least, through the commercial activity of its Catalonian colony. See on this Julio González, *Repartimiento de Sevilla*, Madrid, 1951, I, pp. 343-344.

[12] See Baer, *Untersuchungen über Quellen und Komposition des Schevet Jehuda*, Berlin, 1923, p. 29.

[13] *Qoveẓ 'al Yad*, v. 3 (XIII), part I, p. 66 (verses 10-11).

[14] *loc. cit.*, p. 128.

[15] See *Cuarta Crónica General*, in *Colección de Documentos Inéditos para la Historia de España*, CVI, p. 105, and Ortiz de Zúñiga, *Anales Eclesiasticos y seculares de . . . Sevilla*, lib. IX, año 1391 (Madrid, 1795, p. 237), who relied,

it appears, likewise believed that the number of Jews killed in Seville by far exceeded that of those slaughtered in Valencia or Barcelona. Regarding Seville, he says: והרגו בה עם רב ("in it they killed a multitude"), which suggests a massacre on a large scale.[16]

There is another piece of evidence that speaks very clearly in favor of our supposition. Replying to a complaint lodged against him by the leaders of the Jewish community of Seville (in February 1388), Ferrán Martínez stated, among other things, that 23 synagogues had been built in Seville against the prohibition of canon law. Commenting upon this, H. C. Lea said: "The twenty-three synagogues evidently refer to all in the diocese of Seville. At the time of the outbreak [of 1391] there were but three in the city" (*History of the Inquisition of Spain*, I, p. 104, n. 2). The great historian, however, is here mistaken both with regard to the number of the synagogues and the meaning of the reference. For this is what Ferrán Martínez stated: ". . . si yo derecho fisiesse, que veynte é tres sinagogas que están en la judería de esta Cibdat adeficadas contra Dios é contra derecho, serian todas derribadas por el suelo."[17] There can be no more precise statement, or one less open to misinterpretation. Martínez speaks of *one* judería (Jewish quarter) and of *this city* (Seville), and not of all the juderías in all the cities of the diocese. Furthermore, this

for that figure, on "many memorials" (*ibid.*). Similarly, Baer's attempt to present the "4,000 killed" in Seville as originally identical with the "4,000 converted" (ד' אלפים) found in Zacuto's *Yuḥasin*, ed. Filipowski (p. 225a) must be rejected for reasons indicated above, p. 241, and also, as B. Dinur (in *Zion*, XXXII [1967], p. 169, n. 60) pointed out, because it contrasts the plain meaning of Zacuto's statement which speaks of those converted in the whole of Spain, and not in Seville only.—In addition, a *Yuḥasin* MS. of the Bodleian Library, Oxford (copy of which I saw in Madrid in the summer of 1968), spells out the figure of 200,000 clearly (MS. Heb. d. 16, p. 180b: והמירו דתם יותר ממאתים אלף יהודים.

[16] "Letter to the Jews of Avignon," *loc. cit.*, p. 128. See also the figure that Amador de los Rios (*Historia de los Judíos de España y Portugal*, II, Madrid, 1876, pp. 362, 398, n. 1) found for the Jews killed in Cordova ("over 2,000"), which likewise suggests that the aforesaid information concerning Seville was not based on a substitution of "killed" for "converted."

[17] See Amador de los Ríos, *ibid.*, *ibid.*, 588: ". . . if I were to do what justice requires, the twenty-three synagogues that were built in the *judería* of this city against God and against the law, would all be rased to the ground."

was not an utterance made during some inflammatory speech. It was part of a formal, carefully prepared testimony, given in reply to charges made in a court of law, and attested to by Sevillian public notaries.[18] To be sure, from Ortiz de Zúñiga's account on this matter in his *Anales de Sevilla*, one may gather that, before the riots of 1391, the Jews of Seville had only three synagogues.[19] But Amador de los Rios has already proven that Zúñiga's data on this point were distorted, and that beside the three synagogues mentioned by Zúñiga, and some that were destroyed, others were taken over by the Crown.[20] This further supports the factual element in the aforecited statement of Martínez; and if the number of synagogues is any indication of a community's size, Seville's community was very large indeed (Toledo, by comparison, had only 14 synagogues).[21] Thus, the sources cited speak a different language and tell us a distinctly different story from what is suggested by the readings of Loeb and Baer.

It is true that the information yielded by these sources does not "square" with some or most of the "known estimates" for Seville's total population in 1391. But the question is to what extent these estimates are correct. As we see it, they are based on incomplete data—hardly adequate for the Christian population, and not at all adequate for the Jewish population.[22] Nor has any

[18] See the whole documentation concerning this in Amador de los Ríos, *ibid.*, pp. 579–589. Ferrán Martínez presented his reply 9 days after the leader of Seville's Jewry brought charges against him in court.

[19] Zúñiga, however, it should be pointed out, specifically speaks of *three synagogues that were originally mosques*, donated to the Jews by Alfonso X shortly after the conquest of Seville (see *Anales de Sevilla*, lib. II, año 1252, ed. Madrid, 1677, p. 61a), two of which the Christians transformed into churches. He says: Entonces la ciudad, de tres Sinagogas que tenian *en otras tantas Mezquitas* que les dió el Rey Don Alfonso el Sabio. . . . ocupó las dos para hazerlas Iglesias (*ibid.*, lib. IX, año 1391, p. 252ab).

[20] See Amador's criticism of Zúñiga (*Historia de los Judios*, II, 358–359, n. 2; 389–390, n. 1), and especially his summation of the royal cedula of January 9, 1396 which authorized the transfer of the "communal property" formerly owned by the Jews of Seville, "*together with all the synagogues*," to magnates and favorites of the king (*ibid*).

[21] See Cecil Roth, "The Hebrew Elegy on the Martyrs of Toledo, 1391," in *JQR*, XXXIX (1948), pp. 123–150, and especially 133–134.

[22] The Sevillian census of 1384 (comprising some 15,000 souls), on which

evidence ever been offered regarding the proportion of the Jewish community to the totality of Seville's residents. The estimates referred to are, therefore, in our opinion, not sufficiently well-founded for us to reject all contrary data included in the sources. Furthermore, should we do so, and accordingly conclude that the Jews of Seville in 1391 numbered, say, 5,000 souls, we would still be faced with the same problem for the period of 1470-1480 (on which our interest is focused). For the existence in that period of a Marrano community of a size in the neighborhood of our estimate (see above, pp. 240-241) can be gathered, we believe, quite independently from sources other than those cited.

A statement of the historian Alonso de Palencia—the first of the witnesses we are about to summon—throws a valuable side-light upon our problem. Describing the Sevillian Marranos' preparations against a possible mass onslaught by the Old Christians (in 1473), Palencia says, among other things, that "they [namely the Marranos] secretly recruited a militia of 300 horsemen and 5,000 foot soldiers . . . prepared to resist any attack" (*Crónica de Enrique IV*, Madrid, 1905, III, p. 134). Baer accepts Palencia's figures, but interprets "recruited" as meaning "hired."[23] Yet, this interpretation is flatly denied by the very source on which it relies.

To be sure, the statement just quoted from Palencia is in accordance with the version offered in the Spanish translation of Paz y Mélia.[24] The translator, however, correctly conveyed the

---

some of these estimates lean, is no doubt far from reflecting the true size of Seville's population at the time. Apart from Jews and Moors, it failed to represent the clergy, "foreign" Christians, and doubtlessly also other Christian residents who did not qualify as taxpayers (see Julio González, *op. cit.*, I, pp. 316–317, 336–337). On the basis of the figures offered by that census, and considering its particular aim—to establish the tax potential of Seville's Christian population after the plague of 1383—, "it would be impossible," says González, "to calculate the total volume of the [Sevillian] population" in 1384 (*ibid.*).

[23] *Toledot*, p. 399.

[24] ". . . los conversos sevillanos alistaron secretamente una milicia de 300 jinetes y 5,000 peones armados . . . preparados para resistir todo ataque" (Palencia, *Crónica de Enrique IV*, transl. Paz y Mélia, III, p. 134).

meaning of the original Latin sentence, and he obviously considered it self-understood that the militia referred to in the above cited passage was a *Marrano* militia, that is, an underground military organization whose membership was recruited from Seville's New Christians. Perhaps because this fact was not fully spelled out in the translation (although, in our opinion, it is clearly implied), Baer felt that the term "alistaron" (enlisted) used by the translator could have, in a way, stood for "hired". Yet the Latin original negates this interpretation, for it makes it quite clear that the enlistment referred to was effected not only *by* the conversos, but also *among* the conversos;[24a] and so it becomes unquestionably evident that the testimony before us does not speak of any "hiring" of professional soldiers to defend the Sevillian Marranos, but of placing these Marranos themselves in a state of preparedness for defensive action.

To be sure, the enlistment of such a force (5,300 men) appears to be beyond the normal capacity of a community of 40 or even 45 thousand souls. Nevertheless, when total mobilization is ordered, and when normal recruiting standards are abandoned, and, above all, when the community involved sees itself in a state of mortal danger, it is by no means excluded. It can hardly be doubted, besides, that the Marranos—in Seville, as well as in other cities—possessed a considerable military potential.[25] As

---

[24a] The Latin original (MS. of the Academia de la Historia, Madrid, 9/6482, Decada secunda, liber XVIII, c. II, p. 363) reads here as follows: "lustrum secretum fit *inter* neophitos Hispalenses trecentorum equitum cetratorum et peditum armatorum quinque millium."

[25] See, for instance, Palencia's report on the extensive military preparations of the conversos in Toledo in 1467, their apparent proficiency in the employment of weapons and confidence in their ability to overcome their opponents (*Crónica de Enrique IV*, II, pp. 48–51). Similarly suggestive along the same lines is the historian's account concerning the Sevillian converso group that "marched gladly" to Gibraltar in 1474, at a time when the city was "in great need of soldiers" no less than of artisans. Soon thereafter, we are told, the Marranos in Gibraltar launched "terrestrial and maritime expeditions" which, although they proved "fatal," according to Palencia (*ibid.*, III, p. 233), demonstrate the Marranos' basic preparedness, as well as capacity for military action.

full-fledged Christian citizens for decades, they were *bound* to participate in the militias of the cities,[25a] and many of them, therefore, were trained soldiers whose military prowess, though belittled by their opponents, was highly respected by members of their own group.[26] In Seville, particularly, the Marranos proved their strength in an encounter with their foes in 1465; and, as the diarist Garci Sánchez tells us, "since then the conversos retained their honor" and no one would dare offend them in Seville even "in so much as a single word."[27] In view of all this, it is not at all impossible that, in the perilous situation in which they found themselves, the Sevillian Marranos recruited for their defense all available manpower in their community.

More proof can be offered in support of the contention that the force mentioned by Alonso de Palencia consisted of Marranos, sons of Seville, and not of Old Christian mercenaries. Codex 2041 of the Biblioteca Nacional in Madrid contains an eyewitness account of the hostilities that erupted between the Old and New Christians in Toledo in July 1467. It is a cautious, and apparently unbiased account, written, it seems, by a moderate Old Christian whose name did not come down to us. It reads in part as follows:

> Supporting Alvar Gómez was the Count of Cifuentes and one Fernando de la Torre, leader of the conversos, who had at his disposal four thousand men capable of taking action

[25a] Concerning the militias in Castile's medieval cities, see the still highly valuable work of Antonio Sacristán y Martínez, *Municipalidades de Castilla y Leon*, Madrid, 1877, pp. 278-292.

[26] Against the depreciative opinions of some Old Christians about the Marranos' martial valor (Palencia, *op. cit.*, III, p., 230), see the laudatory view of the Marrano leader Pedro de Córdoba (ibid., p. 233), and especially that of Alfonso de Cartagena, *Defensorium Unitatis Christianae* (ed. Manuel Alonso), Madrid, 1943, p. 215.

[27] See *Los Anales de Garci Sánchez, jurado de Sevilla*, published by J. de M. Carriazo in *Anales de la Universidad Hispalense*, Seville, año XIV (1953), p. 53 (item 239): "e de aqui adelante quedaron los conversos con su honrra, que no les osan decir sola una palabra que no la vengan bien." The above was written shortly after the events mentioned. It is not impossible, however, that the memory of that success, together with their known defensive capability, was a factor in saving Seville's Marranos (in 1473) from the fate of their brethren in Cordova, Jaen, and other Andalusian cities.

in battle, so that it is said that they [i.e., the Marranos] told the Count, who favored and aided them, that there were five or even six conversos for each Old Christian, and that they were well armed and equipped, beyond the need, with a large artillery of *espingardas*[a], culverins, *pasavolantes*,[b] strong crossbows, and many other arms, defensive and offensive.[27a]

According to this account, then, the Marranos of Toledo mastered, prior to the outbreak, a military force of 4,000 men, *all of whom were members of their own group*. There cannot be the slightest doubt as to the meaning of the passage cited. It is in relation to the existence of that force that the author presents the Marranos' claim of being able to place against every man—or rather, *fighting* man—of the Old Christians five or even six conversos(!)—obviously, again: converso *fighters*—whom he describes as "heavily armed" and whose varied weaponry he proceeds to list. Hence, if the Marranos of Toledo could boast a force of 4,000 men, there is no reason to doubt the capacity of Seville's conversos to mobilize a militia of over 5,000—Seville having owned, in all probability, a larger Marrano community than Toledo.

Now, if the Marranos of Seville could mobilize a force of 5,300 men, it is clear that their community was of the magnitude indicated by our inquiry; and this, in turn, suggests that the Old Christian community was at least as large, or, most probably, larger, so that the total population of the city may have well surpassed the 100,000 mark.[28] Obviously, if Palencia's figures are

a. small canons.          b. culverins of very small caliber.

[27a] ". . .e favorecia a este Alvar Gomez el conde de Sifuentes e un Fernando de la Torre caudillo de los conversos, el qual tenia de su parte *quatro mil hombres de pelea*, en tal manera que diz que dezian al conde, que los favorecia y ayudava, q *havia cinco y aun seis conversos para un cristiano viejo*, e en demasia muy armados e pertrechados de gran artileria de espingardas, culebrinas, pasavolantes, vallestas fuertes, y otras muchas armas defensivas y ofensivas (italization is mine; see MS. 2041, Biblioteca Nacional, Madrid, p. 36ᵛ); and cf. above, note 25.—Alvar Gómez was a Marrano notable, whose quarrel with the *Iglesia Mayor* of Toledo sparked the outbreak of 1467.

[28] The size of Seville's total population in the 1480s is not, it seems, better known than in the 1380s. Lea, for instance, thought that it consisted of

accepted, there is no escape from any of these conclusions. If, on the other hand, they are rejected (say, on the ground that he was misinformed as to the actual strength of the Marranos' defense force), these conclusions need not be basically altered. For Palencia lived in Seville for many years, and was doubtless aware of the size of its population, as well as that of its various components. He was also familiar with military matters, and knew how to assess military needs. Therefore, even if he quoted wrong figures, *the fact that he believed that they could be true* substantiates our position.[29]

Other data offered by another Sevillian, who was also well-in-

"nearly half a million of inhabitants" (*op. cit.*, IV, p. 519), while others cited much lower figures. This brings us back to the census of 1587 (see above, p. 240) which, in our opinion (supported by M. Colmeiro's view of the early censuses in Spain: *Historia de la Economía Política en España* [first ed., 1863], Madrid, 1965, I, pp. 298–299), is not exaggerated (its figure for Seville being confirmed also by Mariana [*Historia de España*, lib. XIII, cap. 7, ed. BAE, vol. 30, p. 378b], who states that in his time [1572] Seville had 24,000 households). While this census cannot tell us anything definitive concerning the situation a century earlier, it cannot disprove our calculations either. Granted that Seville's population increased in the course of the hundred odd years following the establishment of the Inquisition, this growth, it should be stressed, took place in the *second* half of that period (c. 1530–1585), while in the *first* half Seville witnessed a sharp decline in the number of its inhabitants. The major causes of this decline were: (a) the flight of Marranos from Seville since 1481 (see below, p. 266); (b) the pestilences that visited the city since 1502, and especially the one of 1507, which decimated a major part of its population (see Bernáldez, *op. cit.*, capit. 219, and F. de B. Palomo, *Historia crítica de las Riadas . . . en Sevilla*, Seville, 1878, I, 52–56); (c) the mass starvation that followed the pestilences (see Bernáldez, *op. cit.*, cap. 219, and the evidences cited by Santiago Montoto, *Sevilla en el Imperio*, Seville, 1938, pp. 43–44); (d) the migration of many Sevillians to the Indies which reduced the city's male population to an extent that it could impress the Venetian Ambassador Navagero (1525) as if it were controlled by women (see A. María Fabié, *Viajes por España*, Madrid, 1879, pp. 272–273). For all these reasons it is not unlikely that while in the period of, say, 1530–1580 Seville's population was more than trebled, in the period of 1480–1530 it was reduced to approximately a third of what it had been.

[29] The same argument may be applied also to Garci Sánchez who noted that 18,000 men "were armed" in Seville on July 24, 1465 (see above, n. 25). Considering Sánchez' position in, and familiarity with, Seville, one is inclined to assume that he might cite a *wrong*, but not an *impossible* figure.

formed on the point in question, confirm this conclusion. We refer to the chronicler Andrés Bernáldez and his statement concerning the Inquisition's victims. "Within 8 years," says Bernáldez, the Inquisitors of Seville "burned more than 700 persons and reconciled more than 5,000."[30] If we add to these the *minors*, who were immediate relations of the burnt and the reconciled, (say, a third: 1,900),[31] and the otherwise uninvolved heirs of condemned dead,[32] the number of persons involved in the Inquisition's activity will easily rise to 8,000. And to these we may add, of course, the *absentees*—i.e., the Marranos who left the area in that period and whose number was no doubt much larger. Indeed, according to Pulgar, "more than 4,000 houses" were deserted by Marranos who fled the Inquisition, "especially in Seville, Cordova, and other cities and towns in Andalucia."[33] To be sure, Pulgar does not tell us how many of these houses were in Seville or its archbishopric; but considering the share of Seville's territory in Andalucia, plus the duration and severity of the Sevillian persecution, we can safely assume that at least half of these desertions occurred in the archbishopric of Seville.[34] Accordingly, we may conclude that the Marrano fugitives from that

[30] See *op. cit.*, p. 601ab.

[31] Children below the ages of 14 for boys and 12 for girls, and especially below the ages of 7 and 6 respectively, were generally not subject to prosecution. See Lea, *A History of the Inquisition of Spain*, II, p. 3.—Our calculation for the minors is based upon the assumption that they constituted a quarter of the Marrano population.

[32] That is, the heirs of dead Marranos who were condemned as heretics and whose inheritance was confiscated by the Inquisition. According to Bernáldez, the number of condemned dead in Seville was "infinite" (*op. cit.*, p. 601b). Most of these, however, may have been parents of Marranos who were executed or reconciled and, therefore, included in the categories mentioned.

[33] Pulgar, *Crónica de los Reyes Católicos*, ed. J. de M. Carriazo, Madrid, 1962, I, 337. Since the *Crónica* ends in 1490, the development under consideration occurred, most probably, in the 8 years referred to by Bernáldez.

[34] According to Pablo de Espinosa, the historian of Seville, the number of abandoned houses in the archbishopric of Seville amounted to 3,000 (en sola Sevilla y su Arzobispado se hallaron tres mil casas vazias; see *Historia y Grandezas de Sevilla*, II, Seville, 1630, p. 70b). The figure, no doubt based on some authentic record, is nevertheless not accompanied by any time limits. We prefer, therefore, to apply it to a longer period than the one suggested by Bernáldez and Pulgar. See below, p. 267.

area comprised about 14,000 souls (an average "house" representing 7-7.5 persons).[35] This would make a total of some 22,000 souls—or, according to our calculations, about 30% of the Marrano population in the archbishopric—that were directly affected by the Inquisition's activity—certainly a high percentage for the brief period referred to by both chroniclers.

This assessment is also supported by a later summation—from 1524. In that year, "there was placed over the gateway of the Castle of Triana, occupied by the tribunal [of the Sevillian Inquisition] an inscription signifying that, up to that time, it had caused the abjuration of more than 20,000 heretics and had burnt nearly 1,000 obstinate ones."[36] "This," says Lea, "is probably an understatement, if we are to believe Bernáldez" (*op. cit.* p. 519). But compared with Bernáldez' data, cited above, the figures of the inscription may be regarded as too low only if we assume, as Lea indeed did, that they refer to the whole period of the Inquisition's functioning—that is, from its establishment to 1524. Yet such an assumption would seem inadmissible. For actually, what the inscription tells us in this connection is that the summary it offers relates to a *shorter* period—*that which followed the expulsion of the Jews* (i. e., from 1492 to 1524);[36a] and if so, the toll of the Inquisition in the *longer* period (1481–1524)

[35] Cf. the summarized figures for houses, families and persons in the Sevillian census of 1565, cited by Santiago Montoto, *op. cit.*, p. 43, and the similar listing in the 1597 census of Madrid, in Granville Edge, "Early Population Records in Spain," in *Metron*, IX (1931–1932), pp. 240–241.—"Houses" here stand for *casas*, while "households" or "families" represent *vecinos*.

[36] See Lea, *op. cit.*, IV, p. 519.

[36a] The original Latin text of the inscription, preserved in Zúñiga's *Anales de Sevilla*, p. 482, reads, in its opening part, as follows: "Anno Domini M. CD. LXXXI . . . sacrum Inquisitionis Officium contra Haereticos Iudaiçantes . . . hic exordium sumpsit, ubi post Iudaeorum & Sarracenorum expulsionem ad annum usque M. D. XXIV, . . . XX. M. haereticorum, & ultra, nefandum heareseos crimen abiurarunt, necnon omnium fere M. in suis haeresibus obstinatorum . . . ignibus tradita sunt & combusta."

The inscription, then, clearly differentiates between the period of the Inquisition's existence, which began in 1481, and that for which it offered a summary of achievements: from the expulsion of the Jews [1492]. It would be far-fetched to assume that by this expression (*expulsio Iudaeorum*) the reference was to the expulsion of the Jews from Seville (1483). An inscription

was considerably heavier—perhaps 27,000 reconciled and c. 2,000 burned—if we may rely on what we gather from Bernáldez for the first eleven years. In any case, even if we follow Lea's reading of the inscription, and use that "probable understatement" as a starting point for our calculation, we find that the number of the Sevillian Marranos may have easily exceeded several tens of thousands. For, if we add to the groups mentioned the related minors (7,000), the fugitives whose number must have risen by that time (21,000),[37] the otherwise uninvolved offspring of dead heretics, whose number, by 1524, must have also become substantial (say 3,000),[38] and reduce the resulting total by a third, since the period referred to spanned a generation and a half, it would appear that the Inquisition's activity in the archbishopric directly affected some 35,000 persons, or, according to our estimated population, one out of every two Marranos living in the area in the course of one generation.

This is certainly a high rate of involvement, but not nearly as high as that suggested by Zurita who, in his *Anales de Aragon*, beside presenting the estimate he once rejected as too low,[39] also included the higher appraisal, for which, as we have seen, he offered strong support in his note to Valera's *Crónica*.[40] That he still considered that appraisal as more truthful is evident from the praise he has for its author ("a most diligent [researcher] in

placed over the gate of the Castle of Triana was obviously directed to all who would visit the spot, and not merely to those who were especially informed of Seville's local history. Accordingly, the phrase *the expulsion of the Jews*, with no reference to date and place, could only be taken to mean the well-known expulsion of the Jews from Spain in 1492, just as by *the expulsion of the Saracens*, we may add, a similar national event was meant—the ousting of the Moors from Spain in 1502.

[37] See above, note 34.

[38] See above, note 32.

[39] See above, p. 245.—Even according to this estimate (4,000 burned, 30,000 reconciled in the archbishopric of Seville), the number of the Marranos directly involved comprised 65% of the Marrano population (if we follow our line of computation).—Zurita introduces this estimate in the *Anales* with the words: *segun escriven*; evidently, he found it repeated by several authorities, and therefore could not ignore it.

[40] See above, p. 246; and see Zurita, *Anales*, IV, lib. XV, cap. 49, ed. Saragossa, 1668, p. 324a.

this area"); from the fact that he records the latter's assertion that the lower assessment is "very defective;" and also from his inclusion of that researcher's evaluation of the higher figure as both "certain" and "ascertained."[41] Of course, Zurita may have been wrong in his adherence to, or inclination toward, that view. Yet, what is at issue here, after all, is not the reliability of the figures he quoted as far as they reflect upon the activity of the Inquisition, but *their value as indicators for the number of Seville's Marranos*; and from this standpoint their value is great. For it can hardly be assumed that the author of Zurita's source—that "autor en esta parte muy diligente"—was so ignorant of Seville's conditions that he cited figures for its Judaic culprits larger than that of its Marrano population.[42]

Other considerations, too, it seems, lead to the same conclusion. To prepare an account of the Inquisition's actions, with the aim of presenting it to the public, was a task which no one, in 1521, could approach lightly. It meant, in a way, dabbling in the affairs of the Inquisition, and in an area to which it was most sensitive—i.e., that of its record and public image. One, therefore, would tread carefully in that area, and would, first of all, seek to "verify" his statement— if possible, by the Holy Office itself, and if not, by some authoritative sources (note the word *averiguado* in the passage cited, note 41, which may well allude to this situation). Caution, then, would dictate "verification," and the need of "verification" would dictate restraint and keep one from making exaggerated statements. But even more significant than this and other deductions that may be

---

[41] *Ibid.*: ". . . affirma que este numero, que aqui se señala, es muy defetuoso, y que se ha de tener por cierto, y aueriguado, que solo en el Areobispado de Sevilla, entre viuos, y muertos, y absentes, fueron condenados por hereges, que judayzauan, mas de cien mil personas."

[42] Similarly, it would be most unlikely for that writer not to have been a native, or at least a citizen of Seville. A *non*-Sevillian in the 1520s would lack, it seems, the incentive to dedicate himself to an investigation of the history of *Seville's* tribunal; nor would he have the necessary facilities to undertake such a task. Also, in all probability, in 1521 there were still Sevillians, New and Old Christians, who could recall the numbers of their respective communities, say, in 1480. All this suggests that the afore-cited author, while he may have computed a factually wrong figure, could have hardly arrived at a theoretically absurd one.

drawn in favor of the above assumption is the telling fact that *all three accounts* of the Inquisition's activity in Seville to the 1520s—including one of the Inquisition itself!—speak of *tens of thousands* of Marranos who were subjected to inquisitional action. To this common denominator, there must have corresponded a common notion about the size of the Marrano community. Yet such a notion could not have developed against the public record, or the popular tradition.

It seems, then, that our view of the matter under consideration is substantiated by all the aforesaid evidence, coming as it doe from a variety of sources, with dates spanning about a century and a half (1388-1524). To be sure, these testimonies do not contain overall figures for Seville's conversos; but *they all point in the same direction*—the one which leads to the conclusion we have reached concerning the numbers of the Marranos in Seville (the city and the archbishopric) at the time of the founding of the Spanish Inquisition. Thus they offer support for that conclusion, and indirectly also for the general figures suggested for the Marranos by Spain's Jewish scholars from 1487 on.[43]

[43] The low estimate of Seville's Jewish population before the riots of 1391 (500 *vecinos*) suggested by A. Collantes de Teran, apart from being contradicted by the aforecited evidence, is unacceptable because of the paucity and questionable meaning of the data on which it relies (see his *Sevilla en la baja edad media*, 1977, pp. 206-207).

## Addendum

In assessing the number of the Spanish conversos in the last two decades of the fifteenth century, certain data we possess about the size of Spanish Jewry on the eve of the Expulsion may be of special value. The first is provided by Isaac Abravanel in the following statement, which he wrote in 1494:

> I present as my witnesses the Fear of God and the Honor of His Divine Presence that the number of Jews in the lands of Spain's King in the year in which [Israel] was robbed of its glory [namely the year of the Expulsion] was three hundred thousand souls.[1]

In his Commentary on Kings, completed a year earlier, Abravanel quoted the same number (three hundred thousand) for the Jews who *left* Spain in the course of the Expulsion.[2] But the later statement must be given greater weight. What endows it with that weight is (a) his specific reference to the Jews *who lived in Spain before the Expulsion*, and (b) the opening of the statement, which reinforces the validity of the information it imparts. Abravanel *virtually calls God as his witness* that what he says is the truth. What led Abravanel to make that oath-like declaration?

It seems that the number cited by Abravanel in his Commentary on Kings was met with some criticism. He might have been informed that the overwhelming proportion of the Jewish aristocracy of Spain did not leave with the exiles; they converted, and their conduct served as a model for many of the lower classes.[3] Abravanel,

---

[1] See his Commentary on Prophets and Writings, 1960, p. 274a. Obviously, Abravanel meant: *about* 300,000, as he said *ibid.*, p. 413a; and cf. his Comm. on the Latter Prophets, 1956, p. 207a (on Isaiah 43.1).

[2] See his Comm. on the Early Prophets, 1955, p. 422b (introd. to Kings).

[3] See A. Torrutiel [ = Ardutiel], in A. Neubauer, *Mediaeval Jewish Chronicles*, I, 1887, p. 112.

apparently, did not believe that these conversions were so numerous as substantially to affect the number of exiles. Nevertheless, when he referred to this matter in the following year, he found it necessary to make it clear that he had cited the figure of 300,000 on the basis of the number of Jews who lived in Spain prior to the Expulsion, and that concerning this number he had such definite knowledge that he could affirm it upon the "Honor of the Divine Presence." We must accept this statement as factual.

Naturally, we are still curious to know what gave him that assurance; and to this we may give the following answer. Once the leaders of Spanish Jewry understood that the decree of the Expulsion was irrevocable, they began to think of the measures they would take in order to be able to face the catastrophe. The first thing they obviously had to do was to obtain full and precise information on the scope of the problem that faced them, and this meant, first of all, to establish the number of Jews who were to leave Spain.

According to an anonymous Hebrew document surviving from those times, a "long and elaborate inquiry" was conducted in this matter,[4] and the Spanish historian Bernáldez preserved important data that were probably secured through that inquiry. From these data we gather that 6,000 Jewish families lived in Aragon (including Catalonia and Valencia) and 31,000 families in Castile, the latter item stemming from a letter that Meir Melamed wrote to Abraham Señor.[5] Señor was the Chief Rabbi of Castilian Jewry, and both he and Melamed, his son-in-law, were responsible for supplying the royal treasury with the taxes imposed on Castile's Jews. The above information, however, must have represented a summary of the *first* phase of the inquiry, for according to the anonymous account we have mentioned, Spanish Jewry on the eve of the Expulsion comprised 50,000 families![6] Furthermore, this figure was, according to that account, the "most agreed upon"—presumably by those aware of the relevant data.[7] That Abravanel was informed of this later summation, as well as of the earlier one communicated by Bernáldez,

---

[4] See A. Marx, *JQR*, 20 (1908), p. 250.
[5] See A. Bernáldez, *Memorias del reinado de los Reyes Católicos*, ed. Gómez-Moreno and Carriazo, 1962, p. 255.
[6] See Marx, *loc. cit.*, p. 250.
[7] *Ibid.*

can hardly be doubted in view of his standing among the Jews of Spain. He is usually mentioned after Señor and Melamed as one of the three men who led Spanish Jewry. In fact, however, he was the chief of this trio, or, as he put it:

"I was the head of my entire people. . . . they anxiously awaited my instructions, and would not go beyond my orders."[8]

As the occupant of such a position of leadership, Abravanel must have concentrated in his hands all the information required for organizing the exodus. Consequently, he must have known not only how many Jews then sojourned in Spain, but how many lived in each Spanish province. Moreover, the conflict between the numbers cited by Bernáldez and those found in our anonymous document is actually much smaller than it seems. Bernáldez referred to the Jews of four lands: Castile, Aragon, Catalonia, and Valencia. But in listing the domains of King Ferdinand, Abravanel mentions, besides the above countries, "Sicily and the Islands of the Sea" (i.e., Sardinia and Majorca),[9] whose Jewish population in 1492 numbered, most likely, about 10,000 families.[10] This would bring the total Jewish population close to the 50,000 families which was commonly viewed as the "most acceptable estimate" for the size of Spanish Jewry. But the anonymous reporter gives us, in addition, a fuller account of the lands from which the Jews were expelled, including Galicia, the Basque country, and Minorca.[11] Thus, if we add the Jews of these countries to the common estimate mentioned above, we could easily reach the higher figure (53,000 families = 265,000 souls), which the same reporter indicated as the one preferred by some of his contemporaries.[12]

Thus, the more we examine the available evidence, the closer we come to the figure quoted by Abravanel (300,000 souls) and the more convinced we become that his account was sound. The summary he gave us was probably based on information that included

[8] See Abravanel's *Zevaḥ Pesaḥ*, Constantinople, 1506, introd., p. 1.

[9] See his Comm. on the Early Prophets, 1955, p. 422ab.

[10] According to A. Milano, *JSS*, 15 (1953), the number of Jews in Sicily alone at the time of the Expulsion was 37,000 souls (7,400 families).

[11] See Marx, *loc. cit.*, p. 249.

[12] *Ibid.*, p. 250.

later, fuller, and more accurate data than those acquired by our other informants. Hence, we prefer it to any summary coming from less central, less authoritative, and therefore less reliable sources.

Having thus established the number of Jews in Spain in the decade before the Expulsion, we may be helped by this figure in our attempt to estimate the number of the conversos during that time. In his commentary on Deuteronomy (30.1), Abravanel says that the "majority of [our] people abandoned their religion," while those who adhere to it are "few out of many" (*mĕat me-harbēh*). In its Hebrew original, the expression indicates a *remnant of a multitude*, and in this particular case, a small minority in contrast to the large majority of converts. To be sure, Abravanel wrote the above comment *after* the Expulsion of 1492, but he used an expression applied by Spanish Jews *before* the Expulsion to describe their numerical condition. In a letter written from Castile to Rome and Lombardy in 1487, we read that owing to the great troubles and tribulations undergone by the Jews of Spain, they remained "few out of many" (*mĕat me-harbēh*).[13] The expression no doubt reflected the *impression* that the size of the Jewish group made upon its members when they compared it with that of the converso community (whose large numbers they kept stressing[14]). This, it seems, may permit us the following deduction. Had the number of the conversos been, say, 300,000, as has been suggested by Cecil Roth,[15] the faithful Jews would have constituted *half* of Spanish Jewry, and it is most unlikely that in this condition they would have seen themselves as "few out of many." Such a view, however, *could* be formed if the Jews were reduced to much less than a half—say, to a third of what they had been—and the converso population was, correspondingly, double that of the Jewish, namely, of a size close to the one suggested by Abravanel (over 600,000).[16]

---

[13] *Ibid.*, p. 247.
[14] See, for instance, above, pp. 234–235.
[15] See his *History of the Marranos*, 1958, p. 27.
[16] See above, pp. 244–245.

# On Myths, History, and Scholarship

## I

The name of the Latin author Terentianus (2nd century) is today known only to very few, but his saying, "Every book has its fate," remained alive for more than eighteen centuries and is still a common byword in the civilized world. This saying now comes to my mind when I am about to consider the scholarly reaction to this book in the three decades that passed from its first appearance to the publication of its sequel and concluding parts in my *Origins of the Inquisition in Fifteenth Century Spain.*

It was in many ways an odd reaction that I found hard to understand for a long time. Apart from full supporters whose number was limited, most of the reviewers lauded the book for the scope of its sources, the nature of its analysis, the way it was presented, etc. But when it came to its thesis, the attitude changed. Here one could notice in the writers' expressions discomfort, perplexity, or hesitation, if not outright opposition to the thesis as a whole or to some of its main parts. There was an evident discrepancy between the evaluation of the book as a general scholarly effort and the evaluation of the conclusions in which that effort was brought to its natural climax.

I originally thought that the book would attract the fire of some determined opponents because of the complete departure of its views (on the Jewishness of the Marranos and the purpose of the Inquisition) from the notions that had dominated public opinion for almost five centuries. Then I came to think that much of the opposition would be generated by the powerful religious organizations and established schools of thought, both Spanish and Jewish, that had cultivated the theories attacked in my book. Both assumptions were

275

basically correct, and had much to do with the peculiar reaction displayed toward this work, or rather to its thesis. Yet both failed to explain the nature and contents of some recurring criticisms. For real antagonism to new ideas and the common defense of institutional positions are usually expressed in reasoned expositions of arguments opposed to the ideas censured and those supporting the established theories. But in our case, I saw nothing of the kind. What I saw was a flight from reason, reliance on known scholars rather than on sources, and the employment of assertions irrelevant to the subject, expressed with the assurance of preachers of dogma, who cannot be contradicted.

I finally realized that what characterized these cases was something different from mere adherence to old views, or the usual attachment of famous institutions to theories they had been used to uphold. What we have here is the influence of certain conceptions that had become so widespread and so deep-rooted as to assume the character of *myths.*

To fight a myth, I know, is extremely hard, and to fight two myths, as our case requires—involving as it does both the Marranos and the Inquisition—is doubly difficult. But I also know this, which is more decisive: in the oft-repeated strife between myth and history, which has marked the course of modern historiography, history has always emerged the winner; and I have also seen confirmation of this rule in the scholarly reaction to this book. The number of supporters of its thesis has increased, constantly and markedly, in the past three decades, and the controversy that began with its first appearance and has continued unabated ever since is gradually changing into a consensus of agreement with most, if not all, of its major conclusions.

This seems, then, to be the "special fate" of this book. But better to understand it, we should take a closer look at some of the arguments that were raised against it. This may serve as a lesson in the ways of scholarship, which sometimes deviates from its common patterns for reasons not always apparent.

## II

The impact of myth is by no means limited to ordinary human beings. Myths often affect the feeling and thinking of the strongest and most independent minds. I shall later note their impact on some of the views expressed about this book by various authors. But before I come to that, I would like to show how the double myth with which we are concerned influenced the understanding of the Marrano question of two great historians of the preceding century. It will help us comprehend our case.

The historians I refer to are Karl Josef von Hefele and Marcelino Menéndez y Pelayo, whose great fame rightly matched their outstanding scholarly achievements. Both championed the traditional notion that the Spanish Inquisition was created for the purpose of suppressing a dangerous Judaic heresy; and both claimed that the aim of the Judaizers was not merely to bring back to Judaism the conversos who had become true believers in Christ, but also to proselytize Old Christian Spaniards—in fact, all the Christians of the Spanish kingdoms. Elsewhere I have shown, I believe quite clearly, the hollowness of this grotesque charge,[1] but here I must touch on it briefly again because it bears directly on our subject.

In our quest for a source of this incredible charge, we did not exclude even the evidence offered by Lucero, the infamous criminal inquisitor of Cordova, who sought to advance his inquisitorial career by precisely this kind of accusation. Hefele and Menéndez y Pelayo, however, could not rely in any measure on Lucero, who was so vehemently denounced by Cordova's Old Christians, and was exposed for what he was by Cardinal Cisneros, who ordered his imprisonment and put him on trial. So to prove their claim that the conversos were seeking to proselytize all of Spain's Old Christians, both scholars went as far back as the first and second centuries, when many Jews were engaged in a campaign of proselytization, and they both tried to prove that the same desire persisted in later times, manifesting itself especially under Visigothic rule, as well as in subsequent conducive circumstances, including those leading to the Spanish Inquisition.

One is not only amazed but bewildered when one sees himself compelled to explode such claims coming from renowned scholarly authorities. In the first and second centuries of the Christian era the Jews were indeed trying to convert to Judaism many of the vari-

---

[1] See my *Toward the Inquisition* (1997), pp. 186, 191.

ous groups of pagans who then populated the Roman Empire—a phenomenon that formed an integral part of the great Hellenistic-Jewish conflict over the spiritual mastery of the ancient world. But this had nothing to do with what happened in Spain thirteen centuries later! As for the Visigothic period, both Hefele and Menéndez Pelayo found evidence for their thesis in the frequent attempts of the Jews to "Judaize" their Christian slaves. The phenomenon, however, was not peculiar to Spain, and its motives were not purely religious. In their efforts to undermine the Jewish economy, the Christians in the East, and later in the West, urged the rulers to prohibit the Jews from acquiring Christian slaves (pagan slaves having become progressively less available); and to counteract the laws issued to this effect, the Jews tried to de-Christianize their slaves by "partial" or complete proselytization. In no circumstances, however, could these attempts affect the religious structure of the general population, and of course the whole activity stopped completely in the seventh century (from 613 on) during the anti-Jewish fury of the Catholic Visigoths.[2] Had there been in those circumstances the slightest movement of proselytization, it would have been seized upon and used as a major argument in support of the fiercely anti-Jewish measures repeatedly urged by kings like Receswinth and Erwig, sworn enemies of the Jews. And here, too, a tremendous gulf of time—a gulf of eight centuries!—separates that period from the Spanish Inquisition.[3]

Is it possible that such elementary facts, and such self-evident conclusions, escaped the thinking of the two great scholars? "Impossible!" is our immediate answer. But if so, what led them to present the aforementioned arguments and contend that they prove their case?

[2] Sisebut's gravest punishment for proselytizing Christian slaves was not decapitation of the slave, as asserted by Menéndez Pelayo (*Hist. de los Heterodoxos Españoles*, ed. E. Sánchez Reyes, 1963[2], II, p. 464), but decapitation of the Jewish proselytizer (see *Fuero Juzgo*, lib. XII. tit. II, ley 14; ed. 1815, p. 182, col. 1).

[3] No actual evidence is available for proselytization of Christians (free or enslaved) in the Christian Spanish kingdoms during the Reconquest. Laws decreeing death for such an action, which were included in the codes of these kingdoms, traditionally followed old enactments (such as those of Theodosius, *Novellae*, III, and Justinian, *Code*, I, tit. 10, law 1; I, tit. 9, 1. 15), although they also served as deterrents.

There seems to be only one solution to this riddle. Both Menéndez y Pelayo and Hefele knew that the Inquisition was reportedly
established to suppress a Marrano group that preached return to
Judaism among the Christianized conversos. They considered this,
of course, a worthy aim. But is it possible, they asked themselves,
that this was the sole object for which the famed tribunal was established? There seemed to have been a marked imbalance between
the rather small scope of the projected task and the power of the
instrument fashioned to perform it. The task of the Inquisition, they
presumed, must have been far greater, both more extensive and
more significant; and having formed a theory that agreed with that
presumption, they looked for evidence on which it could lean.

As I have already pointed out, they could not find such evidence.
But it seems they believed that they noticed some clues to the situation that the Inquisition was meant to combat. Thus, they read in
the Sovereigns' statement (included in the first declaration of the
Inquisitors) that the Judaizers were "infecting their sons and daughters and also *others with whom they had conversed.*" Who were the
"others"? they may have wondered. They also read that the Sovereigns created the Inquisition in order to "protect their *subjects* from
evil." Who were those "subjects" they sought to protect? Our scholars may have concluded that these undefined terms alluded to the
main goal of the Inquisition: the heretics' aim was not only to re-
Judaize their "sons and daughters" and other relations, as well as
their other Christianized brethren, but also to Judaize all of Spain's
Christians—i.e., the "subjects" of the dual monarchy. Spain was thus
faced with the "imminent" danger of being lost to Christianity; the
Inquisition came to save it from that horrid fate.

We cannot, of course, say with any measure of certainty that either
Hefele or Menéndez y Pelayo was led to his conclusion regarding
the aim of the Marrano heresy by following the above process of
thought. But whether they did so or not, the conclusion they arrived at was not based on any source. It was essentially a product
of their speculation; and yet it became so implanted in their minds
that they regarded it almost as an article of faith. Actually, of course,
it was no more than a myth; but a myth when so believed is defended by all means, even by the most irrational explanations. Ernst
Cassirer, who is known for his works in the field of neo-Kantian phi-

losophy, touched also on the measure of estrangement from reality that myths may attain in their self-defense. Without entering into his weighty discussion, I shall mention only one of his observations, which seems to me most applicable to our case. The answers that myths offer to perplexing phenomena, including those related to our human behavior, may appear to us, he says, "absurd and fantastic"; but "the strangest and most extravagant motivation is better than no motivation at all."[4]

## III

The above remarks may be helpful as preliminaries to our forthcoming comments on various opinions expressed by scholars on the present work. I do not intend, of course, to survey all the cases that formed that varied and manifold reaction, but merely to dwell briefly on a few of them that may illustrate characteristics of a special kind. I believe the instances I shall touch on will suffice to prove that modern scholars, of even the highest rank, are not more immune to the impact of myths than their great forerunners in preceding generations.

Professor S. W. Baron dealt with my book in a number of places in the thirteenth volume of his *Social and Religious History of the Jews* (1969). I have the highest respect for this great scholar who, by his vast erudition and manifold inquiries opened new pathways of investigation and shed new light on many obscure areas. His treatment of the conversos in the above volume, however, falls short of what is required by the subject. Baron fails to explain to us what happened in Spain following the catastrophe of 1391. Nor does he give us a true image of the Marrano as it changed in its social and religious transmutations—the image that is clearly depicted in the sources. Instead, Baron offers us a camouflaged portrayal of a human type that lacks distinctive features, which is nonetheless assumed to conform to the view of the "Jew at heart" he was brought up to believe in. In discussing my present work on the Marranos, he says that I "subjected to a careful analysis the varying attitudes of the medieval rabbinate to forced converts" and the "different reactions to

---

[4] E. Cassirer, *Symbol, Myth, and Culture* (1979), p. 249.

these converts' post-conversion behavior";[5] but he completely fails to indicate any of the conclusions supposedly attained by my "careful analysis." Above all, he fails to mention the crucial phenomenon that our sources reflect very clearly—namely, the process of assimilation and Christianization that the converts had undergone from their entry into Christendom to the beginning of the Inquisition's operation, when most conversos had already been alienated from Judaism and regarded themselves as fully fledged Christians.

But Baron not only fails to refer to the final stages of the evidence offered in this book; he also fails to present properly the evidence he discusses. Thus, he says that the rabbis did not view as a full-fledged Jew even a Marrano "who observed most Jewish laws the best way he could."[6] The reader who is familiar with the contents of this book knows that such a view or proposition could never have entered the mind of any rabbi or any Jewish religious authority. In fact, Baron's assertion was not only wrong, but the very opposite of what the sources attest. And just as misleading was his assertion that Spain's Jews felt deep sympathy for the victims of the Inquisition, which made the rabbis less stringent about the conversos' peccadilloes. This may have applied to some isolated cases, but the overwhelming majority of Spanish Jewry, who considered the conversos of the Inquisitional period not only *apostates* but also *gentiles*, and, moreover, *enemies of their people and religion*, were not moved by their suffering to feel pain and sorrow, but only joy and exultation. Baron ignores the powerful testimonies to this effect of men like Arama, Jabez, Berav, and others, which clearly nullify his argument.

Yet, the most far-reaching misrepresentation of my conclusions—and, I do not hesitate to say, of the sources—appears in Baron's discussion of the decision concerning the conversos made by Solomon Duran. Duran was confronted with the prevalent view that the conversos, "sons of uncircumcised apostates," were full-fledged Christians who should be considered *gentiles*. Duran argues that such a position would contravene the age-old Jewish law stipulating that the offspring of an ethnically Jewish woman, even if converted to

---

[5] S. W. Baron, *A Social and Religious History of the Jews*, vol. 13 (1969), p. 305 n. 5.

[6] Ibid., p. 350.

another religion, must be regarded as a member of the Jewish people —and hence, not as a gentile. He extends this law to as many generations as the mother is known to be of Jewish stock, and he also objects to regarding sons of forced converts, who were brought up as Christians by their parents, as ordinary apostates. Real apostasy, he argued, can be only the result of one's free, conscious choice of a different religion; but the "apostates" in question could not make such a choice. Just as their forebears were forced to convert under the impact of overwhelming fear, so were their children coerced to be Christians by their parents' education, teaching, and behavior.[7] They too, therefore, must be viewed as *forced* converts, unless they had somehow been given the opportunity of becoming aware of the principles of Judaism, and then, knowing them, rejected these principles in favor of the dogmas of Christianity.

Duran here opened a discussion of an issue that was raised repeatedly again in later years, especially under the Inquisition, when the overwhelming majority of Spanish Jewry, including almost all its rabbinic authorities, rejected the notion of treating renegades and apostates, who openly denied Judaism and all it stood for, as "forced converts," and not as gentiles. They considered such a treatment a farce and, of course, a misrepresentation of reality. Baron, however, in discussing this controversy, not only failed to refer to its outcome (a rabbinical decision according to which all descendants of Spain's Marranos were *gentiles*,[8]) but presented Solomon Duran's arguments as if they were mainly directed to prove the Jewishness of the conversos on *ethnic grounds*. But was this the main problem that concerned him, and was this the chief issue in which we can find his new approach to the Marranism of his time? In referring to Duran's specific position, Baron says that he discussed the "*Jewish character*" of second and third generation Marranos who were not circumcised and who *assimilated many religious doctrines and practices from their Christian environment.*"[9] But was it the "Jewish character" of these generations of Marranos that Duran was concerned about, or their pronounced *non-Jewish character?* Did he refer to Marranos who

---

[7] See above, pp. 70–71, 215.
[8] See above, p. 215.
[9] Baron, *op. cit.*, p. 353 n. 24 (emphasis added).

merely "assimilated many Christian doctrines and practices," or to such who were considered outright *apostates* and *Christians* in the full sense of the word? And what is more: Did he speak of the adoption by the Marranos of those doctrines and practices from the "Christian environment," as Baron put it, or from the *education of their parents*, who not only took care to acquaint them with Christianity, but also denied them any knowledge of Judaism, so that they were totally cut off from it. Nowhere would Baron allow himself to use the plain, striking terms "apostates" and "gentiles," which are at the core of Duran's discussion and without which his whole argument is incomprehensible. Instead, he paraphrases Duran's statements in a way that clearly avoids the essentials of the dilemma. Why? I have only one explanation to this perplexing presentation.

What we have before us is a clear example of a great Jewish scholar struggling on behalf of an established myth against a long series of conflicting testimonies touching the Marrano question. He was not, as I said, the only scholar to whom the present book, its sources and conclusions gave that kind of trouble. I shall now refer to another Jewish scholar, Frank Talmage, who displayed the same pattern of reaction.

## IV

Talmage, who does not spare praise for my work, although "one cannot *fully* accept its major thesis,"[10] believes that by "synthesizing" the materials I presented with those found in the earlier literature, one obtains a more balanced view of the Spanish Marranos. He sees the essence of this balance in the recognition of the fact that the Marranos included both faithful Jews and renegades. But for this recognition no "synthesis" is needed, since it was observed by almost all scholars who dealt with the Marrano problem. Naturally, my own inquiry did not seek to prove the existence of two types of Marranos, but to *determine the numerical relationship between them across the century that followed the first mass conversion.* It is in this, or rather in the conclusions I arrived at, that I radically differed from all my predecessors. While the latter believed that the great ma-

---

[10] See *Judaism* 17 (1968), 376 (emphasis added).

jority of the conversos remained faithful to their religious heritage, my own explorations led me to the conviction that the Marranos— or at least their overwhelming majority—were true Jews upon their conversion and also a short time thereafter, but that they soon became subject to a process of assimilation, which gradually led them to Christianization, and with it to alienation from the Jewish people. Consequently, when the Inquisition was established, the majority of Spain's Jews considered them "gentiles" and enemies of the Jewish people. Of course, even then, as I have stated, small pockets of Marranos who were "Jews at heart" survived in the Marrano camp, so that the two types referred to—renegades and "faithful Jews"— continued to exist even then, except that my view of their numerical relationship was the very opposite of the one that had hitherto prevailed.

Talmage found it difficult to yield to the evidence I adduced in support of my thesis. He tried to find flaws in this evidence or counterargue the conclusions I drew from it. Thus, while citing Solomon Duran's statement that "all Marranos violate the Sabbath publicly," he hastens to throw doubt on the validity of that statement by telling us that Solomon's son, Zemaḥ, found in Majorca "many Marranos who preserve the laws of the Sabbath." In my discussion of this statement in the present book, I pointed out that it referred to *one* specific place, while Duran's aforesaid statement referred to *all of Spain's Marranos*, and like all broad generalizations, it had some exceptions. Talmage, however, sought to show that the exception was the rule; and as he could not find support for this in the Jewish sources, he turned to the documents of the Inquisition.

But then he encountered a much greater difficulty, which he must have regarded as especially disturbing, and which he naturally tried to remove. I have cited statements of Arama and Abravanel, the luminaries of the last generation of Spain's Jewry, attesting that the Inquisition had *falsely accused* the conversos of secretly adhering to Jewish views and precepts, and that on the basis of these accusations it "burned them by the hundreds and thousands." Thus, we have here most reliable statements from the Marranos' contemporaries in the Inquisition's early decades, confirming what we gathered from many other testimonies, and especially those stressing the Marranos' *Christianization*, that the Spanish Inquisition used *fictitious charges to condemn many Marranos and destroy their group*.

I assume that, confronted with these statements, our reviewer saw himself in straits. But then, he believed, he found a way out. The Hebrew word used for "false accusation" is *'alila*, and the corresponding verb of this noun is *le-ha'alil*. Talmage noticed that in one of the passages I quoted in my book from the Responsa, the term *le-ha'alil* was used in the sense of *accuse* (and not *accuse falsely*), and this is indeed how I translated it in that place. Talmage concluded that this was also the meaning of the term in Arama's statement. For some reason he failed to apply his explanation to the similar statements I cited from Abravanel.

I confess I was dismayed by this manner of treatment of such crucial testimonies by a serious scholar. What Talmage should have stated is that the correct translation of *le-ha'alil* is *to accuse falsely*, and that the usage of the term in the sense of *to accuse* is wrong, irregular, and uncommon. From the one case he noticed of the wrong usage, or from other isolated instances of this kind, he could not deduce the meaning of the word in the many other instances in which it was employed. What is more, even if the erroneous meaning was accepted so that it was commonly used, it would not in any way prove his contention. Many words have different meanings, but their specific meaning in any sentence is determined by the contents of the sentence involved, or of the passage to which it is related. Had Talmage considered carefully the contents of Arama's statement, he would not, I assume, have come to the conclusion that the meaning of *le ha'alil* is there *to accuse* and not *to accuse falsely*. Here is how the passage in question reads:

> For although they [i.e., the Marranos] have *completely assimilated* among the nations [or: the gentiles], they will find no peace among them; for they [the nations] will *always revile and beshame them, plot against them, and falsely accuse them in matters of faith.*[11]

Arama refers in this statement to Marranos who have "radically changed their religious views" and have *completely* assimilated among the gentiles, and consequently were *Christianized*. For could there be such a *complete* assimilation without abandoning the Jewish religion? And if the Marranos had abandoned their Judaism and replaced it with the faith and customs of the nations, would not the charges

---

[11] See above, p. 154.

leveled against them (i.e., that they were secret Jews) have been necessarily false? And if all this is not sufficient to prove the meaning of the passage in question, I think the word "although," with which it starts, should clinch the argument. Confirming this interpretation are also Abravanel's various statements, of which I shall first quote the following:

> Although they [the conversos] and their descendants endeavored to be like *complete gentiles,* they did not achieve this aim; for the native people of the land will always call them Jews [in the ethnic sense], designate them as Israelites against their will, regard them as Jews [in the religious sense], and falsely accuse them of Judaizing in secret and burn them for this in fire.[12]

Here again, the Marranos are portrayed as endeavoring to be like *complete gentiles* — namely, assimilated in every respect, including of course, *religiously,* and we have again the same "although" and the contrasting religious accusations, which in this context may mean only "false."

Abravanel was one of the great hebraists of his time; he knew precisely the biblical meaning of the word *'alila,* and in one place in his commentaries (Deut. 23.14) he elaborates on that meaning. He also knew that this was the *commonly known meaning* and that his statement would be correctly understood. The three relevant passages I have cited from his works[13] should be sufficient for any impartial reader clearly to grasp the meaning of his statements, but perhaps not for those so attached to the old view of the Marranos that they find it extremely hard to part with it. So I shall present here a fourth passage from Abravanel's writings which includes the term *'alila* and in which he refers to the "criminals of Israel," a title he often used to designate the Christianized conversos.

Commenting on Malachi 3.19, which predicts that the evil-doers[14] will be set ablaze, Abravanel says that in these words the prophet may have

---

[12] See above, p. 184.

[13] See above, pp. 184, 187–188.

[14] The corresponding Hebrew word in Malachi is *zēdim,* which was used in medieval Hebrew literature to designate voluntary converts from Judaism. See above, p. 91, n. 20.

alluded to what is happening in our own time when the peoples in their various lands produce, in their wickedness, false accusations against the criminals of Israel—who, like their forebears, left the fold of our religion—by claiming that they judaize and secretly, in their privacy, guard the Law of Moses, and on the basis of this charge they burn them without mercy by the hundreds and the thousands.[15]

Had Talmage paid due attention to these statements and the related testimonies that preceded and followed them, he would not have disposed of the above passages as erroneously as he did. But his urge to defend the old theory was so strong that it led him to disregard elementary logic, the sequence of ideas, the common meanings of words, and the apparent content of crucial sentences, and to try to find reasons for not accepting novel conclusions that he did not like. What was the motive, or rather the factor, which compelled him to involve himself in such escapes from truth and such evident misrepresentations? It was, I am convinced, the impact of the *myth*—of his belief in the *essential piety* of the Marranos[16]—that led him to give wrong explications of the evidence, and assume at the same time—as I am sure he did—that he was acting in the service of truth.

## V

I have presented two examples of reactions to this book by Jewish scholars, which were clearly affected by the old, prevailing notions about the Marranos' Jewishness and the purpose of the Inquisition. I shall now present two assessments of this work by two important Spanish scholars, in which we shall see the same symptoms of escapism, of refusal to face the plain content of the evidence and, instead, of turning to fanciful "solutions," which cannot solve any of the problems involved.

I shall first refer to the review of my *Marranos* by Professor José M.ª Millás-Vallicrosa (*Sefarad*, 66 [1966], 152–153). Millás was a talented

---

[15] See Abravanel's Commentaries on Prophets and Writings, ed. 1960, p. 593ab (*Mashmi'd Yĕshu'ah*, on Malachi 3.19).

[16] Or, as he put it, "the essential reality of Marrano piety" (*Judaism* 17 [1968], 376).

and conscientious scholar whose works reveal his investigative capacities as well as his literary skill. His approach to Hebrew literature was inquisitive and open-minded, and one would expect him to display the same attitude also in his review of the present book. On the whole, indeed, he did. His review is a model of a concise presentation of the main lines of inquiry followed in my work, of its major conclusions, and the main differences between them and those of antecedent studies. He recognizes the "full merit of the new investigations about the Marrano problem, especially those touching the Responsa, as well as the homiletic and polemic literature of that tortured age," and admits that what these sources teach us is that the "authorities involved considered most conversos christianized and lost to Judaism." Yet this "puritan and pessimistic view," he adds, "could not embrace all cases, nor could it always be exact." [17] One wonders at this unnecessary reservation. It is obvious that in such broad assessments of views as those made by the authorities examined—assessments that referred to the whole Marrano group—the aim was to indicate the dominant trends in that group and not specific situations in certain circles or localities. There were, of course, more than a few cases to which the general rule did not apply, but in broad outline the "pessimistic view" of our authorities was the realistic view, if we go by the *outcome* of the trends referred to— i.e., the destruction of the Marrano community, which occurred as a result not only of persecution, but also, as we have shown, of assimilation. There is a retreat here on the part of the reviewer from the conclusions demanded by the disclosed evidence, without telling us even in a single word what justified, in his opinion, that retreat. For a logical and inquisitive scholar like Millás, such a procedure seems strange.

But even stranger is his other reservation. "The note of savagery applied to the inquisitional activity," he says, "cannot of course be accepted in a generic and extensive sense." Of course? That note is the inevitable consequence of our inquiry; it is clearly and repeatedly implied in our conclusions, though it does not emerge from them directly. Our additional studies in the Spanish and Latin sources, to which we refer in the Foreword to this book, have fully

---

[17] See *Sefarad* 66 (1966), 153.

confirmed that note. The Inquisition, though established by the
Spanish sovereigns, was actually the achievement of a popular movement, whose aim was the destruction of the conversos, as one must
conclude from the tirades of its spokesmen, who intended and hoped
to have the Inquisition serve as the engine of that destruction.[18] The
"religious" charges which these spokesmen hurled at the allegedly
"Judaized" conversos were riddled with absurdities and false claims,
as we have clearly shown in our studies;[19] and their real motives,
which were social and political, were exposed—and denounced—
by Old Christian men of truth, by great personalities like Montalvo
and Oropesa,[20] and by outstanding conversos like Cardinal Torque-
mada.[21] Millás-Vallicrosa, however, was habituated to believe that
the Inquisition was an instrument of religious purification and that
no other reason save religious improvement could possibly be ascribed to such a court. That our implied conclusions could not fit the
Inquisition in a "generic and extensive sense" was therefore to him
a matter of course. Why? Our answer is: the scholar here found the
road to freethinking blocked by the myth that dominated his mind;
and the scholar had "of course" to retreat.

The other Spanish review I referred to was written by Antonio
Domínguez Ortiz.[22] Elsewhere I have dealt with a portion of that
review,[23] and now I shall address another part which relates to our
present discussion. Domínguez Ortiz evidently tried to fit some developments discussed in my book into the framework of his own
conceptions about the Marranos and the Inquisition. Thus, in referring to the "religious crisis"—largely the product of Averroistic
teachings—that affected Spanish Jewry following the first mass conversion, he fails to point out what I repeatedly did—namely, that
the crisis affected many converts only among those of the *first* gen-

[18] See my *Origins of the Inquisition in Fifteenth Century Spain* (1995), pp. 500–
504, 844–846.
[19] *Ibid.*, pp. 360–362, 370–373.
[20] *Ibid.*, pp. 627, 893–894.
[21] *Ibid.*, pp. 444–447, 449.
[22] See *Saber/Leer*, no. 90 (December 1995).
[23] See *The Howard Gilman International Colloquia*, ed. C. Carrete Parrondo,
M. Dascal, and F. Márquez (1999).

eration, whereas their descendants from the second and third generations were brought up as fully fledged Christians. Consequently, there were few Averroists among the conversos of the later generations, since Averroism had hardly any following in Spain's Christian society.[24]

Domínguez Ortiz, nevertheless, makes the assertion that "according to the authors" cited by me, "the majority of the conversos were either Christians or unbelievers." Since the works of these authors were produced during a long period (120 years from 1391), "the conversos" to whom our reviewer refers without any limitation or qualification are presumed to have been qualitatively the same *throughout that period;* and when he speaks of them as "Christians *or* unbelievers," the reader may easily assume that the two groups were always more or less of equal strength. Both assumptions, however, would be wrong. For what we truly gather from the authors I cited is that those who lived close to the second mass conversion (1412–1415) stressed the large number of *unbelievers,* while almost all of those who lived under the Inquisition emphatically pointed out that the conversos were *Christians.* This correct summary of the sources, however, would promptly raise the question: *Why the Inquisition?,* while Domínguez' inaccurate and ambiguous summary allows the reader to assume that the unbelievers were numerous under the Inquisition, too, and that these unbelievers were obviously heretics who had to be rooted out.

But Domínguez Ortiz, I should add, also takes up separately my claim that when the Inquisition was established, the overwhelming majority of the conversos were Christians. "This affirmation," he says, "may be accepted with respect to the communities north of the Tajo," where the "converso problem did not exist" or was not "grave";[25] it is not valid, however, for the southern part, and especially for Andalusia, which was teeming with false converts.[26] We must refrain from going into the unsettled question of this division of Spain into two different halves, as it has nothing to do with our problem. For when our sources describe the transformation of

---

[24] See above, pp. 164–165.
[25] *Saber/Leer,* no. 90 (December 1995), p. 5 cols. 3, 2.
[26] *Ibid.,* col. 2.

the converts from faithful Jews to sincere Christians, from lovers of Judaism to its avowed enemies, they refer of course to *all* conversos of Spain, the southern part included; and when our "cited authors" say that the Jews of Spain saw in the conversos' inquisitional tribulations a *divine retribution for their religious betrayal*, they referred, above all, to the *southern* conversos who supplied most of the Inquisition's victims. Domínguez Ortiz cannot answer the challenge of these irrefutable, powerful testimonies. By calling our attention to that alleged "division," he explains nothing and merely avoids the issue.

But the issue, it seems, does not let him go. The reaction of the Jews to the heavy punishment that the Spanish conversos suffered at the hands of the Inquisition[27] must have caused him no little disturbance. "It is indisputable," he says, "that in the course of its long history, the Inquisition has condemned good Christians, authentic conversos."[28] This, he explains, happened for two reasons, the first of which was that, "like all courts, the Inquisition has committed judicial errors." By this comparison of the Inquisition to all other courts, Domínguez Ortiz evidently wants us to believe that the judicial errors of the Inquisition were rare. But this is a belief we cannot entertain. For the Inquisition was *not* like other courts, even if only for its evidential system. In the secular tribunals of Spain and other countries, witnesses were admitted after careful examination of both their past lives and personal qualities. But in the Spanish Inquisition, says Lea, when it came to testimonies *against* the accused, "all witnesses were admissible, however infamous." When, in addition, one bears in mind the concealment of the accuser's name from the accused and the latter's inability to cross-examine his accuser, one must conclude that the errors of judgment committed by the Inquisition *had* to be very numerous indeed.

Finally, a word on Domínguez' second reason for the Inquisition's condemnation of the innocent. This, he says, was the "processal procedure of the Inquisition which often made it more convenient for the accused to admit guilt and receive a light sentence rather than keep denying what the Inquisitors considered sufficiently proven,"

[27] See above, pp. 171–175.
[28] See *Saber/Leer*, no. 90 (December 1995), p. 4, col. 4.

and thereby bring upon himself an extremely harsh verdict.[29] Such cases of self-incrimination, which likewise resulted from errors of judgment, were *many*, Domínguez Ortiz says; and yet together with the ordinary errors, which, as we have concluded, were also numerous, they formed only a minority of the cases. The majority, he believes, consisted of true judgments, based on correct identification of the accused as Judaizers and other heretics.

This is Domínguez Ortiz' position as one may deduce it from his various assertions. But it is not a position that matches what we gather from the relevant Jewish sources. For the Jews of Spain knew *both* converso types—the Christianized and the Judaizers—and had they even suspected that most of the burned, and most of the tortured and robbed by the Inquisition, or even a minority among them, were Jews—in thought and, as much as they could, in deed—they would not have been happy over their fate. It is only because they considered them all traitors, deserters of their people and enemies of its faith, that they could celebrate their "downfall."

What, then, does Domínguez Ortiz' review teach us? In spite of all he knew of the Inquisition's flaws and faults and of many other factual contradictions to his view, he remained attached to that view because of a concept, which he aptly summarized as follows: *"The Inquisition was an ecclesiastic tribunal established for religious motives."* [30] This was the concept by which he judged everything essential related to the Marranos and the Inquisition, for this was the myth that governed Spain's thinking for more than five centuries; and from this national belief he would not part.

The reviews examined represent a group of authors whose views on this study were preconceived. As we see it, what formed these views was not a particular idea of their own, but a common opinion, entrenched for generations, and generally considered to be beyond doubt. When upheld by religion and national sentiment, it often takes on the power of myth, which may sway the thinking of scholars and experts as well as ordinary men. The reactions to this book such as those we have presented show that the old myths about the

[29] *Ibid.*
[30] *Ibid.* (emphasis added).

Marranos and the Inquisition still hold a variety of authors in their grip—among them, in full accord with custom, some well-known scholars of the highest rank.

We have seen the lengths to which such authors go in support of their beliefs against opposing demonstrations: evasion or avoidance of damaging evidence, attempts to misinterpret conflicting testimonies, and even the construction of groundless theories to sustain assumptions clashing with fact and logic. In the end all these measures will prove futile. For myths are created to fulfill certain functions that multitudes of people consider useful. But the myths we are concerned with have outlived their usefulness; and this is why their influence must wane and vanish. Indeed, we can see clear symptoms of this process also in the present book's reception, which is marked by the increasing number of historians who identify themselves with its thesis.

# INDEX

## (*of* persons, places, subjects)

Abba Mari, see Isaac ben Abba Mari
Abba Mari ben Moses of Lunel, 115, 136
Abner of Burgos, 102
Abraham ben Moses, 100
Abraham ben Solomon of Torrutiel (Ardutiel?), 242
Abraham Isaac ha-Levi of Gerona, 114
Abraham of Regensburg, 40
Abravanel, Isaac, 90, 136, 162, 177–203, 205, 206, 108, 218, 231, 235, 243, 244, 245, 247
Adret, see Solomon ben Adret
Agde, Council of, 35
Ahaziah, 150
Akiba ben Joseph, 7
'Akrish, Isaac, 85
Alami, Solomon, 96, 99, 103–106, 111, 120, 225
Albalag, Isaac, 100
Albèri, Eugenio, 247
Albigenses, 82, 109
Albo, Joseph, 96, 116, 117–120, 122–127, 136
Alfasi, Isaac ben Jacob, 17
Alfonso V, King of Aragon, 37
Alfonso X, King of Castile, 260
Alfonso de Valladolid, see Abner of Burgos
Algeria, 54, 218
Algiers, 22, 23, 32, 51, 54, 252
Almohades, 16, 28, 145
Amador de los Ríos, José, 16, 43, 239, 257, 259, 260
Amador de los Ríos, Rodrigo, 65

Anus, anusim, use of term in Responsa, 9; rarity of this use in Spanish writings, 78; and see Marranos; Forced Converts; Crypto-Jews
Apostates, see Converts
Aptowitzer, A., 19
Apulia, 219
Aragon (Kingdom), 34, 37, 51, 65, 86, 90, 117, 122, 222, 239, 242
Arama, Isaac, 136, 137–157, 163, 164, 165, 182, 208, 228
Aristotle, 7, 102, 107
Asaf, Simḥa, 5, 20, 55, 71, 73, 212, 216
Asher ben Yeḥiel, 11, 12, 13, 20, 27, 42
Ashkenazi, E., 101
Atlas, E., 22
Averroes, Averroists, Averroism, 88, 100, 102, 106, 108, 113, 115, 116, 136, 139, 140, 164–165, 197, 228
Avignon, 90, 239
Ayala, see López de Ayala, Pero

Bacher, W., 59
Baer, I. F., 2, 3, 16, 21, 28, 67, 102, 119, 122, 164, 165, 223, 224, 238, 240, 243, 255, 258, 260, 261, 262
Balan [Bulat?], Judah, 71, 215
Balearic Islands, 22, 156
Barbary States, 218
Barcelona, 30, 100, 257
Baron, S. W., 255, 256
Bédarride, I., 239

Belasco, G. S., 90
Benedict XIII, anti-pope, 223–225
Ben-Sasson, H. H., 108
Berav, Jacob, 66, 69, 70, 71, 206, 215
Berliner, A., 17, 27
Bernáldez, Andrés, 167, 213, 216, 217, 265, 266, 267
Bibago, Abraham, 133, 135, 136, 140, 179, 228
Binyamin ben Matityahu, 73
Blas, Agustín de, 245
Bonafed, Solomon ben Reuben, 78, 107
Boton, Jacob, 75
Bougie, 49
Brainin, R., 94
Branner, J. C., 219
Buber, Solomon, 79, 89, 201

Caballero, Fermín Agosto, 66
Cagigas, Isidro de las, 66
Cantera Burgos, F., 223, 225
Capsali, Elijah, 73, 213
Carmona, 244
Caro, Isaac, 157–169, 170, 196, 236
Caro, Joseph, 20, 72, 74
Carriazo, Juan de M., 246, 251, 263, 266
Cartagena, Alfonso de, 263
Caspi, Joseph ben Abba Mari, 100, 101
Castile, 34, 37, 51, 64, 65, 70, 117, 122, 206, 211, 239, 242, 247
Castro, Américo, 27
Catalina, Queen of Castile, 239
Catalonia, 51, 65
Cifuentes, Count of; Álvaro de Silva, 263, 264
Cohen, Martin A., 242
Colmeiro, M., 240, 265
Colon, Joseph, 73
Converts, Conversion (from Judaism to other religions), dual policy toward conversion in

Judaism: in Geonic period, 17, 39–40; position of Rashi, 17–18, 40; position of Maimonides, 17–18, 40; position of later rabbinical authorities, 19–20, 40, 45–46, 61–63, 67–68, 70–71; opinions on reasons for conversion, 97–98, 103–104, 138, 160–162, 172–173, 179, 181, 190, 200; traditional view of converts in Jewry, 52, 129, 163, 197; apostasy in Spain prior to 1391, 16; differences between conversions of 1391 and 1412, 120–121; causes of conversion movement of 1412, 107, 116–120, 122–123, 162; impact of philosophy upon this movement, 97–121, 139–140; conversionist agitation among Jews and Marranos, 88–90, 93, 94, 126, 131–132; conversion movement in the 1460's, 227–228; in the 1470's, 140, 162, 165; conversions in Spain and Portugal in 1492–1497, 176–177, 212–213; appellations for converts in medieval Hebrew literature, 90, 91, 94, 129
Cordova, 251, 256, 259, 263, 266
Corominas, J., 59
Crescas, Ḥasdai, 86, 87, 93, 99, 102, 106, 112–115, 221, 222, 239, 240, 241, 256–259
Cuenca, 66
Crypto-Jews, 29, 47, 51, 62, 66, 121, 133, 142, 146, 157, 158, 163, 165–166, 198; early decline of Crypto-Judaism, 26, 29–30, 92; its continued diminution, 36–38, 49–50, 53; crypto-Jewish awakening prior to Inquisition, 187–188, 207, 235–236; impact of pre-Inquisitional persecutions upon the "return" movement, 144–145; Crypto-Juda-

ism at the time of the Inquisition, 55, 56, 57, 58, 59, 60, 62, 198, 207, 235–236; types of Crypto-Jews, 165–166, 170, 199, 236; sincerity of "returners" since the 80's suspected, 143–144, 171; prospects of Crypto-Judaism and of ultimate Marrano "return," 142, 145, 147, 168, 171, 190, 233–235; number of "returners" at the time of Inquisition, 218–220, 248; Crypto-Judaism in Portugal, 214. And see Forced Converts; Marranos; Inquisition

Danvila, Francisco, 257
David ibn Avi-Zimra, 72
David ha-Kohen, 18, 73
Dinur, B., 259
Donin, Nicolaus, 89
Duran, Profiat (Profeit); also *Efodi*, 84, 85, 86, 88, 89, 90, 91, 92, 93, 114, 221–223, 226
Duran, Simon ben Solomon, 54, 55, 56, 57, 58, 60, 61, 64–67, 70, 71, 73, 220
Duran, Simon ben Ẓemaḥ, 21, 22, 32–44, 46, 49, 62, 67, 75, 101, 114, 116, 125, 130, 131, 136, 207, 212
Duran, Solomon ben Simon, 44–50, 51, 62, 67, 68, 69, 75, 126, 204, 231
Duran, Ẓemaḥ ben Solomon, 50–54, 67, 68

Ecija, 247
Edelmann, Z. H., 13, 54
Edge, Granville, 267
Efodi, see Duran, Profiat
Egypt, 218, 252
Eidelberg, S., 9
Eisenstein, J. D., 14
El'azar ben Judah, 12

Elfenbein, I., 8
Eliezer ben Nathan of Mayence, 19
Eliezer ben Samuel of Metz, 12, 19
Eliezer ben Yoel ha-Levi of Bonn, 19, 20
Elijah, 63, 150
England, 95
Ephraim ben Jacob of Bonn, 9
Epstein, Isidore, 22, 32
Escolano, Gaspar, 241
Espinosa, Pablo de, 226

Falaquera, Shem Tov ben Jospeh, 100
Farinelli, A., 59
Fernando I, King of Aragon, 242
Fernando III, King of Castile, 27
Ferrer, Vicente, 239, 242
Fez, 69
Filipowski, H. P., 132, 212, 239, 241
Finkelstein, L., 9
Fita, Fidel, 257
Flanders, 72, 253
Forced Converts, dual attitude toward such converts in Judaism, 6; origins of this dualism, 6–8; Franco-German view of forced conversion, 8–13; the Maimonidean policy, 13–15; rules of conduct considered proper for forced converts, 10, 12, 15, 24, 25, 26, 27; the view of later Spanish rabbis, 21–22, 24, 32–35, 157, 158; test of forced conversion according to Albo, 122–124; difference between position of forced converts in Spain and in other countries, 19–21; forced conversion in Portugal, 214. And see Crypto-Judaism, Marranos
France, 16, 217

Franciscus de Sant Jordi, 119, 132
Freimann, A. H., 19
Freimann, J., 83
Friedländer, J., 92, 221, 222

Gascogne, 82
Gerlach, Stephan (the older), 219
Germany, 16, 95
Gerona, 114
Gershom ben Judah (Meor ha-Golah), 8, 9, 18
Gershon, Isaac, 75
Gersonides, 100, 101
Gibraltar, 251, 252, 262
Ginzberg, L., 9, 17, 39, 40
Gog, 153
González, Julio, 258, 261
González, Tomás, 237, 242, 244
Graetz, H., 22, 32, 43, 87, 133, 155, 213, 221, 222, 223, 224, 229, 230, 231, 238, 245, 247, 248
Granada, 54, 220, 239
Grünbaum, S., 89
Grünhut, E., 69
Guillén, Claudio, 253
Guttmann, Julius, 102

Habermann, A. M., 96, 104, 118
Haebler, C., 242
Ḥagiz, Moses, 211, 212
Hai, Gaon, 17, 20
Halkin, A. S., 145
Haman, 175
Ḥayyim ben Isaac of Vienna, 10, 12, 20, 40
Ḥayyim ibn Musa, 131, 132, 136
Heilpern, P. M., 225
Herculano, A., 219
Hershman, Abraham M., 22, 23, 32, 241
Hesqueto, Baruch, 200
Huesca, 132
Huici Miranda, A., 27

Husik, Isaac, 96, 118

Ibn Caspi, see Caspi
Ibn Danan, see Saadia ben Maimon ibn Danan
Inquisition (Spanish), difference between its formal and real purposes, 4; its charges concerning Marrano Jewishness regarded as untrue, 154-155, 184, 187, 188, 208; its influence upon the Marranos in general, 54, 156, 166, 168; its impact on Crypto-Judaism, 3-4, 144-145, 187-188; its effect upon the "return" movement, 60-61, 72, 156; Jewish reaction to its persecution of the Marranos, 149-150, 168, 171-172, 173-174, 176, 200-201. And see Marranos; Crypto-Judaism
Isaac bar Sheshet Perfet, see Perfet, Isaac bar Sheshet
Isaac ben Abba Mari, 52, 65
Isaac ben Asher ha-Levi, 20
Isaac ben Joseph Israeli, 90
Isaac ben Moses of Vienna, 40
Isaac ben Samuel of Dampierre, 19
Isaac Napaḥa, 195
Ishmael ben Elisha, 7, 8
Isserlein, Israel ben Petaḥyah 20, 40
Italy, 217, 253

Jabeẓ, Joseph, 136, 175-176, 177
Jacob ben Asher, 20, 40
Jacob ben Ḥaviv, 73, 74, 214, 215
Jacob ben Reuben, 82, 93
Jaén, 263
Játiva, 51
Jaulus, J., 22, 23, 32
Jerez de la Frontera, 247
Jerusalem, 252
Jesus, 80, 89, 126, 223

Joel ibn Shuaib, 172–175, 190
Joronimo de Santa Fe, see Joshua
  ha-Lorki
Joseph Abram, 92
Joseph ben Isaac Kimhi, see
  Kimhi, Joseph
Joseph ben Lavi (Vidal Ben-
  venist), 89, 126
Joseph ben Leb, 75, 215
Joseph ben Meshulam, 227
Joseph ben Nathan Official, 94,
  125
Joseph ben Shem Tov, 85, 87, 93,
  95, 97, 98, 106, 107, 135, 140
Joseph ben Zaddiq of Arevalo, 78,
  153, 242
Joshua ha-Lorki, 89, 97, 105, 126,
  132, 180, 196
Jost, Isaac Marcus, 35
Juan II, King of Castile, 37
Judah ben Asher, 8
Judah ben Joseph Alfacar, 100

Kaminka, A., 78, 107
Karaites, 42, 46
Katz, Jacob, 17
Kaufmann, David, 32, 136
Kayserling, M., 43, 132, 212
Kimḥi, David, 100, 101, 139
Kimḥi, Joseph, 89
Kirchheim, R., 100, 224
Kohn, J., 92, 221, 222
Korah, 227

Landau, L., 89, 97, 105
Lattes, M., 213
Lea, H. C., 66, 156, 246, 259, 264,
  266, 267
Leon, David Messer, 73
Levi ben Gershon, see Gersonides
Lewin, B. M., 17, 39, 40
Libowitz, N. S., 169
Lieberman, Saul, 7, 59, 147
Lipmann-Muhlhausen, Yom Tov,
  125, 129

Lisbon, 176, 212, 213
Llorca, Bernardino, 1
Llorente, J. A., 239
Loeb, Isidore, 82, 258
Lope de Barrientos, 66
López de Ayala, Pero, 240
López Martínez, Nicolás, 2, 167
Lorki, see Joshua ha-Lorki
Los Palacios, 216

Maimonides, 6, 11, 13, 14, 15, 16,
  17, 18, 20, 24, 25, 27, 30, 33,
  34, 35, 37, 40, 42, 46, 52, 61, 63,
  68, 71, 79, 80, 89, 99, 100, 102,
  103, 104, 114, 115, 125, 126, 144,
  158, 228
Mairena, 216
Majorca, 32, 43, 48, 49, 51, 52,
  65, 156, 257
Malaga, 54
Mandelbaum, B., 79
Marchena, 216
Mariana, Juan de, 242, 265
María Fabié, A., 265
Marineo Sículo, Lucio, 217, 220
Marranos, origin of term, 59;
  other terms by which Marranos
  were indicated, 79–80, 89–90,
  94, 129, 179; the question of
  their Jewishness, 1–2; position
  of Jewish historians on this
  question, 2–3; basic components
  of Marrano camp, 95–96;
  changing policies of rabbinical
  authorities toward Marranos,
  23–25, 32–36, 46–47, 48–49, 53,
  61–62, 67–68; Marranos described as estranged from Judaism, 141–142, 153, 172; dese-
  crate the Sabbath, 36, 38, 42,
  44, 49–50; worship a foreign
  deity ("idolaters"), 36, 37, 38,
  44, 67, 70, 146, 152, 159, 165,
  170, 176, 181, 183, 197, 201;
  eat "defiled food," 38; drink

wine of gentiles, 43; are uncircumcised, 45, 67, 198; disregard
the commandments in general,
29, 44, 125, 127, 166, 180,
193–194, 195, 197; observe the
laws of the gentiles, 29, 159,
218; refuse to migrate from
Spain, 26, 27–29, 36–37, 38, 55,
56, 58, 60, 70; denounce Crypto-
Jews to the authorities, 29; have
relations with Christian women,
31; intermarry with Old Christians, 55, 57, 61, 64, 65, 66, 70,
71, 186; bring up their children
as non-Jews, 42, 46, 180, 231–
232; assimilate with the gentiles, 70, 71, 141–142, 146,
154–155, 179, 181–182, 184–
186, 191–192, 198–199, 201, 206,
232; spread of Christianity
among them, 42, 46, 60, 61, 84,
88, 90–92, 93, 126–127, 130,
131, 132, 141–142, 180, 193,
199, 231–232; Marranos as
"heretics" and "Epicureans,"
62, 125, 127–129, 193–194, 195,
196–197; their enmity for Jews
and Judaism, 125, 128, 147, 149,
173, 174, 175, 176, 180, 220,
231; hostility of Jews for Marranos, 128, 147–149, 174, 175;
diverse opinions on Marranos'
belonging to Jewish people,
61–63, 67, 70–71, 73–74, 124–
125, 168, 178, 183; advocacy of
sharp distinction between Jews
and Marranos, 39, 151–152,
169, 172, 178–179; disqualification of Marranos as witnesses
before a Jewish court, 30, 38,
42, 49, 212; defined as apostates,
30, 42, 45, 50, 52, 53, 55–56, 57,
60, 66, 72, 124, 127, 147, 179,
184, 187, 195, 196; regarded as
gentiles, 45, 55, 56, 60, 64, 66,

70–72, 153, 154, 180, 206, 215;
their "returners" seen as proselytes, 45, 53, 55, 57, 61, 64,
68, 71, 72, 152–154, 191; objections to these definitions, 45,
53, 62, 63, 64, 66; "returners"
viewed as penitents, 55, 58, 65,
66, 71–72; attitude of Spanish
rabbis toward Marranos at time
of Inquisition, 68–72, 158, 173–
174, 215; their major characteristics at that time, 205; their
number, 232, 245, 255–270;
their military capacity, 261–
264; their contries of refuge,
216–218, 251–254; Christian
view of Marranos, 62, 167–168,
193, 200; Jewish attitude toward
Marranos in Portugal, 74–75,
211–212, 214. And see Crypto-
Judaism; Conversion; Forced
Conversion; Inquisition
Martínez, Ferrán, 259, 260
Marx, Alexander, 62, 169
Matityahu [ha-Yiẓhari?], 127, 128
Medina, Samuel ben Moses de, 211
Medina Sidonia, Duke of; Enrique
de Guzmán, 251, 252
Meir ben Todros ha-Levi Abula-
fia, 100
Meir of Rothenburg, 11, 12, 17,
18, 19, 20, 40, 41, 42, 52
Menahem ben Solomon of Per-
pignan, 53
Millas-Vallicrosa, J. M., 108
Mimi, Simon R., 176
Mintz, Judah, 73
Mizraḥi, Eliyahu, 73
Montoto, Santiago, 265, 267
Mordecai ben Hillel of Nurem-
berg, 20
Morocco, 71, 218, 252
Moses ben Ḥasdai Taqu, 100
Moses ben Joshua of Narbonne,
100, 101

Moses ha-Kohen of Tordesillas, 82, 90, 93
Moshe ben Maimon, see Maimonides
Moshe ben Naḥman, see Nahmanides
Mostaganem, 54
Müller, J., 9

Nahmanides, 6. 19, 20, 45, 46
Naḥshon Gaon, 39, 40
Naples, 156
Narboni, see Moses ben Joshua of Narbonne
Natronai Goan, 17
Navagero, Andrea, 265
Navarre, 172, 217
Neubauer, A., 9, 11, 20, 78, 242
Niebla, 251, 252

Obadiah of Bertinoro, 218
Og, 201
On ben Peleth, 224
Ortiz de Zúñiga, Diego, 237

Pacios López, Antonio, 126
Palencia, Alonso de, 251, 252, 261, 262, 263, 264, 265
Palestine, 65
Palma (de Majorca), 43
Palomo, F. de Borja, 265
Paul of Burgos (Paulus de Sancta Maria), 85, 89, 90, 105, 132, 223-225
Paz y Melia, A., 251, 261
Pedro de Córdoba, 263
Pedro de Luna, see Benedict XIII
Perfet, Isaac bar Sheshet, 22-32, 33, 34, 37, 46, 49, 89, 124, 204, 212, 213
Peturs Alphonsi, 132
Pollak, H. J., 156, 155, 228
Polemical Literature (Jewish), 80 ff.; new direction of Jewish polemics after 1391, 81-84; two types of polemical literature: for Marranos and for Jews, 83-84; share of philosophy in polemical literature, 101, 108; mode of campaign adopted by Efodi, 85-86; mode of campaign favored by Crescas, 86-87; effect of renewed polemical literature, 93-94
Portugal, 65, 74, 157, 162, 169, 175, 211, 212, 213, 214, 215, 216, 217, 219, 239
Posnanski, Adolf, 82, 86, 221, 222, 223
Provence, 82
Providence, 110-120 (its relation to conversion movement), 125, 127-128, 136, 139, 164, 181-182, 183, 197, 230
Puig y Puig, Sebastian, 224
Pulgar, Fernando del, 217, 220, 266
Pulgar (Policar), Isaac ben Joseph, 90, 91, 100, 101

Quintanilla, Alonso de, 245
Quirini, Vincenzo, 247

Rashba, see Solomon ben Adret
Rashbash, see Duran, Solomon ben Simon
Rashbaẓ, see Duran, Simon ben Ẓemaḥ
Rashi, 6, 8, 9, 10, 12, 17, 18, 19, 20, 25, 27, 40, 45, 89, 139, 153, 154, 212
Rava, 8
Regensburg, 11
Reggio, Isaac Samuel, 227, 228, 229
Repentance (of converts and forced converts), 7, 10, 11, 55, 56, 57, 58, 124, 141, 143, 144, 150, 152, 168, 170, 171, 189

Reuben ben Nissim Gerundi, 241
Ribash, see Perfet, Isaac bar Sheshet
Rome, 216
Rosanes, S., 219
Rosenthal, Judah, 82, 222
Roth, Cecil, 260

Saadia ben Maimon ibn Danan, 54–59, 61, 62–64, 67, 68, 71, 73, 76, 207, 220
Saadia Gaon, 100
Saba, Abraham, 169–172
Saloniki, 74, 211, 212, 214, 219
Samuel ibn Tibbon, 99
Sánchez, Garci, 251, 263, 265
Sanctification of the Name, 7, 12, 13, 14, 157, 158, 169; position of Maimonides, 13–14; position of German rabbis, 12–13; position of Spanish rabbis after the Expulsion, 157–158
Santotis, Cristóbal de, 224
Sasoon, D. S., 256
Schirmann, J., 129, 258
Schor, J. H., 226
Serra, J. R., 224
Serrano, Luciano, 224
Seville, 21, 27, 240, 241, 245, 246, 251, 252, 253, 254, 255–270
Shalom, Abraham, 135, 136
Shalom Gaon, 17
Shem Tov ben Joseph, 135, 136
Shem Tov ben Shem Tov, 98, 110, 111, 116
Shem Tov ben Yizhaq ben Shaprut of Tudela, 16
Sherira Gaon, 40
Sicily, 156
Sihon, 201
Silveira, Joaquim da, 59
Simon ben Zemah Duran, see Duran, Simon ben Zemah
Solomon ben Abraham of Montpellier, 100

Solomon ben Adret, 17, 19, 20, 22, 24, 40, 116, 136
Solomon ben Simon, 9
Solomon ben Simon Duran, see Duran, Solomon ben Simon
Solomon ben Yizhaq, see Rashi
Solomon ha-Levi, see Paul of Burgos
Starr, J., 35
Steinschneider, M., 82, 132
Stern, Moritz, 9, 11, 20

Tam, Jacob ben Meir, 9, 19, 45, 46
Taqu, see Moses ben Hasdai
Tlemcen, Sultunate, 22
Todd, James H., 109
Toledo, 66, 100, 262, 263, 264
Tortosa, 49, 107
Turkey, 73, 157, 169, 218, 219

Urbach, E. E., 19
Usque, Samuel, 239

Valencia, 21, 22, 51, 66, 241, 256, 257, 258
Valera, Diego de, 242, 243
Villanueva, J. Lorenzo, 257

Weiss, I. H., 136
Wiener, M., 239
Wistinetzki, Judah, 83

Yeda'yah of Béziers, 100
Yehiel of Paris, 89, 91, 94
Yehudai Gaon, 39, 40, 67

Zacuto, Abraham, 132, 212, 239, 241, 242, 256, 259
Zalva, Martín de, 224
Zahalon, Yom Tov, 75
Ze'ira, Rav, 8
Zeitlin, Solomon, 59
Zimmels, H. J., 5, 71, 215
Zuñiga, see Ortiz de Zúñiga
Zurita, Jerónimo de, 242, 243, 244, 256, 268